WILLIAM FAULKNER IN HOLLYWOOD

THE SOUTH ON SCREEN

Edited by R. Barton Palmer and Matthew H. Bernstein

WILLIAM FAULKNER IN HOLLYWOOD

SCREENWRITING FOR THE STUDIOS

Stefan Solomon

The University of Georgia Press *Athens*

Paperback edition, 2020
© 2017 by the University of Georgia Press
Athens, Georgia 30602
www.ugapress.org
All rights reserved
Designed by Erin Kirk New
Set in 10/14 Chapparal

Most University of Georgia Press titles are
available from popular e-book vendors.

Printed digitally

Library of Congress Cataloging-in-Publication Data

Names: Solomon, Stefan, 1986– author.
Title: William Faulkner in Hollywood : screenwriting for the
    studios / Stefan Solomon.
Description: Athens : The University of Georgia Press, [2017] |
    Includes bibliographical references and index.
Identifiers: LCCN 2017003985 | ISBN 9780820351131 (hardback :
    alk. paper) | ISBN 9780820351148 (ebook)
Subjects: LCSH: Faulkner, William, 1897–1962—Motion picture
    plays. | Faulkner, William, 1897–1962—Radio and television
    plays.
Classification: LCC PS3511.A86 Z972725 2017 | DDC 813/.52—dc23
LC record available at https://lccn.loc.gov/2017003985

ISBN 9780820357898 (paperback : alk. paper)

FOR MONICA

Contents

List of Illustrations ix

Acknowledgments xi

List of Abbreviations xv

Title Sequence	William Faulkner, Screenwriter 1
One	First Run: MGM 16
Two	Second Run: Universal, Twentieth Century–Fox, RKO 53
Three	Independence: *Absalom, Absalom!* and "Revolt in the Earth" 97
Four	Winning the War with Warners 115
Five	The Great Migration to Hollywood 157
Six	Stage Play and Screenplay: *Requiem for a Nun* and "The Left Hand of God" 195
Seven	Writing for the Small Screen: Faulkner and Television 218
Curtain Call	*Land of the Pharaohs* 241

Timeline: William Faulkner between Cinema and Literature 251

Notes 259

Works Cited 281

Index 295

List of Illustrations

1. *Today We Live* 29
2. *Min and Bill* 44
3. *Smilin' Through* 48
4. *Air Force* 127
5. *Air Force* 129
6. *Background to Danger* 138
7. *Background to Danger* 139
8. *The Southerner* 170
9. *The Southerner* 171
10. *Requiem for a Nun* 208
11. *William Faulkner* 221
12. *William Faulkner and Dan Duryea* 224
13. *Grandeur et décadence d'un petit commerce de cinéma* 242
14. *Grandeur et décadence d'un petit commerce de cinéma* 242
15. *Grandeur et décadence d'un petit commerce de cinéma* 242
16. *Grandeur et décadence d'un petit commerce de cinéma* 242
17. *Wooldridge Family Monument* 243
18. *Land of the Pharaohs* 246
19. *Land of the Pharaohs* 248

Acknowledgments

In completing this book, I am indebted to two people most of all. In its former life as a dissertation, this project was guided by Julian Murphet, whose insight and bold approach to all of his work sets an example I continue to follow. Julian prompted me to continue my interest in Faulkner's writing and encouraged me to conduct the archival research that was so integral to this work. A conference and book that emerged from our collaborative work were together crucial to my growth as an early-career academic. I have been lucky enough to have worked closely with another Faulkner scholar, Sarah Gleeson-White, whose generosity and thoughtful approach to her work have been an inspiration for me in my scholarly journey over the last decade, from her supervision of my undergraduate thesis until today. Working with Sarah on her own research into Faulkner's Hollywood career gave me an unparalleled opportunity to discuss my project with a colleague and friend on a regular basis, and I am sure it has made all the difference.

In my visits to archives in California, Missouri, and Virginia, I was ably supported by Julian's Discovery Project grant from the Australian Research Council, by grants from the University of New South Wales's Postgraduate Research Support Scheme, and by the Faulkner Society's John W. Hunt scholarship. The archives would not be the same without the archivists, and I owe a great deal to them: Ned Comstock at the University of Southern California, whose enthusiasm and depth of knowledge is well renowned; Sandra Joy Aguilar and Jonathan Auxier at the Warner Archives, who were incredibly helpful before and after my visit and made my stay there enjoyable;

and Robert W. Hamblin and Christopher Rieger at the Center for Faulkner Studies at Southeast Missouri University, whose dedication to their work is remarkable. Thanks should also go to Cindy Chang and Roni Lubliner at NBC Universal for allowing me to publish excerpts from the "Sutter's Gold" screenplay, and to Shannon Fifer at Warner Bros. Entertainment, Inc., for allowing me to publish excerpts from screenplays written for both Warner Brothers and RKO.

At the pointy end of the writing process, my work was made possible by a visiting research fellowship from the University of Sydney, where I was again able to call on Sarah as my mentor. Her in-depth comments and sharing of resources were needed at this stage of the project, and I won't forget it. At the Australian National University, I was helpfully granted the status of visiting fellow, which enabled me the time and space to complete the lion's share of the work. Here I must thank Monique Rooney and Russell Smith for their kindness in hosting me and providing me with opportunities to engage with colleagues from the School of Literature, Languages, and Linguistics, which helped to push the book in new and interesting directions. At this point I was lucky enough to have the advice and criticisms of Ben Robbins, an expert in the study of Faulkner and film, and his feedback kept me on my game and helped to improve much of this book.

Thanks go to Walter Biggins, senior acquisitions editor at the University of Georgia Press, who had faith in the project from the beginning and was incredibly patient with me as I revised the book. Thanks, too, to Thomas Roche, who guided me through the editing process and was extremely helpful in explaining the different steps involved. For the existence of The South on Screen as a book series, I am grateful for R. Barton Palmer and Matthew H. Bernstein. Barton also provided kind and encouraging feedback on the first draft of my manuscript, for which I am thankful. Another anonymous reader gave my work the critical interrogation it deserved, spurring me on to rewrite much of the book, and even to reconsider some of my conclusions. I am certain that the insights of this reader have led to a much better end result than I would have arrived at on my own. I know now that the advice of my copyeditor, MJ Devaney, will stay with me for some time—her attention to detail was phenomenal, and her comments and suggestions have made for a far more coherent book.

I would like to thank my parents, Debra and Matthew Solomon, for taking visible joy in my achievements and in the support and love they have given me all my life. And finally, I dedicate this book to Monica Gill, who has been understanding, compassionate, and increasingly caring during the years I have wrestled with this project. If my concern was for the words on the page, then hers was elsewhere, and that at times proved to be far more important—her patience, wisdom, and love in this period sustained me more than anything.

List of Abbreviations

To minimize the documentary apparatus of this book, the following abbreviations of Faulkner's works and of major repositories of his works are used for in-text citations. Also, each chapter's endnote citations are condensed; for complete documentation, consult the works cited section.

CS	*Collected Stories of William Faulkner*
CL	*Country Lawyer and Other Stories for the Screen*
ESPL	*Essays, Speeches and Public Letters*
FMS	*Faulkner's MGM Screenplays*
F	*Faulkner: A Comprehensive Guide to the Brodsky Collection*
"FH"	Furry, "Faulkner in a Haystack."
FU	*Faulkner in the University*
HHP	Howard Hawks Papers, MSS 1404, box 13, folder 5, Howard Hawks Papers, 1925–70, Brigham Young University, Provo, Utah
KG	*Knight's Gambit*
LG	*Lion in the Garden: Interviews with William Faulkner, 1926–1962*
N	*Novels*
SL	*Selected Letters of William Faulkner*
US	*Uncollected Stories of William Faulkner*
WFATCF	*William Faulkner at Twentieth Century–Fox: The Annotated Screenplays*

WFFC	William Faulkner Foundation Collection, series 4: Writing for Television and Movies, box 10, William Faulkner Foundation Collection, 1918–1959, accession #6074 to 6074-d, Special Collections, University of Virginia Library, Charlottesville.
WFM	*William Faulkner Manuscripts*

WILLIAM FAULKNER IN HOLLYWOOD

TITLE SEQUENCE

William Faulkner, Screenwriter

Q: How do you like Hollywood?
A: I don't like the climate, the people, their way of life. Nothing ever happens and then one morning you wake up and find that you are sixty-five. I prefer Florida.
—Interview with Lavon Roscoe, 1951

Facing a market with little appetite for high modernist experimentation, William Faulkner decided to write for the movies, relocating from Mississippi to the studio backlots where he hoped to earn a consistent salary that would support his family back home. Screenwriting disrupted his preferred working habits and presented him with material that was not necessarily of interest to him, but above all else, the felt effect of screenwriting was one of geographical dislocation: isolation engulfed him on the West Coast, and even when he returned to his "own little postage stamp of native soil" (*LG*, 255), he felt distant.

These feelings come through clearly in the letters he wrote during these years, connecting him to his home state when he was away from it. Excepting a few light-hearted anecdotes, the bulk of Faulkner's correspondence is resolutely scathing in tone, painting a miserable portrait of a literary artist imprisoned in a cultural Babylon. His initial stint at Metro-Goldwyn-Mayer (MGM) beginning in May 1932 was by all accounts a disorienting one, and Faulkner's unhappiness over being exiled from the South comes through with force in his early letters. After he had completed his first three months' work, he wrote to his agent, Ben Wasson, apologizing for his radio silence: "I was too busy and too mad all the time I was in California to write to you. But now I am home again, eating watermelon on the back porch and watching it rain" (*SL*, 66).

Five years later, he wrote his wife, Estelle Oldham Faulkner, this time concerned that another studio—Twentieth Century–Fox—might "hold me overtime" (*SL*, 101). And in 1942, Faulkner would write naively of an arrangement with his new employer, Warner Brothers, that would "allow me to stay in Oxford practically for whatever periods of time I desire" (*SL*, 162). The anticipated agreement would soon prove more elusive than he had expected, and upon his return to the studio in early 1943, Faulkner would complain that he "hated like hell to come back" (*SL*, 167). In another hopeful formulation of a career poised between screen- and prose-writing (and one that has since become shorthand for the critical division of his work), Faulkner would inform his greatest advocate, Malcolm Cowley, in late 1944 that "I can work at Hollywood 6 months, stay home 6, am used to it now and have movie work locked off into another room" (*SL*, 186). But clearly this strategy was taking its toll. At the very end of his time with Warner Brothers, he wrote openly of his feelings for the film industry: "I feel bad, depressed, dreadful sense of wasting time, I imagine most of the symptoms of some kind of blow-up or collapse." Faulkner attributed these feelings to his time being split between supporting "a divided family, that is myself here in hotels, etc., and a house at home whose expenses dont alter whether I am there or not" (*SL*, 199).[1]

And while he struggled to keep the Hollywood work "locked off into another room," Faulkner also repeatedly wrote of the "symptoms" of screenwriting that manifested "whether I am there or not." Although as a screenwriter he was subjected only to a series of short-term contracts, the work seemed have a lasting effect on his very body. Reporting on the physical manifestations of screenwriting, he noted that Hollywood had inundated him "up to my neck" (*SL*, 96), that it had found its way into his "lungs" and "reflexes" (*SL*, 205, 248), and that even when he was free of its clutches, he would still "have it in my head" (*SL*, 243) that he would have to report back to the site of his secondary employment. And this was true, in a sense, as in the 1940s Faulkner was contractually obliged to produce work for the studio before doing anything else: "[Jack] Warner seems to insist he owns everything I write, and so Faulkner wont do any writing until he finds out just how much of his soul he no longer owns" (*SL*, 210). Whether stationed on the alienating West Coast or safe in the comfort of his hometown, Faulkner almost always seemed distracted or unable to write as he pleased, the film industry always proving more than a mere hindrance to his more favored career: "I have realised lately how much trash and junk writing for movies corrupted into my writing" (*SL*, 248–49), he wrote in 1947. Such are the sentiments of an author who was compelled to sell his time to an industry and to a craft for which he showed no particular interest, and we should certainly remember them as we consider this aspect of Faulkner's career in closer detail.

However, Faulkner's sentiments represent only one side of the story, and in this book I attempt to think through and past them in order to better understand what he managed to produce—and even what he managed to gain—from his Hollywood experiences. On paper, it is quite an achievement: all told, Faulkner was affiliated with five of the eight major film studios in Los Angeles—MGM, Universal, Radio-Keith-Orpheum (RKO), Fox, Warner Brothers—on and off for over two decades (1932–54), and the cumulative time he spent living and working in Beverly Hills, Burbank, and Culver City added up to around four years.² His efforts as what he modestly called a "motion picture doctor" (*LG*, 57)—fixing those scenes in films that required the touch of an accomplished author—earned him six screen credits, most notably for *To Have and Have Not* (Howard Hawks, 1944) and *The Big Sleep* (Hawks, 1946) but also for *Today We Live* (Hawks, 1933), *The Road to Glory* (Hawks, 1936), *Slave Ship* (Tay Garnett, 1938), and *Land of the Pharaohs* (Hawks, 1955). From this list, it should be clear that Faulkner had the greatest success with Howard Hawks, and indeed the prolific director was Faulkner's patron in Hollywood, often requesting assistance from the writer on screenplays that were causing him trouble. Faulkner may have hoped that Hawks would hire him full-time ("I am to be his writer," he exclaimed in 1943 [*SL*, 177]), but he ended up working for many different directors on a wide variety of properties. Altogether, he contributed to around fifty motion picture projects at various stages of the scripting process, and his ongoing presence in California owed in equal parts to his celebrity and his genuine competence as a prolific writer plying an unfamiliar trade as a contract laborer.

Faulkner was probably the most accomplished writer to ever grace classical Hollywood's studio system, but a notorious exchange with Clark Gable suggests that he was not necessarily a household name. At the very beginning of his screenwriting career, Faulkner went "dove-hunting" with Hawks and Gable (according to Bruce Kawin, dove hunts were in fact "wild weekends in rented bungalows in Los Angeles, with drinking and women").³ Gable asked him who he thought the best living writers were, and he replied, "Ernest Hemingway,

Willa Cather, John Dos Passos, Thomas Mann, and William Faulkner." Gable, who was not familiar with the literary talent in front of him, asked the Mississippian if he was a writer, and Faulkner famously responded: "Yes, Mr. Gable. What do you do?"[4]

Interestingly, of the five living writers that Faulkner listed that day, only he would maintain a direct, ongoing relationship with the industry. His closest rival, Hemingway, managed to avoid the business of screenwriting altogether, instead only selling the movie rights and leaving the task of adapting them for the screen to other writers (Faulkner included). One of Cather's works, *A Lost Lady*, was developed into a silent (Harry Beaumont, 1924) as well as a sound film (Alfred E. Green, 1934) at Warner Brothers, but Cather played no part in the adaptations. The German émigré and 1929 Nobel laureate Mann did live and work in Los Angeles for a time; he did not write screenplays when he was there, however, but instead completed his acclaimed novel *Doctor Faustus* (1948). Dos Passos was contracted to work on Josef von Sternberg's *The Devil Is a Woman* (1935) at Paramount, but he spent most of the five weeks of his contract in bed suffering from rheumatic fever and never returned to the studio.[5]

Like these authors, Faulkner is today more renowned for his literary prowess. His Nobel Prize–winning chronicle of life in the South that is depicted in the novels and short stories of the fictional Yoknapatawpha County (a disguised version of his own Lafayette County, Mississippi) traces the history of the region from its antebellum days up until the mid-twentieth century. His reputation as one of the most revered authors in the history of American letters rests on a series of dense and difficult modernist masterpieces: *The Sound and the Fury* (1929), *As I Lay Dying* (1930), *Absalom, Absalom!* (1936), and others in a long catalogue of inimitable works.[6] In Faulkner's use of language, there is an ambitious coupling of identifiable regional color with a fresh modernist sensibility. His narratives are brought into being through a creative process that makes the old South new, as he locates the legacies of slavery, the Civil War, and Reconstruction in unexpected places, manifesting the sentiment voiced in the most quoted line from *Requiem for a Nun* (1951): "The past is never dead. It's not even past" (*N*, 4:535). Faulkner's is the kind of prose that demands—but does not always reward—close reading; its polysyllabic Latinate words, its tendency toward the verbose and the baroque, and its notoriously unending sentences, all appear to say too much while at the same time withholding key narrative secrets. Across his entire body of work, Faulkner's writing displays his syntactical and narrative skill and also shows him to be an attentive secretary of southern history, attuned to the multitude of voices that make the region what it was and is.

But when we come to his voluminous output as a screenwriter, a different reading practice is required. A Faulkner screenplay rarely provides anything like the ludic experience one might gain by becoming lost in the vertiginous twists and turns of a Faulkner novel. Instead, we are confronted with a mostly recognizable formula, a combination of scene text that provides the setting and direction for the narrative, and a set of character names that precede lines of spoken dialogue. Indeed, much of the work that Faulkner produced for Hollywood was broadly in keeping with what Barry Langford has referred to as "the transparency and the self-explanatory qualities of the ideal commercial screenplay," which is written for simple transposition to film and so can "accordingly render 'excessive' critical interrogation redundant."[7] The screenplay form is not a simple genre but one defined by a variety of documents at different stages of the filmmaking process, prompting us to consider draft materials along with a "final" script (throughout this book I make specific reference to "treatments," "continuities," "screenplays" and other items that fall within the remit of the screenwriter). In his work for the studios, Faulkner adapted to both a new and unfamiliar craft and to a genre that changed in form over the twenty years he was associated with Hollywood.

How, then, are we to read Faulkner's screenplays? And how are we to relate them to the novels and short stories that he wrote at the same time? While it might seem that Faulkner the novelist and Faulkner the screenwriter are irreconcilable figures, two distinct writers whose works could not be more dissimilar, it is nevertheless crucial to "put these two Faulkners and their separate canons in the same croker sack," as Vincent Allan King has helpfully recommended.[8] Indeed, in spite of the absolute singularity of his writing and his mastery of the novel form, this book attempts to demonstrate that it is impossible to fully understand Faulkner's career without a serious consideration of what happened out West, a task for the critic that means not only acknowledging Hollywood's presence but reading and responding to the work Faulkner completed for the film industry. While his screenwriting may never be held in the same esteem as the novels and short stories, it was something more than a mere irritation in his career. Indeed, Faulkner's authorial stock continued to rise even as his engagement with Hollywood intensified, his belated critical following and Nobel Prize win only arriving after his last major contracts with the studio system. His novelistic output during those years runs the gamut from the derided to the critically acclaimed, and the Hollywood career covers both the majority of his self-proclaimed "matchless time" (*LG*, 149)—1929–42—and what Lawrence Schwartz has referred to as his "years of despair"—1940–46—the majority of which he spent at Warner Brothers.[9] If the critic is aware of Faulkner's own dismissal of his studio work and has made only a cursory comparison of the literary writing and the screenwriting, he or she may be tempted to consign the screenplays to the cutting room floor, sight unseen. Fortunately, however, although there remain some subscribers to what John T. Matthews has referred to as the "myth of the artist corrupted by newly dominant commercial media like the movies and magazines," for the most part contemporary Faulkner scholarship is quite attuned to the worth of the screenplays, and the result has been a boon for the field of Faulkner studies more broadly.[10]

Truth be told, there is a tradition of critical analysis of Faulkner's screenwriting, even if it has often been coupled with more wide-ranging associations of cinema with Faulkner's prose style.[11] As early as 1958 (less than a decade after Faulkner had secured the Nobel Prize), George Sidney surprisingly wrote an entire dissertation on the topic and laid much of the groundwork for the research that followed. In 1977, Bruce Kawin published *Faulkner and Film*, in which he ambitiously catalogues all of the screenplays to which Faulkner had contributed, notes their relevance to many of the novels, and also interprets what he describes as a kind of "montage" in his writing. *Faulkner and Film* remains the yardstick in this subdivision of Faulkner studies, and my book owes a great debt to it. In the year following the publication of Kawin's book, the annual Faulkner and Yoknapatawpha conference was devoted to the same theme; presentations responded to the various adaptations of Faulkner's work, to what might be called the "cinematic" quality of his prose, and to the screenplays themselves. And in a moment of institutional repetition, the 2010 iteration of the conference was devoted to the same topic. In between, the 2000–2001 issue of the *Faulkner Journal* focused on the author's various entanglements with cinema, and in 2004, Peter Lurie's *Vision's Immanence: Faulkner, Film, and the Popular Imagination*, which explores the filmic imaginary as a catalyst for Faulkner's writing during the Depression, was published.[12] The screenplays themselves have enjoyed a renaissance of late: articles by Sarah Gleeson-White and Ben Robbins and a landmark critical volume of Faulkner's Twentieth Century–Fox scripts recently edited by Gleeson-White are especially noteworthy in this regard.[13]

Bearing all of this scholarship in mind, *William Faulkner in Hollywood: Screenwriting for the Studios* offers a comprehensive overview of many of Faulkner's screenplays and analyzes them from a number of different and innovative angles. Most importantly, I have tried throughout to contextualize the screenplays by connecting them to the prose fiction Faulkner was writing at the same time, understanding the two forms of writing as more porous and intertwined than he himself would have us believe. Thomas Strychacz has described Faulkner as a "cinematic" writer, suggesting that his masterstroke was to appropriate the "formal elements" of cinema while at the same time eliminating any direct influence of Hollywood in his work and thus evading the industry's commercialism and the risk of becoming "an ideological sellout." "While Faulkner's work might seem cinematic in some abstract sense," Strychacz remarks, "it will not be held to owe its existence to Hollywood."[14] By way of contrast, this book argues for the particularity of Faulkner's "cinematic" writing, offering an empirical analysis of his debt not only to Hollywood but even more to the craft of screenwriting.

Rather than simply positing a generalized relationship between the fiction and the screenplays, I examine Faulkner's writing habits in close detail and aim to understand precisely how Faulkner's frequent shifts between different work practices and different scenes of writing might have had concrete implications for his career (see the timeline at the end of this book for a detailed chronology of Faulkner's back-and-forth passage between cinema and literature). My argument is not just that much of what Faulkner wrote in Hollywood has a vague affinity with his Yoknapatawpha work but that there were clear cross-pollinations between the two around the same time and sometimes even on the same page. It is worth remembering, for instance, that Faulkner wrote works as intricate as *Absalom, Absalom!*—which he would claim as "the best novel yet written by an American"—while he was stationed in Hollywood and likewise that he put some of his ideas for the silver screen on paper while he was back home in Mississippi.[15] But by paying even closer attention to his writing schedule, we also discover that Faulkner's composition of the celebrated short story "The Bear" was interrupted by a week's work on a treatment for Warner Brothers—"The Damned Don't Cry"—the call from the studio came so suddenly, in fact, that he was compelled to suspend his writing of the short story in the middle of a word.[16]

Faulkner references the competition occasioned by his oscillating work schedule in his letters and interviews, and it is clear that it affected his literary writing. In a number of places throughout this book, I speculate that this ongoing struggle becomes internalized in Faulkner's work, with the narrative content emerging as a complex reflection on the art of adaptation itself. In so doing, I have been guided especially by Fredric Jameson's theory that film adaptation, which encompasses more than the creation of an "imitation" from an "original" and more than the author's own decisions about what to include or exclude, stages a competition between different media (written and visual), allegorizing the "unresolvable struggles for primacy" between them.[17] In my discussion of short stories like "Elly" and "Golden Land," and of "The Bear" section of *Go Down, Moses*, I consider how the difficult disjunctions between writing and speech and between writing and visualization play out as a response (intended or otherwise) to a media ecology in which literature both resists and submits to cinema.

These tensions and divisions in Faulkner's literary work are all the more pronounced in his studio work, since the screenplay is a strange intermediary, occupying a particularly awkward position between page and screen. In his important 1965 essay, the Italian director Pier Paolo Pasolini describes the screenplay as a "structure that wants to be another structure," a "kinetic" text that never considers itself a finished product the way that a novel does. As a piece of writing, the screenplay is unique: it at once wants to be considered writing, a static and legible work that might be understood in isolation, but it also aspires to be a film, which requires that the words on the page be left behind and converted into the material that we will eventually see on the screen. This double status of the screenplay, both as a thing in itself and a blueprint for a potential film, means that it is "*a structure morphologically in movement*," a restless and unfinished object that is in motion, destined for another place even as we read it.[18] Embedded within the form itself is a paradox: the screenplay distills the content of its source text, creating a new, condensed version of a longer narrative; at the same time, however, as it prepares the text to be transformed into moving images, the screenplay is aware of its own obsolescence, a text that will find few readers once it has been used to produce the film itself.

While Pasolini's ideas are foundational to this book, my account of Faulkner's work in Hollywood is also supported by a more exact understanding of the idiosyncrasies of the screenplay and its role in film production. As Jack Boozer has argued, the screenplay has yet to be fully understood as the heart and soul of adaptation, to be recognized as the transmedial text that troubles the historical binary of source literature and finished film.[19] In the last few years, the emergent field of screenwriting studies has taken some important strides in righting this imbalance, not only treating the screenplay as an object worthy of study in its own right but also drawing attention to its centrality in Hollywood and in global filmmaking cultures. Thanks to the work of scholars like Claudia Sternberg, Steven Price, and Claus Tieber, and to the establishment of the Screenwriting Research Network and the *Journal of Screenwriting*, we now have a much better understanding of screenwriting as a unique form of art that requires a unique form of reading.[20] As this research shows, although it seems to have exhibited a certain degree of stability over its lifetime, the screenplay as an object has changed in many ways since its emergence in the silent era. There have been modifications to the genre both in terms of its textual form (adjusting it to sound cinema by the inclusion of written dialogue, for example) and in terms of its industrial function (the screenplay affording the writer a credited role in the filmmaking process).[21] In considering Faulkner's explorations in the genre, it is especially important to take both of these aspects of the screenplay into account. His first foray into screenwriting, for instance, coincided with the beginning of a broad shift in the industry toward the now-standardized "master-scene" screenplay (which I discuss in chapter 2). He also wrote television drama in its earliest days, working with the technically separate form of the teleplay (the focus of chapter 7). Each of these formats made different demands on Faulkner, and taking stock of the documents he produced at each stage of his Hollywood career requires a certain awareness of the particularities of the form.

The changing nature of Faulkner's screenwriting also owes a great deal to the seemingly minor differences between studios. As Tom Stempel has helpfully pointed out, the major studios in Hollywood each cultivated a peculiar "house style" for their screenplays, a fact we can observe by examining a few of Faulkner's contributions to the form. Although the parameters of the film script were broadly the same for all writers in the classical period, variation is nevertheless in evidence, often dictated by their respective heads of production. Irving Thalberg's MGM, for instance, often adopted an episodic structure for its stories that emphasized individual scenes for its star actors; Hawks's *Today We Live* (1933) bears this out, insofar as it modifies its Faulknerian source material—the short story "Turnabout"—by adding a female lead, Joan Crawford. Twentieth Century–Fox, meanwhile, displayed more regard for narrative flow because this studio did not have access to the same screen idols as

MGM. Warner Brothers, on the other hand, coupled popular actors with an "insistent and driving" style and preferred that its writers work serially rather than simultaneously.[22] When Faulkner worked on *Mildred Pierce*, for instance, his screenplay was tendered as one of eight from five different writers.[23]

Because elements of screenwriting escaped Faulkner's control, this book focuses less on the singularity of his style and more on a process that involves managerial oversight and multiple authorship, that is governed by industrial textual models, and that is subject to technological restrictions. On the one hand, then, the power customarily conferred on the author is transferred to a far more impersonal structure. By necessity, all work for a film studio—that of the screenwriter, director, and actor alike—must be understood with respect to what André Bazin once called the "genius of the system."[24] The success of the filmmaking process in Hollywood depended on the sublimation of idiosyncrasy into the larger design of the respective studios; because of this, as Thomas Schatz has observed, "any individual's style was no more than an inflection on an established studio style."[25] Indeed, following Jerome Christensen's recent and even more strident argument, we might say that Hollywood filmmaking is a kind of "corporate art"—even more than just a "house style"—in which the films made by each studio act as vehicles to further the studio's brand.[26] Although Christensen is well aware of the various human agents at work in the production of every commercial feature film, he boldly assigns the studio a status even greater than the cast and crew: "It is as important," he claims, "for a student of Hollywood to know that *The Big Sleep* (1946) was a Warner Bros. feature as it is to know that Howard Hawks directed the picture."[27] Never mind that Faulkner was one of its screenwriters!

If we were to embrace Christensen's persuasive thesis, then we would have to allow that Faulkner had little control over his material, since it proposes such a high level of commercial influence. Following his argument, Faulkner was either unconscious of this influence, or he was completely beholden to it and thus powerless to circumvent it. But even when we attend to the screenplays themselves, we discover another way in which the author's control was diminished, as Faulkner's signature was regularly just one of many in a series because multiple writers worked together on the same script. In spite of his noted distaste for the "compromise" (*LG*, 240) that studio writing represented, Faulkner was more often than not required to work cooperatively with fellow screenwriters, whether that meant adding dialogue to a treatment, altering a scene or two, or even dividing up the adaptation of a novel, chapter by chapter, as he would do with Leigh Brackett for *The Big Sleep*. The collaborative nature of the work makes it nearly impossible to identify Faulkner's precise contributions in many of the screenplays under discussion, and conflicting accounts of his level of involvement only hinder such an investigation. Howard Hawks emphasized Faulkner's contribution to *Land of the Pharaohs*, for example, while the author himself deflected the praise to cowriter Harry Kurnitz. And after the release of *The Southerner* (1945), Jean Renoir would claim that Faulkner was instrumental to the film, even though it appears that he only wrote two very brief scenes. Faulkner's name thus at times appears to serve as a simple kind of window-dressing on the screen.

Beleaguered by a system that traded on his name while also downplaying his contributions to its products, Faulkner can appear as a shadow of his former self in Hollywood. When we look past the credit sequences and into the screenplays themselves, however, we find a far more complex narrative. And by positioning his screenwriting alongside his work as a writer of prose fiction, we see that some of his own material followed him from the South to Hollywood, just as some of his ideas for the screen would accompany him on the return journey to Yoknapatawpha County. In what follows, I explore Faulkner's foray into and out of the film industry, locating his unique touch even in the relative anonymity of the studio system.

In chapter 1, I explore Faulkner's freshman experiences from 1932 to 1933 in Hollywood, where he worked initially for the most successful of all the studios, MGM. During his year at MGM, Faulkner worked mostly on film treatments, but he also contributed dialogue on a couple of occasions. At this time, the studio system was still in its honeymoon phase with sound cinema, and the screenplay was itself adjusting to that momentous change. The introduction of dialogue in the early 1930s necessitated an influx of novelists and playwrights experienced in writing speech for characters, and as Faulkner became accustomed to the new craft, he appears to have taken the importance of dialogue into account. Assigned to *Today We Live*, Faulkner was made to think about real, spoken dialogue in a way he hadn't done before, and it had a certain influence on the fiction he wrote immediately after his stay, the short stories "Elly" and "Two Dollar Wife." The star system at MGM under Thalberg that led the studio to center its films around its most prominent actors so as to ensure a series of box office hits also had an effect on Faulkner's literary work. While Faulkner was helping to consolidate this system, he was at the same time creating Yoknapatawpha County, his own fictional universe in which the repeat appearance of certain characters was crucial. If we read Faulkner's stories about the Sartoris brothers alongside his screenplay featuring the same pair, some intriguing overlaps and discontinuities emerge between the different strategies of the studio and the author.

Shortly after his year with MGM, Faulkner spent some time working for Universal, Twentieth Century–Fox, and RKO. Chapter 2 focuses on the years from 1934 to 1937, a period in which Faulkner wrote his masterpiece *Absalom, Absalom!*, his novel of aerial daring, *Pylon*, and a number of short stories that would collectively make up *The Unvanquished*. But at the same time, he managed to contribute to a handful of full-length screenplays and earned his second and third screen credits. At Universal and RKO in the midst of the Depression, Faulkner worked under his own steam. But at Fox, he was often joined by one or two cowriters and became acquainted with the process of the "story conference," in which his work was scrutinized by studio head Darryl Zanuck.

At the end of his final contract with Fox, Faulkner managed to write an adaptation of *Absalom, Absalom!* with the avant-garde director Dudley Murphy. In chapter 3, I examine the treatment, which was titled "Revolt in the Earth," that Faulkner composed with Murphy under the auspices of the independent production company, Associated Artists. A script that has been criticized for failing to live up to its incomparable source text and that indulges in some questionable primitivist aesthetics, "Revolt" remains interesting for its experimentations with sound and its life outside of the studio system. In fact, it is worth analyzing for all the ways in which it is unlike Faulkner's novel, and it provides a fascinating example of the author adapting his own work. This chapter offers a close comparison of Faulkner's works and also considers how Murphy's own filmography might provide one key to analyzing this screenplay that was never produced.

For the five years after he left Fox, Faulkner was able to get by without screenwriting work. But in 1942, he was back again, this time at Warner Brothers. It was here, under the terms of a notoriously unfair contract (which could have lasted for seven years but in fact ended in 1945), that Faulkner managed to write what he himself later nominated as "the best work I knew how on 5 or 6 scripts" (*SL*, 204). Chapters 4 and 5 follow Faulkner's ups and downs at Warner Brothers. Chapter 4, "Winning the War with Warners," examines Faulkner's work on a variety of projects encompassing the different aspects of the conflict at a studio that was more attuned than most to the impending war. His first projects were large-scale, big-budget works like "The De Gaulle Story" and "Battle Cry," which were later shelved, but he most notably cowrote the script for *To Have and Have Not*, an adaptation of Hemingway's novel that would feature Lauren Bacall and Humphrey Bogart in the leads. Although many of the films on which he worked were less ambitious in scope, Faulkner learned much from his writing during wartime, and it was during this time that he conceived his epic allegory, *A Fable* (1954), the novel born as a film treatment. The last short stories he wrote before making his way to Warner Brothers also focused on the war, and in some ways even resembled the studio's approach to the battle.

In an industry that prioritized war films in the first half of the 1940s, Faulkner was still able to write a number of screenplays set in the South. He wrote "The Damned Don't Cry" just as he was putting the final touches on *Go Down, Moses* (1942), although he was so preoccupied at Warner Brothers that he would not publish another novel until 1948, when *Intruder in the Dust* appeared. That work, along with the crime story "Knight's Gambit," reflects a region that was undergoing major changes during the war and also tessellates with some of Faulkner's screenwriting completed during those years. Chapter 5, titled "The Great Migration to Hollywood," argues that the major exodus of African American labor from the South in the 1940s not only had an enormous impact on Faulkner's fiction but also had an indirect effect on cinema in the decade. Here I argue that film noir, which routinely excluded black characters from its narratives, responded to a changing South by repressing on screen the mass influx of black citizens to Los Angeles. Faulkner's contributions at Warner Brothers widened the focus slightly, as he included a black maid in his screenplay for *Mildred Pierce* and charted a cross-generational saga of black and white families in "Country Lawyer." While Hollywood seemed unwilling to accommodate the New South on its screens—even Jean Renoir's *The Southerner* seemed slightly out of touch—the fading traditions of the region were also cause for concern in Faulkner's Yoknapatawpha fiction.

After winning the Nobel in 1950, Faulkner was for all intents and purposes freed from screenwriting as a necessity. Nevertheless, he made some late, important additions to his film portfolio in the 1950s. Chapter 6 takes as its focus "The Left Hand of God," a screenplay about a mercenary posing as a Catholic priest in postwar China that Faulkner wrote for Hawks at RKO. That script is linked to *Requiem for a Nun*, a novel incorporating several sections resembling stage plays that Faulkner was writing at the same time, in unexpected ways. In fact, some scenes from *Requiem for a Nun* were written on recycled manuscript pages that had already been used for "The Left Hand of God," so that their respective narratives at times literally overlap one another. In this chapter, I also analyze another intriguing connection between the highly stylized voiceover narration that Faulkner wrote for a character in the screenplay and the narrative voice in the novel, each of which are mediated by radio.

In 1953, Faulkner secured work writing for a medium that would become more popular than cinema: television. Chapter 7 follows the writer to New York, where he turned out adaptations of two of his own narratives—"The Brooch" and "Shall Not Perish"—for *Lux Video Theatre*, learning the difference between a screenplay and a teleplay in the process. Here we see Faulkner taking his own work and shaping it to fit the half-hour, two-act structure of the anthology drama, a process that also required him to consider the place of the sponsor's commercial interlude within the program. After the relatively quick completion of these two teleplays, Faulkner wrote an independent teleplay—an adaptation of the "Old Man" section of *If I Forget Thee, Jerusalem*—but was unable to attract any interest from the networks. In any case, these three teleplays offer fascinating insights not only into the form of the Golden Age television drama but also into the original works themselves, which negotiate some of the key factors shaping the new medium: the leveling of the wall separating "high" and "low" culture, the rivalry with a host of competing media in the postwar years, and the final triumphant spread of modernity to all parts of the nation.

After writing for the small screen, Faulkner turned his attention to television's polar opposite—CinemaScope—writing one final screenplay for Howard Hawks. *The Land of the Pharaohs*, the focus of the coda in this book, was Faulkner's last foray in Hollywood and came after his rise to fame as an author was complete. Above all else, the subject matter—the massive amount of collaborative labor it took to build the pyramids—offers an interesting reflection on filmmaking itself as an art form that buries words within images and that at the same time grants them immortality. Many of Faulkner's words survive on film and in screenplays buried deep in archival collections. It is my task in what follows to unearth their remains.

In *William Faulkner in Hollywood: Screenwriting for the Studios*, I consider the most interesting screenplays that Faulkner wrote, electing especially to analyze those works that produce interesting dialogues with his novels and short stories. Of necessity, I have had to omit some of the important scripts. Most notable in its absence is "Dreadful Hollow," a vampire narrative adapted from Irina Karlova's 1942 novel of the same name that Faulkner wrote for Hawks, probably soon after November 1944 when the director purchased the rights.[28] I have also omitted any discussion of Faulkner's work both before and after the years of his Hollywood career, as well as the years from 1937 to 1941, during which time he had no formal contractual engagements with any studios. And finally, I have elected not to discuss any of the adaptations of Faulkner's work in which he did not play a part: neither *The Tarnished Angels* (the 1957 adaptation of *Pylon* by Douglas Sirk) nor James Franco's recent *As I Lay Dying* (2013) and *The Sound and the Fury* (2014) feature in this book.

But there is more than enough to gain from studying Faulkner's screenwriting alone (too much, indeed, for this one book to cover). By privileging his Hollywood career and the screenplays that resulted from it, I also hope to shed new light on some of the works of prose fiction that have already been the subject of countless articles, chapters, dissertations, and monographs. Above all, my wish is that the analysis here will offer readers a more capacious understanding of Faulkner the writer and will encourage further scholarly interest in the close connections between page and screen in his body of work. In spite of Faulkner's feelings about Hollywood and his broad dismissal of the work he completed there, examining the materials for ourselves will not diminish our image of Faulkner but rather enrich our appreciation of his life and of his art.

CHAPTER 1

First Run

MGM

This chapter focuses on a few key elements of Faulkner's experience at Metro-Goldwyn-Mayer (MGM) between 1932 and 1933 and hypothesizes about their potential ramifications for his writing more broadly. First, Faulkner's involvement at MGM would offer him a different perspective on the role of women in the culture industry, as authors, screenwriters, actors, and characters. His first foray in screenwriting would alert him to the fact that Hollywood was carving out a place for women that the South had hardly contemplated, and (at least for this brief moment) it would throw the gender politics of his region into sharp relief.

Second, Faulkner's freshman attempt at screenwriting coincided with Hollywood's turn to sound, the technological and industrial revolution that created a demand for capable screenwriters in the first place. Among the majors, MGM became the largest importer of writers and in 1932 had "sixty-eight writers under contract, with weekly salaries totaling $40,000."[1] Commercial sound cinema implied dialogue, necessitating the expertise of literary authors accustomed to writing convincing lines that could be spoken by the studio's actors. Such work was customary for many of the playwrights who made the journey west, but novelists like Faulkner, whose dialogue was formerly spoken only by fictional characters on the page, would have to consider the way in which their writing would be delivered by living persons before the camera. Screenwriting had always functioned as a contingent art form, but the difficulty in maintaining authorial control became even greater with the talkies, which solicited carefully crafted lines of dialogue from writers only to hand them over to the actors, whose unpredictable interpretation of them could change the meaning the author had intended.

Actors had a lot of power at MGM, which prided itself on its wildly successful "star system," built on the casting of particular recognizable male and female actors as leads again and again across many different films produced by the studio. As I explain, this aspect of the studio was absolutely crucial to the production process there, and as certain stars were earmarked (and contracted) for certain films before even the storyline had become clear, the star system made itself felt in the screenplay. Faulkner may have discovered some parallels between the star-driven films of MGM and his own burgeoning Yoknapatawpha County, which was from the beginning bound together by the repeat appearances of several staple characters.

By now, the story of Faulkner's enigmatic arrival in Hollywood is a familiar one. He showed up in Culver City on May 7, 1932, reporting for duty under Sam Marx, head of the story department at MGM. Taking the initiative, Faulkner made some unexpected suggestions as to his possible assignments: "How about my writing newsreels?" he inquired. "Newsreels and Mickey Mouse, these are the only pictures I like."[2] Instead, he was assigned to work on *Flesh* (John Ford, 1932), a wrestling picture designed as a vehicle for Wallace Beery. Beery was seemingly unknown to Faulkner, who was shown some of the actor's recent screen appearances in a projection room. But no sooner had the show reel begun than Faulkner started acting up, discussing dog ownership with the hapless projectionist, and asking that the film be stopped, at which point he left the backlot and apparently absconded to Death Valley. He returned under a shroud of mystery ten days later, during which time his contract had been canceled. He was welcomed back to the studio, however, and then began work on the first of his nine properties for MGM.

From this account, one that is often repeated and embellished, Faulkner appears as a parochial interloper, a troublesome novice in the film industry who had little idea of the world he had entered. But there is more to this false start (or "mild fiasco" [*SL*, 293] as he later called it) than meets the eye. Although his proposal of a Mickey Mouse picture, for instance, was met with incredulity, it was perhaps more prophetic than critics have allowed. Even though the cartoon character's stories were then being written at Walt Disney Studios, Mickey would make a cameo alongside Jimmy Durante in MGM's comedic anthology film *Hollywood Party* (1934). That odd picture played on the so-called Grand Hotel plot that had been consecrated a couple of years earlier, but the combination of animated characters with living actors was also symptomatic of the changing face of the studio's fabled star system. Even in his seemingly wayward comments, Faulkner appeared to have more than a little knowledge of the studio's operations.

His early antics also contrasted with his contributions as a screenwriter. Even his first effort, "Manservant," reveals his canny awareness of some of the formal features of a screenplay. The treatment was adapted from Faulkner's story "Love," which he had been unable to sell to the magazines in 1921. Although on the reverse of one of the draft sheets for "Manservant," Faulkner wrote, "I am not settled good yet. I have not got used to this work. But I am as well as anyone can be in this bedlam," he had come equipped with a lexicon appropriate to his new craft, inscribing in the screenplay a "CLOSEUP" as well as several crane shots, indicated by "THE CAMERA FOLLOWS" and "WE FOLLOW" (*FMS*, 24, 8, 7).[3] And, perhaps making good on his desire to write newsreels, Faulkner also deployed insert shots of newspapers to show the passing of time (*FMS*, 15, 16). At the treatment stage, he already had a good idea of how the film would look on screen. And more than this, he was familiar with the actor for whom he may have been writing. "Manservant" was possibly intended as a vehicle for John Gilbert, an ailing star of the silent screen who had failed to adjust to sound cinema and was in his final years at the studio.[4] Although at one point, Gilbert had been "a very important element in MGM's valuation of itself," his image alone was no longer enough to sustain his popularity.[5] While Faulkner's description of Blynt, the character Gilbert would have played, is fairly vague—he is "about thirty. He wears several decorations" (*FMS*, 8)—he had already acknowledged Gilbert's beauty in *Sanctuary*, Popeye being referred to at one point as "a right pretty little man, even if he ain't no John Gilbert" (*N*, 2:336).

Dialogue was not only important for actors in 1932 but for screenwriters, too; the first stage in screenwriting was the treatment, in which the screenwriter outlined the story, and so if a screenwriter wrote dialogue, it meant that the studio had approved of the narrative and had authorized the writer to move on to the next stage. Dialogue also allowed for the fuller development of characters that previously only had form in narrative description. The first four properties that Faulkner worked on at MGM—"Manservant," "The College Widow," "Absolution," and "Flying the Mail"—never made it past the treatment stage, and Faulkner was not asked to write extensive lines of dialogue for any of them. While there are a few lines of speech in "Manservant" and though

"The College Widow" ends with a crucial barb uttered by its protagonist, for the most part Faulkner was imagining his screen characters solely through the descriptors he wrote in the scene text.

But this would change with a property that would also earn him his first screen credit. Faulkner's adaptation of his short story "Turnabout," which became *Today We Live* (Howard Hawks, 1933), not only saw him including a female character in a work that didn't originally have one but also forced him to consider how a real, speaking actor would enunciate the words he wrote. This foreign method of writing for actual voices recalibrated Faulkner's work and guided his changing approach to the idea of the New Woman, changes in evidence in a number of short fictions he produced immediately after his stint with MGM. In both "Two Dollar Wife" and "Elly," stories that show a special interest in the grain of the female voice, he is particularly mindful that the sexual, moral, and economic liberation of women in the United States was not a universal phenomenon. Women in the rural South could not as easily lay claim to the benefits of New Womanhood as their urban counterparts in the North.

Over the course of a year, Faulkner's screenwriting was subject to the peculiarities of MGM as a studio under the command of Irving Thalberg, head of production. Faulkner had to adjust to idiosyncrasies of a house style and to accept the focus on certain genres and, most importantly, the centrality of the star system that Thalberg had set in place. From the beginning, Faulkner became accustomed to preparing star vehicles for actors like Beery, Gilbert, and Crawford and was given to understand how the stars in question were to dictate the terms of his screenplays *avant la lettre*. But at the same time as he was creating different roles for the same stars—"sublimating the actual into the apocryphal" (*LG*, 255)— he would also begin to reuse his fictional characters in his screenplays, a practice of recycling he would engage in throughout his career. Here, at MGM, he had begun to think about how his newly minted fictional county, Yoknapatawpha, might itself constitute a star system, or, as he would put it, "a cosmos of my own" (*LG*, 255).

New Woman, Southern Woman

In a 1926 letter to Anita Loos, Faulkner admitted that he was "still rather Victorian in [his] prejudices regarding the intelligence of women, despite Elinor Wylie and Willa Cather and all the balance of them." Faulkner wrote in admiration of Loos's *Gentlemen Prefer Blondes* (1925), the novel in which Dorothy Shaw (the brunette) was constructed "through the intelligence of that elegant moron of a cornflower," her blonde friend, Lorelei Lee. But his "envious congratulations" were not unqualified, and in the context of the letter, his closing note—"But I wish I had thought of Dorothy first"—contains more jealousy than goodwill. In Faye Hammill's astute reading of the letter, Faulkner's initial praise of Loos against what he saw as her obtuse readership is overshadowed by his suggestion that she may not have been fully aware of her own powers—"you have builded better than you knew" (*SL*, 32). "Initially," Hammill writes, "Faulkner rightly associates Loos with the witty Dorothy, but subsequently he seems to consider her as another Lorelei—clumsy in her jokes but usually funny by accident rather than design."[6]

Faulkner's "Victorian" prejudices about Loos—who contributed far more as a scenarist in Hollywood than as a writer of fiction—would appear all the more outmoded by the time he arrived in Hollywood in 1932.[7] At this time, the industry was affording opportunities to Loreleis and Dorothys both; female screenwriters were some of the most sought after by directors and female actors commanded the most auspicious roles. Indeed, under the watchful eye of Irving Thalberg, Loos would replace the unreliable F. Scott Fitzgerald on *Red-Headed Woman* (Jack Conway, 1932), after he had tried and failed to write a screenplay for the picture.[8] Its star, Jean Harlow, was one of MGM's brightest lights during her short career, and a few years later made her way into Faulkner's *Pylon* (1935), where Laverne Shumann is noted for her "Harlowcolored hair that they would pay her money for in Hollywood" (*N*, 2:804). The first footage that Faulkner watched in Hollywood probably included scenes from *The Champ* (King Vidor, 1932), written by one of the highest paid screenwriters of the era, Frances Marion. She would go on to win the Academy Award for Best Story for that film and was supposed to have been earning $7,500–$10,000 per week in the period of Faulkner's first contract. Marion also enjoyed a fruitful working relationship with several female stars, including Marie Dressler, for whom she wrote often.[9]

The real success of women in the industry found its counterpart in a body of films depicting the so-called New Woman, who was regularly associated with economic independence, active participation in American political and civic life, and above all, a freedom to express sexual desire. Although women had entered the professions in greater numbers during the 1910s and had won suffrage in 1920, it was not until the early years of the Depression that the figure of the New Woman would truly gain representation in film. Cinema depicting women in the early sound period was initially torn between the new and the old-fashioned: between, for example, rural sweethearts like Lillian Gish and the liberated, boisterous "It" girl, Clara Bow, who was, as Molly Haskell observes in her classic account *From Reverence to Rape*, "the twentieth-century pitted against the nineteenth, urban against rural society, the liberated working girl against the Victorian valentine."[10] The liberation of cinematic women, whether vamp, flapper, or working girl, from the confines of domesticity and submissiveness is depicted as largely associated with urbanization, as the modern city offered a variety of occupations, chance encounters with members of the opposite sex, and changing modes of fashion rather than the stolidity of tradition.

Such aspects of life were simply unavailable in the South, a region that by the dawn of sound cinema was synonymous with the shrinking violets of D. W. Griffith's films, and it would be some time yet before Scarlett O'Hara could claim her precarious place as the "antebellum version of the flapper" in *Gone with the Wind* (Victor Fleming, 1939).[11] Even so, New Womanhood in the South was in this case only discovered in a return to a bygone era, and in the case of Fleming's film even seemed premised on the existence of the premodern institution of slavery. Michael Rogin has argued that Scarlett is allowed to be rebellious because "order has broken down in civil war" and there is no longer "any legitimate patriarchal authority" in the wake of the South's resounding defeat at the hands of the North.[12] In the ravaged landscape of Georgia, the social order must be reconstructed, and Scarlett must discover the limits of her freedom in this new age. Although much has changed during the war, at least part of Scarlett's independence, Rogin suggests, is helped by the continuation of black servitude in the nation (even if Scarlett's servants also prevent her from achieving complete independence): Scarlett's rebellion is made possible because of her servants' inability to rebel and is kept in check by their willingness to protect her.[13] Even with the material conditions and power relations in place, in the final analysis Scarlett longs after the husband she has rejected.[14]

But this was a film set in the South of old—what about the region on the road to modernity? Of course there had been many dramatic changes that had accompanied the region's passage through Reconstruction and into the twentieth century. And yet for women, in some respects it was much the same. Indeed, Faulkner wrote of the fact that the possibilities women were afforded in urban centers and in Hollywood cinema were perennially out of reach for women in his part of the nation. In an early draft of "Dry September" (1931), his story about the obvious lag between modern screen fantasy and the lived reality of the South, Faulkner describes the plight of the southern woman in towns like his fictional Jefferson: "Life in such places is terrible for women. Life in all places is terrible for women. But in such towns as this, bound by the old traditions of genteel idleness, to which the old defeated cling, and by the genteel poverty, which that engenders, they must see the boys and youths grow into men and depart and return not at all or with foreign city-bred wives while they, bound by the traditions, have in their bone and flesh the hot sun of the land and the stubborn feminine counterpart of that which bred a tradition and which could outlast victory or a defeat and which behind the doomed monotony of their day and nights lay like gunpowder in a flimsy vault" (WFM, 24:264).

A melancholic disparity had opened between the prospects of the urbanized New Woman—especially as she was depicted on the silver screen—and those of her southern equivalent. The latter wanted what the former had, but because of the persistence of hoary traditions and the geographical immobilization they entailed, such opportunities were not made available to her. Too much depended on keeping southern women in place to allow them to shake off their traditional roles. But by the 1930s, the tide was turning, and new possibilities for women were coming even to the South. Faulkner's response to this was complex, as his fiction both reflected and reimagined the issue of the New Woman in the South. He had by this point created several important "stubborn feminine" characters: Caddy Compson, the lost object of desire in *The Sound and the Fury*, Addie Bundren, the void around which *As I Lay Dying* coheres, and Lena Grove, the symbol of pregnant possibility of narrative progress in *Light in August*.[15]

Each of these figures troubled the age-old patriarchy and the cavalier myth of the region by resisting or interrogating the sustainability of women as southern belles: virtuous, docile, obedient. And in *Sanctuary*, readers discovered a more openly defiant and worrying instance of the emancipated woman in the South. Here, Temple Drake's refusal to remain "bound by the old traditions" signals her downfall, and the novel seems to come down particularly hard on her decision, punishing the protagonist for her actions. Temple comes painfully close to securing the rewards of New Womanhood, only to have them brutally snatched away from her at the hands of a criminal. The work is disconcerting in this apparent tendency toward misogyny, and Faulkner was widely disparaged in this instance for peddling the grotesque fictions of the South as a means of enticing northern readers. Its stance on the future of women in the South is far from unequivocal: while for Leslie Fiedler, Temple is "desecrated" at the hands of her author for her "betrayal of her traditionally submissive role," there is also a sense in which the explicit condemnation of female desire in *Sanctuary* might actually appear as its tacit endorsement and thus a denunciation instead of the very society that suffocates such desire.[16]

But this is certainly far from evident, and the dominant reading at the time was quick to note the unsavory elements of the novel. In this way, Faulkner's pulp modernist experiment had a negative effect on Hollywood and its representation of liberated women. Although Faulkner could not have known this would happen at the time, his sale of *Sanctuary* to Paramount Pictures and its appearance as *The Story of Temple Drake* (Stephen Roberts, 1933) helped to bring the full force of the Motion Picture Production Code to bear on the industry. Although the code was established in 1930, its more serious enforcement came in 1934, with the installation of Joseph Breen as its director. Faulkner's novel and the film adapted from it was in part what incited this more serious enforcement. In 1933, the Screen Writers' Guild and the Writers Branch of the Academy together voiced their concerns over "the production of stories based on perversion, or containing sequences showing it." Although it would affect the type of work they were able to do for the next three decades, the writers were here taking it on themselves to prevent unsavory content from making it to the screen, declaring a "war on filth" at the level of the screenplay itself: "If you want a job today in pictures at big money, all you have to do is to write a dirty book. Look what has happened recently. One of the most revolting novels ever published is William Faulkner's 'Sanctuary,' but Paramount is making it under the 'The Shame [sic] of Temple Drake,' and another major company has hired the author for its writing staff."[17] It was bad enough that screen sirens like Harlow were bringing Hollywood into disrepute. But to add insult to injury, here was a rural girl, Temple Drake, trying to emulate the independence reserved for her urban sisters. Worse still, Faulkner himself promised to bring more "filth" with him on his journey to MGM.

In a sense, the guild was right to be concerned, as Faulkner's first thought for Hollywood was something firmly in the *Sanctuary* mold. On a trip to New York late in 1931, the author had met a fellow southerner, Tallulah Bankhead, and began writing a short play for the young actor. Bankhead, who had recently begun her Hollywood career at Paramount's Astoria studios on Long Island, hoped that Faulkner could write her a screenplay once he had made his way westward, even if he had his reservations.[18] "I'd like to help a Southern girl who's climbin' to the top," he told her. "But you're too pretty an' nice a girl to play in anything *I'd* write" (a comment that suggests Faulkner's lack of familiarity with her work).[19] Rather inauspiciously, *Variety* magazine announced the Bankhead collaboration along with the publication of Faulkner's "Idyll in the Desert."[20] That story follows a woman from the East through to Arizona, where, after being jilted and fruitlessly waiting eight years for her lover's return, she contracts tuberculosis, makes her way to Los Angeles, and breathes her last after seeing her lover now married to another woman. But surely with Faulkner's help Bankhead would have better luck out west than his character?

She had first properly arrived on the screen as Nancy Courtney in Paramount's *Tarnished Lady* (George Cukor, 1931), making her a clear choice for Faulkner's brief story outline, "Night Bird," which he wrote before arriving at the studio. The narrative follows a young college girl who has been prevented from marrying the man she loves. She ends up dating a number of students at the local college (at which her father is a professor) and has an encounter with a strange older man who haunts her thereafter. Attempting to leave her past behind her, she marries her earlier sweetheart, but he kills her old pursuer in a struggle, after which he seeks a divorce. She returns to her dalliances with college boys and subsequently reencounters her ex-husband, now married with a child. As Faulkner explained in a letter to his wife, Estelle: "I am writing a movie for Tallulah Bankhead. How's that for high? The contract is to be signed today, for about $10,000.00. Like this: yesterday I wrote the outline, the synopsis, for which I am to get $500.00. Next I will elaborate the outline and put the action in, and I get $2500.00. Then, I write the dialogue and get the rest of it. And then likely we will go out to the Coast, to Hollywood" (*SL*, 53).

Although the work didn't quite unfold as planned (especially as concerned financial predictions), Faulkner was able to revisit "Night Bird" in May 1932. The single snippet of dialogue that Faulkner wrote for it was its final line, the sardonic toast: "To the mother of my child" (*FMS*, 33). When he converted the outline at MGM into the longer treatment, "The College Widow," the protagonist's final line was changed to the more emphatic "To the mother of my son!"[21] The story had been altered somewhat, too; the protagonist, Mary, was given greater psychological depth and made a little more malicious than naive. In "Night Bird," Faulkner originally had her undergo a miscarriage, which was a more believable motivation for her sudden divorce, but he had edited that out; in "The College Widow," this key plot point was reinstated. Although she still only speaks the single capstone of dialogue, other suggested lines betray a conflicted mind. While publicly refusing to marry her college beau, "She says that perhaps later, when people have forgotten it, she will come to him. She does not know herself whether she means this nor not. She is too busy thinking about her disappointment" (*FMS*, 43).

At the treatment stage, Mary certainly has things to say, but more often than not she internalizes what she can't express. She is attracted to a mysterious stranger who stalks her, but as she is unable to adequately communicate just why he is alluring, her actions don't always comport with her thoughts. In this way, she bears a keen resemblance to Temple Drake, another difficult female character who struggles to articulate her thoughts. Indeed, as a reader at the studio would comment two years after the treatment had been handed in, the story that emerged suggested that "Faulkner would obviously develop another SANCTUARY."[22] For this very reason, "The College Widow" was never approved for the addition of dialogue, but the importance of the only dialogue in the treatment shouldn't be understated, not least of all since Faulkner was clearly aware of its monetary value. The future of "The College Widow" depended on the power of its climactic, ironic, and tragic final words, which although inconclusive gestured toward the promised value of dialogue if the studio were to take up Faulkner's script. The single line, as Bruce Kawin has put it, forms a "paradoxical site of coherence," as it rounds out the treatment on an ironic note.[23] The plot is unresolved, but so too is the screenplay itself, as its final words demand the addition of further dialogue.

Dialogue in screenwriting generally follows a story outline that has already been tentatively approved. And yet, even though the more detailed account of the actions of characters and events of the plot precede the words intended for actors later assigned to the roles, it is clear from Faulkner's first efforts as a screenwriter that the real, material sounds of spoken dialogue are already present in the mind of the writer *before* the dialogue—and often before the treatment—is written. Before any ink was spilled, Faulkner had real stars, with real voices, in mind for the words that he would write. He knew their mannerisms, knew how they projected their lines on screen, understood the importance of their charisma; above all else, he knew who he was writing for. He was certainly asked to familiarize himself with Wallace Beery's persona in *The Champ* before making an attempt at *Flesh*, and he had probably also seen *Min and Bill* (George W. Hill, 1930), featuring Beery and Marie Dressler, before he wrote "Flying the Mail" in late May 1932.

Tallulah Bankhead was new to the talkies, having entered into Hollywood from the London stage. Her voice in theaters, as in the Paramount studio, had a deep, husky quality. As she later observed, her voice was "likened to the mating call of the caribou, and to the haunting note of a Strad."[24] Not having quite achieved the success she had imagined in Hollywood, Bankhead returned to the stage in the adaptation of W. Somerset Maugham's *Rain*, playing the prostitute Sadie Thompson, a character whose best efforts to reform herself are frustrated by a zealous missionary susceptible to her charms. She had little success in that role (one for which she had unsuccessfully auditioned almost a decade earlier), with one reviewer implying that the detrimental effects of Hollywood had weakened her performance: she was better in the play's "quieter scenes," but when she spoke, she bellowed "with the disturbing rumble of a female baritone."[25] From stage to screen and back again was a long journey.

"Turnabout," "Turn About," and *Today We Live*

Although Bankhead never quite endeared herself to cinemagoers, women in Hollywood in the early 1930s who had the ability to speak like men were generally favored, since the recording apparatus often had difficulties with high pitch. One such talent was Joan Crawford, whose appearance in the film adaptation of *Rain* (Lewis Milestone, 1932) three years before Bankhead's on the stage had marked her voice as one worth listening to. It was not only low but sufficiently neutral, lacking a harsh accent that might run the risk of distracting viewers.[26] As Kaja Silverman has written, such attributes of the voice allow it to "exceed the gender of the body from which it proceeds"—Crawford could resist being put in her place as a woman precisely because her voice had a masculine tone.[27] One of the major female stars of the decade, she could at once appear as the seductive Sadie or as the magnetic stenographer Flaemmchen in *Grand Hotel* (Edmund Goulding, 1932) and—due in part to the power of her voice—hold her own with the best of her male leads. Her unexpected appearance in the adaptation of Faulkner's "Turnabout" would confirm her as a star for whom MGM simply had to find a permanent place.

Written just before Faulkner had arrived in Hollywood and fortuitously recommended to Howard Hawks by Hawks's brother, William, "Turnabout" was a fairly simple story. Captain Bogard, an American pilot, takes the drunk British naval officer Claude Hope on one of his bombing missions. Hope returns the favor, taking Bogard on a mission of his own to prove that life aboard his torpedo boat is nothing to be sneezed at. Bogard meets the midshipman Ronnie, and the trio takes a daring run at a German port, during which their misfiring torpedo endangers the audacious crew. Later, Ronnie and Claude are killed, and Captain Bogard, vitalized after his encounters with the navy men, mounts a successful yet unorthodox raid on an enemy chateau. The eponymous "turnabout" of the story lay in the back and forth between Bogard and Hope, American and British, air and navy.

But a more dramatic switch would take place as the story was put through its paces at MGM. Faulkner completed a full-length script for his story in July—"Turn About," so spelled—which mostly followed the original narrative and also adhered to the MGM house style: the speakers' names in lower case and centered on the page, scene numbers in the extreme left margin, and slug lines and scene text indented.[28] As was custom, the "boy wonder" of the studio, Irving Thalberg, had read the script but had refrained from making any edits. Enthusiastically, he told Howard Hawks to "shoot it as is. I feel as if I'd make tracks all over it if I touched it."[29] Later in July, however, Thalberg's tracks were well and truly there, as he foisted Crawford into the mix, asserting that the actor needed to star in the picture so as to satisfy her contract with the studio. "I don't seem to remember a girl in the story," a dismayed Faulkner told Hawks.[30] Nevertheless, the author was obliged to find room for the female lead and was allowed to return home to Oxford later in the month in order to finish the second draft, complete with a new role for Crawford: she was to play Ann, Ronnie's sister, who would later fall in love with Bogard, while her first love, Claude (a ward of Ann and Ronnie's family) is later killed along with Ronnie.

As John Matthews has pointed out, Ann becomes the very focus of the screenplay. Beginning with a scene featuring three of the leads as young children playing in an English brook, Faulkner has Ronnie complaining about the presence of his sister, who protests that "I have just as much right here as you have." Claude allows her to stay, "so long as she doesn't muddy the water" (*FMS*, 129).[31] Of course, as Matthews observes, this is precisely what she does, both in the content of the screenplay—where, as an object of desire, she comes between a male friendship—and in the adaptation process, which demands that Faulkner's story, if it is to become a film, include a prominent female character. In this way, Matthews writes: "Joan Crawford *is* the movie."[32]

This first scene, which did not make it to the screen, proves this point. It also bears an affinity to the scenes of childhood in *The Sound and the Fury*, which stage in miniature the tense dynamics of filial desire and resentment that characterize the relationship between Caddy Compson and her three brothers (although the lasting memory of Caddy's "muddy drawers" is a far more potent version of Ann's muddying of the waters in "Turn About").[33] These opening exchanges also manage to encapsulate neatly the shift from published short story to screenplay, and they foreground the effect of the production process on the narrative, as changes made in writing transmuted into tangible, embodied changes. Even more than the addition of a female character, this adaptation would insist on the addition of a female voice that would deliver so much more than the single line designed for Tallulah Bankhead. Sensing her "intrusion" into the all-male story, Crawford apologized to Hawks and asked that her dialogue be written in a clipped, British style that would lend itself to snappier delivery and requested a more robust character that would be on a par with that of her male counterparts. The speech patterns attributed to Claude's character in Faulkner's story were now also shared by Ann, who would prove her worth by pacing her speech like an Englishman. But the resistance from its author is there from the very beginning, as Faulkner opens his screenplay by characterizing the two boys while offering nothing specific in the way of Ann's disposition:

Claude is lively, talkative, vivacious; Ronnie is sober, almost dour. He and Claude are quite busy when Ann comes up.

RONNIE
(Turns upon Ann)
Why do you have to tag along after me all the time?

ANN
I'm not tagging after you. I have just as much right here as you have.

CLAUDE
We're busy. We can't be bothered with girls. Go away.

ANN
I won't. (*FMS*, 129)

Although the female voice offered Faulkner the prospect of being able to work further on "The College Widow," this scene as written seems to suggest a certain reluctance to admit a woman into the adaptation of his own work. It was the problem of voice itself that would see the screenplay's opening

FIGURE 1. *Today We Live* (Howard Hawks, 1933)

sequences culled from the final cut. Initially, Dorothy Gray, one of the highest paid child actors at the time, was selected to play Ann in part because of her "adeptness in acquiring a British accent."[34] But the first scenes were excised from later revisions to the screenplay, since the children hired (Gray included) were apparently unconvincing in their adopted nationality, with Hawks recalling that their accents "sounded terrible."[35] Faulkner altered the narrative to accommodate the addition of Crawford to the film only to have the additional scenes—written precisely in order to better contextualize her role—excised.

Faulkner followed instructions by carving out a role for Crawford in the screenplay, and it was one that allowed her to vocalize her thoughts in a "clipped" form, emphasized by the ubiquity of monosyllabic lines. When Ann first falls for Claude, the pair discuss how they will break the romance to Ronnie, trading lines in rapid succession, with Ann taking charge of the conversation:

>ANN
>
>Are you going to tell him we are in love?
>
>CLAUDE
>
>What? Love? O good gad.
>
>ANN
>
>Don't lie to him any more. Claude.

First Run   29

                                CLAUDE
No. But aren't we?

                                 ANN
Are we?

                                CLAUDE
Right. You know. I don't. Are you?

                                 ANN
I don't know either.

                                CLAUDE
Right. I shan't lie. (*FMS*, 194)

The capacity of such exchanges to place Ann on an equal footing with her male leads depended not only on the content and the staccato rhythm of the lines but also ultimately on the way in which Crawford delivered them. Faulkner's intention with "Turn About" was to create the conditions of possibility for Crawford to come across as bold and self-assured. But what would eventually come out of Ann's mouth in *Today We Live* would be far less predictable, for the basic reason that dialogue as written was never the sole determinant of how the dialogue was spoken. As Sarah Kozloff points out, on set and in postproduction, lines "are improvised, cut, repeated, stammered, swallowed, paraphrased; changes may be minor or major, but the results represent the unique alchemy of *that* script in the mouth, mind, and heart of *that* actor."[36] For the first time in his career, Faulkner had to relinquish control over the way in which his writing was expressed, with writing ultimately bowing to speech on this occasion. Of course, he had always had to deal with the revisions of his editors, but this was something qualitatively different from what Faulkner had experienced up to that point. With Addie Bundren in *As I Lay Dying*, Temple Drake in *Sanctuary*, and Lena Grove in *Light in August*, Faulkner had provided a space of interiority, of inner speech and thought (whether unmediated or by way of free indirect discourse), lending varying degrees of psychological weight to female characters who were otherwise sidelined in the South.[37] But when writing for cinema, round characters would of necessity become flat, since on the screen it was far more difficult to suggest the complexities of mental processes or attitudes toward given situations. If any inner feeling articulated in the screenplay was to translate to the screen, it would need to register at a surface level.

In light of these constraints, Faulkner constructed Ann as a shallow character. She is built from visible actions and audible words alone and in certain places, Faulkner uses the commentary of others around her to make her seem more robust. Depth is not the priority here, and indeed, as is clear from the first scene, Ann is not even afforded a character profile. Most of what is depicted in the script and on screen is what Stanley Aronowitz has referred to as "the outer shell of social character" that leaves the core "unrepresented" in cinema.[38] Aside from her gestures, expressions, appearance, and one private scene of letter writing, Joan Crawford would depend on the clipped British dialect that Faulkner had written for her and would speak in such a way that her audience might believe that she was not a Hollywood actor but a real Englishwoman.

In October, however, while working with the young screenwriter Dwight Taylor on a third draft of "Turn About," Faulkner began to eliminate some of Ann's more masculine dialogue, rendering many of her best lines melodramatic. He also softened the contours of her character: Ann's antipathy toward Bogard blossoms into love, and her anger at his absence from the front line (after the deaths of her own father and mother) evaporates, as she is reduced to crying in her new lover's arms. Ann's trajectory—from self-assured female lead to a damsel-in-distress—is perhaps most clearly mapped in the difference between her thoughts and her words, a discrepancy that, as Kawin notes, Taylor targeted when he suggested that the changes Faulkner had made were "not an adequate substitute for the expression of a thought."[39] In their first meet cute, Ann is seething at the fact that Bogard will attend university instead of joining the war effort (*FMS*, 153–54). Her frustration over this is even more apparent in their next encounter, during which Ann becomes so incensed that she storms off and writes a letter to Claude in order to properly express herself:

> Ann, looking back, sees Ronnie and Bogard enter the door. Her face is hard, almost contemptuous. Turns and walks fast. Returns home, sits at desk and writes furiously to Claude:
>
> ". . . sickening. Beasts filthy strong and hale, going to school with fathers safe in New York, getting richer and richer because of the war. Why don't you hurry and be eighteen so you and Ronnie can go out there and kill them and kill them." (*FMS*, 157)

These are fighting words from Ann, and writing certainly confers power on Ann in the narrative, allowing her to articulate something that might otherwise go unsaid. But her speech here has been diverted into a written form because she has been discouraged from voicing her opinion in public. In her confrontations with Bogard, Ronnie tells her to "shut up" because "girls have no sense" (*FMS*, 154) and her brother also mentions to the American that Ann is a "silly girl. Child yet" (*FMS*, 157). Indeed, while Ann has moments of powerful self-representation on screen and at times lives up to her status as a "regular fire-eater" who wants to "kill all Germans out of hand," her reputation precedes her, since it is discussed among and managed by the men who circulate around her (*FMS*, 155). Indeed, Bogard discovers the origins of Ann's anger when he is told by a male companion, and with this knowledge he is ultimately able to seduce her:

BOGARD
I know why you hate me. I didn't at first. But I do now.

ANN
Know what?

BOGARD
About your mother and fa . . .

ANN
Stop. Don't you dare!
(She is breathing hard)
You're so safe, you Americans. It can't touch you. And we——I——Ronnie and me—
(She begins to cry hard not hiding her face, her fists clenched at her sides. Bogard goes to her; suddenly she is in his arms, crying hard.)
He was so damn fine! I liked him! I liked him! Things ought not to happen! They ought not to! God ought not to let them!
(She is crying uncontrollably, on the verge of hysteria. Bogard holds her. Her hands wander about him, clutching him)

BOGARD
Now. Now. I'll get you out of it. Away from it. We'll go back to America, where——

ANN
(She springs free, looking at him)
What?

BOGARD

We'll go back to America. I have been to school, enough.

ANN

(She slaps him hard, taut, furious)

You coward.

(She breathes hard.)

BOGARD

(Falls back, looking at her)

Coward, am I?

(He moves slowly toward her. She holds her ground, defiant, glaring at him. He takes her in his arms She resists. He kisses her by force. For a moment longer she resists. Then she succumbs, crying again. He holds her quietly now. From outside the window the tramp of soldiers begins and passes and dies away. He listens to the sound, turning his head as it passes.) (*FMS*, 163–64)

Although in previous scenes Ann makes damning, undiplomatic remarks about Bogard's absence from the war, here Bogard breaks her down. Of course, although it is Bogard's doing, the character is only acting at his author's behest; it is Faulkner himself effectively silencing the fictional woman he had brought into being. Following Dwight Taylor's criticisms of Faulkner's changes to Ann's dialogue, Marx assigned another writer to develop her character in more detail, although as Kawin asserts, the results of those revisions were "extremely sentimental."[40] Edith Fitzgerald, who had recently written additional dialogue for Crawford on *Laughing Sinners* (Harry Beaumont, 1931), then wrote some additional scenes for the actor, "focusing on her activities as a nurse and her friendships with other women."[41]

It is unclear just why Faulkner made the changes to the script that he did, but his revisions of Crawford's dialogue may have been part of an effort to regain control over his own work and to downplay the importance of the only female character in the story. In a letter he wrote to Ben Wasson, his Hollywood agent, while he was in Oxford working on the screenplay, Faulkner revealed how unhappy he was over Thalberg's instruction that he include Crawford and explained how he had arranged with Sam Marx "to work on TURN ABOUT alone and no interference from any Jew in California" (*SL*, 68). Later, at the premiere of *Today We Live* in his hometown, Faulkner mentioned that "writing a play and dialogue for the screen was somewhat different from writing a book. As a novelist he has absolute say as to what appears therein, while writing the play was subject to changes by the scenario authorities and the picture director."[42] The major change here was the introduction of a female character, and a female actor who would give her a voice. In Faulkner's first screen credit, it was ultimately the intervention of Ann and Joan Crawford that would highlight the differences between short story and screenplay in the adaptation process.

"Elly" and "Two Dollar Wife"

Once Faulkner had left MGM, Hollywood's approach to women seemed to change overnight. Robert Sklar describes the shift after 1933 as one from an "age of turbulence"—in which pre-code licentiousness allowed for the foregrounding of bold, self-determining female characters—to an "age of order," wherein women in cinema experienced a near reversal of fortunes, the more conservative nature of film in the middle years of the decade being less amenable to their social rise.[43] In these more orderly films, as Veronica Pravadelli points out, "emancipatory plots often had a negative outcome, while the formation of the heterosexual couple became the new model of reference, the era's dominant lifestyle."[44] On the one hand, there emerged a number of films in the 1930s that appeared to delight in punishing women who appeared to overreach their assigned societal roles. On the other, there was a tendency toward plots of integration, with the so-called comedy of remarriage normalizing stable relationships between men and women that seemed to stay safely within the bounds of what was socially acceptable.

Although he did not experience the full force of the Hays Code in his first year as a screenwriter, Faulkner completed two pieces of work immediately following his time at MGM that offer intriguing parallels with Hollywood's reaction against the New Woman. "Elly" is a haunting story of a young woman desperately trying to rebel against her parents and grandmother, principally through her relationship with a man who may be black. It continues the meditation on the entrapment of southern women that Faulkner had remarked on explicitly in "Dry September," but it ends on an even more brutal note than that story. In "Two Dollar Wife," on the other hand, Faulkner offers a bizarre tale of university romance, derived from his treatment for "The College Widow," albeit far lighter in tone. This story, styled as a kind of comedy of remarriage, sees a young couple almost pulled apart by the intervention of a rival at a drunken dance. Although its faux-serious ending is quite jarring, the comical interplay between the male and female betrothed is in marked contrast to the interracial and incestuous couplings elsewhere in Faulkner's work of the period.

Bearing some similarities with the types of films produced at MGM and elsewhere in the early 1930s, Faulkner's two stories also interrogate the repression and standardization of women in Hollywood by subjecting the female characters to the equally stifling atmosphere of the South. Faulkner's recent experiences with writing female voice for the screen proved useful here, since it is voice that is thematized most intriguingly in both "Elly" and "Two Dollar Wife." Where the thoughts of women like Temple Drake and Addie Bundren are refracted through the narrative voice in Faulkner's previous works, here, the prose is full of verbal articulation, important even if it falls on deaf ears (as in "Elly") or is traded loudly between an engaged couple (as in "Two Dollar Wife"). While both stories were conceived before Faulkner's MGM stay—"Elly" in 1929, as "Salvage" or "Selvage" and "Two Dollar Wife" as early as 1925 under the title "The Devil Beats His Wife" and then in 1927 as "Christmas Tree"—he revised both after that time, framing the first by a flashback and attempting to incorporate some of the material from "The College Widow" into the second (US, 701–2).[45]

In the manuscript of "Dry September," Faulkner had suggested that women in the South had little hope of sharing in the progress of women in urban areas. In "Elly"—one of the stories written after what he called his "sojourn downriver" (SL, 72)—the protagonist herself expresses this hopelessness; the "little dead" (CS, 212) town of Jefferson holds nothing for her. Indeed, it does not even allow her to be "caught in sin" (CS, 211), as she attempts to seduce her (probably) black lover, Paul, in front of her grandmother under the shrubbery of the family lawn. So reduced are the opportunities for young women like Elly in the South that she is forced to concoct her own drama. "I don't want to be idle," she pleads. "Just find me a job—anything, anywhere, so that it's so far away that I'll never have to hear the word Jefferson again" (CS, 212). Elly's attempts to escape her town are thwarted: she resigns herself to marrying a respectable assistant cashier, but after she is later rebuffed by her true object of desire, Paul, with no alternatives in sight, she forces the car she, Paul, and her grandmother are driving in over a precipice; although she survives, they die. In the final analysis, her actions seem desperately and psychotically selfish. But perhaps there is more here than the simple punishment of southern female desire? Indeed, as Alice Hall Petry has pointed out, "Elly" is not just an attack on the "flapper" type that appears grossly out of place in the region.

Both the Old and the New South come under fire here, as the stubborn and traditional grandmother is also faulted for her domination of the childlike yet ambitious Elly.[46]

A flashback that Faulkner added to the revised manuscript just as he was leaving MGM in 1933 begins the story just before the fateful car crash, but it also places front and center the gaps between thought and speech that consistently plague Elly. If Faulkner's original intention in "Selvage" had been, as Edmund Volpe argues, "to allow the story action to portray the heroine's inner tensions and her psychological collapse," the supplementary flashback reveals much more about her character.[47] In the first version of the story Elly's motivation was largely muddled, even though the clearest explanation of it came in the form of a direct thought, and so Faulkner now opted to enhance the character's inner turmoil by way of a couple of externalized devices—the objective correlative of the winding road and Elly's later use of writing as a means of communication. Having surveyed the limits of inner and outer character in "Turn About," now Faulkner would put them to the test in the short story form.

Ominously beginning on the bend on which the tale also finishes, the flashback has Elly desperately asking for Paul's commitment one last time, but there is something else, something "dreadful" and "terrible" (CS, 207) that is on her mind—her grandmother. Her desire for Paul, expressed openly and without reservation, is hampered by her silent thoughts of the woman who is the obstacle to that desire. The yearning to which Elly gives voice is also literally obstructed by the woman's "dead hearing" (CS, 208). The grandmother has been deaf "almost fifteen years" (CS, 212), and Elly must scream in order to attract the matriarch's attention, to make her desire to leave the South understood. Later, however, while trying to keep Paul from hearing, she manages a conversation with her grandmother by quieter means. Writing on the back of a dance program, Elly insists that Paul is not who he is rumored to be: "*He is not a negro he went to Va. and Harvard and everywhere*" (CS, 218). The exchange continues in this way, before Elly writes something she quickly regrets: "'Wait,' Elly cried thinly, whispering, tugging at the card, twisting it. 'I made a mistake. I—' With an astonishing movement, the grandmother bent the card up as Elly tried to snatch it free. 'Ah,' she said, then she read aloud: *Tell him. What do you know.* 'So. You didn't finish it, I see. What do I know?'" (CS, 218). Elly goads her grandmother in writing, since her most daring gesture of defiance would not be audible to the older woman. In "The College Widow," as we have seen, Faulkner vocalizes the narrative's most sardonic line, its protagonist voicing the cruel irony of her situation, which is left unresolved even as the line appears to resolve the treatment. There, the line heralds the potential for further dialogue, even though a dialogue continuity was not forthcoming. In "Turn About," the written lines of dialogue are themselves turned about by Joan Crawford, pointing to the unpredictable power of the recorded voice that emanates from the contingent words of the screenplay. In the screenplay, writing yields to images and to speech but is itself left behind once the adaptation process has been completed.

Here, the tension between writing, voice, and thought plays itself out differently, since we are privy to Elly's desires even if she can't or won't articulate them. In the forced translation of her thoughts into words, Elly is uncertain of what can and cannot be said, unsure what words will ultimately liberate her. Because Elly must transcribe her speech for her grandmother, the potential of her voice is diminished. Afterward, speaking to Paul furtively through the wall of his room, she is depicted "whimpering quietly to herself." She speaks only by "cupping her voice into the angle" of the wall; she holds "her breath while the dying and urgent whisper" to her lover "fail[s] against the cold plaster" (*CS*, 219). In the final tableau, Elly sits by the side of the road; she has survived the crash but is likely doomed to remain in her hometown, more than ever unable to leverage her voice against her restrictive environment. Although she has radically thrown off the burden of her grandmother, Elly seems to have regressed to a childlike state. All she can muster now is a whimper, and indeed, that word is repeated in different forms five times in the story's final paragraph: "she whimpered"; "She moaned a little, whimpering" (*CS*, 223); "She sat whimpering quietly"; "she said, whimpered"; "she whimpered" (*CS*, 224).[48] For Faulkner's New Woman, punished in her attempt to flee her place of birth, the "gunpowder" remains firmly inside the "flimsy vault" of the South and is more likely to produce a whimper than a bang.

The emancipatory plot of "Elly" has a decidedly negative outcome, ending with the failure of a woman's voice to have any bearing on her situation. But Faulkner follows another, different trajectory for the voice in the South in "Two Dollar Wife," the critically derided short story that has the embarrassing prestige of failing to place in a $500 short-story competition run by *College Life* in 1936. The magazine branded the piece as a tale of "madcap matrimony" and a "pungent panorama of reckless youth." Such alliterative hype may have helped sell copies of the magazine, but James Ferguson's opinion—that it "is without question one of the worst pieces of fiction ever produced by a major American writer"—likely represents the general consensus as to the literary quality of the story.[49] The criticism of it largely stems from its lack of believability: Maxwell Johns and Doris Houston become engaged and then break up only to be farcically reunited by way of a drunken dance, the appearance of a rival from Princeton, and the use of a forged marriage license. Faulkner himself "forgot the characters' names" (*SL*, 77) by the time he came to rewrite the story, and it is certainly not the most memorable example of his work.

But "Two Dollar Wife" has much more to offer if we read it with Hollywood in mind; indeed, this was a story that in part grew out of Faulkner's treatment "The College Widow." Before this, however, it started life as "The Devil Beats His Wife," which Faulkner began writing when he returned from Europe in 1925. A fragmented story that opens with dialogue "in the fashion of a play script," it features a young married couple, Doris and Harry. She taunts him, and he responds by hitting her, while their maid Della provides quiet commentary: "Hey, hey . . . devil beatin' his wife."[50] The story was left unfinished, but at least some of its elements remained intact when Faulkner came to rewrite it soon after as "Christmas Tree" and attempted unsuccessfully to have it published in the *Saturday Evening Post*. Now, the newlyweds are Doris and Hubert, and their tribulations are watched over by Ruby, another maid figure who gently intervenes in the relationship. When it is discovered that Doris has faked a pregnancy, Hubert abandons her, until Ruby sends a telegram revealing that there really is a child on the way: "*You come on home to your family.*"[51] After this point, the story also picks up the remnants of "The College Widow," seeking to strike a balance between the tragic and the comic. Perhaps with some awareness of Hollywood's newfound prudishness and distaste for the more immoral scenarios he had proposed, Faulkner turned to the past, reaching back to the early 1920s and the flapper-era characters of Fitzgerald for his inspiration.[52] While "Elly" condemns the flapper ethos, "Two Dollar Wife" revels in it. Here is a story, then, that was initially written for the magazines and rejected by them, had taken a detour through the MGM backlot, where it was also rejected, and had come out the other side, emerging as something strange and new that stood in contradistinction to another piece written in the same year.

Sending the story to Morton Goldman in 1934, Faulkner initially suggested it would "run about 20,000 words, maybe less," and that he could also "send a kind of synopsis of the rest" for the purposes of selling the complete story to "some editor" (*SL*, 77). It is no coincidence that Faulkner used the term "synopsis" to describe his work in progress, and the similarities between showing "Christmas Tree" to a prospective buyer and showing "The College Widow" to the studio could hardly be any clearer. But the stories themselves are quite different, as Faulkner turned the potentially scandalous treatment with the single line of dialogue into a story filled with drunken witticisms and angry one-liners—the stuff of a comedy film. As Edmund Volpe has pointed out, the style of the writing suggests that the story "has the makings of a very weak B grade movie."[53] Perhaps this is true. But in another way, "Two Dollar Wife" loosely follows the plot of a "comedy of remarriage," the genre most readily associated with Hollywood sound cinema, that focuses on the humorous entanglements of the romantic couple.

In his *Pursuits of Happiness*, Stanley Cavell dates the comedy of remarriage to 1934. Here, at this particular point in the Depression, the conditions were in place for a series of genre films that set the New Woman aside and substituted the mutual recognition of men and women for the more shocking narratives that had just preceded them. These films are generally about forgiveness and understanding, moments that are reached only after periods of intense soul searching and major conflict between the two principals and that more often than not necessitate flights into noncity spaces, pastoral landscapes that are removed from the real world.[54] And importantly, they also contain some very witty dialogue. Integral to such films is the consolidation of sound in cinema, specifically the verbal battles husband and wife engage in in which they show themselves able "to bear up under [an] assault of words."[55]

In "Two Dollar Wife," the abundance of dialogue and action seem suited more to the screen than to the page, and the cartoonish similes incline naturally toward visualization: the backside of the "colored maid" is seen "billowing like a high wave under oil," while Doris makes her grand entrance "like a pip squeezed from an orange" (*US*, 412). Furthermore, this revision of the original story has it end almost on a non sequitur: Maxwell, having sewed Doris into her dress, has carelessly left the needle in the seat cover of her chair. We think nothing of it until the story's end and are just as surprised as Max to discover that a baby (introduced here for the first time!) has swallowed the needle, narrowly escaping death. While the story is comedic from the beginning, then, this climactic ending is perhaps unintentionally hilarious and makes almost no sense in the context of the narrative.

As the story begins, we are immediately made party to one of the exaggerated, tempestuous exchanges between Maxwell and his intended as he puts the finishing touches on her dress: "'Here, Unconscious, sew me up!' he interpreted her mumbled words. 'Good God, I just sewed you into it night before last!' Maxwell growled. 'And I sewed you into it Christmas Eve, and I sewed—' 'Aw, dry up!' said Doris. 'You did your share of tearing it off of me! Sew it good this time, and let it stay sewed!'" (*US*, 413). While the first sounds she makes appear unflattering, Doris at least has the fortitude to stand up to the unreliable Maxwell, and her initial riposte—casting Maxwell as the "unconscious" to her subjectivity—affirms a dynamic partnership more at home in screwball features. There is certainly conflict between the two, and it is only in the excursion to a country club that this tension is finally resolved and the two are tentatively reunited. Although Doris does not feature very heavily in the narrative, when she does, it is dramatic. Disappearing with Maxwell's rival, Jornstadt—who changes the names on the marriage license—before returning to reluctantly marry her original fiancé, Doris triumphantly announces that "from now on you're taking orders from me—Mrs. Johns!" (*US*, 421). Unlike in *Sanctuary*, in which a night of drinking leads to tragedy for Temple Drake, and unlike in "Elly," in which there is little hope on the horizon for young women in the South, here the female protagonist holds her own and for a time enjoys some of the sexual and social freedoms denied elsewhere to women in Faulkner's oeuvre, although she is wedded in the end.

"War Birds" and the Star System

Movie stars, as Faulkner learned early on, were instrumental in the construction of film narratives. Directors, producers, and cinematographers would all help to transform a finished screenplay in their own way, as he well knew, but at MGM, the entire enterprise revolved around the star, and their fit within a greater star system. Screenwriting, especially its process of characterization, was often tempered by actors even before pen was put to paper, as is clear from Faulkner's first few efforts. And, importantly, the experience of working in Hollywood over many years meant that a screenwriter like Faulkner could produce a number of treatments and dialogue continuities for the same stars.

Stars were often contractually attached to a particular studio and often became synonymous with the films of their principal employers, although they could go on loan to rivals. This strategy was designed to ensure that viewers in search of a Clark Gable film would invariably look to the roaring lion of MGM, too. "MGM became the studio of stars," as Jerome Christensen has pointed out, "so that it might establish itself as the star studio—an intangible value that may not have shown up in the box office receipts for every MGM product but which accrued to the company's earning power and long-term profitability."[56] Indeed, adopting an idea first conceived by Adolph Zukor, founder of Paramount Pictures, MGM under Irving Thalberg became a studio chiefly concerned with acquiring and maintaining its stable of star actors, often assigning their players to films before they were written. *Grand Hotel*, which premiered just before Faulkner's arrival, was a case in point, which featured many of MGM's best and brightest in its cast and integrated all of them within a larger whole.

But midway through Faulkner's term at MGM, when Thalberg suddenly fell ill, the studio's historical reliance on stars began to fade. The abandonment of the system wasn't abrupt by any means—Faulkner's "Louisiana Lou" script had parts that may have been destined for Marie Dressler and Jean Harlow—but as Thalberg was taking some time off, it slowly shifted away from it.[57] Writing to studio president Nicholas Schenck from his sickbed in the first half of 1933, Thalberg noted that a successful Hollywood studio needed to retain its key players were it to continue to thrive during the Depression. "Without stars a company is in the position of starting over each year," he implored. Schenck's desire to churn out more pictures was causing the studio to lose hold of what had made it so prosperous: "The destruction of stars is a very subtle process," Thalberg commented. "You scarcely notice that it is happening. . . . Sometimes what seems to be quite a good picture somehow tends to destroy the background of glamour and interest that has been built up in the star."[58] Although he was key to its survival in these years, Thalberg's days at the studio after his illness were numbered, and the emphasis on star power was never quite as pronounced at the studio after he died in 1936.

Just as the star system was beginning to slide off the radar at MGM, Faulkner was starting to consolidate his own fictional universe in which the repeat appearances of characters in his novels and stories would lend weight to the apocrypha that was Yoknapatawpha County. Following in the footsteps of Balzac, one of his most admired predecessors, Faulkner would reuse a wide variety of his own characters—Gavin Stevens, Temple Drake, Flem Snopes—and slightly modify others—V. K. Suratt became V. K. Ratliff, Shreve MacKenzie turned into Shreve McCannon—cementing the connections between his works as he sought to provide the South with its own human comedy. And the two maps of his county that were published at the back of *Absalom, Absalom!* in 1936 and revised for the *Portable Faulkner* a decade later created the sense that the "postage stamp of native soil" was a real and living thing.

The reappearance and consolidation of Yoknapatawpha's characters was propelled in part by Faulkner's interactions with magazines. In 1931, an editor at *Scribner's* rejected a war story and made it clear to Faulkner exactly what his readership expected—more stories about Flem Snopes, the malevolent interloper who rises from storekeeper to power plant superintendent and finally becomes vice president of the Sartoris bank, unconcerned about how his actions affect others in the county. After declaring a "proprietary interest" in the character, the editor proceeded to dictate his demands to Faulkner: "We are so keen on that character that you may have the idea that we are urging you to turn yourself into a Flem Snopes machine, whether it is good for you artistically or not. In a measure, that is true; we do want the Flem Snopes in which the old boy is the mean, cagy creature of 'Wild Horses.' . . . We want him triumphant to the point where everybody in America will hate him in unison. Then it will be time for his downfall."[59] Even before his first visit to Hollywood, then, Faulkner was becoming aware of the star power of his own characters and was considering how the development of a single character—however loathsome—in different stories over time might contribute to the author's own success. But the mechanics of the studio were also now suggesting themselves to Faulkner, proposing the instantiation of stars as a factor as equally crucial as the molding of a plot or experiments with style and structure.

While the MGM star system and Yoknapatawpha County certainly bore similarities, it is important to note the differences between the repeat appearances of a fictional character in literature and the repeat appearances of a certain actor on film. Marked most obviously by iterations of a proper name, fictional characters are always of necessity composed of "words, of images, of imaginings, and are not real in the way that people are real."[60] We are always too aware of their unreality to mistake characters for persons, since their existences on the page, in traditional visual media, or as digitized combinations of pixels grant them immortality. Even though fictional characters take on many of the attributes of personhood, it is precisely because they outlive their creators that they can never properly pass for human beings.

Nevertheless, as John Frow has reminded us, fictional characters nag at us; their quasi-ontological status means that we cannot separate them completely from ourselves. For every character that we follow through a narrative, whom we may at times identify with and whom we may at other times repudiate, there is a semblance of reality there that "moves us," a haunting and seemingly humanoid excess that emerges through the textual material on which the character is borne.[61] Bound up with this close proximity of fictional character to real person is the notion that we are always ourselves built on ideas of fictional character, that "the non-personal insists at the very heart of the personal."[62] This last point is brought home by the meeting of character and person in the cinema, where fictional roles are grafted on to the bodies of real actors, stars performing a double duty in playing themselves and another. Characters in fictional texts are not "real" of course, but in cinema, the stars that play them are made of flesh and bone and have lives that extend beyond their screen appearances.

This fit of star with character on film can operate in a number of different ways, as Richard Dyer has shown, with differing degrees of congruence between the two.[63] Whether or not the star meshes with her character is often dictated by her prior screen roles; the identity of the star is never completely stable but rather is the aggregation of her turns in multiple feature films as well as of photographic and written representations in fan magazines and appearances at public events. As Dyer has argued, the "roles and/or the performance of a star in a film" often seem "as revealing the personality of the star," a dynamic that has had the effect of flattening of the distinction between life and art in Hollywood.[64] Although there was perhaps some "real" kernel of personality inside Wallace Beery, for example, who could really distinguish this from his countless performances as a lovable, dim-witted yet somehow charming slob?

Although the image and bearing of someone like Beery is easy to picture on screen, the task of the screenwriter is to plot, in words, the intersections of stars with their characters. In the screenplay, as Claudia Sternberg has written, characterization is achieved through a number of means before it is acted out in front of the camera. Initially, the character is introduced, either before the action begins (as in the dramatis personae of a stage play) or in the character's first appearance, in what is known as an "integrated first character profile."[65] At the start of his continuity treatment for "Flying the Mail," a story about daring aviators, Faulkner offers such a profile for the characters Wally and Min, who were in all likelihood based on characters played by Beery and Marie Dressler in *Min and Bill*.[66]

FIGURE 2. *Min and Bill* (George W. Hill, 1930)

1.   CLEVELAND 1912.

    Wally and Min, they are nearing 40. Wally is a mixture of child and tramp and blackguard. He is a swaggerer, yet there is a warm and lovable quality in him. He and Min are not married, yet Min's attitude toward him is that of a nagging wife. We learn that this relationship has continued for some time, during which time Min still hopes that Wally will some day marry her. Wally is always moving about, though probably without any intent of leaving her. A great deal of Min's life consists of trying to keep up with him, in order to take care of him, or perhaps just to have him to nag at. (*FMS*, 84)

This opening statement would have allowed Irving Thalberg to picture both Wally's and Min's characters in action—he the independent journeyman, she the nagging romantic—and both Beery and Dressler in their prior film appearances. The treatment contains very little dialogue; Faulkner instead cements this mode of characterization in his depiction of Wally's and Min's nonverbal behavior, incorporating directions for what Sternberg would categorize as kinesics (facial expressions, eye contact), haptics (touch), and proxemics (spatial interrelationships) throughout.[67] In the second scene, when he is about to make "a record non-stop flight of 300 miles to Chicago," Wally displays elements of all three: "With his chest out and with an expression of majestic condescension on his face, he now stalks through the crowd" (*FMS*, 84). These were characteristics that one might reasonably associate with Beery, too, suggesting Faulkner's intimate knowledge of the star's appearance and mannerisms.

In "Flying the Mail," Faulkner takes the characteristics of two MGM stars and transposes them on to the two main characters of the treatment. But in "War Birds," a later MGM dialogue continuity, he introduces two of his own "stars," the Sartoris brothers, Bayard and John, who had already achieved fame in a number of stories and were instrumental in inaugurating the fictional Yoknapatawpha County. The twins had first appeared in *Sartoris* (1929), which Faulkner had originally written as *Flags in the Dust* (1927). At the beginning of the story, John is already a casualty of war, and Bayard later dies during peacetime. But Faulkner reinstated his dead heroes in the coming years, featuring the Sartoris brothers in the short stories "Ad Astra" (1931), "All the Dead Pilots" (1931), and the unpublished "With Caution and Dispatch" (1932). John and Bayard appear once again in the screenplay that incorporates elements of these narratives, although here Faulkner was rewriting and resuscitating his characters especially for the screen.

Film has been associated with the haunting return of the deceased ever since its inception. The very operations of the medium—which takes a series of still photographs and reanimates them at twenty-four frames per second—create the semblance of movement out of stasis, life out of dead matter. In addition, the cinema allows us to witness the return to life of actors who have long since passed, preserving not only the images of screen stars but their very gestures and mannerisms in the kinetic flow of still frames. As Laura Mulvey has written, the "inanimate images of the filmstrip not only come alive in projection, but are the ghostly images of the now-dead resurrected into the appearance of life."[68] The illusion of the screen reanimates dead bodies, which never properly pass away once they have been recorded and archived in motion. But even before the projector can summon the ghosts of the past, the screenplay must imagine their movements already taking place in words and must conceive of the possibility that the dead could be made to live once more.

Faulkner imagined such procedures both in terms of the medium's specific capabilities and in more literal narrative terms. In late November, after he had finished with *Today We Live*, Faulkner began working on the property initially titled "War Story" but that would later become "War Birds" (or "A Ghost Story," the title Howard Hawks preferred).[69] He was still working on the script, supervised by Hawks, on February 7 in the next year.[70] It drew on *War Birds: The Diary of an Unknown Aviator* (1926) by Elliot White Springs, a work that MGM had recently acquired, as well as on an unsuccessful treatment based on the diary. Faulkner may have already been familiar with the book, which had been adapted from the real wartime diary of

John McGavock Grider, a young man from Memphis who had joined the Royal Flying Corps, trained in England, and later died in France.[71] Much of Grider's war record and family history resembled Faulkner's own. Grider had a great-uncle who had fought in the Civil War, just as Faulkner's own great-grandfather had done.

Faulkner's *Flags in the Dust* charts a similar path to Grider's diary. Set in the period immediately after the end of the Great War, it tells of the death of the reckless John Sartoris, shot down while flying behind German lines. John's twin, Bayard, is burdened by the guilt of his brother's death and lives out his days with an apparent death wish, first causing his grandfather (the Bayard of *The Unvanquished*) to die of a heart attack and then killing himself by crashing an unsafe test plane in Ohio. The boys descend from Colonel John Sartoris, who had led a guerilla struggle against Union troops in Mississippi, while his brother—yet another Bayard—was needlessly killed while mounting a raid for coffee and anchovies. If nominal determinism is anything to go by, the names "John" and "Bayard" are guarantors of dangerous and selfish behavior: like great-grandfather, like great-grandson. But the repetition of character traits is also part of a broader repetition of world events, with the new global conflict appearing to echo the fight between North and South.

Such repetitions were also apparent in the various Sartoris narratives published around this time, each of which approached the reappearance of the characters in a slightly different way. Faulkner included the brothers in what was originally *Flags in the Dust*, but after that manuscript had proved too unwieldy for a number of publishers, it was famously reduced in size and became *Sartoris*. As Theresa Towner has asserted, the ghostly return of the boys' great-grandfather is represented in a far more literal, direct manner in the truncated version, as a revenant "spirit" rather than as the subject of an anecdote.[72] The stories published after the release of the novel would offer further background. In "Ad Astra," we return to Armistice Day. John has already died, but Bayard is still living, although his reckless behavior already seems to have marked him for death. "All the Dead Pilots" goes further back, back to the days leading up to John's death, and intriguingly begins with the narrator looking at "snapshots" of the dead pilots from the war and reflecting on the impossibility of accurately depicting the "not exactly human" (*CS*, 511) men who gave their lives for their country. "That's why this story is a composite," he explains, "a series of brief glares in which, instantaneous and without depth or perspective, there stood into sight the portent and the threat of what the race could bear and become, in an instant between dark and dark" (*CS*, 512). And in "With Caution and Dispatch," the story Faulkner commenced just before his move to MGM, John crashes his fighter plane three times while somehow surviving. These mishaps are a grim reminder of his death—imminent in the Sartoris narrative but already staged three times in Faulkner's output. In the stories themselves, as in the chronology of their composition, John Sartoris hovers as a spirit: his author's interest in repeating his death several times over redoubles the effect of his ghostly presence from *Sartoris* all the way through to "War Birds" and affirms the importance of such characters in the Yoknapatawpha universe.

When the Sartorises migrated to the MGM backlot, this revenant quality would become all the more apparent, since the "War Birds" screenplay was, according to Howard Hawks, inspired by Faulkner's dissatisfaction with a recent "ghost story" he had seen at the theater: *Smilin' Through* (Sidney Franklin, 1932), starring Norma Shearer.[73] That film begins in 1868 with the wedding of a young couple, during which Shearer's character, Moonyeen, is shot dead by a jealous spurned lover (Fredric March). Her fiancée John (Leslie Howard) lives on, as the action flashes forward half a century to 1915. He has looked after Moonyeen's niece, Kathleen (also played by Shearer), who is now in love with the murderer's son, Kenneth (also played by March). Although John attempts to prevent their matrimony, Kenneth's commitment—both to his nation in the Great War and to Kathleen—shows him to be a better man than his father, and John gives the couple his blessing.

The narrative of *Smilin' Through* has some obvious resonances both with *Flags in the Dust* and with Grider's diary, including an emphasis on both the inevitability of warfare and continuities of certain undesirable family traits and a son who is able to avoid repeating the sins of his father. Importantly, this mixture of influences also led to Faulkner altering the characterizations and fates of John and Bayard in his screenplay. Most notably, Bayard dies in the earlier novel but survives in "War Birds," where he functions as a more mature character who keeps alive the memory of his departed brother and resists the temptation to kill the interloping German character Dorn, who is responsible for John's death. Faulkner was here both developing and preserving the characters he had already created and redeployed several times in the preceding few years, maintaining the Sartoris brothers as staples of his budding fictional universe but also allowing them to grow and develop for the screen. In addition to using profiles and nonverbal behaviors as methods of characterization in the screenplay, in "War Birds" Faulkner also put the effects of editing to good use in constructing his protagonists.

FIGURE 3. *Smilin' Through* (Sidney Franklin, 1932)

And indeed, the specificities of cinema would add to the sense of immortality all the more. While he experimented with a variety of different transitional effects—kaleidoscopic dissolves, cuts, double exposures—one of the most prominent devices Faulkner used was possibly inspired by the film he had apparently disliked. In *Smilin' Through*, Moonyeen is able to communicate with John from beyond the grave, and Shearer's ghostly image is projected in many scenes throughout even as she also portrays the flesh-and-blood Kathleen. Even after her on-screen death, Shearer—who was Thalberg's wife and was earmarked for many important roles at the studio—would not really die but could live on as both a spirit and as a younger doppelganger, thanks to the magic of film. The double exposures in the film were commended for their technical accuracy in *American Cinematographer*.[74] And as Maureen Turim has observed, this trick doubling of Shearer's role also had much to do with expanding the possibility of the star vehicle—what could be better than one lead role for Norma Shearer but two?[75]

Faulkner would use double exposures and other similar effects in the same way as Sidney Franklin. Often, he uses dissolves to effect prosaic transitions between scenes, but he also uses them for the appearance of the ghost of John

Sartoris, a gesture that allows the character to live on in the film even after he has died and to live on in Faulkner's work, too. John's ghost is visible on screen on a number of occasions, as when his hand is seen writing the diary from which his wife reads after he is gone or when his plane appears, still airborne after its destruction:

249. BAYARD CRUISING ALONE.
He approaches a cloud as though it were a rendezvous. As he reaches cloud, ghost of John's ship resolves as though waiting for him. John lifts his hand. Bayard points forward. John nods, the two ships go on together, Bayard looking this way and that through binocular. Steadies glass, turns, waggles his wings. John waggles back. Bayard indicates a flight of ships in distance. John nods. They turn and fly toward ships, Bayard watching them through glass. (*FMS*, 383)

Such visualization of the dead was already suggested in Grider's diary. Against the irreversibility of death, he wrote that "it's hard for me to believe that a man ever becomes even a ghost. I have sort of a feeling that he stays just as he is and simply jumps behind a cloud or steps thru a mirror."[76] John's ghost, complete with his ship, indeed does exist up in the clouds and remains present to Bayard as though it were real, even influencing his actions in the earthly realm.

When Dorn, the German responsible for John's death, is captured, Bayard has the chance to shoot him. However, out of consideration for Antoinette—the Frenchwoman who loved John—and for John's child, Johnny, he refuses. His actions in the following scene are completely at odds with the Bayard Sartoris known to readers of Faulkner's prose fiction, changing our earlier picture of the character by suggesting that he is capable of a degree of selfless self-restraint:

Dorn
Well? Why do you wait? Your brother is slain, but my country is slain; fallen from a greater height than my Camel has ever reached. Shoot, Captain.
Antoinette watches Bayard, her hands to her face, poised as though to run. Bayard looks at Dorn, his face wrung, terrible. Slowly the pistol rises, covers Dorn's chest, steadies. They look at one another. Tableau. Then Bayard flings pistol through window. The fractured glass is in the shape of a star. Antoinette runs forward, falls at Bayard's feet, clutching his knees.

> Antoinette
>
> Thank God! Thank God!
>
> Bayard stands, his head bent. As DISSOLVE begins, the star shaped fracture in the glass begins to glow faintly as daylight begins behind it. It is brightest at the instant of complete dissolve, then it begins also to fade. (*FMS*, 409)

Bayard's radical decision to lay his weapon aside rather than seeking revenge elevates his character. It is an action helped along, too, by the expressionistic effect that Faulkner suggests: after Bayard throws his gun, the glass shatters in the shape of a star, which allows the light to pierce through it even as the image dissolves. The particular shape of the broken glass allegorizes the resting place of John Sartoris in the celestial realm but also suggests the waxing and waning of the star characters that Faulkner had here attempted to introduce to Hollywood: Bayard and John would never make it to the screen, but in this, their final appearances in Faulkner's work, they would certainly develop in new, exciting directions. And this story comes to an end in a markedly different manner than the other stories they appear in:

> 323   IN DISSOLVE there passes behind Bayard the ghost of John's ship, John looking down at them, his face bright, peaceful. The ship goes on in dissolve; sound of an engine dies away.
>
> THE END (*FMS*, 420)

Faulkner creates his Sartoris twins anew in their single screenplay appearance, giving them traits they did not possess in his fiction and enabling them in different ways to experience life after death: Bayard lives on instead of dying as he does in the fiction, while John's ghost pervades the script in a more vivid, palpable way than in the fiction, projected as a visual effect that could be realized only on the screen.

Midway through his time at MGM, Faulkner was writing with one eye on the studio's fabled star system and the other turned to his own newly networked narrative system that he was developing to ground his own region in a fictional register, a system whose reiterated characters and stories were key to its continued well-being. While a great economic, industrial, and artistic gulf lay between the studio's vision and Faulkner's own, what we might prise from the author's work on "Turn About" and "War Birds" is the a priori influence of stars and characters alike on the stories they would come to inhabit; in both cases, before pen was put to paper, the proper names, voices, and personality traits of studio actors and fictional men and women were bringing new narrative worlds into being and solidifying those that had already been set in motion.

Return to Oxford

The final three properties to which Faulkner was attached at MGM—"Honor," "Mythical Latin-American Kingdom Story," and "Louisiana Lou/Lazy River"—emerged during a strange period for the studio. Sam Marx records that Thalberg had been "ill and away almost the entire first half of 1933" and that during this time vice president Louis B. Mayer, operating in his stead, "never read a script."[77] What Mayer did do was to deliver a bracing diatribe to his staff in Culver City, informing them that under his regime he expected them to "try and accomplish things" on a daily basis and indicating that the writers specifically were to be "pinned down to story material" and "were not to be allowed to play around with hazy and fantastic ideas."[78] And it was at this confusing time, when Faulkner had finished one contract with the Joyce-Selznick agency and was about to start another through William Hawks, that he reflected on his conditions of employment: "The arrangement is like that of a field hand; either of us (me or M.G.M.) to call it off without notice, they to pay me by the week, and to pay a bonus on each original story" (*SL*, 71). MGM was feeling the pinch of the Great Depression, and a staff-wide 50 percent pay cut was introduced in March of that year:[79] Faulkner himself would see his salary reduced from $600 to $300 per week.[80]

"Honor" was based on Faulkner's short story of the same name, although he told Marx that he "did not change it or do any work on it at all, being at the time engaged on the WAR STORY" (*SL*, 73). In March 1933, he began to write an untitled full-length dialogue continuity that was later referred to as "Mythical Latin-American Kingdom Story," an adventure narrative featuring American characters in an unnamed nation caught up in a revolution. As Kawin observes, the script recalls Faulkner's earlier short stories "Black Music" and "Carcassonne," and also looks forward to *Pylon* in its characterization of the aircraft mechanic Otto Birdsong—a prototype, perhaps, for Jiggs.[81] This screenplay was apparently made possible because of Thalberg's absence, too, since it "had not been cleared in advance with Marx or Hawks."[82] In Oxford after the birth of his daughter, Jill, he completed work on the piece, attempting to make something more of it, perhaps even to turn it into a novel. Although Marx had found the script to be "very unsatisfactory," Faulkner was granted permission to rewrite the narrative as a novel, with some faint hope on Marx's part that from it would emerge "a better basis for a motion picture."[83] It was never to be.

Faulkner's final project for MGM, Tod Browning's ill-fated "Louisiana Lou"—which became *Lazy River* (George Seitz, 1934)—must have initially seemed like the perfect material for the Mississippian.[84] It followed the travails of a group of convicts who choose not to participate in a prison break and are rewarded with pardons for honorable behavior and who subsequently make their way to a Louisiana shrimping village (a plot that Faulkner may have recalled while writing his "Old Man" section of *If I Forget Thee, Jerusalem*). Faulkner later recounted some absurd facets of the project; for example, the crew built an artificial shrimp village instead of buying one already constructed. In part owing to the need to tighten the budget after the expense of shooting on location in Louisiana but also to the studio's dissatisfaction with the work in progress, Browning was soon fired, and Faulkner dismissed along with him (*LG*, 243). His last contribution at MGM, although firmly in the southern tradition, was cut short, and Faulkner returned home to Oxford.

CHAPTER 2

Second Run

Universal, Twentieth Century–Fox, RKO

In the year after his MGM contract had expired, Faulkner turned to short story writing as the lesser of two evils. Writing short stories might have been almost as much of a commercial endeavor as writing screenplays, but he clearly preferred it and would resist the siren call of the studio by working prolifically for the magazines—even if it was, as he called it, "orthodox prostitution" (*SL*, 85). Hollywood was "flirting with me again," he wrote late in 1933, "but if I can make a nickel from time to time with short stories, I will give them the go-by" (*SL*, 75). For the most part, this was possible, and these were fruitful times; these stories contributed to Faulkner's expanding magazine portfolio, and many served as the embryo for the beginnings of several later novels.

Notably, nearly all of the stories that made up *The Unvanquished* (1937) were published between 1934 and 1936: "Ambuscade," "Retreat," and "Raid" in 1934, "Drusilla" (or "Skirmish at Sartoris") in 1935, and "The Unvanquished" (or "Riposte in Tertio") and "Vendée" in 1936. This period also saw the germination of *Absalom, Absalom!* in the short story "Wash" (1934), *Go Down, Moses* in "Lion" (1935), and *Knight's Gambit* in "Monk" (1937). And in 1934, Faulkner was able to publish *Doctor Martino and Other Stories*, a collection of published and unpublished pieces. But short fiction would lead him elsewhere, too. *Variety* magazine's brief review of *Doctor Martino* gestures toward the potential afterlives of the stories: the reviewer mentions the successful adaptation of "Turnabout" before noting that "'Death Drag' is another that could be filmed" and that "'Smoke' is a cinch for picturization."[1]

At the time, however, Faulkner was far from enamored with the idea of screen adaptations and had expressed as much in his plans for a text with the working title "A Child's Garden of Motion Picture Scripts." "They will be burlesque of the sure-fire movies and plays," he wrote his agent, Morton Goldman, "or say a burlesque of how the movies would treat standard plays and classic plays and novels, written in a modified form of a movie script" (*SL*, 79). The clearly pejorative association of the child with the screenplay suggests that Faulkner's view of film adaptation was that the screenwriter could do little but bowdlerize that which had already been written. Even so, after the graduation of "Turnabout" to the screen, Faulkner did eagerly attempt to sell his own novels to the studio system. And soon enough, screenwriting itself would beckon again.

From July 1934 to July 1937, Faulkner worked for three separate studios: Twentieth Century–Fox, Universal, and Radio-Keith-Orpheum (RKO). Universal and RKO were the smallest studios he would write for over the course of his screenplay career. He worked on only one property at Universal, "Sutter's Gold," and only one at RKO, "Gunga Din." At Fox, he was assigned to seven: "The Road to Glory," "Banjo on My Knee," "The Last Slaver/Slave Ship," "Four Men and a Prayer," "Submarine Patrol/Splinter Fleet," "Dance Hall/The Giant Swing/The Bouncer and the Lady," and "Drums along the Mohawk."[2] All told, the three years of intermittent work were more intense than his time at MGM, as Faulkner attended story conferences with Fox vice president Darryl Zanuck, wrote extensive dialogue continuities, and participated fully in the adaptation process, developing novels and scripts and even incorporating existing footage into his work.

And it was work that both subsidized and influenced his prose writing during the worst years of the Depression. At Universal, Faulkner wrote a 108-page treatment for "Sutter's Gold" that borrowed from an earlier script written by none other than Sergei Eisenstein. The story, about a Swiss adventurer who finds gold in America, was a perfect fantasy for the era. Faulkner learned much from Eisenstein in his rewriting of the script, and the particular formal innovations Faulkner introduced into his revision would worm their way unexpectedly into his novel about daring barnstormers, *Pylon* (1935).

Contrary to the message of "Sutter's Gold" (but consistent with the film's poor box office returns), money was drying up in Hollywood. "Golden Land," the one short story Faulkner wrote that addressed the chimera of Los Angeles, depicted speculative real estate and tabloids in place of material riches, as the city seemed to lose touch with the real world. At the same time, however,

Faulkner's craft concretely benefited from screenwriting during his time with Fox. While at Fox, he also continued work on *Absalom, Absalom!*, borrowing stylistic and thematic elements from his screenplays. That novel was finally published around the same time he was working on the screenplay for *Slave Ship* (Tay Garnett, 1937), a film that also addresses the mysteries of the triangular trade and one that perhaps inspired a late revision to the author's magnum opus.

Overall, Faulkner's work in Hollywood during the mid-1930s proved that it did not simply "interrupt" his preferred writing practice. With the experience of regularly writing long dialogue continuities adapted from the works of fellow novelists, he was able to consider how his own prose fiction might incline toward the screen, although he had mixed success in his efforts to sell *Pylon*, *Absalom, Absalom!*, and *The Unvanquished* to studio producers. In fact, the screenwriting he carried out for Universal, Fox, and RKO should be counted in the reckoning of Faulkner's "matchless time," for without his experiences at these studios, the prolific output of novels and short stories in the decade simply would not have been possible.

"Sutter's Gold" and *Pylon*

In July 1934, Faulkner found himself back in Hollywood once more. He was again working for Hawks, although this time the two were reunited at Universal Studios, assigned to "Sutter's Gold." This property was an adaptation of Blaise Cendrars's best-selling novel of frontier life, *L'or* (1925), which was translated into English in 1926 as *Sutter's Gold*, but Faulkner wasn't the first to attempt to translate it for the screen. Sergei Eisenstein, who had been in Hollywood since 1930 at the behest of Paramount Pictures' Jesse Lasky, had already tried his hand at the narrative, albeit unsuccessfully—his script was rejected on the grounds that it would cost $3 million to produce.[3] Although, as the Soviet director pointed out, there were probably other factors counting against him: "'What? Let the Bolsheviks get at the subject of gold . . . ?' They shook their heads and finally shelved the project with all its ramifications."[4] In any case, after Paramount's rebuff, the script reverted to its owners at Universal. Another writer completed a screenplay there in November 1933, but evidently it was not to the satisfaction of the studio.[5]

Universal was at the time renowned for its B pictures, excelling most notably with horror films like *Dracula* (Tod Browning, 1931), *Frankenstein* (James Whale, 1931), and *The Mummy* (Karl Freund, 1932). Under studio chief Carl

Laemmle Jr., however, it began moving into new territory, with woman's pictures such as *Imitation of Life* (John M. Stahl, 1934) and musicals such as *Show Boat* (James Whale, 1936), notable attempts to compete in the difficult first-run market. But the studio—continuing to produce its bread and butter genre films while also expanding its repertoire—could not have it both ways. John Stahl's *Magnificent Obsession* (1935), a critically successful film that was financially ruinous for the studio, begins with an episode that cruelly allegorizes the problem: a spoiled playboy and a generous surgeon lie dying in the same hospital, but there aren't enough resources to resuscitate the two, and the better man loses out. In the midst of the Depression, Laemmle's gamble ultimately failed to pay off for the company, and *Sutter's Gold*, with its liberal location budget, eventually became part of the problem that ushered in a 1936 change in ownership.[6]

Hopes had been high for Universal, however, before this crisis. Faulkner was writing a script for a major historical epic, one that could carry its lead, Edward Arnold, to stardom, and see the studio riding out the storm of the mid-1930s. *Sutter's Gold* was even named as one of four "special" features that Universal would release in the 1934–35 season, the perfect fodder for a nation in financial turmoil. The studio allocated $500,000 to its production. It had originally been attached to director William Wyler early in 1934 before Hawks took the reins later in the year.[7] Among the other films announced was *The Good Fairy* (William Wyler, 1935) with Margaret Sullavan, a rising star. This comedic "crisis affair" (*SL*, 82) was another project for which Faulkner wrote a treatment (for Hawks), but it ultimately amounted to nothing, and the treatment has not survived.

The "Sutter's Gold" treatment remains, rediscovered only recently by Sarah Gleeson-White in the Howard Hawks Papers at Brigham Young University. Faulkner began writing in early July 1934, making "a synopsis of the play" (*SL*, 81), and was still apparently working on the "moom pitcher [moving picture] script" (*SL*, 83) when he went back to Oxford at the end of the month, at which point he estimated it would take perhaps a month more to complete. He had finally "caught up with the movie" (*SL*, 84) at some point in August, and then proceeded to move on with other work. Cendrars's novel, which is based on a true story, follows Johann Sutter as he travels from Switzerland across antebellum America to California in search of wealth. After gold is discovered on his estate, New Helvetia, Sutter is invaded by prospectors from all over the nation. His children, whom he had abandoned to build his empire, follow him to America only to find the estate in financial ruin, and his son ends up perishing in the fire that burns the whole edifice to the ground.

This narrative, as Gleeson-White has pointed out, may sound familiar in some respects for readers of *Absalom, Absalom!*, the novel that Faulkner had begun to write in earnest in January 1934 but that he put on hold at this time, taking it up again in March the following year.[8] It, too, follows a determined man, Thomas Sutpen, who is hell bent on completing his utopian "design" of building a Mississippi plantation with slave labor. He has a Haitian wife and (possibly) multiracial son, Charles Bon, however, who cannot possibly enjoy the fruits of this labor. This plantation is threatened by the onset of the Civil War, and it later goes up in flames, taking with it his other son, Henry. In a number of ways, as suggested by the tantalizing near-homophony of "Sutter" and "Sutpen," Faulkner appears to have drawn on his experiences working with Cendrars's novel to fashion *Absalom* into the epic narrative of filial destruction that it became.

And yet Faulkner appears to have drawn not only on Cendrars's work but on Eisenstein's, too. The roots of at least one scene in Faulkner's work derive from Eisenstein's screenplay, as Gleeson-White points out: in *Absalom*, Thomas Sutpen regularly fights his slaves so as to keep them in line; in Eisenstein's script, Sutter boxes a "giant Negro" at a New York circus in order to win "one hundred dollars and a young slave."[9] This is but one example of Faulkner's borrowing from Eisenstein, whose influence might be seen not only in narrative terms, as Gleeson-White argues, but also in the way that it prompted the author's "grappling with the ideographic representation of sound."[10]

In these very early years of sound cinema, Eisenstein was struggling with the new technology in a different way from the Hollywood studios. He was acutely concerned with the possibility that sound would have the effect of reaffirming rather than denaturalizing the realism of the film image. In 1928, he and Vsevolod Pudovkin and Grigory Alexandrov wrote their famous statement on film sound, which approached the new technology with caution, recommending that sound be mobilized as a "counterpoint" to the image instead of being synchronized with it.[11] He would have the chance to put this philosophy into practice when he came to write his version of "Sutter's Gold" two years later: indeed, had it been produced, it would have been Eisenstein's first sound film (in the end he reached that milestone with *Alexander Nevsky* [1938]). Eisenstein also had very particular (if inconsistent) opinions about the function of the screenplay in relation to the finished film, opinions that had a direct impact on dialogue and sound direction more broadly.

Over the course of the 1930s, screenwriters in Hollywood would gradually (albeit unevenly) adopt the common "master-scene" form that is still prevalent today: essentially, this was a screenplay that was broken into scenes rather than individual shots, included action and dialogue, and could be used for shooting even without the technical details of camera directions. The form was designed primarily to deal with the introduction of sound, a fact reflected in the typographical layout—centered character names with dialogue below; stage directions to the left; scene numbers in the extreme left-hand margin—but, as Steven Price has argued, it would be some time before it was adopted in a uniform way throughout the industry.[12] On the whole, the master-scene format was designed to function as a shooting script, which would give the director enough leeway to determine his or her own shot choices but would offer enough of a guide for predicting the action and speech that would be recorded by the camera.

Eisenstein arrived in Hollywood several years before the master-scene format was coming into use, and instead of relying on existing models, he imported some of his own ideas about screenwriting, coupling them with the incorporation of sound. The notable incompleteness of Eisenstein's scenarios created a strange paradox: they conformed to the notion of the screenplay as blueprint, and yet at the same time their unfinished nature had the effect of keeping authorial control of the finished product in Eisenstein's hands. Each one was "a statement of a kind of artistic authority over the whole production," since unlike the majority of studio screenplays, Eisenstein's scripts resisted simple adaptation.[13] Over the course of his career, he approached the task from a number of different angles, at times numbering each and every shot and—as he did for *October* (1928)—adding "literary qualities in excess of the requirements of any blueprint."[14]

Once the cameras began rolling, Eisenstein could just as easily ignore the shot descriptions as given. His scenarios—or rather, "prose poems" or "librettos"—were at once self-contained and resistant to adaptation but at the same time always open to revision and subject to being rewritten even as filming was under way. This is evident in the "Sutter's Gold" scenario, a team effort by Eisenstein, Alexandrov, and Ivor and Hell Montagu. Eisenstein verbally narrated the treatment he had planned, and then Alexandrov wrote it out. After it was typed and translated, Ivor Montagu brought the English version back to

Eisenstein, and they made emendations. Ivor added some rewrites, and Hell typed the finished version, after which it was handed over to the Paramount staff, who created additional copies.[15]

In this case, the "Sutter's Gold" scenario was divided up into seven separate reels and written in a series of paragraphs (often as short as a single sentence), with each paragraph corresponding either to "a single shot or a group of shots."[16] Although the copy of the screenplay that has been preserved appears to be a version at an advanced stage, gesturing from its first pages toward the screen with a camera that "tracks back," there is scant dialogue throughout.[17] Instead, there are far more nonhuman sounds than speech, a sign of the group's reluctance to produce a film in which sound was synchronized to the image in an uncomplicated way. A variety of intertitles begin each of the reels and are interspersed at certain dramatic moments, at times combining with the sounds and voices in the screenplay in a way that suggests a call-and-response structure. One example is in reel 4, when Sutter unwraps a package containing the first grains of gold:

> His fingers, trembling, hold the paper, with, on it, some tiny grains of metal.
>
> *Title*: GOLD?
>
> *Title*: G O L D ?
>
> *Title*: G O L D ?
>
> Hands completing a chemical test on the grains and Sutter's voice answering softly and definitely:
> "Gold."
>
> Sutter is standing at the table, with the gold and reagent in his hands and grief on his face. He repeats yet lower:
> "Gold!"
>
> *Title*: GOLD.
> *Rushing up from small to fill screen and, in a simultaneously rising inhuman roar the word "GOLD!"*[18]

As is clear from the dialogue, this is not a silent film script. Nevertheless, Eisenstein's version of *Sutter's Gold* does represent a transitional moment in the history of cinema, bearing witness to the conversion from intertitles to spoken words in Hollywood. Despite his best efforts, the script as written does not comport itself well with the Soviet director's philosophy of film sound, as Gleeson-White has argued. The images—both of words and of gold itself—in the scene in which Sutter opens the package are matched by his synchronized response, as he says exactly what he sees.

Interestingly, then, it would fall to Faulkner to write the more "Eisensteinian" adaptation. In his treatment the division of sound and image is mapped via two parallel, split-page, columns. Faulkner's process in adapting *Sutter's Gold*—from Cendrars's novel but even more obviously from Eisenstein's scenario—was to disaggregate sound from image by assigning sound directions, as Gleeson-White has noted, "in typescript in the left-hand margins on 61 of the treatment's 108 pages; on average, that means one on every one-and-a-half pages."[19] In the early 1930s, as Steven Price has observed, this was a mode of presentation that was actually practiced quite widely in the industry, used for "films of strikingly different genres at several studios." Price offers examples from Fox and Paramount, as well as a rare instance from MGM.[20] But it was at Universal that the split-page format seems to have been quite consistently adopted, especially in the horror film cycle from the early years of the decade: the shooting scripts for *Dracula*, *Frankenstein*, and Frankenstein's sequel, *The Bride of Frankenstein* (James Whale, 1935), all contain the parallel columns that Faulkner used around the same time at the same studio for "Sutter's Gold."[21] While the studio differentiated its prestige from its genre pictures, the two would at least share the same screenplay format. There are two differences, however: Faulkner's scene text appears on the right, and his sound on the left, and his sequences are not alphabetically ordered (indeed the treatment only contains page numbers).

In any case, Faulkner was able to change the screenwriting style he had used at MGM and adapt to this different—and seemingly more archaic—form. Faulkner employs a multitude of sounds throughout his script: knocking on doors, gunshots, the discontented rumblings of a mob, tramping feet, laughter, horses hooves, falling snow, and at one point the more abstract "sound of progress" (50).[22] But as it is only at the treatment stage, Faulkner's script (like Eisenstein's) includes very few lines of dialogue, with the words of his characters mostly paraphrased in the scene text on the right, while the sounds of their voices are indicated in the sound text on the left. This means that any nonhuman noise made over the course of the screenplay is on the same plane as human noises, as both are eventually assigned to the same soundtrack. Here, in a moment of crisis, Sutter looks back on the wrongdoings that helped him earn a land grant for his utopia, the repression of black and Native American lives, lives that were sacrificed for the sake of New Helvetia, and refuses to answer to the imaginary voices of the wife and children he left behind:

Voice, etc.	Swift PAN as SUTTER whirls to: Mended statue of justice. RESOLVE behind statue face of OCTOROON as she was dragged from ship.
Sound of chair knocked over; SUTTER'S voice	Swift PAN as SUTTER whirls to: Grant, Spanish [s]word, RESOLVE behind grant and sword faces of three crucified Indians. He denies charge, harsh, fanatic; recounts what he has accomplished, dares any one to reproach him; justifies himself by mad philosophy and logic while faces DISSOLVE to (73)

The return of the repressed is manifest here in both images and voices, with the two columns acting in concert to upset "the richest man in the world" (72). But a less noticeable point of interest is the rendering of Sutter's distressed voice alongside the prosaic sound of the fallen chair. Not only does this reduce the importance of the protagonist's voice on paper, but it also forces the reader to consider the disentanglement of voice as noise (left-hand column) from voice as meaning (right-hand column).

In this format, the treatment presents the fascinating idea that the voice is always what Mladen Dolar terms the "bearer of an utterance," a container for words, but that it also simultaneously has qualities in excess of this: as Roland Barthes writes, the voice has a certain style, a timbre, an expressivity —a "grain."[23] Faulkner's procedure tears the signifying capacity of the voice away from its manifestation as pure sound—Sutter's voice on the one side, his words on the other—and so confers meaning on both. Although difficult to see once a script is committed to celluloid (where in commercial cinema, soundtrack is habitually subsumed to the image track), the difference between the sound of the voice and its words comes to the fore in the parallel-column screenplay, emphasizing the fact that film is from the beginning composed of discrete modes of representation.

Although this particular form of the screenplay encourages such a neat distinction, there are points throughout the script at which Faulkner conflates sound and dialogue and places both in the left-hand column, which indicates the difficulty of separating words from their sounds. When Sutter's son

August arrives at New Helvetia, his father has been stripped of his riches. Planning an appeal to the governor, Sutter describes the "imaginary city of gold" he will build:

SUTTER'S voice	Valley, tents. DISSOLVE tents to: city, lights flowing. PAN back to:
	SUTTER'S and AUGUST'S faces, leaning forward while SUTTER talks of gold, their faces increase in glow
Words: Gold! Gold! (88)	w~~ords~~! g~~old~~! gold! DISSOLVE

Although earlier he had written Sutter's words on the left-hand side of the page before transferring them to the right-hand column, here Faulkner places dialogue in the scene text column before correcting himself (12). The attributions of voice and words are not at all consistent in "Sutter's Gold," as Faulkner struggled to master the parallel-text method as he wrote. A form he would use only once more in "Battle Cry" at Warner Brothers, the parallel-text method does, however, seem to have had an impact on Faulkner's next novel, *Pylon*, a book that experiments in interesting ways with the connections between sound, voice, and environment.

At this point in his career, Faulkner had just begun work on *Absalom, Absalom!*, but he laid it aside while he was writing "Sutter's Gold" and only returned to it in early 1935, after he had completed *Pylon*. The style and content of the these novels are radically dissimmilar, and one is tempted to make sense of this disparity by way of Faulkner's remark that he wrote *Pylon* "because I'd got into trouble with *Absalom, Absalom!* and I had to get away from it for a while so I thought a good way to get away from it was to write another book. . . . It seemed to me interesting enough to make a story about, but that was just to get away from a book that wasn't going too well, till I could get back at it" (*FU*, 36). In spite of Faulkner's appraisal, *Pylon* is not simply the lesser of the two novels, and to read it in the shadow of *Absalom* is to tar it unfairly with what Michael Zeitlin has called "the stigma of the minor and the secondary."[24] Perhaps, however, we should give the author the benefit of the doubt here and allow that *Pylon* did provide a kind of relief for Faulkner at this stage. But instead of *Pylon* having been a means for Faulkner to "get away" from what he called the "inchoate fragments" (*FU*, 76) of *Absalom*, perhaps it was a means of working through his experience writing "Sutter's Gold."

Although Faulkner had paid close attention to the spoken word in his earlier fiction, with *Pylon* we see the first serious intrusion of artificial and mechanized sounds, especially of the voice as it is projected through a loudspeaker. The intersubjective "phenomenal voice" and the descriptive voice tags—"he said," "she said"—that marked his first novels are for the first time superseded, as Stephen Ross points out, by the "artificially created language of machines or print."[25] This turn away from the human and toward the mechanical is anticipated by the graphophone of *As I Lay Dying* and the "competitive radios and phonographs" (*N*, 2:257), adding to the din of *Sanctuary*. But in *Pylon*, the sustained attention to the "brazen, metallic, and loud" (*N*, 2:790) noise emitting from the loudspeaker dominates the writing for the first time, and it is to "Sutter's Gold" that we should look in order to understand these peculiar, disembodied sounds.

In Faulkner's treatment, as we've seen, sounds are disaggregated from images—and the voice is at times disaggregated from its words—in the form of split-page, parallel columns. But Faulkner is not consistent, and sometimes dialogue appears among other sounds, while at other points it is fully integrated in the "image" column, written as part of the scene text, or indented, as is more common in screenplays of the period. What takes place in *Pylon* is something like the reconstitution of this split: the ideographic bringing together of voice and image, sound and scene, adjective and noun, in the form of composite, portmanteau words, including "corpseglare," "wirehum," "gasolinespanned," "pavementthrong," "trafficdammed," "machinevoice," "gearwhine," "slantshimmered," "typesplattered."[26] With the jamming together of machinelike and natural sounds, of artificial and embodied voices, Faulkner transmutes his writing practice in "Sutter's Gold" into the form of the novel, bringing image track and soundtrack together in much the same way as they are eventually joined on screen. At least, that is what such words strive to achieve. For *Pylon* offers a more complex mediation between sound and image, human and machine, than the portmanteau would allow. Consider our introduction to the "amplifyer" in the novel's first chapter:

> There was an amplifyer in the rotunda too and through it the sound of the aeroplanes turning the field pylon on each lap filled the rotunda and the restaurant where the woman and the reporter sat while the little boy finished the second dish of icecream. The amplifyer filled rotunda and restaurant even above the sound of

feet as the crowd moiled and milled and trickled through the gates onto the field, with the announcer's voice harsh masculine and disembodied; then at the end of each lap would come the mounting and then fading snarl and snore of engines as the aeroplanes came up and zoomed and banked away, leaving once more the scuffle and murmur of feet on tile and the voice of the announcer reverberant and sonorous within the domed shell of glass and steel in a running commentary to which apparently none listened, as if the voice were merely some unavoidable and inexplicable phenomenon of nature like the sound of wind or of erosion. Then the band would begin to play again, though faint and almost trivial behind and below the voice, as if the voice actually were that natural phenomenon against which all man-made sounds and noises blew and vanished like leaves. (*N*, 2:791–92)

In such a passage, sound emanates from a variety of overlapping and competing sources: aeroplanes, feet, the announcer, the band. The first and third of these are filtered through the "amplifier," which allows the engine noise to fill the space and, more importantly, transforms the announcer's voice into a "natural phenomenon." Like "the sound of wind or of erosion," the voice forms part of the background, making plenty of noise but not signifying anything very meaningful. Here, Faulkner expertly and unexpectedly transmutes the voice emitting from the machinic "amplifier" into an accident of nature, and in the space of a paragraph pits the "masculine" voice against the "man-made sounds and noises" of everything else in the scene, reflecting, as John Matthews has argued, his complex fascination with modern technology as an extension of the human body: the amplifier here makes the voice equivalent with the inhuman "snarl and snore of engines" but in so doing suffuses the entire airfield with its sound, breaking its ties to "a single body, a single place."[27] Situated human voice becomes, through the miracle of technology, the sourceless sound of the natural world, decoupled from the mouth but all the more natural for its being so.[28]

Pylon is a novel that is outwardly invested in the changes wrought by the machines of modernity, at once disgusted and spellbound by aeroplanes, loudspeakers, and the printing press. But keeping in mind Faulkner's work on "Sutter's Gold," we can see that this otherwise quite sudden turn to what Julian Murphet has called "techno-mediation" in the prose fiction also has its origins in Hollywood.[29] In the separation of the scene text from the sound text in "Sutter's Gold" and the occasional migration of the voice itself as noise rather than dialogue to the left-hand column, the treatment presents us with the tearing asunder of meaningful words from the meaningless voices on which they are carried—the first are assigned to the right-hand column, while the second are positioned on the left, as the sonic background to the narrative images and dialogue.

In the scheme of film production, this division at the treatment stage of image track and soundtrack and of dialogue and noise is only temporary. Eventually, in what Michel Chion has described far more broadly in cinema as an "instantaneous perceptual triage," the columns are sutured back together, and the sounds of the film are fully synched to its images.[30] So too the noise of the voice is fully wedded to the dialogue, with nothing to distinguish the words spoken from the grain of the speaker's voice. In *Pylon*, we read of a voice—*the* voice—that begins in a human "masculine" body, is fed through the loudspeaker, and becomes a "natural" part of the scenery. The fusing of the human with technology in that novel is first imagined in "Sutter's Gold," and the end result in both is a union that seems completely natural.

For these reasons and more, *Pylon* has been seen as the polar opposite of *Absalom*; *Pylon* is set in the present, outside of Yoknapatawpha, and shows more concern for the contemporary "dead wirehum" (*N*, 2:825) of a telephone than for the insistent whispers of ghosts of the Civil War dead. In contrast to the oral storytelling mode in *Absalom*, *Pylon* offers the mechanical objectification of human speech (indeed, in December 1934, after he had finished the first draft of the novel, Faulkner was also considering sending it to Howard Hawks for potential adaptation: the mechanical voice would have been truly mechanized then [*SL*, 86]). And here, if we consider *Pylon* as a novel that is fully inflected by—and that reacts to—the structure of "Sutter's Gold," then we can gain a fuller understanding of the surreptitious effect of writing a 108-page film treatment on the novel, the way it introduced a series of sounds and images on their way to being reconciled into the novel and forced its author to think through the technological entanglements of the human voice. I explore *Absalom* a little more at the end of this chapter and in fuller detail in the next chapter. But for now, we should consider that while "Sutter's Gold" clearly influences the central plot of *Absalom*, it also has a less obvious bearing on the stylistic singularity of *Pylon*.

"Golden Land"

In "Sutter's Gold," Faulkner had written the backstory of San Francisco's development as a city, which had been chiefly determined by the discovery of large deposits of gold. In "Golden Land," Faulkner wrote the story of Los Angeles, a city with no gold of which to speak. The sprawling metropolis had originally been built on the back of derivatives, a real estate empire that had found investors even before the first brick had been laid. This was late in the nineteenth century, but by the time Faulkner had arrived, a new, even flimsier substance propped up the houses and streets: film. In Faulkner's story, Los Angeles is "that city of almost incalculable wealth whose queerly appropriate fate is to be erected upon a few spools of a substance whose value is computed in billions and which may be completely destroyed in that second's instant of a careless match between the moment of striking and the moment when the striker might have sprung and stamped it out" (CS, 719). Even more hazardous than a house built on sand is one built on the flammable strips of celluloid on which Los Angeles stood, yielding an economy prey to the whims of cinemagoers, with the potential to combust at any moment.

At bottom, then, this is a story about Los Angeles as a deceptively bright—but perhaps predictably dark—city, where all are slowly but surely corrupted by the Midas touch of the land. Here the sun certainly shines, but it is always "strained by the vague high soft almost nebulous California haze," resulting in "a kind of treacherous unbrightness" (CS, 706). In these "changeless monotonous beautiful days without end" (CS, 726), the Ewing family, who hail from Nebraska, seem to have fallen from their former bucolic state: Ira, the patriarch, has become a Beverly Hills realtor who makes more money than he can spend but is a poor father, husband, and son. His mother lives alone in a house away from her only family. The Ewing children are an embarrassing pair (at least in their father's eyes): the son, Voyd, has been caught cross-dressing, while the daughter, Samantha, has changed her name to "April Lalear" in order to pursue a career in acting. Only Ira's mother has the right idea, as she desperately tries to save enough money to catch a train home to Nebraska. At seventy years of age, she will likely die back in her home state come the first winter, but there is apparently no fate worse than the one she is left with in the story's final line: "I will stay here and live forever" (CS, 726).

As treacherous as it might have been, Los Angeles was also something of an easy target for the literati of the 1930s, many of whom were forced to go there for the purposes of employment. The sentiments expressed in "Golden Land" thus appear as simple restatements of complaints that Faulkner would often express about the city in letters and interviews, and it is difficult to shut out the author's biographical voice while reading the story. But as Robert Jackson points out, "Golden Land" presents a far more complex picture of regional difference than it might seem, with Faulkner exchanging his customary North-South axis for an East-West opposition (Nebraska-California), and in the process holding idyllic country life and perverted urban existence in tension. For Jackson, although Los Angeles is condemned in the story "as a representation of the monstrous, soulless North," it also forces Ira Ewing to reconcile two different sets of regional values and demonstrates how regional identity itself is a constructed, rather than inherent, phenomenon.[31] The story certainly allegorizes Faulkner's own westward migrations and complicates his own excoriations of Hollywood. And yet it does more: for "Golden Land" is also about the filmmaking process, concerning itself both with the transformation of words into images at the behest of the screenwriter and also with the way that stars and writers alike must necessarily petition film producers to keep their careers alive.

The story picks up where *Pylon* left off, with "not only news but the beginning of literature" (*N*, 2:991) in the form of a series of newspaper headlines laying bare the Ewing family's very public problems: "APRIL LALEAR BARES ORGY SECRETS" (*CS*, 705); "LALEAR WOMAN DAUGHTER OF PROMINENT LOCAL FAMILY" (*CS*, 711); "LALEAR WOMAN CREATES SCENE IN COURTROOM" (*CS*, 721). April shames her father by having to appear in court, an incident represented in the paper along with "five or six tabloid photographs" (*CS*, 705). She is on trial after being caught naked with another woman and a producer, a stunt in which she participates in order to improve her chances of being offered "extra parts" (*CS*, 713) in a film project. And certainly, April appears to succeed: all press is good press, and she manages to remain a fixture in the papers for the duration of her trial. In her mind, the first step she needed to take to break into the film industry was "to change her name" (*CS*, 713), and so "Samantha" carefully edits herself to become "Miss April Lalear of the cinema" (*CS*, 708). But then, as Ira puts it to his bewildered mother, "Can't you understand that you don't get into the pictures just by changing your name? and that you don't even stay there when you get in? that you can't even stay there by being female? that they come here in droves on every train—girls younger and prettier than Samantha and who will do anything to get into the pictures? So will she, apparently; but who know or are willing to learn to do more things than even she seems to have thought of?" (*CS*, 714).

In one obvious sense, he is referring to April prostituting herself to gain a part in a film. But what she also does is to take her name and fashion it into a set of images in which she "alternately stared back or flaunted long pale shins" (*CS*, 705) for the reader of the newspaper. Print media is ever present in the story, and the newspaper plays a crucial role in the production of movie stars: Ira steps on it in the bathroom, Voyd uses it as a means of sun protection, and

Mrs. Ewing's gardener all too eagerly brings her the latest humiliation to the family name.

But so effective is her media strategy that April's image survives even without the paper to host it. Ira is unable to stop thinking about his daughter's face, which had "sprung out at him, hard, blonde and inscrutable, from every paper he opened; doubtless he had never forgot her while he slept even, that he had waked into thinking about remembering her" (*CS*, 705). April leverages text and image to edge her closer to those "extra parts" she seeks, and even though she is now on trial, she still manages to "CREATE SCENE IN COURTROOM" (*CS*, 721). But like daughter, like father: Ira is also a shrewd media operator and publishes a photograph of himself with a caption—"APRIL LALEAR'S FATHER" (*CS*, 715)—linking his company to the paper's far more newsworthy item involving April. After the dust clears, Ira too hopes that prospective clients will remember his name and his image, at once hitching his future success to his daughter's scandal and hoping that her misdemeanors will, with time, fade into the past.

"Golden Land" is clearly a story about Hollywood. But it is also less obviously a narrative of the screenwriting process, first and foremost a literary craft, yet one that makes the word an expedient to the image and that necessitates that it take a backseat once the camera takes control. Unlike the overly literary screenplays of a filmmaker like Eisenstein, the Hollywood screenplay was written for simplicity, receding from vision over the course of the adaptation process. And yet while screenwriting was in many respects an ephemeral occupation, its effects would stay with Faulkner long after he had ceased studio work. Sometime after "Sutter's Gold," and months before his next contract, Faulkner anticipated the enduring impact of screenwriting on his work: "The trouble about the movies," he wrote, just before the publication of "Golden Land," "is not so much the time I waste there but the time it takes me to recover and settle down again; I am 37 now and of course not as supple and impervious as I once was" (*SL*, 90). Before the year was out, he was back in Hollywood again.

The Road to Glory

Although "Golden Land" and a number of other short stories were published in 1935, in this year Faulkner began to work in earnest on *Absalom*, meaning that he was unable to earn much from publishing in the magazines. Eventually Morton Goldman secured him "a nibble from movies" (*SL*, 94), and he left for

Los Angeles once more, beginning work there on *The Road to Glory* (Howard Hawks, 1936) on December 16. This time around, Faulkner was stationed at Twentieth Century–Fox, a newly incorporated studio that had just appointed Darryl F. Zanuck as its vice president in charge of production. Zanuck, who had quit Warner Brothers a couple of years earlier and had since achieved independent success, was installed in a central producer arrangement, which made him responsible for many of the studio's quality pictures. In fact, he controlled almost all aspects of filmmaking at Fox, reading over 150 story synopses each week and scheduling daily story conferences with writers and producers during which he pored over scripts line by line, making suggestions for improvement.[32]

Even though Zanuck had already been earmarked as the next Thalberg, he undoubtedly had a lot more to prove than his MGM counterpart, and Faulkner's dealings with the Fox man were undertaken at close quarters.[33] This need to assert himself was especially pronounced in Zanuck's contributions at story conferences. He was still finding his feet at this time, trying to carve out a house style for the studio that would draw on nostalgic Americana and westerns for its strength, since many of Fox's theater holdings were located to the west of the Mississippi.[34] But Zanuck also had international audiences to consider and was especially concerned that *The Road to Glory* not show anything that would have them fall afoul of the French censors (*WFATCF*, 82n6).

Faulkner would again have the chance to work under Howard Hawks, whose 1926 silent film of the same name—his first—would give this picture its final title (although the screenplays adopted the working titles "Wooden Crosses" and "Zero Hour"). The film concerns the enlistment of new French soldiers in the First World War and follows their struggles in the trenches of Champagne, where their squad is outnumbered and outgunned by the German opposition but always manages to find new recruits. When the troops first convene, they are addressed by their captain, Marache (La Roche in the film):

> MARACHE
> Soldiers of France! You are now members of the 5th Company of the 2nd Battalion of the 39th Regiment of the Line. This regiment was created by General Bonaparte and served with him gloriously through many campaigns. It also served in the Crimea, in Indo-China, and in Africa. Since November, 1914, it has been fighting on this front. Its record of valor has not yet been damaged. I do not expect any man, or any platoon, or even this entire company, to add stature to this record—but I do and will require that no man in it will detract from that record! (*WFATCF*, 74)

When these soldiers are annihilated in battle, Marache is forced to recruit once more, and he gives the same rousing speech. Finally, after Marache himself dies heroically alongside his father, his rival in love—Delaage (Denet in the film)—is promoted from lieutenant to captain, and he delivers the speech verbatim in one of the final shots (*WFATCF*, 179). In their screenplay dated January 24, 1936, Faulkner and his cowriter Joel Sayre made original contributions to the story, such as inserting Marache's father, a veteran who is too old to be on the front line, into the company—Hawks claims to have come up with this idea himself after a chance meeting with an old veteran of Verdun in New York.[35] But influences arrived from a number of different angles, and the repetition exemplified by Marache's speech is evident elsewhere.

Following on from the success of such war films as United Artists' *Hell's Angels* (Howard Hughes, 1930), Universal's *All Quiet on the Western Front* (Lewis Milestone, 1930), and the British-American coproduction *Journey's End* (James Whale, 1930) earlier in the decade, Fox was now hoping to offer a prestige trench warfare picture of its own. But since the onset of the Depression, it had become difficult to budget for such projects. In place of original location shots, then, the studio would save money by using battle footage purchased a few years earlier from the French studio Pathé-Nathan's *Les croix de bois* (*Wooden Crosses*, Raymond Bernard, 1932), based on a novel of the same name by Roland Dorgelès. Further, although the remake would still be set in France, *Variety* reported that it would, like other recent films, have "a magnified American angle."[36] And, indeed, many of the shots from Bernard's film had already been recycled in *The World Moves On* (John Ford, 1934), another Fox film revolving around battle on the frontline.[37]

When it was decided that "the use of battle scenes from the French picture required a more serious story treatment than the outlines so far afforded," Faulkner was brought in.[38] It seems evident that Faulkner and Sayre had familiarized themselves with the film adaptation of *Les croix de bois*, as they identified certain episodes from that film that would be useful for the new project. More than offering additions and revisions to a preliminary screenplay by Stephen Morehouse Avery, then, Faulkner was also appropriating material from another war film. The task of the screenwriter was, of course, intimately connected with film viewing itself; from his first day at MGM when he viewed *The Champ* to his experiences on the set of *Lazy River*, Faulkner had relied on film viewing in writing his screenplays, and now he was again made to consider the place of preexisting footage in his writing and to think once more about how that writing would acquit itself once the cameras started rolling. As was common practice, Faulkner was in attendance on the set of *The Road to Glory* (the film "was coming along fine," he wrote in one letter home [*SL*, 94]).

The first three shots in the screenplay are listed as "STOCK SHOT out of 'Wooden Crosses,'" and there are more distributed throughout the script (*WFATCF*, 54). In total, twenty-six of the shots in the screenplay are taken from *Les croix de bois*: most are those costly sequences titled as "BOMBING PLANES" (*WFATCF*, 61), "BATTLE STUFF" (*WFATCF*, 176), and "BIG GUNS FIRING" (*WFATCF*, 176), showing that the screenwriters were making judicious use of the already purchased footage. In a different vein, shots 217–22 are taken from a scene in a church, where a slow panning camera reveals "the other half of the church, which is being used as a hospital. Beds are filled with wounded men whose groans can be heard above the strains of 'Ave Maria'" (*WFATCF*, 150–51). But perhaps the most economical and productive use of footage from *Les croix de bois* is in the climactic episode in which the Germans plan to blow up the Allied trench. As the French troops hear the German sappers digging underneath them, the tension rises, but the soldiers cannot leave the trench lest the enemy realize their plan has been revealed. Our heroes are safe so long as the sounds of digging continue, for the Germans will not detonate the mine until their sappers are clear. Just before the explosion, the troops are relieved from their posts, but in a cruel twist of fate, Marache and Delaage cannot tell the incoming soldiers about the mine, for it would reveal their knowledge of the German plan. And as they escape, the mine indeed does explode:

105   MED. SHOT—STOCK SHOT FROM "WOODEN CROSSES"
The men are tramping along. They keep glancing back over their shoulders. INTERCUT TO CLOSE SHOTS of Delaage, Marache, Bouffiou, et al. Then there is the explosion. The mine has been detonated. The men watch it. Then they resume their march.

FADE OUT (*WFATCF*, 98)

This event, unemotional in the extreme, probably suggested to one reviewer that the screenplay had been written "with the impersonality of a veteran newspaper man's account of a fire."[39]

To be sure, it is always difficult to determine exactly who wrote what in any given screenplay, and "The Road to Glory," composed by Faulkner and Sayre and later revised by the producer (and fellow southerner) Nunnally Johnson, is no exception. Indeed, the script underwent a number of revisions between

Faulkner's arrival on December 16, 1935, and the final retakes that were shot in late April 1936 (*WFATCF*, 46). William Everson has suggested that Faulkner and Sayre were chiefly responsible for the mine detonation sequence, which cleverly extends the digging scene that only features very briefly in the film *Les croix de bois*.[40] In their screenplay dated December 31, the pair builds up a small amount of tension with the possibility of the German mine being detonated but never cashes it out in any spectacular way.[41] In the screenplay of January 24, the mine is indeed detonated, using the footage from Bernard's film. However, this idea does not appear to have been Faulkner's or Sayre's: in a story conference addressing the problems of the script in progress, it seems that the scene was also shaped by Zanuck (*WFATCF*, 90n9).

Story conferences, which I mention particularly throughout this chapter, were all-important at Fox, and especially so for the autocratic Zanuck. In his work on story conference protocols, Claus Tieber draws attention to the importance of reading such documents in order to understand the screenwriting process. Story conferences underscore the collaborative work practices involved in the writing of a screenplay and complicate the idea of single authorship by showing that all conference attendees "have to be seen as co-authors." Nevertheless, Tieber reminds us "they were without doubt dominated by the producers."[42] This much is certainly true of the conferences for *The Road to Glory*, as many of Zanuck's suggestions were realized in later versions of the script.

It is evident that at least a few of the actors had already been selected for parts in the film, including Simone Simon, Warner Baxter, and Frederic March, who were to form a love triangle (*WFATCF*, 47). June Lang later replaced Simon, but it is fascinating to know that at Fox, as at MGM, Faulkner would have known precisely the actors for whom he was writing. Faulkner's name is itself conspicuous in its absence from these conference protocols, but that by no means diminishes his contribution to the property. Faulkner finished with the screenplay on January 7, around the same time he was winding up work on the manuscript of *Absalom, Absalom!* Deservedly celebrating the end of his new novel, Faulkner went on a drinking binge, and it would be another ten days before he was sober enough to leave Los Angeles.[43]

Perhaps owing to what he referred to as his "illness" on *The Road to Glory*, there is a stipulation in the Fox records from January 16 that "Faulkner is not to return here on same deal."[44] He would be back very soon, however, and it was not just studio work that would lure him to Hollywood this time. Over the

New Year period, he had begun a passionate affair with Fox continuity adviser Meta Carpenter Wilde that would sustain him for the next eighteen years in California, off and on. She was, as Philip Weinstein puts it, "a Southern oasis in the great Babylonian desert," a fellow Mississippian to whom Faulkner was drawn and who was responsible for assisting him with his screenwriting during his time with Fox.[45] Carpenter Wilde dropped Faulkner off at the station at the end of this stint, and a telegram he wrote from the train reveals his early infatuation: "9 P.M. on the Golden State Limited. Darling, love, dear love, dear, dear love—I had to be cold and still when we said goodbye; if I had let myself go and hold you, I would not have let you go and boarded the train."[46] They would be reunited before too long.

Although everything seemed to have been wrapped up for Faulkner on *The Road to Glory*, he would revisit the set during filming, probably continuing to advise Hawks, and revise the script as it was being shot (*WFATCF*, 46). But there was more still. Several years later, in 1939, Faulkner was summoned to Washington for a trial to determine the originality of the film's screenplay. The claimant was not Pathé-Nathan, who supplied the footage from *Les croix de bois*, nor Dorgelès, who had expressed fears that the remake wouldn't do his book justice.[47] Rather Robert Sheets, a young soldier, had filed suit against Twentieth Century–Fox for $1 million, claiming that he had written the original scenario for the picture and that the plot had been changed so as to become a "false, absurd, and perverted presentation of [his] thoughts, ideas, and meanings," leading to his humiliation.[48] The case dragged on for nearly three months, but it was finally decided that Sheets had "copied the story from a serialization of the film in a fan magazine."[49]

Banjo on My Knee

When Faulkner returned to Los Angeles in February, he continued to visit the set of *The Road to Glory* but worked principally on *Banjo on My Knee*, a "rich-as-earth Southern tale."[50] "Getting along fine," he wrote Estelle, "am well and busy at new picture, though I go and see the making of the other one every day" (*SL*, 94). After his illness in January, his wages were reduced, and his new short-term contract contained a clause under which it could be terminated at will, either by Faulkner or Zanuck.[51] As such, he was taking care to complete the script in a timely manner and at the same time looking toward the future, "arranging to be offered a long contract" (*SL*, 95).

Faulkner's second property at the studio played to his strengths, concerned as it was with a collection of parochial southerners who live on the Mississippi bayou and are content to remain in blissful ignorance of the modern world. A treatment from March 3 and a revised treatment from March 10 both outline the comical tale of Pearl and Ernie, destined to be together but prevented from marrying when the groom believes he has killed another man and is forced to flee. Ernie is followed to New Orleans by Pearl and her father, Newt, but a rival, Leota, is also in pursuit, and threatens to upset the planned matrimony. Pearl attracts unwanted suitors of her own, like the hapless Chick Bean, but the upbeat tone of the narrative suggests that it will only ever end happily, and indeed it does. The script was based on a novel by Harry Hamilton, for which Fox had paid $10,000, but from the beginning the film was also marketed as being similar to the studio's *Steamboat Round the Bend* (John Ford, 1935) and Jack Kirkland's 1933 Broadway play, *Tobacco Road* (based on the irredeemably grim novel by Erskine Caldwell).[52] Indeed, in the first treatment to which Faulkner contributed dated March 3, the foreword brands the family of *Banjo* as "Tobacco Road" people, "but a profound and unquestioning faithfulness to the river gives them a certain integrity" (WFATCF, 195). In fact, constant mentions of that play in advertisements for *Banjo* almost landed the film in hot water, with the theater producer wanting to sue Fox for riding on the coattails of *Tobacco Road*.[53] However, the film was clearly a more light-hearted take on the Depression South, as even a cursory glance at the screenplay materials reveals.

Faulkner's contributions to *Banjo* were to the fifth and sixth—the final two—sequences of the treatment, which he later revised after a conference with Zanuck.[54] As Steven Price points out, segmenting screenplays into sequences like this was common in a significant minority of films in the sound period, whether at the treatment stage or later. In Faulkner's treatment, as was often the case, the boundaries of the sequences were defined by FADE IN and FADE OUT directions at the beginning and end of each one.[55] This much is standard practice, and we can see it in several full-length screenplays that Faulkner completed at Fox. But what is perhaps most interesting about his fifth sequence is the way in which it begins. At this point in the treatment, Pearl has all but lost hope of seeing her betrothed again, and working dispiritedly as a dish washer at the Creole Café in New Orleans, she is now preparing to compromise with the sympathetic Chick: "We FADE IN on Pearl and Chick Bean seated side by side in the balcony of a moving picture theatre, the locale of more than one love scene. On the screen, though we do not see it, is a terrifically exciting newsreel. All we get of it is Lowell Thomas's voice, or the voice of any hysterical announcer, describing the hair-raising events that are taking place on the screen. But neither Chick nor Pearl ever notice it. To Chick this is a place to make his plea in privacy."[56] Immediately, the voice of this "hysterical" announcer that goes unnoticed by Chick and Pearl calls to mind the all-pervasive—though easily ignored—voice of the announcer in *Pylon*. But here that announcer is given a name, and one that would have drawn attention to the studio to which this property belonged: Lowell Thomas narrated Fox's Movietone newsreels from their inception in 1928 until 1952, when he became involved with Cinerama technology. His inclusion here is meant to lightly mock, as is done elsewhere in the treatment, the shanty people's general lack of interest in modern contrivances: the earnest "plea" of the lovelorn Chick easily trumps the "hysterical" and the "hair-raising" tone of the voice from the screen. And indeed, further down the page we read that "Lowell Thomas continues his harangue while Pearl, troubled and deeply moved by Chick's urging, confesses to herself that what he says is true."[57]

Furthermore, the announcer can be seen as mimicking the task of the screenwriter himself. Faulkner considers that the newsreel footage will not be visible from the balcony of the cinema but that the voice that accompanies it will provide the energy and detail necessary to convey the events "taking place on the screen." The strained attempts of the announcer to gain the attention of two uninterested moviegoers was also the effort of Faulkner himself to evoke the "terrifically exciting" images of the off-screen newsreel, but it too fell on deaf ears. Although the sequence began promisingly enough, a story conference with Darryl Zanuck two days after the treatment was submitted forced Faulkner to change it significantly: "Mr. Zanuck did not think the newsreel episode would work out. He felt that we should give this scene between Pearl and Chick as colourful a background as possible—moonlight—the bales of cotton on the jetty—far-off whistles from freighters—and the crooning voices of darkies singing off-scene" (*WFATCF*, 212n22).

Against the inventive addition of Lowell Thomas to the scene, Zanuck instead suggests the tried and tested stuff of the romantic setting (even if, for Faulkner, the theater was "the locale of more than one love scene"). More notably, the production chief replaces the announcer's newsreel commentary with the "crooning voices" of black extras, evoking not only local color and providing a softer substitute for the "hysterical" Thomas but also perhaps reminding the viewer of Chick's own incompetence as a crooner. For in the fourth sequence, we discover that Chick has never had much luck in his profession and has just been replaced by Pearl's father, Newt, who has appeared from nowhere with a strange musical "contraption," his accordion. Indeed, the overlaying of Chick's plea with the "crooning voices" accords well with his character description at the beginning of the revised treatment, where we read that he "realizes his own futility, and that he is always doomed to failure, in his dispirited love for Pearl as well as in his profession" (WFATCF, 195).

In any case, Faulkner was not one to argue with his employer. Much later, when asked how he could stand to sit through these story conferences, Faulkner famously replied: "I just kept telling myself, 'They're gonna pay me Saturday, they're gonna pay me Saturday.'"[58] Zanuck held such sway in the conference that in the revised treatment submitted on March 10 Faulkner follows his suggested edits almost to the letter, with one clear exception: "A matter of two or three weeks has passed. We FADE IN on the wharf in back of the Creole cafe. Pearl and Chick are sitting side by side on a cotton bale. Occasionally the far off whistle of a freighter can be heard. The night sounds are augmented by strains of music drifting out from the cafe. Pearl is no longer a dishwasher. She is wearing a fancy yellow dress that Newt bought for her. This is the thirty minute period that Chick has between appearances. He is smoking a cigarette and trying to get up enough courage to say what he wants to say to Pearl" (WFATCF, 211–12). Absent from this revision is not only Lowell but also the "crooning voices," replaced instead by "strains of music," with Faulkner disregarding the one fetishized trope that was perhaps too hackneyed even for this property. The film as produced, however, features a striking rendition of W. C. Handy's "St. Louis Blues" by Theresa Harris and the Hall Johnson Choir (acting as stevedores on the dock) in the scene just prior to the Pearl and Chick sequence. This was the film's eventual refrain, a song that Faulkner had originally recommended should be played by Newt to close out the story and that begins with a line that the author had famously used in an earlier short story: "I hate to see that evening sun go down."

David Hempstead—Nunnally Johnson's assistant who was supervising Faulkner's work on this script—was evidently displeased with some of the dialogue the author had prepared: "Bill wrote magnificent things. . . . practically blank verse, sometimes two or three pages long. They were beautiful speeches, but they were written for actors like Tony Martin, and I couldn't show them to Zanuck."[59] And sure enough, Zanuck rejected Faulkner's contributions to the first treatment and didn't retain him on the screenwriting team for *Banjo* after the revisions were in. But at least something of the film remained with Faulkner long after he had left the project: returning to Hollywood with his family in their Ford phaeton, his daughter Jill sang "Oh! Susanna"—the Stephen Foster song from which *Banjo*'s title is derived—the whole way there from Mississippi.[60]

Gunga Din

In between projects at Fox, Faulkner was offered a short contract at RKO, working on a property the studio had recently acquired: the 1892 Rudyard Kipling poem "Gunga Din." One of the smaller of the majors, RKO was known for its rather erratic production philosophy.[61] The studio had experienced a year of brief success in 1935, with *The Informer* (John Ford, 1935) a critically well-received picture. But it was short lived, as RKO struggled through the rest of the decade.[62] The mood at the beginning of 1936 was a somber one. The new production chief Sam Briskin believed RKO would need to churn out more A pictures if it were to keep its head above water, and there were plans to spend more money than ever before on releases for the 1937 season.[63]

The studio was banking on two films in particular, which it planned to "roadshow." This essentially meant screening them in limited release before they were more widely circulated so as to draw attention to the most costly flagship pictures that RKO had to offer. One was *Mary of Scotland* (John Ford, 1936), a property that was almost taken up by Hawks in mid-1934 and that Faulkner imagined at the time would be his next task after the "Sutter's Gold" treatment: "Finished another synopsis today, and am waiting now to hear about making a movie of the recent play, Mary of Scotland. Will get to work on that right away, as it is the next job" (*SL*, 82). The other film that RKO had selected for roadshowing was *Gunga Din*, although various events conspired against it, and the film, which was eventually directed by George Stevens after Hawks had been dismissed, wouldn't be released until 1939.

Part of the reason for the delay was its cost: the film's lavish outdoor scenes and abundance of extras brought the budget to nearly $2 million, making it the most expensive picture that RKO had produced to that point. But even the source material was pricey. The rights to the titular poem were purchased from the Kipling estate by Edward Small for his company Reliance Pictures, their eleven stanzas fetching a sizeable £4,700.[64] Small was to produce the picture, and it was under his watch that Faulkner was assigned to write the initial scenario. But the work that Faulkner did complete—notes from April 10 and 13, two separate sequence outlines from May 14, and an incomplete rough draft of a story outline dated May 15—shows very little reliance on Kipling's poem. As Rudy Behlmer points out, there was "hardly enough narrative in the poem for a full-fledged commercial feature film," and so Faulkner—who had once referred to his own short stories as "third-rate Kipling"—instead sought inspiration for the script in one of his own Hollywood treatments.[65]

It seems clear from Faulkner's first notes that his version of the story, called "Pukka Saib" (a Raj term that can be roughly translated as "true gentleman"), was modeled on the first treatment he had completed back at MGM: "Manservant." The plot of "Pukka Saib" revolves around a British colonial, Captain Holmes, who has a son with an Indian woman in the Khyber Hills. Holmes promptly disowns the boy, Das, and his mother, but the son gains his revenge by letting his father die when he could have rescued him. Holmes also has another son with an English woman, alongside of whom Das fights during the First World War. The two are loyal to one another, even when their blood relationship is revealed, and the outline ends with Das sacrificing his life for the British regiment by poisoning himself before his half brother is able to stop him.[66]

But this story truly had no connection with the poem, as one reader duly noted, and it appears that Faulkner left his MGM plotline behind as he moved on to write further material. On April 15, five days after his first attempt, Faulkner turned in more notes, this time for an untitled story that changed "Das" to "Din," and did away with the hints of miscegenation and oedipal revenge. The narrative still ends with Din's death, however. This time, he fakes orders from the colonel of the battalion so that Holmes might visit his dying wife. Din is found out, and, rather than being executed, takes his own life with the revolver Holmes gives him. As a reader noted, this was more closely connected with the Kipling text—both end with the British officer raising a toast to his fallen servant.[67] While not producing the final line verbatim here— "You're a better man than I am, Gunga Din!"—Faulkner's sequence outline of May 14 ends with a close paraphrase of Kipling's words: "Robert, sobered by what has happened, says Din was a better man than he was."[68]

The focus on the final line of the poem, precisely in the form of a toast, curiously calls to mind the unresolved irony of Mary Lee's tribute to her rival that closes "The College Widow," although in "Gunga Din," Faulkner was working with a more troublesome paradox: the sacrificial death of a native water bearer for the good of the British Empire. Indeed, it was a problem that Bertolt Brecht observed while watching the film, noting that Gunga Din might be viewed not as a hero but as a "traitor" who "sacrificed his life so that his fellow countrymen should be defeated."[69] To be fair, Din is supposed to be an untouchable (Dalit) in the film, so his fellow countrymen are not necessarily his friends. In his various story outlines, Faulkner seemingly wanted to soften any potential contradictions by setting Din up as the fall guy, who is at first "a liar, braggart and petty thief"[70] who neglects his wife and child and later constantly on the receiving end of "a beating he justly deserves."[71]

It is unclear just why Faulkner spent over a month producing only a handful of pages for the property, but it is likely that his rewriting of *Absalom, Absalom!* at this time was occupying his mind. This would go some way to explaining the miscegenation of the first "Gunga Din" notes, as well as the fraternal bond reminiscent of the Henry Sutpen–Charles Bon dynamic before it sours in his novel in progress. So too would it make sense of his reported comment to Meta Carpenter Wilde at the time: "The trouble with the script . . . is that these damned fool people . . . don't begin to realize that Gunga Din was a colored man."[72] If Faulkner had earlier imagined himself through Kipling, now he was imagining Kipling—and India—by way of the South. His comment was also quite prescient, as the "colored man" of Faulkner's adaptation was progressively edited out of his later story outlines, replaced the very white "soldiers three" that headlined the film as released: Cary Grant, Victor McLagen, and Douglas Fairbanks Jr.

Faulkner had nearly finished with the script in mid-May and wrote Estelle that he had hopes for another picture, having agreed to write "a short synopsis for Gloria Swanson, will see her Monday and find out about that."[73] But Swanson was essentially sidelined from Hollywood activity at that point, and it would be five years before the famous actor of the silent screen would make her next appearance, in RKO's *Father Takes a Wife* (Jack Hively, 1941). Faulkner's next sojourn in Hollywood, however, was only a few months away.

"The Last Slaver" and *Slave Ship*

Fearing for his future in a precarious industry, Faulkner had signed a contract with Fox back in March, securing twenty weeks of work at $750 per week, with six-month options thereafter and the prospect of a $250 raise per week (*SL*, 95).[74] He started back at the studio on August 7, where, as he wrote Goldman, he was "going to try to make some money without having to borrow it" (*SL*, 95). There he was assigned to "The Last Slaver" (based on the 1933 novel of the same name by George S. King), later released as *Slave Ship*, a project focused on a historical reality close to Faulkner's heart: the horrors of the triangular trade. Based on a true story (as a newspaper article reprinted in its postscript confirms), King's novel follows the *Wanderer*, a yacht that is converted into a slave ship in the years before abolition. The ship's Yankee navigator, Kane, expresses an ethical objection to his working on such a vessel, and the conflict onboard escalates until, with the help of an African cook and a European crew more enlightened than their American counterparts, he overthrows the captain and nobly returns the *Wanderer*'s slaves to the Congo.

Although earlier treatments and screenplays by Sam Hellman and Gladys Lehman that date to as early as March 14, 1936, had clearly established a thrilling narrative, Darryl Zanuck felt the script needed serious revision. He was evidently concerned with the dialogue in particular, which as Sarah Gleeson-White suggests, "probably explains Faulkner's assignment to the property" (*WFATCF*, 222). In a later interview, Faulkner responded to a question about his precise role in *Slave Ship* by simply stating that "I'm a motion picture doctor. When they find a section of a script they don't like I rewrite it and continue to rewrite it until they are satisfied. I reworked sections in this picture. I don't write scripts. I don't know enough about it."[75] And indeed, Faulkner's claim that he only "reworked sections" (*LG*, 57) of "The Last Slaver" accords with the fact that many of the changes to King's narrative had already been made in the earlier script by Hellman and Lehman. The Kane character, now named Lovett, is captain of the ill-fated *Wanderer*, who sets sail for Africa with the intention of purchasing slaves but changes his mind about the mission once he falls in love with the abolitionist Nancy. His crew, led by Beery's character, Thompson, is understandably unhappy with this turn of events, and after carrying out a mutiny, they proceed with the voyage as planned. Unbeknown to them all, a marine, Duncan, has disguised himself as a crewmember, intending to halt the ship's progress. Eventually he is found out, the ship catches fire, and Duncan escapes (romantically) with Nancy, leaving both Lovett and Thompson behind to die.

This much had already changed, then, when Faulkner arrived to make his revisions with Johnson, but he may have had a hand in notable emendations subsequently made to the dialogue. In the screenplay as it was developed, Lovett's lines were altered so that he could show his softer side in his conversations with Nancy. After they are married and before Nancy discovers the reason behind the ship's journey, Lovett promises her an eternal honeymoon in the West Indies:

147   TWO SHOT—LOVETT AND NANCY
      INT. MASTER'S CABIN—NIGHT
      Lovett is holding her in his arms.

                    NANCY
                (laughing happily)
      I can hardly believe it—that we're actually married—and on a ship going
      to sea—to a home of our own!

                    LOVETT
                (amused)
      Shall we just sail around first—for a week or so—like millionaires? Or
      head straight for Jamaica?

                    NANCY
      Straight for Jamaica. Is it a very large house?

                    LOVETT
      It isn't much at all now—so it can be whatever you want it to be—and
      we'll stay at the inn until you're satisfied with it.

                    NANCY
      And that'll be our future?

                    LOVETT
      It'll be our whole life.
           As he kisses her. (WFATCF, 293)

But Faulkner and Johnson also cooked up some lustier exchanges, which become especially heated after the mutiny. The following scene takes place just as Thompson has seized control of the ship; Lovett is being held at gunpoint by the hostile Lefty, a character who did not appear in the earlier treatment:

                    LOVETT
                (grimly)
      Before this is over I'm going to have the head off every shoulder in here.

                    LEFTY
                (disgustedly)
      Aw, drop him over the side and forget it.

                    THOMPSON
      No, no. Just let me talk to him a minute! Jim and me's—

> LOVETT
> Stow that! What are you getting at?
>
> THOMPSON
> (freezing on him)
> All right, my lad, if that's the way you want it . . . We're going to Africa—to get a cargo. Maybe you're going with us—maybe you ain't. It's up to you.
>
> LOVETT
> And if I say no. (*WFATCF*, 307)

Realism was the order of the day here, whether it was sincere romance or aggressive sparring. And accurate historical details, not just convincing dialogue, were necessary to present a realistic depiction of seafaring in the mid-nineteenth century. When the screenplay was submitted to Zanuck in late September, Johnson attached his own comments, outlining a remaining problem: "One thing more is that the marine terminology in this script leaves a great deal to be desired. Faulkner's naval experience was on a cat boat on the Mississippi while mine was spent in the bar of the Normandie. Sam Hellman was in the Navy but that was before sail was invented. Gladys Lehman nearly met the fleet. There may be somebody versed in sail ship jargon on the lot. . . . At any rate the seamanship in the script certainly needs going over."[76]

With the property already being compared to the recent nautical success *Mutiny on the Bounty* (Frank Lloyd, 1935), it was imperative that the screenplay present itself as an accurate historical document, especially considering that King's novel was itself well versed in the jargon of the sea: not only had it included an article outlining the travails of the real-life *Wanderer* but it also contained within its pages a cross-section of a slave ship, illustrating the real, historical "METHOD OF STOWING NEGROES IN THE 'TWEEN DECKS OF A SLAVER."[77] In keeping with the work's unflinching portrayal of the conditions of slavery, this image appears as a throwback to the late-eighteenth-century abolitionist movement in Britain, in the course of which Thomas Clarkson, seeking to overthrow the slave trade, tendered similar evidence to a parliamentary committee.

The image is also a sign of the novel's desire to break free of the shackles of narrative; its inclusion of pictorial evidence both supplements its horrifying account of slavery and pushes the work away from the confines of the page and toward the screen. In the novel, King spends a good deal of time down in the hold with the slaves, documenting the shocking conditions of their captivity. He also creates a rounded black character, Kavla, the ship's cook, who is instrumental in Kane's mutiny and who productively triangulates the relationship between the black slaves and their white masters: "Kavla scanned each of the captives' faces intently. 'This been Kavla's country—back there,' he said, as he pointed beyond the hills. 'Good country before slave man come ketchem black man; now very bad—most all black mans go 'way. Slave man go far to get black man.' 'Can you talk to these blacks?' asked Kane. 'Yes,' replied the negro. 'I know what he say. For twelve years I no talk; I talk all right now; no forget.'"[78] This question of talking is important in the scheme of things, since only one line is spoken by a black character in the screenplay—at one point a "Negro boy" hands an envelope to the first mate, Thompson, saying: "White man gimme this to give you" (*WFATCF*, 283).[79] Thompson also takes the place of Kavla as translator, and he is far less sympathetic to the slaves in bondage:

> Thompson is questioning the slave in Swahili, the slave answering with many gestures.
>
> LOVETT
>
> How old does he say he is?
>
> THOMPSON
>
> He doesn't know but he says he remembers Noah and the ark and the flood like it was yesterday.
>
> (to slave)
>
> Bwana Noah?
>
> (slave nods eagerly)
>
> He says he liked Noah personally.
>
> LOVETT
>
> (to Danelo)
>
> Call his grandchildren to put him to bed.
>
> 40   MED. SHOT—INT. HOLD OF YACHT—NIGHT
>
> This is the slave hold, dark, cramped, lighted by torches, as Lefty directs the stowing of the slaves, who are packed like spoons in tiers, men on one side, women on the other.
>
> LEFTY
>
> (to the sweating sailors)
>
> Pack 'em tighter—closer! You can get a dozen more over there!

> At this point we can use whatever SHOTS we want or need to show the handling and storing of slaves aboard ship. (*WFATCF*, 241)

There is, then, some aspiration in the script to depict the harsh brutality of slavery, the description of the shot here mirroring the image reproduced in King's novel. And it was apparently enough for Carl van Vechten to later recommend the film to his friend, James Weldon Johnson: "Have you seen 'Slave Ship'? This goes a little further in the direction of realism than most movies on this subject & you get a glimpse of how the Africans were packed into the holds of the ships & treated."[80] A "glimpse," perhaps. But ultimately, Faulkner's and Johnson's screenplay seemed to be edging the film closer to a mediation of slavery by white characters, savior figures who performed unlikely heroic deeds or ignoble masters who failed to see the harm they were doing, even in the face of overwhelming evidence. The recurring appearance of one particular novel throughout the screenplay—indeed, the best-selling novel of the nineteenth century—not only confirms the ignorance of the crew on the *Wanderer* but also a further shift away from any potential black agency in the script:

> 289 MED. CLOSE SHOT—THOMPSON IN FO'C'S'LE—NIGHT
> He is reading "Uncle Tom's Cabin" to two seamen.
>
> > THOMPSON
> > (reading)
>
> "Listen, you black beast. Ain't I your Master? Ain't you mine—body and soul?" That's what Lee-gree says. Now listen to what Uncle Tom says to him. "No, no, my body is maybe yours, but my soul isn't—it belongs to someone greater than you—and you can't harm it!"
>
> > 1st SEAMAN
>
> That's pretty fancy, coming from a darky.
>
> > 2nd SEAMAN
>
> That's pretty fancy coming from anybody.
>
> > SCOTTY
> > (entering)
>
> Cap'n wants you in the chart room—right away.
>
> > THOMPSON
> > (rising)
>
> A book like that just about breaks your heart. (*WFATCF*, 357–58)

The idea of Harriet Beecher Stowe's popular abolitionist novel appearing in Thompson's hands as a way of indicating the ironic disconnect among the crew was apparently suggested by Zanuck at a story conference with Johnson and Faulkner on August 10.[81] But it is also fascinating to consider it in light of Faulkner's own work on the script, especially since he was at that time just finishing up his revisions of the galleys of *Absalom, Absalom!*[82] This, too, is a novel about the slave trade, although the slaves within its pages are never more than shadowy figures in the margins and the nature of slavery itself is more than a little unclear.

In his reading of *Absalom, Absalom!* alongside "The Last Slaver," Jeff Karem argues that in both texts, Faulkner "is actively repressing vital historical connections between the United States and the Black Atlantic."[83] And certainly Karem seems right to point this out: over the course of writing the novel, Faulkner steadily cut the representations of the West Indies from the manuscript, so that in the end it appears as a strange, mythical place. This is also true of the screenplay. Ellen Scott argues that Zanuck was ambivalent from the beginning about the commitment to realism where slavery was concerned, worrying more about the commercial appeal of the film and about "impugning the protagonists": "It is evident that Zanuck sometimes saw slaving more as a masculine sport—a last frontier for the toughened white man—than as part of a brutal institution at odds with America's democratic promise of freedom."[84] King's focus on African characters and locations had thus been well and truly buried by the time Faulkner began working on the screenplay; the slaves had been reduced to the background in line with Zanuck's wishes to avoid representations of brutality, and the plot even skirted around the trade routes as mapped out in the source text.[85] The reason for Faulkner's unwillingness to properly engage with the historical facts of the slave trade, Karem tells us, is that he harbored a deep fear of the Caribbean and of its explosive revolutionary history and the apocalyptic promise that it would "conquer the western hemisphere" (*N*, 3:311), as Shreve predicts at the end of *Absalom*.

But it is not simply Faulkner's subjective "fear" that led to his repressing the historical truth of slavery and backgrounding of black characters: it is rather Quentin Compson's fear that his family is implicated in the slaveholding past that leads to his actively repressing its history.[86] Outside of the novel, we must consider, too, the close proximity of *Absalom, Absalom!* to "The Last Slaver," and how Faulkner might have thought to mold the latter in the image of the former as he completed both. We can see something of this crossover, perhaps, in the first chapter of *Absalom* that was published in the *American Mercury* in

August 1936. The story printed in the *Mercury* was taken from the pages of a preliminary typescript of the novel's first chapter that Faulkner had sent to his publishers in early April. This typescript contains many suggestions and critical comments from the editors, all of which were incorporated into the magazine publication. What the *Mercury* story does not include, however, are Faulkner's own later edits of this chapter, which he appears to have completed in early August. These include his important naming of Sutpen as "Thomas," correcting the version in the *Mercury*, wherein he is referred to as "Charles" (*WFM*, 13: 17).

Candace Waid has argued that the most conspicuous difference between the versions of the chapter in magazine and novel lies in the first of *Absalom*'s "italicized echoes," those words of Miss Rosa Coldfield that Quentin incorporates into his own narration. This "reverberating echo form" is crossed out in the preliminary typescript and is absent from the *Mercury* excerpt but present in the published book, and Waid argues that it is this passage that makes the novel the "provocative masterpiece of modernist narrative" that it is:[87]

> *It seems that this demon—his name was Sutpen—(Colonel Sutpen)—Colonel Sutpen. Who came out of nowhere and without warning upon the land with a band of strange niggers and built a plantation—(Tore violently a plantation, Miss Rosa Coldfield says)—tore violently. And married her sister Ellen and begot a son and a daughter which—(Without gentleness begot, Miss Rosa Coldfield says)—without gentleness. Which should have been the jewels of his pride and the shield and comfort of his old age, only—(Only they destroyed him or something or he destroyed them or something. And died)—and died. Without regret, Miss Rosa Coldfield says—(Save by her) Yes save by her. (And by Quentin Compson) Yes. And by Quentin Compson. (N, 3:9)*

In its rapid condensation of the novel's entire plot, this synoptic passage makes clear from the beginning Quentin's refusal to admit the truth about Sutpen's labor force, whom he will never refer to as "slaves" in his narration. Here, they are simply "a band of strange niggers" who, along with Sutpen, "came out of nowhere and without warning upon the land." Quentin's opening summary (with the intrusion of Rosa Coldfield) pervades the remainder of the narrative, during which various other voices affirm or interrogate this early assessment of the Sutpen story.

Written just as he was beginning to work on "The Last Slaver," this supplement to *Absalom, Absalom!* offers a brief overview, very early on, of all of the novel's key details, and it is precisely the kind of overview that could hold appeal for a producer, as the passage somehow makes sense of a piece of writing and a piece of history that is otherwise narratively fragmented and completely abstruse. If we recall that Faulkner began work on his screenplay as he was finishing off his novel of the slave trade at the same time as he dealing with its horrific effects in the South, then it is certainly plausible that the synopsis was even designed to help *Absalom* ride to the screen on the coattails of *Slave Ship*. Indeed, Joseph Urgo has provocatively nominated the italicized additions as the "story idea" that Quentin obtains from listening to Rosa, akin to the treatments Faulkner was asked to write while at MGM.[88]

The associations are more than suggestive. Indeed, just as he was finishing up on "The Last Slaver," Faulkner expressed his desire to adapt *Absalom* as a motion picture in letters on September 4 to Morton Goldman and Harrison Smith (his editor at Random House). To Goldman, he wrote: "I am going to undertake to sell this book myself to the pictures, first. I am going to ask one hundred thousand dollars for it or nothing, as I do not need to sell it now since I have a job. I am going to try it first and if I don't have any luck I will write you later" (*SL*, 96). Faulkner's letter to Smith was in much the same vein and was coupled with a request for "clean galleys" (*SL*, 96) that he could show to prospective producers. According to Joseph Blotner, Faulkner's first port of call with the galleys was Nunnally Johnson, a logical choice at Fox. The galleys were accompanied by a note indicating that Faulkner had halved the price he had quoted to Goldman: "Nunnally, these are the proofs of my new book. The price is $50,000. It's about miscegenation."[89] Only a few months earlier, Margaret Mitchell had agreed to sell the rights for her Civil War saga, *Gone with the Wind*, for precisely that amount to the new independent company Selznick International Pictures.[90] But owing to its similar subject matter and with only a pitch like this to recommend it, *Absalom* failed to find a willing studio, and talk of its adaptation almost disappears from the record thereafter (although not completely, as I discuss in the next chapter).

"Splinter Fleet" and *Submarine Patrol*

Faulkner had more difficulty with his next assignment than he had with his previous Fox screenplays. The property was based on *The Splinter Fleet of the Otranto Barrage* (1936) by Ray Millholland and was eventually released as John Ford's *Submarine Patrol* (1938). The story revolves around a fleet of hastily assembled wooden submarine chasers that are resting in an Italian port in 1917 but are eventually called into action when other naval ships are occupied elsewhere. In an unlikely display of military prowess, the ill-equipped vessels prove their worth, countering claims from within the navy of their impending obsolescence. The narrative victory of those makeshift boats points forward to the war films Faulkner would write for Warner Brothers and back to his work on *Today We Live* (a film that documents, as John Matthews has shown, the way "the limitations of modern technology actually produce old-fashioned pride in manual work").[91]

At a script conference on September 4, Zanuck stressed that the film should concern itself less with the romance plot (nowhere in sight in Millholland's book) and more with the story of the splinter fleet. And here at least he was listening to the suggestion of his screenwriter: Zanuck was apparently amenable to Faulkner's suggestion that Craig, a lieutenant in charge of the submarine chaser 1X2R, be killed off in the narrative (although he does not in fact die in the screenplay as it is written) (*WFATCF*, 377). Interestingly enough, at this stage the script already included a southern character—Jefferson Davis Schultz—who was "a fat, comic-looking youth" (*WFATCF*, 387). As such, Faulkner's contributions would not take the form of supplying a stock southerner. The conference was concluded with a plan for Faulkner to "block out a new treatment" and with Zanuck stressing the need "to fight away from FORMULA" (*WFATCF*, 377).

More than the crew of eccentrics that people Millholland's novel, the film would require a detailed understanding of naval warfare. Coincidentally, the producer, Gene Markey, would become a rear admiral in the U.S. Navy. But according to Markey, Faulkner was not particularly knowledgeable about battle at sea, evidenced in his view by the fact that the dialogue Faulkner was producing was more suited to aviators than seamen. "It was good Faulknerian dialogue," Markey recognized immediately, "but it had nothing whatever to do with our story."[92] And it wasn't just the dialogue that was causing trouble, as Zanuck now appointed Kathryn Scola—who had collaborated many times with Markey at Warner Brothers and in the pre-code era—to the project to "keep an eye on the story line."[93]

It is difficult to verify precisely what was wrong with Faulkner's dialogue or how he failed to see the storyline based on the scripts titled "Splinter Fleet" that bear his name—a screenplay dated December 7 and a first draft continuity dated December 22 that contains revisions, both of which were written in collaboration with Scola. Indeed, the writing displays a keen grasp of the technical language that Millholland uses in his yarn of naval life, and accusations of Faulkner's inability to understand the lingo of the seamen appear misplaced. After all, Faulkner had already earned a credit for dialogue that related specifically to naval warfare, and it appears he didn't forget it, since here he seems to have repurposed earlier material from "Turn About." Consider, for example, the scene from the MGM script that recounts Claude's and Bogard's reaction when the torpedo "drops only part of the way out" of the ship's gun:

> CLAUDE
> (Cheerfully)
> Didn't go that time.
>
> BOGARD
> Go? It didn't——the torpedo——
>
> CLAUDE
> (He and one seaman drawing the torpedo back into tube)
> No. Clumsy. Always happening. Should think clever chaps like engineers——happens, though. Draw her in and try her again.
>
> BOGARD
> But the nose! The cap! It's still in the tube?
>
> CLAUDE
> Absolutely. But it's working now, loaded. Screw's started. Get it back and drop it clear. If we should slow up or stop, it would overtake us. Drive back into tube. Bingo! As Mac says, What? (*FMS*, 211)

Contrary to Markey's estimations, Faulkner had learned from his work on the "Turn About" script the precise differences between the language of aviators and seamen. The use of naval jargon in "Splinter Fleet" perhaps owed itself to Karl Tunberg's earlier screenplay of September 4, but it may also have indicated Faulkner's and Scola's reading of Millholland's novel, which includes several passages about the Y gun, as well as a diagram of the weapon on its inside cover and a photograph in the book. Millholland describes how the Y gun was deployed: "The depth mines were first bolted to the end of smoothly machined plungers, the plungers slipped down into each of the Y-Gun's bores, and the double projectiles were discharged simultaneously by a black powder cartridge inserted in the breech at the base of each gun."[94] Faulkner and Scola adapt this raw information in their screenplay, transforming complex procedure into a tense scene that also draws on the plot point from the "Turn About" screenplay:

169   CLOSER SHOT AT Y GUN

The men watch while Fender puts a cartridge into the gun—takes up one of the depth bombs and loads it into the gun.

FENDER
(indicating)

The cartridge here shoots the bomb out of the ship. But the *first* thing the cartridge does is to drive the plunger into the bomb and set off the timed detonator.

BENNY

What if it don't quite shoot the bomb out of the gun? Won't it blow up the ship?

FENDER

What if it does? You won't mind—you won't be here!
(to the men)
All right, grab two of them ash cans and load the gun.

BENNY
(nervously)

Wait, chief. Ain't it time enough to do this when we got to?

FENDER

Come on—get the ash cans. (*WFATCF*, 452–53)

Not long after this scene, Benny's worst fears are realized when a depth charge becomes stuck in the gun, but luckily he manages to heroically save the ship by releasing the charge.

Scola's and Faulkner's interest in the technical components of the submarine chaser also allowed them to develop a scene that does not derive from Millholland's book. One of the screenplay's comic foils, Benny, is part of the "Black Gang," the ship's engine-room crew. But after he wins a stereopticon in a dice game, he quickly asks to be transferred to the gun crew, and we soon find out why, as he constructs a rudimentary device using the stereopticon and the breech of the ship's gun. Soon, all the sailors are attracted by Benny's mysterious advertisement—ONE MINUTE, FIVE CENTS. PROGRAM CHANGED DAILY—and queue to see a provisional peep show:

155 EXT.—DECK—AT GUN—GROUP SHOT
A number of the sailors are crowded around the breech of the gun.
Brett has his eye to the breech. All watch him.

BRETT
(his voice muffled)
Oh, baby! Hit that gun barrel, somebody. Maybe she'll drop it.

SEAMAN
What do you see? Let me have a look.
(he tries to push Brett aside. Brett holds him off) (*WFATCF*, 448)

But Lieutenant Craig quickly disrupts proceedings:

158 CLOSER SHOT—INSIDE GUN BARREL
The huge figure of a FAN DANCER.

159 CLOSE SHOT—CRAIG—MOVING CAMERA
He straightens, takes the stereopticon lens from the breech, looks at it.
Goes to the muzzle and peers into it.

160 CLOSE SHOT—MUZZLE
A tiny picture of the fan dancer is pasted on a piece of glass,
fixed inside the gun muzzle. (*WFATCF*, 449)

A nineteenth-century viewing device that creates a composite picture from two almost identical images, the stereopticon had appeared in Faulkner's work before—Thomas Sutpen may have "swapped the Indians a stereopticon" (*US*, 583) for his land in "Evangeline," and in a metaphorical register the plantation ledgers in *Go Down, Moses* come to encompass what Ike McCaslin refers to as "the stereopticon whole" (*N*, 4:220). These two references, as Stuart Burrows deftly argues, are not accidental: "The optical technology that Faulkner uses as a metaphor to express the doubled relation of the plantation is thus . . . potentially the very thing exchanged for the land in the first place."[95]

In "Splinter Fleet," the stereopticon appears in a quite different manner, first and foremost as a means for creating a licentious spectacle. But in the scheme of the narrative, its inclusion offers more than meets the eye. For the stereopticon is, in 1917, a largely anachronistic device that properly belongs to the prior century. With the plot of "Splinter Fleet" in mind, the appearance of the fascinating stereopticon begins to make sense: for this is a script all about the value of seemingly obsolete technologies, of the sudden importance of an armada of retired wooden ships in the Great War. Like the stereopticon, the splinter fleet here proves its enduring worth in the film's battles and makes a case, too, for its capacity to surprise and enthrall modern viewers. In spite of the skillful writing of such narrative set pieces, Faulkner and Scola were released from the project, and *Submarine Patrol* was completed with the aid of a number of additional screenwriters.

Drums along the Mohawk

By 1937, Americans were spending 75 percent of their leisure money on motion pictures.[96] As such, there was still plenty of work left for the willing screenwriter: Faulkner's earnings at Fox by the end of 1936 had totaled a very respectable $19,374.99.[97] He had spent a holiday "layoff" period away from the studio after he finished work on "Splinter Fleet" in early December 1936. But starting on March 18 in the new year, as per the contract he had signed in August 1936, Faulkner's pay rate was due to rise from $750 to $1,000 a week. And he would return to work at this rate even earlier than expected, signing on once again toward the end of February. Back at the studio he was assigned, along with Scola and fellow southerner Lamar Trotti, to work on a property at that stage known as "Dance Hall"—but later released as *The Giant Swing* (Irving Pichel, 1941)—but only lasted a couple of days on it.[98]

His swansong project was a far more sustained one, however, as he began an adaptation of *Drums along the Mohawk* (1936), Walter D. Edmonds's vastly popular novel of frontier life during the Revolution. The story begins with the wedding of Gilbert and Lana Martin, who start their married life by moving into the relative wilderness of the Mohawk Valley in New York State. As the Revolutionary War looms, Gilbert and Lana have a hard time establishing their home and increasingly come into conflict with British and Seneca forces alike. Before too long, Gilbert is fighting alongside the Yankees, and Lana is pregnant and left to fend for herself. Suspenseful and romantic, *Drums* would not appear out of place in James Fenimore Cooper's Leatherstocking Tales, and it proved extremely popular with readers. In fact, it had sold a hundred thousand copies by the time Fox purchased it.[99]

The studio was prepared to allow Edmonds to write a script for his own work, but, as was not often the case, Faulkner was initially able to adapt the work under his own steam, turning in a twenty-six-page treatment in mid-March 1937.[100] As George Sidney indicates, since the novel had proved so popular, Faulkner "could not very well have discarded Edmonds's story" in his adaptation, and so he seems to have mostly adhered to the existing narrative, at times reining in some of its more sprawling, picaresque tendencies.[101] However, it is unclear whether Faulkner worked directly from Edmonds's novel or from a treatment by Bess Meredyth dated January 9, which may have already made some changes to the original story. The most obvious difference between the novel and the treatment lay in the condensation of the novel's ten separate sections into the five sequences of the treatment, part of an effort to trim the epic saga into something more manageable. The treatment offered a more character-driven story, the troubled Martin marriage serving as the anchor point for all other narrative strands. There were obvious casualties of this decision: Edmonds's Loyalist John Wolff was excised from the story altogether, and Blue Back, an amiable Oneida Indian, is treated with less respect by the whites and relegated to a bit-part player. Faulkner also heightens the conflict among the farmers and government of the emerging nation, which, as Sarah Gleeson-White has observed, draws attention away from the battle between British and American forces.[102]

Over the following months, Faulkner would continue with "Drums along the Mohawk," working it into what was labeled by the studio as a "dialogued treatment" of 237 pages (although it is in fact what is typically thought of as a dialogue continuity).[103] He followed through with many of the narrative plans he had laid out in the treatment and indeed supplemented the longer script with a list of locales for each sequence, of which there were now six. A six-page list of characters precedes the screenplay, too, accompanied by a list of figures that correspond roughly with those in Edmonds's novel. Indeed, various excerpts of dialogue and other narrative events are lifted directly from the book (perhaps via Meredyth's treatment). In both texts, for example, Gilbert is paid precisely $4.27 for his service to the United States Congress, less than the $5.52 he had expected, but is consoled by the belief that they will prevail: "it sure is fun to lick the British" (*WFATCF*, 633).[104] But soon afterward, when the pedantic company man, Collyer, requisitions crops from his farm, Gilbert's heart is hardened not against his foreign enemy but against the Congress itself. Playing on a joke from Edmonds's novel about the overly formal papers carried by the soldiers, Faulkner depicts the struggle as follows:

> Gilbert takes the paper, looks at it. His face becomes grim and sardonic. The others watch him.

MRS. McKLENNAR

Well?

GILBERT

Maybe I'd better read it aloud.

(he reads)

"Mrs. McKlennar, Widow, Greeting:"

HELMER

Greeting?

GILBERT

That's what it says.

(he reads)

"You will, on reception of this, surrender at once to the presenting officer of the Continental Army of the United States all corn, wheat and other grain in your possession, in return for which you will receive a receipt in full, signed by the said presenting officer. By order of the Continental Congress of the United States. T. Collyer, Commissioner."

HELMER

Greeting. Well, well, well!

GILBERT

And right pretty written, too. Would anybody else like to see It first?

(he offers the paper around)

No? Well then!

He throws the paper into the fire. (*WFATCF*, 637–38)

Following on from this scene, Faulkner has Gilbert leading a group of starving farmers to (nonviolently) take back the crops that are rightfully theirs:

GILBERT

All right, men. Load the carts. Hurry now.

With the exception of the ones who hold the sergeant, the settlers hurry into the granary.

SERGEANT

You'll pay for this.

A SETTLER

Sure. That's what you told us when you took the corn.

SERGEANT
The requisition to Congress ain't gone through yet. As soon as it does, you'll get your money.

SETTLER
We ain't used to requisitions in this country, and there ain't nobody here we can requisition of for a field of wheat or corn. We have to plant it and work it.

2ND SETTLER
That's right. It ain't like we were going to take the wheat and corn and eat it up. We're just going to put it in the ground. Any time he wants it, he can come and dig it up again. (*WFATCF*, 646)

These sequences, in both novel and screenplay, must have surely piqued Faulkner's interest, for at that very moment he was collating his recent Civil War stories for *The Unvanquished* and revisiting some very similar sequences involving Granny, Bayard, and Ringo. In that book, Faulkner depicts the breakdown of order in the South, as the Union army burns the Sartoris home and steals the family silver. In response, the unlikely trio robs both Yankee and Confederate forces of mules and freed slaves, forging orders that allow them to repeat the scam and sell the property they receive, until Granny is betrayed and shot, and the two boys seek revenge by bushwhacking her killer. Faulkner's Civil War narratives share common ground with the novel of Revolutionary America in their depiction of lawless, retributory theft. Overall, as Gleeson-White has argued, the script forges an implicit connection between "the rifts and conflicts present within the nation from its inception, conflicts that would of course erupt more fiercely nearly a century later."[105] And Faulkner's simultaneous reworking of *The Unvanquished* certainly helps to explain his inclusion of the acts of requisition in the "Drums along the Mohawk" screenplay.

The last story of the collection, "An Odor of Verbena," was completed toward the end of July, around the same time as he discovered that his contract with Fox was not to be renewed (*SL*, 100). "It's hot here and I dont feel very good," he wrote Estelle, "but I think it's mostly being tired of movies, worn out with them" (*SL*, 101). Nevertheless, by the time he returned home in August, Faulkner had amassed over $21,000 in earnings from the studio for the twenty-one weeks he had been on contract in 1937—which is quite a lot considering that he had really only written one screenplay during this time, and one that was uncredited at that.[106] Ultimately, although "An Odor of Verbena" would not find a home in the magazines, Faulkner was able to execute a far more impressive feat by selling the rights to *The Unvanquished* to MGM for $25,000.[107] While he was able to purchase a 320-acre farm with the royalties, the film would never appear, as Faulkner later recounted: "A producer named David Selznick bought *Gone with the Wind*. M-G-M wanted to make it and he wouldn't let M-G-M make it. He wanted to use [Clark] Gable, who was under contract to M-G-M in it, and they wouldn't let him have Gable, and he wouldn't let them have *Gone with the Wind*. So they bought my book and told him that if he didn't let them make *Gone with the Wind* they were going to make a *Gone with the Wind* of their own—they had no intention of making a moving picture out of my book—and so Selznick let them make the picture" (*FU*, 252). Although this work never made it to the screen with MGM, the money earned from the sale meant that Faulkner could return to Mississippi, and it would be some time before he would make his way west on a contract again. Before he left, however, Faulkner would make an attempt to take another novel, *Absalom, Absalom!*, to the screen.

CHAPTER 3

Independence

Absalom, Absalom! and "Revolt in the Earth"

While Faulkner's packaging of *Absalom, Absalom!* as a work "about miscegenation" had ensured that his attempt to sell it as a film project in 1936 never got off the ground, he would make a more serious attempt in the following year, just as his contract with Fox was finishing up. For a number of reasons, the screenplay that resulted is hardly ever taken seriously, branded variously as a "downright inane" piece of writing, a "ludicrously awful script," and a "justly unmade movie."[1] But "Revolt in the Earth," the sixty-two-page screenplay written by Faulkner with director Dudley Murphy, has much to recommend it, provided we read it with an open mind. While we should of course keep the formidable *Absalom* in our thoughts as we come to "Revolt," there is much to learn from the screenplay in relation not to the novel alone but to the studio system and the difficulties of independent film production.

Contrary to prior claims, "Revolt in the Earth" seems to have been written at some point in July 1937, when both Faulkner and Murphy were stationed in Los Angeles. Murphy had recently directed Paul Robeson in *The Emperor Jones* (1933) and was now making another attempt to break the Hollywood mold with a series of new independent features. Although there are no records of a meeting between the two, an article from that month in the *New York Times* confirms their collaboration. Writing in his column, "Footnotes on Pictures and People," B. R. Crisler announced the arrival of a new independent production company on the scene that engaged Hollywood talent but was located in London: "One of the more interesting and plausible of the newer production ventures, Associated Artists has now advanced to the stage of negotiating for release outlets and Dudley Murphy, the director, fired with a new vision of cooperative-artist enterprise, seems to be the negotiator-in-chief hereabouts."[2] Against the hegemony of the big five studios, with their models of vertical integration, Associated Artists had ideas of creating its own features, with cast and crew dividing the profits fairly among them. Crisler went on to note that in addition to boasting a number of impressive acting names (Leslie Howard, Edward G. Robinson), the new company also boasted a "surprisingly rich fund of story properties." These included "a Dashiell Hammett item," "an unnamed story-in-progress with comedy-musical background, for Duke Ellington"—with whom Murphy had previously worked on *Black and Tan* (1929), and, most importantly, "'Revolt in the Earth,' an original screen story by William Faulkner about Mississippi swampland folk."[3] This first mention of the existence of "Revolt" is dated July 18, 1937, and so refutes previous assumptions that the screenplay was written either in late 1942 or early 1943 (the point at which it was rejected by Robert Buckner at Warner Brothers).

Evidence for the collaboration between these two high modernists remains mostly circumstantial. Murphy certainly seems to have loitered on the West Coast over the summer: indeed, the first (aborted) Associated Artists picture was scheduled for production in Hollywood in July, placing Murphy in Los Angeles at that time.[4] In June, Faulkner was finishing work on a 238-page screenplay for John Ford's *Drums along the Mohawk* (1939).[5] He stayed in Los Angeles until mid-August and aside from fulfilling his contractual obligations at Fox seems to have mostly been cooling his heels at this time. With no further assignments forthcoming at the studio, Faulkner took the opportunity to strike out on his own, attempting once more to sell *Absalom* to the movies.

"Revolt" is not an adaptation of just *Absalom*, incorporating as it does elements from "Evangeline" (1931) and "Wash" (1934), as well as a fragment that perhaps even dates from 1925. It seems far more useful therefore to include the script on what Estelle Schoenberg has called the "Sutpen continuum," positioning "Revolt" among the various artifacts relating to Faulkner's saga of the South, of which *Absalom* is only the most recognizable.[6] The screenplay's point of departure is a familiar one. As with Faulkner's novel, "Revolt" follows Thomas Sutpen's attempt to build a small empire in Mississippi on slave labor, a design threatened by miscegenation, incest, and the Civil War. His daughter, Judith, becomes engaged to Charles Bon, who is then killed by Judith's brother, Henry. At this point, the screenplay diverges from *Absalom*: after both Thomas Sutpen and Henry die in the Civil War, Judith marries a Yankee soldier and subsequently moves to England, so as to escape the torment of the Sutpen family curse, the most obvious symptoms of which are the constant drumbeats that she hears. Years later, Judith's granddaughter Miriam marries Eric, an anthropologist-cum-priest, and together they travel from London to Mississippi for their honeymoon, where Eric takes a keen interest in the voodoo ceremonies in the southern bayou. Here, we discover that Sutpen's grandson Wash has become a voodoo witchdoctor, and he now administers the curse on the Sutpen family and is eventually satisfied only when Miriam—the last remaining Sutpen—drowns in quicksand.[7]

This seemingly more far-fetched version of events (especially the invocation of voodoo), alongside a propensity toward visual and auditory experimentation, certainly hampered the script's fortunes when Faulkner attempted to sell it to Warner Brothers several years later. Faulkner's difficulties selling the movie rights notwithstanding, "Revolt in the Earth" has much to offer to the scholarly study of Faulkner, screenwriting, and literary and film studies. The most important aspects of "Revolt," and those that might usefully govern our reading of the screenplay, are as follows. First, the script presents a bold statement on the use of film sound innovations that elaborates on the sonic dimensions of the screenplay form in a manner different to the majority of Faulkner's other scripts and, indeed, in a manner different from the majority of 1930s film scripts. Second, its major investment in sound when considered with respect to Dudley Murphy's career more broadly prompts more nuanced readings of the screenplay as regards its representation of African American characters. And third, it offers an example of truly collaborative labor in a way that is radically distinct from most other scripts, precisely because it avoids the industrial, studio-based models that direct their composition.

"Revolt" stands as a fascinating example of a screenplay that includes various innovative sound and cinematographic stage directions. Its script is even more technically complicated than "Sutter's Gold," a complexity owing no doubt largely to Dudley Murphy. As Kawin says, it is indeed "Faulkner's most formally experimental screenplay," precisely because of its surprising emphasis on technical invention, which rarely manifested at the screenwriting stage of the filmmaking process.[8] While the use of dialogue in the 1930s was ubiquitous (even if transcribed in a number of different ways), the appearance of additional sound effects in the screenplay was not as common. In "Revolt," however, there is a superabundance of voodoo drumming, laughter, and the constant galloping of horses' hooves, and at least one of these punctuates almost every scene. Sound effects, which often accompany dissolves and so are carried between scenes, pervade the script, governing the narrative in its entirety.

The screenplay begins with "the sound of a galloping horse" that crosses the path of a twelve-year-old Clytie, and the sound continues on over the dissolve to a flashback of the scene of her birth (1).[9] Here, the sound that dominates is written as "sourceless laughter," which grows in volume as Thomas Sutpen seemingly prepares to kill the newborn Clytie. Then, with the mother and an older woman watching on, "Sutpen lifts the child above his head as though he would dash it to the earth" but hesitates at the final moment. At the same time as Sutpen halts his murderous action, we read that "the laughter stops short off, as though it too were watching him" (2). Over the next few scenes, the sound of the hooves gives way to the offensively transcribed "nigger laughter," which continues through several dissolves before paving the way for the sounds of tom-tom drums:

> THE LIBRARY
>   The tom-toms are going. Charles enters the room. Sutpen is there.
>   CHARLES
>   Sir, may I have a word with you?
>   SUTPEN
>   Is this my son's friend Charles who speaks to me, or is it Mr. Bon?
>   CHARLES
>   Charles, sir, and dare I hope more near than ever Henry's friend.
>   SUTPEN
>   Say on, sir.
>   The laughter goes over the dissolve and out of it we hear the drums. They are louder now.
> DISSOLVE TO:
> JUDITH AND CHARLES
>   —alone in the library. They are in each other's arms. (The tom-toms are still going.) Judith is very happy, but suddenly her face becomes grave and she draws back.
>   JUDITH
>   Listen!

					CHARLES
What?

					JUDITH
There, don't you hear them?

					CHARLES
Hear what?
	(he tries to draw her close to him again)
It must be in your mind.

					JUDITH
					(holding back)
Don't you hear anything at all?

					CHARLES
I can hear nothing else but wedding bells.

					JUDITH
But I do hear them.

					CHARLES
Nonsense.
	(he draws Judith close to him; he turns her face up and they kiss)
The drums are still going. (9–10)

In this sequence, the sounds of laughter and tom-toms combine to gloss over what appears to be an important confrontation between Sutpen and Charles. The stopping short of their dialogue mirrors a similar incident in *Absalom*—the decisive quarrel that results in Henry being disowned by his father—although here Charles takes the position of Henry in the novel, arguing on his own behalf for the right to marry Judith. In *Absalom*, sounds frame this key conflict, even if they are only imagined retrospectively, since no one else was privy to the scene: Mr. Compson "can imagine [Henry] and Sutpen in the library that Christmas Eve, the father and the brother, percussion and repercussion like a thunderclap and its echo, and as close together" (*N*, 3:90).

In the equivalent scene in "Revolt," however, real sounds introduce themselves so sharply as to relegate the narrative events to the margin. Since the laughter and drums are not commented on in the Sutpen-Charles meeting, it is safe to say they intrude here in a nondiegetic fashion, disrupting (or dictating the dissolve of) the scene for the reader but not for the screenplay's characters. However, in the next scene, the sound of the drums becomes meaningful within the diegesis for Judith, who (unlike the other characters) can hear what the audience would also hear in the finished film. The sound of the drums that "are still going" as the scene ends evolves organically from the sound of the horses' hooves in the first few scenes to the African American laughter that follows, forming a continuum of sounds.

While the ubiquity of such sounds—which appear to follow the worst kind of primitivist logic—invites reproach from the critic, there is another way we might read the black laughter and drum beats that guide the narrative. In Ryan Friedman's productive reading of another of Murphy's films, he introduces the notion of "surplus diegetic grounding" of African American characters in early sound cinema. Friedman argues that in lieu of addressing real-world instances of African American oppression, *The Emperor Jones*, for instance, instead amplifies the oppression of African Americans within the fictional world of the film. Murphy achieves this by turning his mise-en-scène into a mise-en-abyme from which there is no way out for the black American: Robeson's character constantly gazes at his reflection in a series of mirrors; the jungle is coded as a space of "blackness" that confirms his slide into an atavistic state; and the plot itself is circular, regressive, leading Jones toward a seemingly inevitable conclusion.

While such tropes clearly "participate in the ideological work of primitivism as conventionally theorized," they also attempt to provide a way out,[10] naturalizing "black social immobility by making stasis or entrapment appear natural" and simultaneously drawing our attention to "the sorts of social tensions and hierarchies that are otherwise invisible in the film."[11] That is to say, while it was practically impossible to address the real social struggles of black citizens on the screen in the early 1930s, directors like Murphy were able to smuggle in representations of such tensions precisely by overplaying the distorted, suffocating depictions of black characters. Although Murphy's strategy in *The Emperor Jones* was certainly dangerous and perhaps not as successful as he had imagined, sound cinema offered radically new ways of representing the black American experience.

Although encumbered by a long line of unimpressed readers, "Revolt in the Earth" certainly makes more sense when reckoned against Murphy's long-term interest in both innovative sound technology and racial issues. In 1929, Murphy was hired by RCA Photophone, responsible for showcasing the company's recent advances in sound-on-film technology, and with a pair of two-reelers—*Black and Tan*, and *St. Louis Blues* (1929), Bessie Smith's solitary screen appearance—he was able to demonstrate his true ability. For *St. Louis*

Blues, Murphy set up four cameras, "synchronized to the master sound track, so that I would not have to stop the action for close-ups or moving shots and could run the music and song without a break"—a true advance for early sound cinema.[12] Sounds in *St. Louis Blues* continue over the cuts, just as they do over the dissolves of *The Emperor Jones*—a radical innovation at the time but one that would soon become ubiquitous in editing practices. In *The Emperor Jones*, as James Donald observes, the beating tom-tom drums are a near-permanent fixture and complete a "quasi-anthropological circle" that runs from "African rhythms" to "the Gullah music of South Carolina, to the sophistication of Harlem jazz, and back to the voodoo tom-tom of the conclusion."[13]

It is no coincidence that Murphy's most notable talkies paired innovations in sound technology with attention to African American narratives and characters. Indeed, that particular tendency had emerged elsewhere at the dawn of sound cinema, with films like *Hearts in Dixie* (Paul Sloane, 1929) and *Hallelujah!* (King Vidor, 1929) that feature well-rounded black characters who speak in a manner that is supposedly "better than white voices."[14] But the near simultaneity with which all-black casts and sound films appeared was also problematic, as it could suggest a natural joining of the one to the other and result in African Americans being fetishized as an innately "rhythmic" people.[15] Indeed, such intense cinematic interest in African American culture beginning in the late 1920s—especially from those directors like Murphy that Thomas Cripps refers to as white "Negrophiles"—often risked rehearsing the same black stereotypes that had been deployed so harmfully elsewhere, reducing to distortions the very people it wished to champion.[16]

Murphy's approach to the troublesome axis of race and sound was nuanced in a unique way, taking the fantasy of black rhythm and feeding it through the rhythm of the cinematic apparatus itself. From the jazzed modernism of *Ballet mécanique* (1924) onward, his work expounds what James Donald marks as a "key condensation: a modern rhythm was at the same time the rhythm of the machine and the rhythm of 'Negro music.'"[17] In place of routine categorizations of African American jazz as "primitive," Murphy practices in his films a clever but risky dialectic of enlightenment: in depicting the rhythmic movements of black characters, he emphasizes atavism so as to work through its contradictions, thereby demonstrating "the geometrical discipline and mechanical precision" of such movements. In *Black and Tan*, for example, the Five Hot Shots (a troupe of male dancers) engage in "a style of jazz dancing, attuned to the camera" that, Donald argues, "articulated his sense of a machine aesthetic."[18] Murphy's interest in the intersections of sound and race expanded, as he turned his hand to "soundies," three-minute proto-music videos accompanying popular songs to be played on jukeboxes with projecting capabilities.[19] In one such soundie, *Alabamy Bound* (1941), the Five Spirits of Rhythm (a jazz string band) are subjugated as lowly Pullman porters but at the same time are connected with the locomotive energy of the train, creating what William Moritz has called an intelligent "synoptic" vision that attempts to redeem the implied racism.[20]

It is crucial that "Revolt of the Earth" be read in the context of Murphy's career-long project if the attempt to situate the screenplay in a new light is to succeed. Unless it is positioned with respect to his earlier and later films that address the conjunction of African Americans and sound cinema, the dominant interpretation of the script as a wholesale capitulation to primitivist fantasy seems just about right. Another related difficulty with rereading "Revolt" is that it offers something like the polar opposite of Faulkner's approach to the black history of the Americas. As we have seen, Faulkner's work for *Slave Ship* mimicked the veritable silence in *Absalom, Absalom!* on the subject of the real history of slavery. But now, with the adaptation of his magnum opus, the author would chart a completely different course. Where *Absalom* proceeds by way of rumor and conjecture and features characters (Quentin Compson and Thomas Sutpen) who refuse to utter the word "slave," "Revolt" lacks subtlety and revels in its overemphasis on the sounds and rhythms of voodoo. Much of this undoubtedly has to do with its genre: the desire of the screenplay is always to make itself heard, as is also clear in Faulkner's work for MGM. But here, rather than dialogue, it was a variety of nonverbal sounds that were pleading to be realized on the big screen.

Although the screenplay itself fails to mention slavery, its soundscape serves to cement the narrative's connection to Haiti, from whence *Absalom*'s slaves supposedly hail. In the novel, General Compson, Quentin's grandfather, consorts with Sutpen in the years after his arrival and hears of the younger man's obliviousness to the impending slave revolt on the plantation he oversees on the Caribbean island. Sutpen's innocent overseeing leads to an oversight, "overseeing what he oversaw and not knowing that he was overseeing it." Indeed, "he apparently did not know, comprehend, what he must have been seeing every day because of that innocence—a pig's bone with a little rotten flesh still clinging to it, a few chicken feathers, a stained dirty rag with a few pebbles tied up in it found on the old man's pillow one morning." Although Sutpen retrospectively understands that the French plantation owner's "gallic rage was actually fear, terror" (*N*, 3:203), during the period that

Sutpen works on the plantation, he is strangely unaware of the connection between the hints of unrest encoded in the mysterious objects and the revolt that after eight nights he inexplicably "subdued" (N, 3:204).

In "Revolt," there are several scenes in which ceremonies take place, and so the suggestions of voodoo are made explicit. This certainly follows the lead of *The Emperor Jones*, but there were other films that exploited a combination of slavery, voodoo, and zombie tropes during that decade: *White Zombie* (Victor Halperin, 1932) is easily the most polished of a sorry bunch that includes *Drums o' Voodoo* (Arthur Hoerl, 1934), the Haitian-based *Ouanga* (George Terwilliger, 1936), *Black Moon* (Roy William Neill, 1934), which features a voodoo curse that compels a young woman to return to a tropical island, and (most intriguingly) *Chloe, Love Is Calling You* (Marshall Neiland, 1934), in which a black voodoo priestess leaves the Louisiana swamp in order to gain revenge on a white plantation owner. A few years later, Jacques Tourneur's brilliant *I Walked with a Zombie* (1943) showed exactly what the genre was capable of achieving and what "Revolt" might have aspired to become.

In any case, the subgenre into which "Revolt" falls moves the screenplay away from *Absalom*, taking its foreign invocation of Haitian voodoo and imposing it on the bayous and swamps of Mississippi itself. Indeed, this domestication of exotic ritual is perhaps what makes such ritual more comprehensible. For, although many of the script's white characters remain naive in the face of the strange rituals, some take an active interest in them—Eric is "writing a most profound treatise on primitive religions and their ceremonies," and another character named Wash (this one the son of Clytie and Sutpen) becomes a witch doctor (27). In a scene that plays on the baffling appearance of the pig's bone in *Absalom*, the following ceremony in "Revolt" situates the poor white man at the head of proceedings:

> —in a swamp clearing beside the bayou. An altar faintly lighted. The witch doctor wears cow horns and Prince Albert coat. He is a white man. In a squatting circle, negroes; in the circle a young negro dances, faster and faster as the drums increase. Suddenly an object falls at the dancer's feet. He halts, stoops.
> FOCUS ON it and see that it is a pig's rib with shreds of bloody flesh. He springs up as though electrified and becomes still in attitude with arm raised. (32)

With more than a hint of Colonel Kurtz about him, this Wash is fully aware of the meaning behind the screenplay's voodoo iconography.[21] Here, Faulkner and Murphy have pushed the ritual to the extreme, at which point it is no longer just the ludicrously overplayed ceremony it was but has turned serious in its ensnaring of Wash, a member of the Sutpen family. The sounds of drumming, which have driven Judith to the point of distraction, and have now begun to concern Miriam, emerge from the soundtrack to find a home in the vision of the voodoo ceremony. Those tom-toms are irresistible and have progressed from nondiegetic to diegetic sound and then to the image, as if to demonstrate the inevitability of the family curse.

This scene also points to a recurring technical innovation that is made more explicit in two other places in the script. While here in the ceremony Wash is "electrified and becomes still," we read elsewhere of Judith, who after trying to kill the man that will become her husband is scared into his arms by the worse threat of the drums back home. "She is in the officer's arms; this pose is electrified into a photograph of the same people in wedding dress" (22). And later, a similar scene transfixes the image of Judith's granddaughter, Miriam:

> THE ENTRANCE OF A CATHEDRAL
> —and Miriam and Eric emerge. Eric in clergyman's black. They hold pose for a photographer. The wedding party is behind them; voices in the background as the photographer's camera cloth gradually obscures scene.
>
> VOICES
> A very promising young man. He will go far; at this very moment he is writing a most profound treatise on primitive religions and their ceremonies.
> The voices fade as the photographer's black cloth blots out the scene. OUT OF THE CLOTH THE PLATE emerges as a photograph of Miriam and Eric on their wedding day. (27)

The function of photography in the story exceeds an interest in the simple workings of the machine. Photography is connected with narrative elision, performing the work of a montage or insert indicating a passage of time by petrifying the action. In his earlier romantic comedy *The Sports Parade* (1932), Murphy had privileged the still photograph within the film, zooming in on an image on a café wall, allowing the picture to fill the frame, and bringing it to life.[22] In "Revolt," the photograph not only signals temporal advances and "develops" the characters whose image it captures but also performs the freezing of the narrative in a distinctly Faulknerian attempt to arrest time. Here, the tableaux of both Judith and Miriam hint at the fate of those who carry the Sutpen patronym whose time is limited by the curse placed on the family long ago.

The scene of Miriam and Eric's wedding also invites comparison with Faulkner's mention of the "negative plate" in *Absalom*, the metaphor Mr. Compson uses in imagining how Charles Bon tells Henry about his relationship with an octoroon mistress. "So I can imagine him, the way he did it: the way in which he took the innocent and negative plate of Henry's provincial soul and intellect and exposed it by slow degrees to this esoteric milieu, building gradually toward the picture which he desired it to retain, accept" (*N*, 3:87). Here, the device is mined for its metaphorical resonances. Yet although Faulkner uses the negative plate as a way of framing Henry's newfound awareness of the possibilities of interracial relationships, it is also a technology whose very operations worked through the issue of color and mediated the way that colored skin appeared to the eye.

For Julian Murphet, the deployment of the photograph in *Absalom* is the way the novel acknowledges the transformative power of the image, which offers real, visual evidence in place of oral storytelling, sealing "a gap in the narrative substance" by insisting on its unimpeachable truth. Both Mr. Compson's metaphorical negative plate and the real photograph of Bon's mistress and child stored within his locket present specific, uncomfortable difficulties of racial difference in the narrative. And yet the specific connection of the photograph with racial matters is no mere metaphor but part and parcel of the technology itself. The process through which the photograph becomes a positive image, emerging out of the negative plate and the darkroom into the full light of day, dictates that the truth of the photograph is bifurcated: the original negative print, in which black appears as white, and white black, is in fact rephotographed so that it may become the final positive image representing the world as it appears to the naked eye. Black becomes white, negative becomes positive. In Faulkner's major novel, as Murphet has it, we glimpse "the extraordinary social logic of photography as a process of 'positive' racial figuration via a technique of double negation," which brings to the fore the "dark" negative at the heart of the positive "white" image.[23]

These complex photographic substitutions of white and black are most evident in "Evangeline," the short story that set *Absalom* in motion back in 1931. As Charles Bon goes off to fight for the Confederate Army, Judith Sutpen gives him a photo of herself as a keepsake, one that the reader assumes remains with him during the war. But at the story's end, it has been substituted with the image of another. After the fire that destroys the slaver's mansion, all that remains is the silver locket case, inside of which is not Judith's image but a portrait of a "smooth, oval, unblemished face, the mouth rich, full, a little loose, the hot, slumberous, secretive eyes, the inklike hair with its faint but unmistakable wiriness—all the ineradicable and tragic stamp of negro blood" (*US*, 608). It is Charles Bon's wife, who is unnamed in "Evangeline" but reappears in "Revolt" with a name at the scene of her husband's death.

> THE BEDROOM
> They lay the body on the bed, and while they are doing so the daguerreotype case falls from his pocket onto the bed. The negroes turn and exit, leaving Judith and Clytie alone. Slowly Judith kneels, and as she is looking at Charles, Clytie sees the fallen case and hands it to Judith. She takes it, and believing it is her picture, holds it tenderly between her hands for a moment. The bullet hole has pierced the case, and she feels it is symbolic. After a moment she opens it. There is the picture of the octoroon woman holding the child. Below is the inscription to Charles, "A mon mari toujours. Toinette." (17–18)

In this scene, the screenplay literalizes Faulkner's photographic metaphor from *Absalom* and the ekphrastic description of the image in "Evangeline," making an image of that which was once only described in words, making clear the connections between black and white, negative and positive, which would now manifest in real, existing images.

The desire to express this part of the Sutpen story, however, would have undoubtedly posed problems for Faulkner and Murphy. The potential miscegenation in the marriage between Charles and Toinette was a taboo that the studio system simply could not brook (indeed, the subject seems to have prevented Faulkner from selling the film to Warner Brothers). But London—where Associated Artists was located—was not Los Angeles, and so the screenplay as written was not yet subject to the Hays Code. Although it would have to pass the censor's eye before it could be screened in the United States, perhaps "Revolt" was here beginning to imagine itself as a narrative that was freed from that nation altogether? Indeed, the very setting of "Revolt"—from the Deep South to London, and back again—tantalizingly allegorizes the circumstances of Associated Artists as a production company. Just like Miriam in "Revolt," who moved to London with her husband to distance herself from the curse that haunted her family, Associated Artists relocated to the city to escape the trappings of the US film industry and to rescue its stars from the studios to which they were in thrall. But life imitated art a little too well in this case: safe in England, Judith writes home to Clytie of the family's happiness only to find out that Miriam and Eric have ventured back to the Mississippi bayou in search of Wash's voodoo ceremony. At this news, Judith takes a fall down the stairs of her home and dies, satisfying the curse. For Associated Artists, the attempts to relocate overseas would also prove fatal. The company's efforts to free star Leslie Howard from his Warner Brothers contract were in vain, and essentially ended up bankrupting them.[24]

Murphy had more luck overseas earlier in his career and had worked well in collaborative situations. Aside from *The Emperor Jones*, today he probably remains most famous for his work on *Ballet mécanique* (completed with the help of Fernand Léger, Man Ray, Ezra Pound, and George Antheil), a 1924 experimental film that demonstrated the true potential of a filmmaking collective. And it was precisely this type of collective creative energy that led to the establishment of Associated Artists and to the very possibility of "Revolt in the Earth." As a work written for an independent production company by two modernists working in their respective fields, "Revolt" doesn't conform to the orthodox patterns of narrative screenwriting, which often pretend to a certain artistic collectivism but in actuality bow to the demands of the studio or the industry at large. Like Thomas Sutpen, each of the major studios in classical-era Hollywood had their own unique "design" for industry dominance, one that was not premised on the talents of individual directors, screenwriters, or actors but more on the power of the studio system itself. Under this system, directors, screenwriters, and actors were forced to minimize their eccentricities so as to keep in lockstep with their competitors. Corporate entities subsumed the individual within a vast network of laborers, valuing idiosyncratic contributions only insofar as they might leverage the production model already set in place. For an independent like Associated Artists, however, the filmmaking process was entirely different. For instance, had it been produced, Associated's *Bonnie Prince Charlie* would have seen the star (Leslie Howard), the writer (Hugh Walpole), and the director (Dudley Murphy) all properly collaborating and sharing the profits "in a co-operative basis."[25]

"Revolt" also exemplifies this different style of collectivist creation, and its peculiar process of composition offers a suggestive means for thinking through the Sutpen narrative, which on the one hand concerns a monomaniacal quest for wealth and status and on the other a more cooperative production of history among a group of narrators. As Joseph Urgo has provocatively argued, "*Absalom, Absalom!* marks a break in Faulkner's narrative strategies," a break through which he fully embraces history as the product of dialogic composition.[26] In the novel, Quentin and Shreve together fashion a convincing account of Sutpen's design in their cold Harvard dormitory in 1910. For Urgo, the process by which the two young men achieve this is akin to the process of cinematic production. Just as the raw materials of a screenplay pass from hand to hand in a film studio and are gradually refined by a series of different studio employees until they are fit for the screen, so too is the chronicle in *Absalom* jointly authored, and it is difficult to precisely quantify the submissions of each of its contributors. As Urgo has it, the "question of who did what, who wrote this or that line or who is responsible for this or that scene, is often impossible to pinpoint in film study. In the same way that a machine, or a factory, objectifies human thought in its operations, filmmaking can be said to objectify the human creative process in its operations."[27] The second of these two claims speaks to the distinction between the Quentin/Shreve conversations and the genius workings of the Hollywood studio system: for while their conversations are certainly beset by tension, repression, and prejudice, they do not reflect the objectification of the storytelling process in the way that the operations of a corporate studio might.

It was not just the studio that asked a writer to forget his voice. For screenwriting in and of itself requires a certain amount of forgetfulness, or at least a conscious leaving behind of one's stylistic signature, if a work—a novel, a play, a short story—is to graduate to the screen. The forcible shedding of *Absalom*'s novelistic discourse in the screenplay it generated has led Estelle Schoenberg to wonder why "promiscuous miscegenation, voodoo, cruelty, and curses fulfilled are acceptable and moving in one context but cheap and silly in another."[28] Indeed, "Revolt" reads as a hysterical reworking of just those themes, laying bare the baser ingredients that made up the narrative of what Faulkner himself modestly claimed was the "best novel yet written by an American."[29] But the apparent betrayal of that work carried out by the screenplay's excesses, as we have seen, appears to return the story to the short tale where it all began and to reincorporate that material into the Sutpen continuum.

In recalling "Evangeline," the screenplay also figuratively reinstates the original source of the narrative—not the white Rosa Coldfield, but two black women: Raby (an early model for Clytie in *Absalom, Absalom!*) and her unnamed daughter. Although "Evangeline" is related by Don (a character Faulkner had used elsewhere in his short fiction) and his friend, "a man who writes for the newspapers and such" (*US*, 595), all of the information is gleaned from the mother and daughter, who still live in the Sutpen house. Raby reveals some of her secrets to the narrator, but she also withholds certain crucial pieces of information that would reveal the secret behind Charles Bon's marriage in New Orleans and why it angered Henry to the point of turning him into a murderer: "It seemed that there was something about the New Orleans business that, to Henry anyway, was more disgraceful than the question of divorce could have been. But what it was, she wouldn't tell me. 'You dont need to know that,' she said. 'It dont make no difference now. Judith is dead and Charles Bon is dead and I reckon she's done dead down yonder in New Orleans too, for all them lace dresses and them curly fans and niggers to wait on her, but I reckon things is different down there. I reckon Henry done told Charles Bon that at the time. And now Henry wont be living fore long, and so it dont matter'" (*US*, 599–600).

"Evangeline" reveals very little about the Sutpen story in its few pages, at least in part because Raby and her daughter do not need to satisfy the narrator's desire for historical scandal: "You done heard now. You go away from here. You let Henry Sutpen die quiet. That's all you can do for him" (*US*, 605). Ultimately, the story is a frustrating one in what it does not tell its readers, but importantly, its silence on certain matters is presided over by those who have suffered the most from the legacy of Thomas Sutpen and at least affords the descendants of slaves the right to suppress the horrors of the past.

The spirit of "Evangeline" also makes its way into Faulkner and Murphy's screenplay. Indeed, in keeping with a formal strategy in evidence elsewhere throughout the screenplay, as Eiko Owada has pointed out, "Revolt" attempts to reverse the power relations in *Absalom* between black and white characters. This is not to say that the positions of master and slave are somehow switched but rather to suggest that the screenplay permits a properly collaborative version of historical storytelling by ending with the recollections of its African American participants. Faulkner's novel begins chronologically with the rise of the white plantation owner and ends with two young white men narrating his story. By way of contrast, "Revolt" allows that "the history of the white rulers remains only in the talkings of the black descendants" and does so particularly by means of forgetting that history:[30]

THE RUINED AND JUNGLE-CHOKED STATUE   DAYLIGHT
Clytie stands before it, still brooding. From the background come the voices of invisible negroes, laughing, mellow, not particularly mirthful, laughing and talking.

FIRST NEGRO
Who say so?

SECOND NEGRO
Don't ask me. Old folks, long time ago.

FIRST NEGRO
Wat dey say?

THIRD NEGRO
Ain't you know dat? I thought everybody know dat old sayin'.
Laughter.

FIRST NEGRO
Reckon I done fergot. What was it?

SECOND NEGRO
Come to think, I don fergot, too. What was it, Mymie?

THIRD NEGRO
(chanting in singsong)
When de debbil spawns on Sutpen lan', dye'll be a revolt in earth twell Sutpen lan' done swallered Sutpen birth. Dat uz it.
Laughter.

SECOND NEGRO
It do sound funny. Whut you reckon it mean?

THIRD NEGRO
I don't know dat. I do well to 'member how to say it.

SECOND NEGRO
Ain't dat a fack?
Laughter in chorus, not mirthful particularly, but mellow in pitch as blended ells, which dies slowly in dissolve in which, just before the scene vanishes, a snake writhes down from the statue and away into the jungle.

FADE OUT. (61–62)

While readers will note here the crudeness of the racist dialect, and the insulting reduction of black characters to their laughter, there is something to be gleaned from the scene. In *Absalom, Absalom!* Faulkner strategically elides the barbaric history of the slave trade and the triangular connections between Africa, the Caribbean, and the South. The real horrors of that institution are almost relegated to the dustbin of history and are glimpsed only in brief and shadowy insinuations or in those infamously defensive protestations of Quentin Compson, one of which closes the novel: "*I dont hate it* he thought, panting in the cold air, the iron New England dark: *I dont. I dont! I dont hate it! I dont hate it!*" (N, 3:311).

Slavery in *Absalom, Absalom!* is almost erased from history, omitted from the words of an anxious narrator. But historical revision is positively valorized in "Revolt in the Earth," where what is forgotten is not the terrible plight of the slaves but rather the lives of their masters. The end of the screenplay leaves us with three black Americans discussing the cursed history of the Sutpen family, a saga that has only recently transpired but now is barely remembered. Although the "singsong" riddle remains, its meaning is lost, demonstrating the curse's promise: not only will Sutpen land swallow Sutpen birth, but the patronym—which subsists on the blood and sweat of slaves and extends the privilege of slaveholding to its descendants long after abolition—will be buried along with it. For all its faults (and its racism), "Revolt in the Earth" ends with the descendants of slaves having outlived the descendants of their masters. In the final scene, African American characters control the narrative, partaking in a vision of selective amnesia in which the white slaveholder is eradicated from his own story.

"A Very Badly Conceived Story"

"Revolt" was written at a point in Faulkner's career when his critical success was far from secured, and it was not written for a major studio precisely because a major studio had refused to gamble on its success. Faulkner's initial failure to sell *Absalom* to Twentieth Century–Fox was in part due to his inability to market the script except as a project "about miscegenation," and Associated Artists would fold before it could be filmed under its name.[31] But Faulkner refused to give up and later attempted to sell the screenplay to Warner Brothers. The assumption that "Revolt" was composed toward the end of 1942 is based on a telegram from Robert Buckner to Faulkner dated January 6, 1943. Buckner was a producer at Warner Brothers, most notably attached to *Mission to Moscow* (Michael Curtiz, 1943), and at this point was overseeing Faulkner's work on a screenplay entitled "The De Gaulle Story" (which I discuss in chapter 4). Buckner had already expressed his concerns about the De Gaulle project, asking Faulkner for several rewrites and later remarking that the author's "natural circumlocuitous [sic] style and endless sentences were diametrically opposed to the stringent, telegraphic needs of pictures."[32] "The De Gaulle Story" had been commissioned by the studio, but even with the assistance of various interlocutors, it was finally abandoned.

"Revolt" presented an even more troublesome property to readers at the studio, where it had been circulating. The telegram from Buckner explained the problem, as Blotner paraphrases it: "He couldn't imagine his friend having had any share in it; it was a badly conceived screen story with no possibilities whatever and he hoped Faulkner would not let it circulate with his name on it."[33] In no uncertain terms, Buckner urged that Faulkner submerge his script, and no word of "Revolt" would be heard again until both Kawin and Schoenberg made mention of it in 1977. At Warner Brothers, as I discuss in chapters 4 and 5, the executive had a fairly formulaic notion of cinematic production, which required supervision at various stages of the process. The composition of the screenplay was under a great deal of scrutiny, since the various written documents that guided a film project were scoured by the Hays office for any questionable content and, starting in 1942, also by the Office of War Information, which ensured that each property would conform to the standards of U.S. diplomacy. An independent work like "Revolt" had done without such examinations, ignoring the roles of censor and studio head alike in recommending itself for production. It reads as an act of gross overreaching, insisting on the realization of its wild and noisy narrative, and stood no chance of making it very far at Warner Brothers.

CHAPTER 4

Winning the War with Warners

The following two chapters, which take up Faulkner's time at Warner Brothers from 1942 to 1945, as well as his literary fiction beyond those years, consider the ways in which the South in Faulkner's work (and thus Faulkner's work altogether) morphed during the periods he lived and worked outside of it. For the first half of this decade marked the longest cumulative period in which Faulkner was away from his hometown, often for months at a stretch, and after he published *Intruder in the Dust* in 1948 (his first novel in six years), he seemed to have come back a different writer. But the prolonged stay in Los Angeles was not the only reason that his Yoknapatawpha would be changed forever more. There were historical and economic forces beyond the author's control that were changing the face of the region and the nation, and it is these—war and migration—that are the subjects of the next two chapters of this book.

Two nationwide events—the one (war) also contributing to the other (the Great Migration)—combined to transform the South from a region sustained by large-scale agricultural production, sharecropping, and a predominantly black workforce into a collection of states increasingly affected by federal legislation and divested of its many workers by the lure of metropolitan wage labor. These events were not only instrumental in the overhaul of Faulkner's South, both real and imagined, but were also connected (albeit unevenly) to two major tendencies in the American film industry in the 1940s. The war made itself felt in a fairly obvious way in Hollywood, the subject dominating filmmaking across all major studios even before the United States entered combat late in 1941. But the Great Migration of African Americans to cities outside of the South was cashed out in a less direct way on film, and in chapter 6, I show just how this historical event lined up with the preferences of the studio system at midcentury. While this correlation can in part be discovered in the idyllic landscapes of a number of wistful southern drama pictures, it also manifests itself less obviously in film noir. The connection between war pictures and films noir for Faulkner stems from the mass influx of industrial workers to Los Angeles in the early 1940s, many of them black.

Faulkner's contributions to Hollywood while under contract at Warner Brothers can be categorized along these generic lines, too, as his writing was being pulled in two different directions during wartime, both of which contributed to the makeover of his southern postage stamp. Dana Polan, in his *Power and Paranoia*, helps to make these two directions clear. On the one hand, Polan argues, the war films of the period are defined by their shared desire for national unity, reflecting the power of the country as its citizens stand together in the face of adversity. On the other, the absolute conviction of national consensus and social stability was belied by the anxieties of film noir in the postwar period, in which the prevailing structure of feeling was paranoia.[1]

In part, this division is likewise apparent in the competing aesthetic tendencies at Warner Brothers during the decade between the (mostly) collectivized anonymity of the war pictures and the focus on the individual of the noir and women's films. During the war, Warner Brothers' films stressed the need for reconciliation—of labor and capital, black and white, men and women—national support of the military, and individual self-sacrifice at home and abroad. This changed after the war, however, with the release of a number of films that were not geared toward the war effort and instead interrogated life in the postwar United States.

The before and after distinctions I'm suggesting here weren't always so clear-cut, especially since there were many patterns that Warner Brothers was eager to exploit during the decade. For example, *The Maltese Falcon* (John Huston, 1941), the film that virtually inaugurated the noir cycle, preceded some of the most famous war films from the studio. And Faulkner worked on two films from each of these genres—*To Have and Have Not* (a geopolitical romance) and *The Big Sleep* (a detective story)—that had identical leads: Humphrey Bogart and Lauren Bacall. As much as the first stresses collaboration against a common enemy and the second makes it difficult to identify a single nemesis, they both end with the same leading lady and man in one another's arms. The first is shot through with a variety of noir inflections—its femmes fatales, its lighting, the mercenary tendencies of its hero—and the latter features a former soldier as a detective and makes references to the war throughout. Furthermore, the output at Warner Brothers was by no means limited to the war and noir genres, and indeed, as I show in the following chapter, a few Faulkner-friendly "southerns" also featured in its catalogue.

In any case, dividing the Hollywood cycles of war and noir pictures also offers parallels with Faulkner's own fiction of the 1940s. While he wouldn't complete a novel during his spell at Warner Brothers, he was writing stories about the war before he left Mississippi and finalized work on stories and a novel about crime in the South upon his return. At least some of this output was influenced by his writing at Warner Brothers in the early years of the decade: both the unifying tendency of the war film, on the one hand, and the disrupting aspects of noir, on the other, equally worked to alter Faulkner's representation of a region that had seemed at least a little surer of itself before the United States had joined the global battle. And at the same time, Faulkner's fiction was making its presence felt in several of the screenplays he wrote for the studio.

Short Stories and *Sergeant York*

The early 1940s represented something of a high-water mark for Faulkner's short stories. He managed to write or revise seven in the decade's first few years but wouldn't complete another until after the war. Many of the stories have a similar tenor, taking up the intrusion of the federal government into the lives of isolated southerners via the Works Progress Administration in "Shingles for the Lord" and the nationwide conscription drive in "The Tall Men." "The Tall Men" explores the South on the brink of the Second World War by focusing on the McCallum family, whose two youngest boys fail to register for the army draft. Although, as their father points out, the United States was "not at war" yet (*CS*, 50), there was no excuse for not registering—the South was well and truly part of the nation, and its youth would need to ready themselves once more for battle. Buddy had fought in France in the Great War and remembers that the government "done right by me in my day, and it will do right by you" (*CS*, 53).

After the attack on Pearl Harbor, Faulkner wrote "Two Soldiers," which sees the young Pete Grier enlisting to fight for the "Unity States" (*CS*, 83), while his younger brother, narrating the tale, is left behind. In "Shall Not Perish," the less successful sequel to that story, we read of Pete's death in combat, his brother's indignation at the loss, and the effects of a major world-historical event on an isolated southern family: "One day there was Pearl Harbor. And the next week Pete went to Memphis, to join the army and go there and help them; and one morning Mother stood at the field fence with a little scrap of paper not even big enough to start a fire with, that didn't even need a stamp on the envelope, saying, *A ship was. Now it is not. Your son was one of them*" (*CS*, 101–102). I examine the Grier stories in relation to television in chapter 7, but here it is worth considering the way Faulkner imagines the impact of the Second World War on Yoknapatawpha County. In each of the stories, there is at once a certain antipathy toward the military's and the government's treatment of the South and an acceptance of the changing circumstances of war, accompanied by a recognition of the need to fight for one's country. Although descendants of the defeated Confederate soldiers still harbor some resentment toward the North, the unity of the "Unity States," now in its second major global war, ultimately overwhelms regional fidelity.

In March 1942 Faulkner wrote another story in *The Unvanquished* vein that suggests parallels between different conflicts (Civil War, Great War, Second World War). "My Grandmother Millard and General Bedford Forrest and the Battle of Harrykin Creek" sees Bayard and Ringo back in action, in a humorous story that not only reflects on nostalgia for the antebellum days but also on the nation's current struggle: "I think it's a good funny story," Faulkner wrote his agent, Harold Ober, "and I think it has its message for the day too: of gallant indomitability, of a willingness to pull up the pants and carry on, no matter with whom, let alone what" (*SL*, 150). In *Flags in the Dust* and again at MGM with "War Birds," Faulkner had connected the Sartoris family's role in the Civil War to its role in the Great War sixty years later. Now, with the Grier stories and the modern resonances of "My Grandmother Millard," he had added the Second World War to the mix, with the history of the South in combat overdetermined all the more.

But Faulkner's approach in his short stories to this latest battle—pitting the imagined isolation of his war-weary South against the new interventionist attitude of the United States it had resisted the century before—was also the technique of an immensely popular Warner Brothers film, Howard Hawks's critically acclaimed *Sergeant York* (1941). Faulkner was clearly very familiar with this film, and it is likely that he saw it the year before he took up his post at the studio. Its story of a pacifist rural man (played by Gary Cooper) who ultimately sets aside his religious convictions in order to kill for his country chimes neatly with the short war narratives that Faulkner had written in order to shield himself from the studio. More like the naïve McCallum boys than the eagerly belligerent Pete Grier, Alvin York also bends to the will of the state and reluctantly leaves his Tennessee home behind him so as to merge his southern identity with that of the more expansive United States.

York later became the model for at least two of Faulkner's screen characters. The first was Colonel Robert Scott in *God Is My Co-Pilot* (Robert Florey, 1945), an aerial combat film based on Scott's autobiography. For this film, Faulkner envisioned Scott, who saw action in Burma with the famous Flying Tigers, in a way similar to the Hawksian war hero, insofar as he is a religious man who is assisted by a ghost in the machine. More than just a simple battle story, *God Is My Co-Pilot* would attain almost mystical proportions: "It could be the story of the regeneration of a man's soul. It could be an air-borne Sergeant York. York's problem was the reconciliation of his conscience with what his body was being compelled to do: i.e., defend his country. Scott's problem might be the same problem."[2] Here, York's piety helped Faulkner to reorient the story to which he was assigned. As he revised a script by Steve Fisher, Faulkner realized that the narrative would either have to follow the detailed aerial combat scenes already written or attend to the title of the work and revolve around that. He opted for the latter.[3]

The second character York provided a model for was Fonda in "Battle Cry." In the earlier expanded story treatment for this unproduced epic, Faulkner leans on York when describing Fonda adjusting the saddle on his horse: "He is careful, deliberate. They wait for him, courteously, while he stretches each leather against his arm, putting his finger tips against the slip-hook and measuring the leather against his arm (with that deliberation of Cooper taking the glare off his front sight with his wet thumb in Sergeant York), then slipping the strap through the buckle and measuring again until he gets each one just right" (*F*, 4:88).[4] Thinking back to Hawks's film, Faulkner was modeling his protagonist not only on Henry Fonda but also Gary Cooper, even though, as Thomas Schatz has written, Cooper's "deliberate, soft-spoken, and heroic demeanor was at odds with the Warners type."[5] Back at Fox, Darryl Zanuck had objected to a similar portrayal of southerners as isolated from the rest of the nation and as stereotypically ignorant of the modern world, in *Banjo on My Knee*—"the stuff about not knowing that a war existed was too far-fetched" (*WFATCF*, 200n13)—but it certainly served its purpose at Warner Brothers.

But aside from his value as a fictional character, York also works as something of an exemplar for Faulkner at Warner Brothers. Both southerners faced the same problem—the reconciliation of conscience with what the body was being compelled to do. Unlike York, Faulkner had always wanted to participate in a war effort. Now that that wish was being fulfilled, however, he too had to undertake tasks on behalf of his country for which he had no inclination. Faulkner was not against killing the enemy, but he did have an aversion to the only alternative available to him at the time: screenwriting. Nevertheless, he took significant steps to join the pool of screenwriters working in Hollywood. As early as May 1941, he asked an agent, William Herndon, to market scripts he had completed even before he signed a contract with Warner Brothers. But when Faulkner tried to rid himself of Herndon, their relationship soured, and the agent tried to sue. Faulkner's own wrangling behind the scenes resulted in a potential seven-year contract with Warner Brothers, the terms of which gave it the power to decide how long it would retain the Mississippian.

At the same time as he was negotiating with Herndon, Faulkner had tried to make his way back into the military. He had organized the county Aircraft Warning Service for six months, but he also wanted to teach navigation as a civilian in the navy and seemed destined for a commission as a lieutenant in 1942 (*SL*, 141, 143, 148–50). He was still holding out hope for an air force job a month before he reported for duty at Warner Brothers, and owing to money troubles, he also missed out on the navy job, and so studio work then became the only option (*SL*, 152–53). After being knocked back from both the navy and air force, Faulkner was resigned to carrying out the only service he could in aid of the war effort: writing screenplays that would inspire a unity of purpose in the nation's filmgoers. And the studio he was about to begin working for was taking its patriotic duties very seriously indeed: by the time Faulkner arrived, Jack Warner had signed up for the Army Air Corps and insisted on being called "Colonel Warner" even in interoffice memos. But just before he left for Los Angeles in late July, Faulkner sent in one last story to his publisher, a piece that resonated with the recent entrance of the United States into the war and that chimed neatly with Warner Brothers' own approach to the rise of Nazism.

"Snow" and the Warner Brothers War

Faulkner probably began his short story "Snow" in 1931, since it features the same characters—Don and an unnamed narrator—as two other stories written that year, "Evangeline" and "Mistral." He revisited it in 1942, however, simplifying the apparently obscure plot in an effort to make it fit for publication and adding a frame tale that incorporated the more recent threat of Nazism (*SL*, 149). Rejected by the *American Mercury* on the grounds that it was Faulkner as his "elliptical worst," he "tried to fill the gaps" and "make it explicit as well" (*SL*, 161).[6] But it was to no avail. He was busy in Hollywood a week after he had last sent the story to his publisher, and it would remain in obscurity during his lifetime.

"Snow" begins in a contemporary setting, as a child puts a question to its father just after the Pearl Harbor attack: "What was Europe like before all the people in it began to hate and fear Germans?" (*US*, 665). The man, who is just about to enlist as a "subaltern of engineers," does not answer immediately, since he is busy reading a report titled "*Nazi Governor of Czdonia Slain by Companion*" (*US*, 665). The story is accompanied by two telephoto pictures, of a "handsome Prussian face which he had never seen and would not see now and did not want to, and the woman's face which he had seen once and did not want ever to see again either" (*US*, 665). A fifteen-year flashback takes us to a Swiss alpine village, where the man (now our first-person narrator) and his companion, Don, observe a funeral procession from a mountain parapet. The two Americans initially watch proceedings unfold while debating whether the deceased, a professional climbing guide who plunged to his death from a mountaintop, fell or was pushed.

The mystery that irks Don and the narrator is the same one that plagues the narrator's conscience years later. Brix, a seasoned climber, takes a wealthy German client, the Big Shot, on an expedition. The Big Shot falls off a ledge with Brix and his wife in tow; Brix dies, though the wife and the Big Shot do not, and Brix's body is left under a deep cover of snow until it thaws in the spring. The implication is that the German client deliberately sabotaged the climb, so that he could dispose of Brix and leave with his wife. And indeed, the former Mrs. Brix departs with the Big Shot on a train, only returning to the Swiss valley for the funeral of her late husband. In the opening frame story, the newspaper announces that Mrs. Brix has fatally stabbed the Big Shot, a General von Ploeck.[7]

The two Americans view the funeral through a German-manufactured "half-Zeiss" glass, which has only one lens. It was purchased in a Milan pawnshop for a bargain but has since lost some of its functionality: "But in its day it must have been the best glass Zeiss ever made because now, during the time you could bear to look through it at all, without the other eye to brace against you could feel your eyeball being pulled out of your skull like a steel marble to a magnet" (*US*, 666). The flaw of the half-Zeiss forces the pair to "turn the glass over every few seconds and divide the strain" (*US*, 666). This method works for a time, but soon it is of no use: "Then I had the glass and then I could actually feel it: not just the one eyeball drawing out of my skull but dragging the other one behind it, around behind my nose to fill the vacated socket, and I turned the glass and then again" (*US*, 667).

The glass thus does not serve as a transparent medium through which to view distant events but is instead a distorting lens that forces the viewer to consider both near and far simultaneously. It crystallizes the multiple historical condensations in the story, connecting its original manufacture to its declining use value, in the same way that Mrs. Brix's "peasant's face" has been irrevocably marked by "the four or five years' triumphal pageantry of power and destruction and human suffering and blood" (*US*, 665). The question governing the framing reminiscence—"What was Europe like?"—itself becomes impossible to answer except through the "lens" of the fifteen years between the two events.

The implication is that in the gap between 1926 when Brix's funeral takes place and December 1941 when Brix's former wife stabs the general, the rise of Hitler—the figure Faulkner referred to in *Go Down, Moses* as the "Austrian paper-hanger" (*N*, 4:249–50)—had altered the world order forever, making it impossible to recall one older state of foreign affairs without recourse to another, newer set of circumstances. Caught in this historical bind and no longer able to isolate one series of events within his divided field of vision, the father answers his child: "It was just the same. . . . The people in Europe have hated and feared Germans for so long that nobody remembers how it was" (*US*, 677). In "Snow," the narrator effectively confers on himself the benefit of hindsight, his suspicion that Brix's fall from the mountain was not accidental. The shadiness of the German governor is compounded by his connection with National Socialism, which validates the otherwise xenophobic comment made by a waiter in the Swiss town: "We dont like Germans in this country" (*US*, 675).

As we have seen in Faulkner's other stories of the Second World War, and in his prose and screenwriting about the Sartoris boys, he had a tendency to draw parallels between vastly different social and historical epochs through the extreme events of warfare. In the case of "Snow," as elsewhere in his oeuvre, Faulkner had drawn such parallels via a retroactive premonition of Nazism. In 1945, he wrote Malcolm Cowley about his character Percy Grimm in *Light in August*, belatedly branding him as a "Fascist galahad who saved the white race by murdering [Joe] Christmas. I invented him in 1931. I didn't realise until after Hitler got into the newspapers that I had created a Nazi before he did" (SL, 202). He would say the same in 1962 at the University of Virginia, now referring to Grimm as a "Nazi Storm Trooper" (FU, 41).[8] Here, Faulkner implicates the racist South in the rise of German fascism, seeing in hindsight that the recent emergence of hateful ideology in Europe was already present in one of his own characters; the United States would need to take heed of what was now happening across the Atlantic, as those seeds had already been sown on its own shores.

But the attempt to market "Snow" to a readership now apprised of the threat of Nazism was calculated and was executed with an eye, perhaps, to the strategies of Warner Brothers in the early 1940s. Both the story and the studio had suggested the existence of a Nazi threat years before it had been nationally agreed on, the one trying to broadcast what was already taking place in Germany in the 1930s, the other looking back in an attempt to imply its own premonition of the events to come. As early as 1934, Warner Brothers had expressed a clear concern over the rise of the National Socialist Party by pulling its employees out of Germany, the first studio to take such action. Even if, as Klaus Mann expressed it in 1941, the "American films against Hitlerism come too late," Warner Brothers was ahead of the other major studios when it came to combating the Nazi threat.[9] Its *Confessions of a Nazi Spy* (Anatole Litvak, 1939) was released not only before the United States had officially declared war on the Axis nations but even before Hitler's decisive invasion of Poland. The film showed how Nazism functioned on the ground and depicted its foot soldiers as already infiltrating the United States. Although bold in its confrontation with the enemy, the prevailing national mood wasn't yet right for this kind of interventionist encouragement, and the film failed at the box office.[10]

Moviegoers weren't alone in their disenchantment with Warner Brothers' efforts. Senator Gerald Nye accused Hollywood of producing propaganda that would push the United States into battle, a claim that led to the establishment of a U.S. Senate subcommittee to investigate the film industry's apparent jingoism. President Harry Warner was especially singled out for his anti-Nazi sentiments and when he appeared before the so-called Nye-Clark Committee in 1941, he asserted that his studio was only producing pictures that reflected on current affairs and that a film like that year's *Sergeant York* was "a factual portrait of one of the great heroes of the last war. If that is propaganda, we plead guilty."[11] Warner refuted Nye's conspiracist suggestions that he had a direct and personal line to Franklin Roosevelt and pointed to the fact that a wide variety of cultural organs—fiction, radio, print media—were at the time expressing their own objections to National Socialism. But then, after Pearl Harbor's day of infamy, the conditions became immediately more suitable to the production of war films, and Warner Brothers was at the cutting edge of the trend. Now the studio could truly become, in the words of Jack Warner, "a sort of war industry."[12]

There was still some difficulty, however, in producing pictures that would satisfy the political class. The now favorable attitude toward intervention necessitated the establishment of the Office of War Information (OWI) in June 1942, which liaised between government and the studios and regulated the content of all war-related films, propaganda and otherwise. The studios were thus now more tightly censored than ever before in U.S. film history, as both morality and politics were now in the firing line. However, the OWI, seeking to quell anxieties on the home front, also encouraged the studios to improve their representations of women, African Americans, and labor unions during these years (although the results are ambiguous).[13] The OWI was disbanded after the war, and although the changes it wrought in Hollywood were mostly temporary in effect, a number of lasting shifts in the early 1940s were taking place across the entire industry.

At the beginning of the decade, all of the Big Five had moved from systems with a central producer to the decentralized unit production model, which meant that figures like Thalberg and Zanuck were no longer responsible for all the films that passed through the studios. Hal Wallis, in charge of Warner Brothers' A-class productions, increasingly delegated his work to other individuals, and so Faulkner ended up working for several different producers during his time at the studio. Ultimately, he was just as likely to write for Howard Hawks, contracted at the studio as a powerful "hyphenate" (producer-director), as he was for newcomer Jerry Wald, who would later go on to produce two adaptations of Faulkner's work at Fox: *The Long, Hot Summer* (Martin Ritt, 1958) and *The Sound and the Fury* (Ritt, 1959).[14] But this did not mean an end to the story conferences he had attended at Fox, and Faulkner was still required to regularly discuss his work in progress with Hawks and others. Different producers also took different approaches. Wald, for example, as Tom Stempel points out, was known for using a variety of screenwriters (concurrent and serially).[15]

The films themselves changed, too. While Warner Brothers had cultivated a house style in the 1930s that relied on star-genre formulas—James Cagney and crime, Paul Muni and the biopic, Bette Davis and melodrama—it was also prepared to change tack, resorting to "off-casting," deals with independent producers, and expensive story purchases, in order to remain competitive.[16] *Sergeant York*, for example, was produced by the outsider Jesse Lasky and starred another interloper in the lot, Gary Cooper. During the war, the studio greatly reduced its overall output, setting aside B-movies in favor of prestige films so as to capitalize on a more prosperous market. Under these conditions, Faulkner was assigned to properties like "The De Gaulle Story" and "Battle Cry," which, while aborted, would have been major big-budget productions for the studio.

"The De Gaulle Story" and *Air Force*

Faulkner's first assignment was representative of the general trends at the studio. The project was to be a biopic of the future French president and was imagined alongside a similar film about Winston Churchill (who would become a character in his own right in the screenplay about Charles De Gaulle's life).[17] Faulkner composed many hundreds of pages relating to the property: a nine-page story outline titled "Journey Toward Dawn," treatments of varying lengths titled "Free France," and a revised story treatment, a full-length screenplay, and a revision of that screenplay all under the name "The De Gaulle Story." He first wrote this property in treatment form (three times), as he had done when he worked at MGM, before being authorized to turn it into a dialogue continuity. Unlike Faulkner's first Hollywood screenplay, however, this one was greenlit not by its producer but by two of De Gaulle's representatives in the United States, as well as a member of the Department of State.

Faulkner was initially working from Philippe Barré's *Charles De Gaulle* (1941), but the scripts he turned in moved progressively away from De Gaulle himself and toward the people of France.[18] Even in his first contribution, Faulkner was clearly foregrounding the heroic everyman in his contrast of the narrative's major protagonists: "Georges represents the French individual as De Gaulle represents the abstract idea of Free France" (*F*, 3:7). Warner Brothers had produced a few well-renowned French historical pictures—*The Story of Louis Pasteur* (William Dieterle, 1936) and *The Life of Emile Zola* (Dieterle, 1937), to name the most famous—but "The De Gaulle Story" had as its focus a figure who was still very much alive and whose war was still ongoing. For this reason, Faulkner's representation of the individual at the heart of the screenplay mutated as he wrote and revised his work, becoming something quite different from the figure with which he had begun. As he would later note, the historical figure "becomes colorful and of dramatic value only after he has been dead for years, because only then can a dramatist make him dramatic without challenge from the people who knew him in the flesh and who insist on fact" (*F*, 3:398).

Beginning with the general's time as a tank commander and his rise to power while exiled in England, Faulkner then shifts the focus to Jean and Georges, brothers from Brittany who end up on opposite sides (Vichy and Free France) during the war. In "Free France," we thus see a slightly diminished De Gaulle—not so much the authoritarian leader as a kind of shoulder angel who asks the pro-Vichy Jean to choose what is right: "It must come from inside you or you are no good to us. A man who can be sold by one demagogue can be unsold by the next one who meets him" (*F*, 3:68). A sardonic "5 line description of work in progress" that Faulkner wrote the head of the Warner Brothers story department, James Geller, emphasized the fact that although the film was about World War II France, its characters were interchangeable figures, ciphers for much larger concerns:

GIRL & 2 BOYS MEET FREE FRANCE
FINAL SCORE:
GIRL 1 BOY UP & 1 TO CARRY
1 BOY DOWN 2
1 BOY OUT
DE GAULLE 3 UP (*SL*, 163)[19]

From this memo, written in mid-September 1942, it seems that Faulkner had a basic vision for the screenplay. However, at this point he was temporarily shifted to another project, *Air Force* (Hawks, 1943). The story is centered on a B-17 Flying Fortress, the *Mary-Ann*, which finds itself in the midst of battle when Pearl Harbor is attacked. With its motley crew, headed by pilot Michael Quincannon, the bomber makes its mark in all the most important battles of the Pacific theater, losing its captain and being completely rebuilt along the way. Dudley Nichols, who had won an Academy Award for his screenplay for *The Informer* and had also written the scripts for *Bringing Up Baby* (Hawks, 1938) and *Stagecoach* (John Ford, 1939), had completed writing on *Air Force* by mid-June. But even with that pedigree, Hawks was dissatisfied with two of

FIGURE 4. *Air Force* (Howard Hawks, 1942)

his screenwriter's scenes, and put in a request for Faulkner, who managed to fix them up: "See Air Force," he later wrote in a letter. "I wrote Quincannon's death scene, and the scene where the men in the aeroplane heard Roosevelt's speech after Pearl Harbor" (*SL*, 173).[20]

The latter of the two brings to mind Faulkner's Grier family stories, in which the president's famous "Day of Infamy" speech is also instrumental as a rallying cry. In "Two Soldiers," we read of the brothers "listening to the fellow in the radio talking" (*CS*, 81) about the Japanese attack, and it is not long before the elder of the two decides to enlist. His father intervenes, however, suggesting that "our President in Washington, D.C., is watching the conditions and he will notify us" (*CS*, 85) and reminding his son of his own experience of being drafted in the First World War and the debt that the Grier family has already paid to the nation. But Roosevelt's wireless statement is far more convincing than the father's note of caution, and it sets the young soldier in motion immediately.

In Nichols's scene as written, the voice of Roosevelt travels over the shortwave radio on board the *Mary-Ann* and is followed by the declaration of war by Congress. Then Sergeant White (in much the same way as the Grier father) explains to the second engineer, Williams, the necessity of waiting for an official declaration before going into battle.[21] Faulkner's revision of the scene features a few further responses from the crew. Lieutenant Monk Hauser, who is the son of a famous aviator of the previous war, is of particular interest here:

138. CLOSE ON TOMMY AND TEX
 listening as the clamor of voices comes full volume again and we hear the shouted refrain: "Vote! Vote! Vote!" They are staring at each other, their faces grave and stern.

138a. CLOSE ON HAUSER AND A GUNNER
 beneath top blister, Hauser standing with sextant, taking a sight as the voices come over the radio: "Vote! Vote!" Hauser is motionless, his head turned as he looks down at the gunner, who stands frozen, too, looking up at Hauser.

138b. CLOSE ON QUINCANNON AND WILLIAMS
 in cockpit as the voices come over radio as the vote is taken a state of war officially comes to exist, the voices loud in acclamation. Quincannon and Williams turn their heads and stare at one another as the acclamation rises toward crescendo. Quincannon reaches out and switches the radio off.

> QUINCANNON
> That's it.
>
> WILLIAMS
> Yes. I always like to be notified officially when I am in a war.
>
> QUINCANNON
> I wonder what Monk thinks about it.
> He reaches his hand to radio switch.
>
> WILLIAMS
> (watching him)
> I hope he's thinking about where we are. Why should he think any more about it than we do?
>
> QUINCANNON
> His old man must have heard something like this once. Maybe Monk knows what we ought to be feeling now, even if we don't.[22]

Although not retained in the final screenplay nor in the film as produced, Faulkner's scene as written develops the reaction to Roosevelt's speech in a way that plays on the responses in "Two Soldiers": as the *Mary-Ann* is already in battle, Williams's joke about official notification points to the impossibility of Mr. Grier's suggestion that they wait. The connection between the two

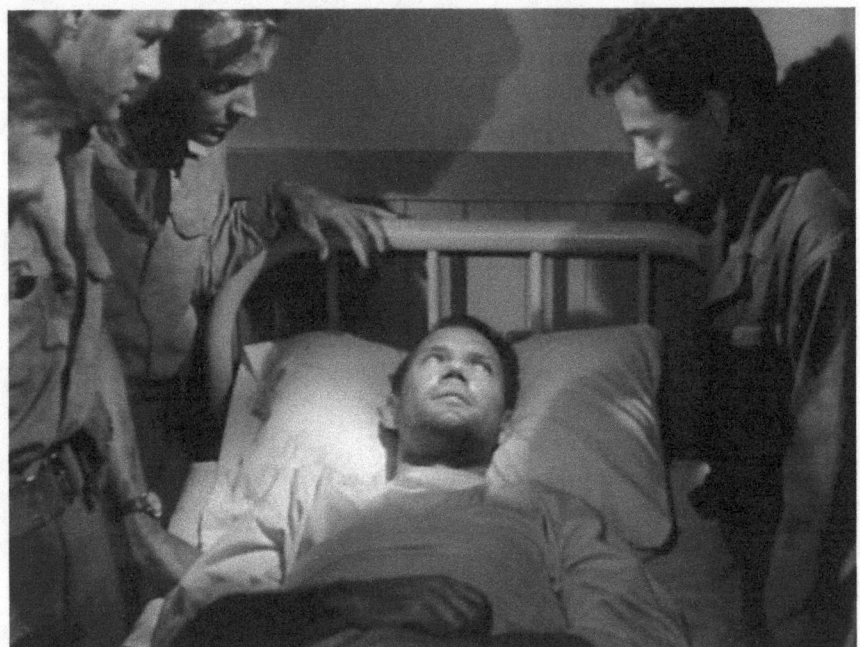

FIGURE 5. *Air Force* (Howard Hawks, 1942)

world wars also carries over from Faulkner's earlier story, and Monk is as keen to emulate his father's exploits in the field of combat as is Mr. Grier's son.

The second scene that Faulkner revised takes place as the *Mary-Ann* flies into battle against an invading enemy fleet. Quincannon is mortally wounded and lies dying in the hospital. Nichols had finished the scene with the captain fading quickly:

QUINCANNON
(feebly—with a kind of panic)
Wait a minute . . . don't go . . . don't go . . . wait for me, fellows. . . .[23]

Bruce Kawin writes of this "original death scene" that it "was sentimental in the extreme; what Faulkner achieved was both moving and professional, emphasizing not the death of one man but the solidarity he inspires in his crew."[24] Indeed, what holds interest in Faulkner's revision is the way in which the men cohere around the inspiring voice of their captain, as Quincannon directs his crew for a last imagined departure:

292f.   CLOSE GROUP SHOT OF THE FACES   QUINCANNON'S ANGLE
As before, in fresh uniforms unscarred yet by war—Rader, Hauser, Williams, McMartin, Weinberg, White. They come into focus for the last time and steady.

QUINCANNON'S VOICE

Stations, Chief.

WHITE

Stations, Skipper.

QUINCANNON'S VOICE

Right. Lock the door. All right, Williams. Get out the bill of fare.
(he begins his responses to the starting of the engines; sound of starting engines begins under scene)
Crew from pilot. Here we go.
Sound of engines revving up as scene begins to darken. The faces fading slowly and continuing to fade toward complete blackness.

QUINCANNON'S VOICE

We're taking off black, but we can see again in a minute.
The faces fade until now only Williams' and White's faces can be seen.[25]

Quincannon continues giving orders from his deathbed, and the crew plays along until he dies, making for a slightly less saccharine ending than the one Nichols had planned.[26]

Of the two scenes that Faulkner wrote for *Air Force*, one centers around a national leader who is only present through his voice, while the other details the unexpected death of a captain. The strength of authority in both lies not in its infallibility but rather in its complete effacement or its physical absence, both of which galvanize the crew to fight for their nation. Indeed, more than Quincannon, it is often the lesser lights of the *Mary-Ann*—mechanic, gunner, navigator—who are integral to its success. The leader was still important, but warfare required a collective effort from the seemingly minor participants, and the captain would not always go down with the ship. Although seemingly insignificant in the scheme of things, the alterations Faulkner made here appear to have had an effect on the other screenplays he wrote at Warner Brothers. After working on *Air Force*, Faulkner returned to "The De Gaulle Story" in November with a renewed sense of how the titular role should shape the narrative, and his new De Gaulle was quite distinct from the one with which he had started the story. As Roosevelt's voice had floated powerfully upon the radio waves, so too would De Gaulle make himself heard in his own call to arms, as he spoke to the French everywhere from his refuge in Britain:

INT. B.B.C. STUDIO   CLOSE SHOT   DE GAULLE AT MICROPHONE

DE GAULLE

All of you whose sons and fathers and husbands and brothers have died, grieve for them but do not despair. All of you whose sons and fathers and brothers and husbands have merely vanished from the places that once knew them—

DISSOLVE TO:

FIVE OR SIX FRENCH PEOPLE

—crouching, tense, listening, watchful. De Gaulle's voice cuts short off. Tramp of army feet increases, the shadow of a patrol, rifles slanted, legs tramping in unison, passes across, disappears, the tramp of feet dies away. The voice comes on again, the people quiet, listening.

VOICE

—do not even grieve. Because they have come to me. They come to me here daily, and our battalions and regiments live again. They are with me today, and they tell you in my voice to believe and hope, for even you who for a little while yet the enemies of France continue to hold, you also are not alone and are not forgotten.

FADE OUT. (*F*, 3:279)

Although De Gaulle was still a formidable presence in the script, he was also beginning to cede some space to the other characters, and his speeches here and elsewhere shift the emphasis from him to his people. In fact, by the time Faulkner had completed his final revised screenplay, the future French president was no longer the lead in the film. Writing to producer Robert Buckner in November, he suggested a radical change to the narrative: "Let's dispense with General De Gaulle as a living character in the story. We will not only be free of the disadvantages and obstructions whose loss will be a gain, we will gain the freedom to make a picture which the American audience whose money will pay for it will understand and believe and not find dull" (*F*, 3:395). In this memo, Faulkner argued that the interests of the Free French script supervisors—to preserve the historical accuracy of De Gaulle as a character and to use the film as a tool to further their cause—were ultimately incompatible with the interests of the studio. "They want to see a piece of Free French propaganda," he wrote, "not a moving picture in which those who see it will recognize their own human passions and griefs and desires." Subtracting De Gaulle from the screenplay would boost ticket sales in the United States and, if it followed the precepts of classical Hollywood filmmaking, would instill in the American audience "a feeling of warmth and affection and pride toward the people like themselves" (F, 3:396).

At this point in his Warner Brothers career, Faulkner had an idea of what the studio required from its product, but he was also invested in the nationalistic stakes of projects like "The De Gaulle Story" and had now come up with a canny strategy for connecting both profits and patriotism. But the problems facing "The De Gaulle Story" later became insurmountable. There were a variety of political and commercial factors working against it, not least of all the studio's prioritization of another Robert Buckner production, *Mission to Moscow* (Michael Curtiz, 1943).[27] Although the studio had committed over $100,000 to the project, it was abandoned, and De Gaulle himself "got a hunk of the money." Although Warner Brothers tried to revive the idea in May 1944—"in time for the invasion"—it never happened.[28] And although it was an interesting script, Buckner did not seem to see the potential in it: "It was a curious ms and perhaps 20 years ahead of its time in technique, more by accident I suspect than prescient genius. . . . [H]e hit on an odd offbeat note, almost 'nouvelle vague' a la Fellini and Bergman. It intrigued me, but worried me, and even baffled Bill in places."[29]

As it happened, Faulkner's most straightforward material contribution to the war effort did not end up taking the form of stories for the screen. As Malcolm Cowley has pointed out, Faulkner's low authorial profile combined with a nationwide resource shortage led to the donation by Random House of the plates of his novels "to be melted down and to make copper jacketings for bullets."[30] On the one hand, his involvement in the production of popular cultural artifacts seemed to him an increasingly meaningless activity. On the other, the destruction of the plates used for reprinting his most prized novels may have achieved just what he wanted from his work—to give material assistance to his nation against its enemies.

Faking the War and "The Life and Death of a Bomber"

Even at its most sincere, Hollywood filmmaking during the war was always a play of smoke and mirrors. No matter the gravity of the production or the persuasiveness of the acting, films concocted in the backlot at Burbank for the purpose of aiding the war effort could of course never be more than approximations of the real thing. Faulkner was clearly aware of the gap between battle and its onscreen representation, as his cruel exclusion from the one (twice over) saw him writing for the other. In "Knight's Gambit," a story that he would revise before and after his Warner Brothers contract, Faulkner writes of the disconnect between the studio and the battlefield.

Set around the time of the Pearl Harbor attack, "Knight's Gambit" is narrated by the young Charles Weddel (later Mallison). It is, in Faulkner's own words, "a love story, in which [Gavin] Stevens prevents a crime (murder) not for justice but to gain (he is now fifty plus) the childhood sweetheart which he lost 20 years ago."[31] Although the evidently noirish plot is mostly centered on his uncle Gavin's detective work and bygone romance, we gain a sense of Charles's own understanding of the world at this crucial stage in his life through his narration. At one point, Charles is ushered out of the house to the picture show, "not knowing what he was going to see and not even caring; it might be another war picture he was walking toward and it didn't even matter, thinking remembering how once a war picture should, ought, to have been the worst thing of all for the heart's thirst to have to endure, except that it was not, since there lay between the war movie and Miss Hogganbeck's world events a thousand times even the insuperable distance which lay between Miss Hogganbeck's world events and the R.O.T.C. pips and the sword: thinking how if the human race could just pass all its time watching moving pictures, there would be no more wars nor any other man-made anguishes" (*KG*, 205–6).

Here, Charles ruminates on the differences between the war picture and his teacher's representation of global conflict and then between his classroom learning and war itself, symbolized for him by the regalia of the ROTC (Reserve Officers' Training Corps). His estimation of the war picture has clearly been altered by the events in the Pacific: before the United States entered the war, Charles was in awe of such films, but now they pale in comparison to the real combat taking place elsewhere. Indeed, now the war picture is not simply a well-meaning representation of battle but its veritable antidote, a form of escapism that would subdue all belligerent feelings in its viewers.

Charles is quite an astute moviegoer, the kind who is willing to suspend his disbelief and submit to the fictional world of the film. But he is also a demanding consumer, one who requires something more from a film now that actual gunfire is being exchanged all across the globe. Combat on film during the Second World War was for the most part simulated and was even difficult to simulate once the West Coast was commandeered for the war. Although Hawks had been able to shoot *Air Force* on location in Florida, as Paul Fussell has noted, many combat films "had to be shot entirely indoors, in sound studios, because the test-flying of planes by the Southern California aircraft industry made outdoor filming impossible."³² Owing to these restrictions, filmmakers were forced to improvise, and these improvisations were deemed by some critics to contribute to a widespread misrepresentation of warfare. For example, in a review of *Air Force*, James Agee remarked that the "well-paid shamming of forms of violence and death which millions a day are meeting in fact seems of an order more dubious than the shamming of all other forms of human activity."³³ Agee likewise derided the manufactured scenes of "air combat on process screens" in *God Is My Co-Pilot*, another Faulkner assignment, images of battle that were "obstructed by the customary close-ups of pilots smiling grimly as they give or take death in a studio, for considerably more than soldiers' pay, a yard above the ground."³⁴

Faulkner seems to have developed a similar suspicion of the industry, even if his own work showed a more complex relation between real and staged combat. While he might have initially had high hopes that his screenwriting would be a way of serving his country, only a few months into his contract, Faulkner admitted that his work was inessential "to winning a war or anything else." He had elsewhere described Los Angeles as a chimera, but now, in a letter to his stepson, Malcolm, he would write more critically of the "moving picture people," a category into which he fell. Faulkner expressed distaste at what seemed to him the luxury of automobility during wartime, complained of Hollywood parasites in the form of "fake doctors and faith-healers and swamis and blackmailing private detectives," and drew a line between these opportunistic rackets and the manual labor of the "aircraft factory people" (*SL*, 165).

These remarks were far from incidental: at the time of writing, Faulkner was working on a script about precisely these people and had visited their workplace in order to better represent them. For "The Life and Death of a Bomber" (also known as "Liberator Story"), Faulkner undertook research at the Consolidated Aircraft Corporation factory in San Diego, where the major project at the time was the B-24 Liberator heavy bomber. Here he "saw not much more than was shown in the picture, 'Wings for the Eagle,'" referring to a recently released Warner Brothers film that was developed for its "publicity value" to Lockheed, the armaments company.³⁵ Faulkner's comments suggest almost the opposite of Agee's criticisms, as the real, working factory conforms to its representation in a feature propaganda film.

After visiting Consolidated in November, Faulkner wrote a few pages of notes in which he observed a quite cheerful production line with a gendered division of labor in which women were assigned such tasks such as "drop hammer, spot welding, painting and doping, sewing linen."³⁶ But more than the factory workers, Faulkner was interested to show the advance of technology itself. The narrative, which he wrote over the winter back home in Mississippi, depicts unionists and bosses as equally greedy in their desire for higher dividends, with a love triangle only serving to highlight the selfishness of the human characters. Far more focused on battle is the bomber itself, which, like the *Mary-Ann* in *Air Force*, is essentially a character in its own right, an anthropomorphized machine that takes matters into its own hands when its makers can not.

This bomber, as Faulkner writes in his outline for the original screenplay, is "a new series, first production job, which if successful will be the forerunner of fleets of new and efficient bombers which will shorten and end the war and so save the lives of many American troops" (*CL*, 63–64). With these expectations, the completed Liberator is transformed in Faulkner's January 1943 treatment into a machine purpose-built to "end the war" and capable of "travelling faster" than expected, its engines seemingly "stronger" than intended (*CL*, 73). In fact, at the beginning of "Act II" of the script, one such bomber moves "of its own accord"—after a delay in production, all factory labor is now redirected toward this particular plane and, as though in response, the Liberator is depicted "trying its best to overcome its handicap" (*CL*, 73). Victory is contingent on the bomber's successful completion, which is achieved on film via a montage of labor, working in sequence so as to put an end to the war. But at the same time, there is something within the machine itself that strives toward battle.

Although his interest in aviation had always been a little guarded (as in *Pylon*), here Faulkner wholeheartedly embraces the machines of aerial warfare over and above their human creators. In the screenplay, this newfound trust in the mechanical is necessary in the face of the defective humans who work on the bomber. Even if he had written with respect for the "aircraft factory people" in his private correspondence, now Faulkner depicts the labor force and other industry stakeholders as altogether greedy and shortsighted, thinking of occupational health and safety and financial reward, before they consider the lives of soldiers they are potentially putting in jeopardy. As the dangerous love triangle forms between the script's main characters, the construction of the bomber is delayed, and the foreman, Halliday, is maimed in an avoidable accident. Later, he returns to the factory and "tells the story of a bomber that arrived too late, because the people who made it let their private selfish motives intervene," an incident that "must never happen again" (*CL*, 80).

The script stresses the urgency of manufacture and the necessity of communicating a message of national unity in this time of struggle. And yet even as the script revolved around the pressing need to arm the United States for combat, James Geller, story editor at Warner Brothers, allowed Faulkner to continue on "The Life and Death of a Bomber" back in Oxford, writing to Robert Buckner that there was "no special rush" required on the property.[37] The project was apparently set to be produced by Jack Chertok, but it was canceled in favor of *Air Force*.[38] More than a simple advertisement for the introduction of a new bomber, "The Life and Death of a Bomber" (had it been produced) would have served as a transparent reminder of the studio's expectations of its employees. Each Warner Brothers picture of course depended on a vast workforce, operating in a way not dissimilar to that of the aircraft factory. But there was always the risk, increasingly so at this point, that one would overlook his or her fidelity to their employer in favor of better working conditions or salary increase. Such temptations marked Faulkner's next two projects, both undertaken for the director Raoul Walsh.

Background to Danger and *Northern Pursuit*

In Jack Kerouac's *On the Road* (1957), Dean Moriarty and Sal Paradise find themselves in a Detroit movie house, watching two films: one a western with "Singing Cowboy Eddie Dean" and the other "George Raft, Sidney Greenstreet, and Peter Lorre in a picture about Istanbul." Occident meets Orient as the pair watch the films six times over: "I heard big Greenstreet sneer a hundred times; I heard Peter Lorre make his sinister come-on; I was with George Raft in his paranoiac fears; I rode and sang with Eddie Dean and shot up the rustlers innumerable times."[39] The actors featured here are certainly memorable enough. But what Kerouac could not have known at this time was that at least one of those Greenstreet sneers had been written into place by William Faulkner. *Background to Danger*, a film he only worked on very briefly, was the second feature in Detroit that night, the first of two properties directed by Raoul Walsh to which Faulkner would make small contributions with another writer, Dan Fuchs.

The film is primarily about the accidental involvement of a normal American citizen—Joe Barton, a machinery salesman—in international espionage. He ends up thwarting a potential geopolitical catastrophe orchestrated by the Germans, which would have seen Russia framed as a potential aggressor of

Turkey, thus forcing the Eurasian country to side with the Nazis in the war. By the time Faulkner came to the script in late November, however, shooting was mostly completed, and Barton's character had been modified substantially. At the request of Raft, who was appointed to play the lead in what would be his last film for Warner Brothers, Barton was no longer a mere traveling salesman as he was in Eric Ambler's thrilling novel *Uncommon Danger* (published as *Background to Danger* in the United States) but was now an American agent, working on assignment in Turkey.[40]

Early on, Barton receives a set of fake blueprints from a mysterious woman on a train bound for Istanbul. He conceals the envelope with the blueprints behind the wallpaper of his hotel room, just before he is kidnapped by the Nazi Colonel Robinson (played by Greenstreet). About to be tortured and probably killed for not revealing the envelope's whereabouts, Barton is rescued by Nikolai Zaleshoff (Peter Lorre), a Soviet spy also out to thwart the conspiracy. Barton reports to his boss, McNamara, concealing how he escaped from Robinson. In the revised version of this scene by Faulkner and Fuchs, he explains exactly what was inside his precious envelope.

McNAMARA
Why'd he ever let you go? I don't get it, Barton. When that baby grabs you, you're out, zero, right away . . .

BARTON
I'm special. He had to let me live.

McNAMARA
What do you mean?

BARTON
He wanted that envelope. I couldn't give it to him if I was a dead man, could I?

McNAMARA
You've got the envelope?

BARTON
I had it. Remzi gave it to me on the train.

McNAMARA
Gave it to you? Well, then, why didn't you destroy it? What were you waiting for?

FIGURE 6. *Background to Danger* (Raoul Walsh, 1943)

BARTON
(wisely)
McNamara, what was in that envelope?

McNAMARA
A set of plans. The Russian general staff's blueprints for the invasion of Turkey.[41]

The scene as written offers a clear explanation of exactly why Barton remains alive, as well as making the audience aware of the information contained in the blueprints. Here, Faulkner's major contribution in these very short revisions was to slow the picture down: "I know what's the matter—too much running around."[42] The instantaneous telegraphing of information in the scenes Faulkner and Fuchs completed helped to make sense of a plot that had become more about the lead actor than anything else. According to Fuchs (who originally gave a veiled description of his and Faulkner's contribution, without naming Faulkner specifically), the rewrites were mostly carried out so as to placate George Raft: "Our star insisted on a scene in which he was given the Congressional Medal of Honor—Cagney had received one, in *Yankee Doodle Dandy*, the camera shooting from behind President Roosevelt's head, and our star threatened bodily harm unless the producer rewarded him in the same way at the conclusion of our picture."[43]

Walsh wasn't his biggest fan, either. In any case, Raft wasn't given his desired sendoff from the studio, but the final scene as rendered by Faulkner

FIGURE 7. *Background to Danger* (Raoul Walsh, 1943)

and his partner at least offered the star a reversal of the famous *Casablanca* ending, with Barton and his love interest, Zaleshoff's sister Tamara, flying to Cairo for their next mission:

362. MED. LONG SHOT   McNAMARA   (FROM BARTON'S AND TAMARA'S ANGLE)

McNAMARA

Hey! What do you think you two are goin' to do in Cairo?

363. REVERSE ANGLE   TAMARA AND BARTON

BARTON
(calling back gaily)

What do you think, Mac? C'est la guerre. We're going to cement Russian-American relations.
    They both laugh into CAMERA as we—

FADE OUT.

In a matter of only a few lines, Faulkner and Fuchs had both pieced together the background of *Background to Danger* and had given Raft a hero's sendoff, leaving Jerry Wald's body intact.

In Faulkner's next project, also to be directed by Raoul Walsh, the narrative of the screenplay likewise came to pivot on a few words. This project was perhaps the only property about which he expressed a problem related to screenplay authorship. Upon his return to the studio from Oxford in February 1943, Faulkner began working on a Nazi invasion narrative with the working title "To the Last Man," eventually released in November that year as *Northern Pursuit*. The film, intended as a vehicle for Errol Flynn, depicted a Canadian Mountie of German descent forced to choose between his distant heritage and the country he serves when a group of Nazi submariners improbably emerges in Hudson Bay, Ontario. The mountie's allegiance to Canada, of course, is never in any doubt, but the moral of the film is clear: one can never be too sure of the potential traitor in their midst (interestingly enough, Flynn's support of the Allied cause was indeed brought into question by Charlie Higham's controversial 1980 biography, but the suggestion of his Nazism has since been thoroughly debunked).

"I am well and quite busy, surrounded by snow, dogs, Indians, Red Coats, and Nazi spies" (*SL*, 167), Faulkner wrote his publisher as he completed work on a preliminary screenplay. These early contributions were critiqued by Bruce Carruthers, a mountie who would later act as technical adviser on *Johnny Belinda* (Jean Negulesco, 1948).[44] His suggested changes are mostly based on careful observances of cultural difference, which were intended to add to the realism of the finished film. But Carruthers's attention to detail as he pulls apart Faulkner's script mirrors nothing less than the plot of the film itself, which revolves around the weeding out of foreign agents from within the Canadian borders and ensuring—by way of a court-martial, if necessary—that one is not secretly in league with the enemy. Although Faulkner had quite a wealth of experience writing war screenplays, Carruthers had the cultural savvy necessary to help refine his early script.

He points out, for instance, and contrary to a line spoken by Errol Flynn's character, Steve, that "a member of the Force does not refer to himself as a Mounty."[45] Later, when Steve is accused of aiding the Nazi infiltration, Faulkner has him admit his fear, but Carruthers ensures that he need not be suspected on account of his idiom:

Top of Page 42:

AS IS: STEVE	SUGGESTED STEVE
Sure I'm afraid.........	Sure I'm afraid........
I get hung.	I get hanged.

REASON: A Canadian never says "Hung" in connection with an execution, It is always "hanged".[46]

These otherwise minute differences in word choice help to draw out the principal narrative concerns of the film, in a context where the use of a certain past participle could be the very thing that prevents one from being hanged.

While Faulkner welcomed changes suggested by an expert, he was more circumspect about the question of screen credit. He had worked with the playwright Thomas Job, as well as Frank Gruber, a genre writer specializing in westerns and mysteries, and Alfred Bezzerides also contributed to the project. Gruber would later complete most of the work with another writer, Robert Rossen, the communist president of the Hollywood Writers Mobilization. But just when it seemed that this pair would be credited on the film, Rossen—as was his right under the articles of the Screen Writers Guild—surprisingly handed his credit to a fellow party member, Alvah Bessie. Bessie, who needed his first credit so that the studio would keep him on, had worked on the screenplay for several months but even so was not expected to have received the credit.[47] Sensing unfairness in the process, Faulkner and Job raised an objection, but Bessie's credit was upheld.

"A person is rehired the next year on the basis of the number of times his name was on the screen this year," Faulkner was quoted as saying only a few years after this incident. "This causes much bribery" (*LG*, 57).[48] Although many appointments and credits throughout Hollywood history have a tinge of cronyism about them, Faulkner and Job seemed particularly incensed by the closing of party ranks here, and Gruber would later recall it as a "Communist conspiracy."[49] Faulkner's next assignment, a much more ambitious project involving many different writers, would require him to think about collaboration more than ever before.

"Battle Cry"

"I am writing a big picture now, for Mr Howard Hawks, an old friend, a director," he wrote his daughter in mid-May 1943. "It is to be a big one. It will last about 3 hours, and the studio has allowed Mr Hawks 3 and ½ million dollars to make it, with 3 or 4 directors and about all the big stars. It will probably be named 'Battle Cry'" (SL, 173–74). Indeed, that would have been the film's title had it ever been produced. With his newly formed company, H-F Productions, Hawks (along with associate producer Charles K. Feldman) had brought "Battle Cry" to Warner Brothers, although the title was an adaptation of more than one narrative.[50] The property relied on at first four and later eight separate sources—including a story developed from a radio script and a news feature—encompassing the different nations represented in the film. The finished film would be eighteen reels, two reels longer than *Gone with the Wind*; indeed, it was subsequently proposed that the film be expanded to an even more ambitious twenty reels.[51] Moreover, an announcement from the studio played up the notion that "Battle Cry" would introduce a new film form altogether, presenting "unconnected episodes" rather than a continuous narrative. These episodes would take up the stories of a number of countries involved in the Allied struggle, depicting American, Chinese, French, Greek, British, and Russian civilians and soldiers in and out of warfare—a projection of the United Nations. The project called for "a blue-ribbon cast of 22 principals" and was to focus on both the "war and the post-war world."[52]

The desideratum to consider the postwar world meant the project was tasked with imagining a time after the fighting had ended; at the same time, the project was about wedding the prestigious Warner Brothers to a time before the war, reassuring patrons that to "win the War with Warners" was not so risible a slogan as it had once appeared. This latest achievement would join a "procession of major projects" that brought back "good memories" of "the pre-war years when Jack L. Warner was spending A-feature money on technicolor shorts extolling Americanism." To go forward was to go back, reminding viewers that the studio had supported the war effort all along and that the artistic successes of its latest prestige pictures—*Casablanca*, *Air Force*, *Yankee Doodle Dandy* (Michael Curtiz, 1942), and *Edge of Darkness* (Lewis Milestone, 1943)—went hand in glove with the exaltation of the United States.[53] Indeed, although this was a picture that depicted the collective efforts of the Allied nations, as with the adaptation of *The Road to Glory* from French material, it was the American story that was privileged here. In an outline used in the earliest treatment from April 1943, the American sequence is divided up into eight separate parts that are punctuated by the various other national sequences and rounded out by an American musical component.[54]

Although the names of up to two-dozen writers were "being withheld to protect those whose contributions are found unsuitable," Faulkner was announced as the author of the "American episode," which described the enlistment of the leading man, Fonda, into a platoon that travels to North Africa.[55] Henry Fonda, the source of Faulkner's protagonist in "Battle Cry" (and who had already starred in *Drums along the Mohawk*), would not go on to star in the film, as he had enlisted in the navy the year prior: "I don't want to be in a fake war in a studio or on location," he said. "I want to be on a real ocean not the back lot. I want to be with real sailors and not extras."[56] Warner Brothers would lose over a thousand employees to the war effort by the end of 1943, but Fonda left the studio voluntarily.[57] The character designed for the actor, however, was less eager to enlist.

One of the sources, a musical cantata titled "Abe Lincoln Comes Home," draws connections between the noble struggle for emancipation in the Civil War and the fight for freedom in the Second World War. Faulkner, as we have seen, often linked wars across the two centuries in terms of their shared aims and outcomes. He had already mined the Gettysburg Address for the title of his contemporary short story "Shall Not Perish," and now he was making associations between the train taking Fonda and other draftees from Springfield, Illinois, to battle, and the Freedom Train that had brought Lincoln's body home to the same town after he had been assassinated. Fonda, who has "a little of the look of Lincoln as a young man" (*F*, 4:3), is naïve and hardly committed to the military, which incenses his grandfather:

FONDA

Aw, I ain't against going. We got to, I reckon, and it ain't any use in fighting against it. But ain't nobody ever told me yet just what I am fighting for.

OLD MAN
(heated)

Fighting for?

FONDA

Hush, Grampaw! Everybody's watching you!

OLD MAN

Let 'em! If there's any more here so poor in spirit they don't know either. You're going to fight for the folks that ain't free, that have been enslaved. And this ain't the first time boys from this town left this very station to go and fight against slavery. Hell fire, there was a man from this very town—

FONDA

Hush, Grampaw! Hush, Grampaw!

OLD MAN

—that said, there ain't room in all North America for a nation to exist half slave and half free. And now we got the same fight on our hands that old Abe had, only worse, because we know now there ain't room even on this whole earth for people to exist half slave and half free— (F, 4:5)

This opening scene's message is driven home in the second temporary screenplay that Faulkner completed in August with the addition of Paul Robeson singing the lyrics to the accompanying cantata, and the suggestion that Lincoln hadn't died but was now freedom incarnate (F, 4:188–90). And yet where this rather uncomplicated condemnation of antebellum slavery is more than welcome in an antifascist screenplay, another scene involving race in the South would prove a little too complex for the script.

Fonda's platoon, marching across the North African desert, includes an English corporal and his two prisoners, one Italian and one German. The troops chance on a house from which they hear a banjo playing: the musician is a southerner, Akers, who is trying to distract his black comrade, portentously called "America," from the bullet lodged in his spine. The men stay to help America, although they soon realize that their position is unsafe and that they will need to make a choice: either to leave before dark or to fight the German army that will soon be on them. Uncertain in command after their lieutenant has died, Sergeant Reagan puts the decision to a vote. All very democratic and American, it seems, until a debate begins between the Italian prisoner and an American corporal, Battson, over the contradiction that divides the United States. Battson points out that there are parts of the country "where America's folks don't have a say," to which the Italian prisoner replies by playing devil's advocate for the anti-Federalist position, namely, that those outside the South should "stop trying to force them to give America's people a vote" (F, 4:102). He continues on in this vein, suggesting what might come of the rifts caused by Jim Crow:

ITALIAN

So they can leave the Jim Crow part of the country, whenever they like. If the rest of the United States' house were as clean as it should be, as it had given its promise to be on that first day of January, 1863, making them as welcome into it as that old promise implied, I think that the Jim Crow people would need much more than just a vote to bribe America's people to remain in the Jim Crow land at all. But perhaps not. Perhaps it is not that simple, not that easy to turn your back on the land, the earth, where you were born and where the only work you know is and where your mother and father and sisters and brothers and children, too, are buried—even if it is only a tenement in Harlem or Chicago or Detroit or a farm in Jim Crow land— (F, 4:103)

This was a remarkably prescient piece of dialogue at the time, and all the more remarkable considering the nationality of its speaker. But it would take a different set of films to respond to segregation and the collective departure of "America's people" from the land of the South. When producer Robert Buckner looked over Faulkner's treatment, he urged a move away from the regional specificity of the episode, with its problematic interrogation of racial politics, and toward the universalism of the struggle against fascism. In particular, Buckner recommended to Hawks that they "cut out the Jim Crow stuff" and instructed that they "watch the use of the word 'niggers'" (a directive Faulkner ignored, the word surviving in the materials submitted in August).[58] The reasons Buckner wished to direct the narrative away from the South were clear: it would be impossible for it to attend to both the immense collaborative project of the Allies, on the one hand, and the internal fractures still evident in the United States, the most prominent nation in the group, on the other. Bringing southern discord to light would weaken an international coalition fighting precisely against race hatred and segregation as they were currently practiced in Nazi Germany. As such, in place of a disquisition on Jim Crow, we have the following revised scene, a paternalistic tableau of black and white harmony:

164. CLOSE SHOT   AKERS AND AMERICA
    They are quiet for a moment. America shakes his head slowly and mutters something under his breath.

                           AKERS
                        (draws closer)
Want somethin', boy?

> AMERICA
> (slowly, almost dreamily—speaks softly)
> Lincoln . . . Abraham Lincoln . . .
>
> AKERS
> (draws out soiled handkerchief)
> What made you think o' him, America?
>
> AMERICA
> Voting.
>
> AKERS
> (mops sweat from America's face)
> Yeah—he gave it to you.
>
> AMERICA
> —give us more'n that. (*F*, 4:354–55)

Although nostalgic wish fulfillment in the extreme, this idyllic scene of the white southerner nursing his black countryman also trades on the sentiment of the project as a whole in its allusion to Lincoln. The great nineteenth-century emancipator remained a powerful figure for those fighting for freedom in the current war. His hope, as suggested in the libretto—"Freedom's a thing that has no ending"—could be exported worldwide (*F*, 4:190).

In gearing the script toward a global narrative, Faulkner made some fascinating additions, especially where music and voice were concerned. The Russian sequence features an entire town gathering together at the behest of a loudspeaker voice to play Shostakovich's Symphony No. 7, with the young, old, and infirm collected in a long montage. Elsewhere, the Italian prisoner tells the transnational story of a Greek hero in an occupied Serbian village: presented as narrative in the treatment, it is converted in the screenplay to parallel text, the scenes playing out on the left side and the Italian's voice-over positioned on the right. This part of the script, reviving the format that Faulkner had used in "Sutter's Gold," was also in evidence in later scenes, this time with "SOUND TRACK" on one side and "SCREEN" on the other. A lengthy episode in the American sequence depicts the singing of the cantata by a large group of African American musicians, but no matter how the story expanded internationally, it would come back in the end to the United States and to the emancipator of the South, giving the lie to the "global" story:

SOUND TRACK	SCREEN
1st SOLO	
Down in Alabama,	DISSOLVE BEGINS.
Nothing but a pulpit and some wooden benches,	
And Mr. Lincoln sitting in the back, away in the back	
CHORUS	
	MONTAGE of 1865 train running. Over it the station signs follow one another:
A lonesome train on a lonesome track,	
Seven coaches painted black,	Washington, Baltimore,
A slow train, a quiet train,	Harrisburg, Philadelphia.
Carrying Lincoln home again. (*F*, 4:310)	

Lincoln's spiritual resurrection, by way of a southern song, would play an instrumental role in changing the overall tone of the screenplay, too. As the composer of the cantata, Earl Robinson, would tell Hawks, "the mood of so much of the picture is a sad one," and it could do with a bit of lightening up.[59] In July 1943, as Russia succeeded on the Eastern Front and Eisenhower launched an Allied offensive on Sicily, it would have seemed reasonable to give the screenplay a more optimistic outlook. As the changing fortunes of the war had influenced the narrative of "The De Gaulle Story," so too would they affect "Battle Cry."

But in the end, the film would not be produced. The film's budget soon ballooned out to $4 million, and, although shooting was only a little over a month away, the studio abandoned production in August. At the same time, Faulkner reported that Hawks was "going to establish his own unit, as an independent: himself, his writer, etc., to write pictures, then sell them to any studio who makes the highest bid." This arrangement, which would have seen Hawks and Faulkner dividing the profits of any film between them, would have been like Dudley Murphy's Associated Artists, just on a far grander scale. For, unlike that failed company, Hawks "says he and I together as a team will always be worth two million dollars at least" (*SL*, 176). This film company would never come to be, but at least Faulkner could take something lasting from the material in "Battle Cry": the beginnings of *A Fable* (1954), his novel about the myth of the Unknown Soldier.

"Who?" and *A Fable*

Starting in mid-August 1943, Faulkner began writing what would become a fifty-one-page film treatment titled "Who?" Over the course of the next decade, he worked up the content of that project into *A Fable*. It was conceived with the assistance of director Henry Hathaway and producer William Bacher, and indeed Faulkner dedicated it to the pair when it was finally published (*N*, 4:667).

"Who?," as Faulkner would tell his publisher, was to be made as an independent picture, after which point he "could write the story in any form I liked: picture script, play, or novel, any revenue from a play or novel to be mine exclusively. The picture rights of course are not for sale." From the very beginning, Faulkner was committed both to delivering the story as a film and as "a magazine and book piece"; he would "smooth it out, give the characters names, remove the primer-like biblical references and explanations, and let the story reveal its Christ-analogy through understatement." In this letter, Faulkner makes clear the genetic origins of his novel—in synopsis form, "sufficient for later picture writing"—that also dictated the "primer-like" administration of its narrative content (*SL*, 178). And indeed, these first "51 pages of the story," though difficult to disentangle from the mostly undated "several hundred pages of preliminary typescript and manuscript," stayed with the work as it evolved into a novel, both in the basic plot and more obscurely in the screenplay, which continued to unnerve Faulkner throughout the decade.[60]

His letters of this time are punctuated by concerns regarding the disposition of the commercial proceeds of the work: in January 1945, for example, Faulkner stressed that a $1,000 loan from Bacher meant that "he owns part of my share of movie rights" (*SL*, 188), and in March 1946, he pledged to "do nothing to jeopardise [Bacher's] rights and wishes" (*SL*, 230). But these considerations of the textual property as a commodity also raise the deeper issue of its process of formal modification. In March 1947, experiencing some trouble with *A Fable*, Faulkner wrote to his publisher once more, stating that he had "just found another serious bug in the ms." The problem, it seemed, was a result of the manuscript's origin as a film treatment, conceived with one eye toward its cinematic production: "Seems to have taken me longer than I imagined to get movie scripting out of my reflexes" (*SL*, 248), he wrote. Faulkner often complained of the cinematic origins of his latest novel over the course of the decade during which he wrote, and so readers have gone looking for signs of the screenplay within its pages.

Robert Hamblin, for one, has commented on the opening chapter of *A Fable* as a cinematic scene, and I have elsewhere discussed the representation of the modern crowd in the novel, a social phenomenon that I argue has cinematic origins.[61] But such interpretations are generally dependent on knowledge of the novel's prehistory as a screenplay: reading through the work, one does not encounter any scene or dialogue text that would immediately suggest the presence of a screenplay in hiding. For this reason, Gene Phillips has rightly noted that *A Fable* exhibits no "special signs of being intentionally based on film techniques, in spite of the fact that this novel was initially conceived as a film scenario."[62] There is certainly a palpable shift in Faulkner's writing style after the war—a more direct political through line is noticeable both in *A Fable* and in *Intruder in the Dust* and in the desire to chronicle Yoknapatawpha County in both the Compson appendix and in *Requiem for a Nun*—and it seems clear that the Warner Brothers stint was at least partly responsible for it. However, although there are some consistencies between early pages of the typescript (which resemble the treatment "Who?") and the overarching plot of the novel, one labors in vain to unearth concrete evidence connecting *A Fable* to Hollywood.

Perhaps a better way to comprehend the shift from film treatment to novel lies in the work's allegorized version of Warner Brothers wartime film style. That is, just as Warner Brothers represented victory in battle by way of collective efforts and the setting aside of individual egos (both in terms of narrative content and in the collaborative labor of filmmaking itself), Faulkner's narrative privileges the collective power of the battalion, which is led by a self-sacrificing Christ-like corporal whose name (Stefan) is mentioned only once in the novel, and even then only to signal his passing: "Stefan was gone; all that was over, done, never to be recalled" (*N*, 4:1033). However, while Warner Brothers was attempting to win a war against almost universally condemned totalitarian forces, Faulkner's novel is ambivalent about war. Confronted with the mindlessness of battle, the corporal manages to convince the entire battalion of which he is part to mutiny, and when they are given orders to attack their German enemies, they refuse to do so. The corporal is court-martialed and eventually executed for his actions, and although the cease-fire between the two sides gives both Axis and Allied forces food for thought, fighting soon resumes, and the war trudges on. Unlike the scripts at Warner Brothers, then, this was a story that exposed the contradictions of global warfare, presenting civil disobedience and the betrayal of one's own country as key to ending the conflict (temporarily, at least). Even though, as Faulkner insisted, it was "not a pacifist book" (*ESPL*, 270), *A Fable* demonstrated that the methods of a major Hollywood studio could be used to move in a different, antiwar, direction.

The setting of *A Fable* confounds the "us versus them" rhetoric of Warner Brothers war films that took aim at the major dichotomy of fascism and democracy in the 1940s. Since it centers on the First World War, *A Fable* by necessity understands that war through the lens of the wars that followed on from it, including the Second World War, the Korean War, and finally through to the noncombat of the Cold War.[63] During his time at Warner Brothers, Faulkner was following a similar logic by writing screenplays that both harked back to films from the previous decade and imagined a world at peace. When he had finished the first draft of *A Fable*, Faulkner reported on his new novel's "argument," one that recalled the different temporalities of the three acts in "The Life and Death of a Bomber": "We did this in 1918; in 1944 it not only MUST NOT happen again, it SHALL NOT HAPPEN again. i.e. ARE WE GOING TO LET IT HAPPEN AGAIN?" (*SL*, 180). This telescoping tendency of Faulkner's was in evidence elsewhere. He had also wanted to adapt Fitzgerald's short story "The Curious Case of Benjamin Button" (1922) in the style of Thornton Wilder's play *The Skin of Our Teeth* (1942); both feature the narrative contraction of large periods of time, and the latter models its characters on biblical archetypes (*SL*, 168). His contract at Warner Brothers precluded him from doing so (*SL*, 172), but the desire to engage with these allegorical frameworks is indicative of Faulkner's work in the period.

When Faulkner sent the fifty-one pages of the manuscript in progress to his agent in mid-November 1943, it was scarcely yet a novel. By early January of the new year, he had finished the first draft and had hopes that the rewrites would be done by February 10, when he would need to report back at Warner Brothers (*SL*, 179). But he could never have known that the novel would require another decade of work before it would be published, and a serious attempt to revisit *A Fable* in 1947 was only the beginning. *A Fable* features briefly once more in the coda to this book, but it is a novel that is certainly deserving of further investigation. Faulkner's self-proclaimed "magnum o" (*SL*, 233) occupies an unparalleled position in his oeuvre as a long prose work that emerged from a short film treatment and tried to shed itself of Hollywood's imprint before taking shape as a late modernist allegory on the dangers of unfettered warfare. While there are several ways one could approach this novel—as a work that engages in a stylistic mode quite distinct from that of his earlier work or as a work that is by and large unconnected to the South (notwithstanding the "Horse Thief" episode in the novel)—*A Fable* is best understood with respect to the operations of Warner Brothers during wartime.

As Faulkner had learned in several instances with "The De Gaulle Story," "Battle Cry," and *Air Force*, legendary historical figures and top studio stars, no matter how deified, could be subsumed in the abstractions of total war, becoming more or less anonymous faces in the crowd and on the screen. Important individuals could hover in the background, orchestrating proceedings (De Gaulle) or providing symbolic encouragement (Abraham Lincoln), but ultimately, the war was fought (or not) by a collective and required the efforts of many in tandem. In *A Fable*, the corporal is executed for his leadership of the mutiny, but at the same time, the cease-fire it created would not have been possible without the assent of the three thousand men who follow him. The plot runs contrary to the less equivocal approach of the studios, and it also marked a significant departure from the spirit of many of Faulkner's own novels: against the psychologized visions of history and affective intensity, here was a novel presenting humanity at its most abstract, as masses and as biblical archetypes, ready-mades with little sense of interiority who were prepared to follow their leaders into battle or out of it. But for Faulkner's next project, which revolved around the Resistance effort on the pro-Vichy island of Martinique, individual characters and stars would ground the narrative once more, and the screenwriting process itself would reveal the complexities involved with committing to a cause.

To Have and Have Not

When he returned to Los Angeles in February 1944, Faulkner was assigned to work on *God Is My Co-Pilot*. However, he told Hal Wallis that he hadn't read Robert Scott's memoir, that he did not want to read it, and that he would rather return to Mississippi.[64] He did, however, manage to turn in fifteen pages of criticism based on Steve Fisher's script, in which he insisted on the presence of "Providence" in battle, a claim that could well have been motivated by his recent preliminary work on *A Fable*.[65] In any case, Faulkner was soon back with Howard Hawks, busy revising Jules Furthman's screenplay for the adaptation of Ernest Hemingway's *To Have and Have Not*.

Hawks had famously joked with Hemingway that he could make a film out of the author's "worst story," and apparently suggested that Faulkner write it, since, as he told Hemingway, "He can write better than you can anyway."⁶⁶ A few years later, speaking to a class at the University of Mississippi, Faulkner would declare that his rival had always played it safe in stylistic terms and had never taken any big risks with his writing (*FU*, 182). True or not, it certainly seemed that "Papa" had turned over a new, more politically conscious, leaf with *To Have and Have Not* (1937). The story largely concerns Harry Morgan's smuggling of contraband (goods and people, both) between Florida and Cuba, but it also is about an alcoholic American writer and his coterie (the haves) and the downtrodden residents of Key West (the have nots). The narrative ultimately forces together the protagonist's maverick entrepreneurialism and the collectivist activities of a revolutionary cadre and ends with Morgan's dying realization that "no matter how a man alone ain't got no bloody fucking chance."⁶⁷

Although an interesting story in and of itself, it would need reshaping: even before Faulkner joined the project, Hawks had cast both Humphrey Bogart and newcomer Lauren Bacall as the leads, and the plot—as the director had worked out with Hemingway a few years earlier—would revolve around their coupling. "A man alone" was no longer just the mercenary throwing in his lot with a greater cause, but even more importantly for Warner Brothers' interests, a popular male actor teaming up with a young, rising female star. The plot was premised on a collectivist struggle, to be sure, but the film's success was truly built on the Bogart-Bacall dynamic at its heart. Another necessary adjustment became apparent during the war, when the Inter-American Affairs Office intervened, concerned that Hemingway's reflections on the tyrannical Machado regime could damage relations between the United States and Cuba. When it was suggested that the setting be changed to the colonial outpost of Martinique, Hawks brought Faulkner in to see if the story could be made to fit with the new location.

Faulkner's idea, undoubtedly borrowed from his work on "The De Gaulle Story," was to make the film a clash between the Free French and Vichy forces, a subject that was not only appropriate to the era but that also invited the attention of the OWI. But as with Hawks's work on *Air Force*, it would be difficult for the studio, or the censors, to keep track of the script as it was being written. According to Bruce Kawin, the shooting schedule demanded that Faulkner write a new scene, on average, only three days before it was shot.⁶⁸ This was a remarkably different practice for Faulkner; although he had likely revised lines of dialogue on set before, he was now being asked to create a large amount of new material (with Furthman), as the cameras had already started rolling. "As soon as I got here, Howard Hawks asked for me," he wrote Harold

Ober. "He is making a picture at our shop. As usual, he had a script, threw it away and asked for me. I went to work helping to rewrite it about Feb. 22. He started shooting about Mar. 1. Since then I have been trying to keep ahead of him with a day's script. I should be through about May 10–15" (SL, 180).

The development of the screenplay, which has been detailed by Kawin and recently expanded on by Ben Robbins, is important for several reasons. Faulkner's handling of the two female protagonists in the story, for example, reveals much about his approach to gender dynamics in Hollywood. In the earliest treatment by Furthman, Harry Morgan's affections are divided between Corinne, a young woman who plays the piano in a Havana café, and Sylvia, an old flame who has since married. In revisions by Whitman Chambers, Sylvia becomes Mrs. Laughton, a comical figure infatuated with Morgan, and eventually morphs into Helen Gordon and then finally Helene de Bursac. All the while, she is a potential love interest for Morgan, and at one stage—had Bacall not been able to handle a starring role—would have been his main squeeze.[69] As Robbins has pointed out, the various rewrites that Faulkner and Furthman undertook from late February to the beginning of May have Helene gradually sidelined in favor of Bacall's Marie, the classic Hawksian love triangle played out not in the film but in the editing of its script.[70] This shift was determined not just by the studio's faith in Bacall but by Joseph Breen, who objected to the relationship between Morgan and a married woman.[71]

The property's approach to fascism necessitated an even more complex modification during the screenwriting process. In Hemingway's novel, the Cuban revolutionaries rise up against General Machado, resisting his violent dictatorship with violent means of their own. This paradox is explored in the first temporary screenplay by Jules Furthman, as Morgan discusses the antifascist "gangsters" with Sylvia:

40.   MORGAN
No, they're not gangsters. These fellows are patriots. They're after
Machado, and I think there'll be kind of a revolution pretty soon.

       SYLVIA
You talk like you were in sympathy with them?

       MORGAN
No, I'm neutral. I'm not interested in local politics. All I want is that eight
hundred and twenty-five dollars I got coming. And if they don't dig it up
come Friday I'm going to do something about it.[72]

Although Morgan has a productive discussion with the Cubans aboard his boat, he ultimately ends up killing all four of them after they murder his harmless friend Rummy. Morgan does not agree with the revolutionaries' claim that "the end justifies the means": the taking down of one fascist leader would only see another established in his place.[73] A knotty problem, to be sure, and one that is perhaps too easily resolved within the confines of the narrative. But how would the narrative have to change in order to accommodate the struggle against the autocracy of the Vichy regime?

In the later screenplay by Faulkner and Furthman, Morgan agrees to collect two Resistance fighters from a nearby island and bring them back to Martinique, but he makes it perfectly clear that he is not one of them: "I'm on any side that pays me," he insists.[74] The distinction between Vichy and Resistance forces is far clearer than the divide between the Machado regime and the Cuban revolutionaries, and Morgan eventually lends the Free French his full support. The adaptation from Hemingway's novel to the film, then, is one in which the unwillingness of a "man alone" to join a worthy cause gives way to a concerted collective effort, with the story's protagonist now willing to lay down his life for his new friends. But in the screenplay's substitution of the modern scenario for Hemingway's Caribbean conflict from the preceding decade, there is a strange remainder. For at the same time that the Cuban revolutionaries of the novel transform into the more trustworthy French in Faulkner's hands, the less noble actions of the antifascists are in the screenplay performed by the Vichy operatives.

The complex transposition becomes clear near the end of the script, as the malevolent Renard repeats the tactics the cruel Cuban revolutionaries had used in the novel and Furthman's earlier temporary version of the screenplay by needlessly mistreating Morgan's innocent friend Eddy (formerly Rummy) as he tries to extract information:

                    MORGAN
                (sitting down in chair)
What are you going to do to Eddy?

                    RENARD
Well, your friend seems to be in a delicate condition, so instead of plying him with liquor and getting stories about a large fish I have decided to withhold it for a while and see what happens.

> MORGAN
> You can't do that. You'll kill him.
>
> RENARD
> You should know.
>
> MORGAN
> He can't stand it. He'll go crackers.⁷⁵

For the most part, the switch from Cuba to Martinique is a smooth one. But in the revisions of the script for *To Have and Have Not*, Faulkner and Furthman attempt to iron out some of the paradoxes of Hemingway's original narrative, revealing the difficulties completing such an adaptation entailed. The contradictions of the Cuban revolution disappeared in the face of the Nazi threat, but it was ultimately very difficult to eradicate all vestiges of cruelty from the source text. "Bill loved working on it because it was Hemingway's," Hawks would later explain. "He wanted to change it."⁷⁶ And certainly, the changes reshaped the story into a film that fit the bill of a Warner Brothers war picture. The work also appears to have reactivated Faulkner's interest in the Vichy issue in "The De Gaulle Story," and it is intriguing to consider that he was now thinking back to some of his earlier, unproduced work for this screenplay.

A letter he wrote while on set, however, suggests that Faulkner had come to a realization that the war film was not providing the great service to the nation that it had claimed: "After being present for a while at the frantic striving of motion pictures to justify their existence in a time of strife and terror, I have about come to the conclusion which they dare not admit: that the printed word and all its ramifications and photographications is nihil nisi fui [nothing if not to be]; in a word, a dollar mark striving frantically not to DISSOLVE into the symbol 1A" (*SL*, 181). This comment, which reveals Faulkner's opinion of the studio system circa 1944, draws a provocative connection between screenwriting and war. Just as Faulkner excoriates the film industry's manipulation of words into images for the purpose of perpetuating Hollywood's existence, so too does he lament the fact that filmmaking for the war effort increasingly appeared as a means of avoiding the draft: the meaning of the "symbol 1A," which signaled one's availability for immediate military service, was widely known at the time. Film witnessed the dissolve of writing into photographs, but this did little (at least to Faulkner's mind) to advance the cause of the Allies. Meanwhile, all those who worked in the film industry desperately tried to turn a profit, lest their services were no longer required and they were instead called up for combat.

The frustration Faulkner felt during his time at Warner Brothers was palpable, as the war never provided him with an opportunity to enlist. But he would take much from his time at the studio, not least of all the kernel of a major novel about the war—*A Fable*—that would put into practice the film industry's effacement of individual characters for the greater good. There was more to his stint with Warner Brothers, besides. In the next chapter, I consider some Hollywood properties that appealed more directly to Faulkner's regional sensibilities and others in which he would unexpectedly locate his South.

CHAPTER 5

The Great Migration to Hollywood

Although the Old South had been represented in bold Technicolor in Victor Fleming's 1939 epic of the Civil War, *Gone with the Wind*, many of the structural remnants of antebellum America were by this point receding into the landscape. In the years following the release of that film, Faulkner likewise reckoned with the changing face of his region, both in literature and in cinema, two media that did not always express the same ideas about the South. While he did not publish much in the way of prose fiction during his years at Warner Brothers, Faulkner completed some interesting work in the second half of the decade—"Appendix: Compson, 1699–1945" (1946), his new preface for *The Sound and the Fury*, was followed by *Intruder in the Dust* (1948), and the collated mystery stories of *Knight's Gambit* (1949). A prolific output for Warner Brothers over the 1940s was inversely matched by a very low yield—compared with the decade before—of novels and short stories. When he returned to writing prose full-time after the war had ended, Faulkner saw his fictional county anew: Yoknapatawpha, just like the South, a place that had changed forever. With the onset of the "second Civil War," the region fended off the various socioeconomic encroachments of the federal government, witnessed the migration of much of its black population to metropolitan areas, and felt the slow decline of its agricultural dominance.[1] The rest of the nation was changing, too, and a number of screenplays that Faulkner wrote responded both to his own region and to a set of shifting urban realities for white and black communities in Los Angeles.

As the Second World War drew to a close, Warner Brothers began to prepare for a different market and to produce films that imagined the various aspects of the postwar world. In a peacetime economy, there would be more latitude for the agonized psychologizing of film noir, and there would be more time for heroic male characters to reflect on the complexity of their individual existence. Freed from the stiff-upper-lip mentality of the war, noir protagonists were now fighting their battles on the urban frontier, uncertain of their surroundings and of the assortment of shady figures that populated them. The crisis of the postwar male subject emerges here, when men are no longer motivated by a desire to defeat a common enemy "over there" and so begin the quest for justice and truth at their own doorsteps instead. That said, there are also strong hints of what was to come even before the war ended: consider the continuities between *The Big Sleep* and *To Have and Have Not*, such as the cynicism of Bogart and the self-assurance of Bacall that are in evidence in both films.

As noir put tormented masculinity on show, the woman's film of this period represented a return to the autonomy of the female subject (and there were productive overlaps between the two genres, as can be seen in Faulkner's work on *Mildred Pierce* [Michael Curtiz, 1945]). The possibility of there being more independent women on screen had already been suggested in films like *Stella Dallas* (King Vidor, 1937). And yet while the pre-code pictures of the early 1930s had afforded filmmakers the chance to explore women as pariahs or liberated characters not bound by the ties of family, the years after 1933 had otherwise largely suppressed female desire by returning women to normative, maternal roles.[2] Temple Drake had not been sighted for some time!

The woman's film of the 1940s seemed to release the female subject once more, featuring emancipated protagonists who would accurately reflect a generation of women increasingly ensconced in the workforce.[3] This is clear in "The Damned Don't Cry," one of the screenplays Faulkner wrote in an effort to woo Warner Brothers in 1941. Here, the leading lady, Zelda, is a social climber from Georgia who manages a successful bordello, has dalliances with several different men, and is rejected by her estranged son. The expression of sexual desire combines with financial aspiration in Faulkner's version of *Mildred Pierce*, too, in which the lead (played by Joan Crawford) leaves both her husband and her domestic confinement, becoming an upwardly mobile restaurateur and property magnate. Nevertheless, these films also promised the restoration of domestic order in the wake of such "transgressive" acts—ultimately, postwar commercial cinema sought to reinstate the status quo where women were concerned, even if it flirted momentarily with other possibilities.

The World War II era also witnessed some brief incremental gains for the nation's black population. On the home front, African Americans had moved in large numbers to cities like Los Angeles for work in the blossoming service industry and then soon after in munitions production. "It used to be that a Negro waiter in the hotel here brought my breakfast up to my room," Faulkner wrote his daughter from the West Coast. "But since rationing started, and men got good jobs in aircraft plants, they have closed the dining-room" (SL, 173). Whatever type of work African Americans were engaged in, it was not the traditional agricultural labor associated with the South. The overproduction of cotton in the 1930s and the subsequent introduction of new agricultural machinery had effectively brought an end to the age-old system of sharecropping, energizing the great migration of blacks from the South that had begun at the turn of the century. The postwar surge belatedly ushered in modernity and dealt a lasting blow to the culture of white paternalism in the region.

While these circumstances were not immediately registered in the films of the period, the early roots of civil rights activism in the military had made possible a number of important black film roles—*Cabin in the Sky* (Vincente Minnelli, 1943), *Stormy Weather* (Andrew L. Stone, 1943), and *The Negro Soldier* (Frank Capra, 1943) were all released in the same year.[4] And in *Bataan* (Tay Garnett, 1943), a black soldier inexplicably fights side by side with white soldiers, even though the armed forces were segregated at the time.[5] But less progress was made after the war was over. Although the later years of the decade saw a few "liberal race pictures" like *Gentleman's Agreement* (1947), *Pinky* (1949), *Home of the Brave* (1949), and the MGM adaptation of Faulkner's *Intruder in the Dust* (Clarence Brown, 1949), the studios in general retreated from such concerns. And, as Ralph Ellison observed of this "Negro cycle" of films, they were not "*about* Negroes at all" but rather about "what whites think and feel about Negroes."[6] And so, even as blacks were vacating the South and migrating in great numbers to cities in the North and West, they were still by and large unrepresented on screen. Ultimately, then, although noir and the woman's film were the two major nonwar genres of the 1940s, genres that responded to the changing postwar environment, African Americans formed film's unseen remainder in the period.

Faulkner may have been aware of this inconsistency, as his work in Hollywood at times proved a minor exception to the rule. In "Country Lawyer," he charted an ongoing "Romeo & Juliet" saga between two white families but remained attuned to the changing nature of race relations over the preceding half century. And for *Mildred Pierce*, his key contribution to James M. Cain's narrative was Lottie, the black maid played by the (uncredited) Butterfly McQueen. As for Scarlett O'Hara, so too for Mildred: their respective successes depended on African American support. Faulkner's involvement in *The Southerner* (Jean Renoir, 1945) and—in a less explicit way—*Stallion Road* (James V. Kern, 1947) also allowed him to engage with his revolutionized South in a new way.

The short stories and novels Faulkner wrote over the course of the decade also responded to changes in the region. *Go Down, Moses* suggested a more concerted turn toward narratives of African American life; the stories comprising *Knight's Gambit* charted the new course of the South through the lens of detective fiction; and *Intruder in the Dust* layered its own criminal plot over a more far-reaching story of race relations, offering a comparatively future-oriented and progressive image of Mississippi. And while Faulkner was appropriating the tools of noir for his prose writing, so too was Hollywood taking the last vestiges of the Old South into the studios. On the one hand, the cinematic reproduction of antiquated Souths during the 1940s often obscured historical reality in favor of plantation nostalgia. On the other, Faulkner sought to preserve the relevance of his novels by keeping his vanishing region alive, even as he repudiated the less salubrious aspects of southern history.

"The Damned Don't Cry"

With Hollywood and Yoknapatawpha jostling for possession of his pen, Faulkner wrote his first treatment for Warner Brothers just as he was finishing work on the final novel of his "matchless time." In November and December 1941, he made several attempts to win the affections of the studios, writing off contract, at the suggestion of his Hollywood agent William Herndon, "5 20–25 page story lines for various studios or individuals, none of which came to anything" (*SL*, 159). One of these was "The Damned Don't Cry," a story of a poor white girl set in Georgia and based on the Harry C. Hervey novel from two years earlier. Warner Brothers had sent Faulkner a script that was unsatisfactory and asked him to revise it, a task to which he had become accustomed.

Faulkner was in the midst of completing *Go Down, Moses* when he received his new freelance screenwriting gig. The story that he had yet to finish was the book's lengthiest and most enduring piece: "The Bear." Although it had already been accepted by the *Post* for publication, Faulkner was now augmenting it by inserting the argument between Isaac McCaslin and Cass Edmonds in chapter 4, over their right to possess land worked on by slaves and originally inhabited by Native Americans, material that Faulkner considered to be the story's most noteworthy. In the midst of a story originally concerned with the hunting of "Old Ben," the legendary bear of the title, this section would ambush the narrative by recreating the idiosyncratic plantation ledgers of Buck and Buddy McCaslin, Isaac's father and uncle, which contain a complicated history of the slaves who were bought and sold and died on their property. With this addition, Faulkner reported that there was "more meat" than he had first thought; it was "a section now that I am going to be proud of and which requires careful writing and rewriting to get it exactly right" (*SL*, 146).

Even as he turned with purpose to this last section of his novel, screenwriting diverted his focus. In fact, he had even sent his new editor, Saxe Commins, an "incomplete section, incomplete chapter, ending with half an incomplete word" from *Go Down, Moses*, because he "had to drop the whole thing for a week and take a shot at a treatment for a movie job" (*SL*, 147).[7] The incomplete manuscript words in question relate to the way in which the ledgers represent "a whole land in miniature, which multiplied and compounded was the entire South." Faulkner began a litany of objects that compose the South—"that slow trick-"— leaving off in the middle of the word to complete "The Damned Don't Cry" before returning a week later to continue the sentence: "le of molasses and meal and meat" (*WFM*, 16.2:320–21). Because they were composed simultaneously, it is worth considering the two in tandem and thinking not only about their shared thematic concerns but also about how Faulkner's concerns about characterization in "The Damned Don't Cry" overlap in some interesting ways with Isaac McCaslin's task as an interpreter of the ledgers.

Unlike his new novel, "The Damned Don't Cry" was slender and would, he informed his Warner Brothers liaison, benefit from a little "beefing up" of "the dialog and incidents in the script as it is" (*SL*, 145). The problem with the existing script in his estimation was that Zelda, the protagonist at the heart of the tale, was too weak to carry the film: she keeps her child, born out of wedlock, although she doesn't possess the temerity or selflessness to make the choice believable. She is a character who "wants a lot but she just sits and wants it until enough people rally around to attend to getting it for her" (*SL*, 145).

Faulkner's new vision for the script presents Zelda as a character with far more pluck and none of the histrionic shrieking and fainting that had marked her appearance in the earlier version. This "beefed up" Zelda is also less dependent on the three suitors in the script and is in fact instrumental in transforming her aristocratic admirer Carter, a complacent heir to a large fortune, into a socially minded advocate of the downtrodden: "Zelda sees in him the aristocrat, with background and gentility and grace, even though she sees his weaknesses: his lack of ambition, his willingness to condone injustice rather than struggle against it, his backward-looking toward the dead past and veneration of family merely because it is old. She sets out to buck him up, make him ambitious to improve himself and the world, too. To her, he was born with so much that he should try himself to attain all the rest: to become morally and mentally what he is by physical accident" (*CL*, 89–90).

Despite being encumbered by old money, Carter manages to "take without pay the case of a falsely accused, dissolute and penniless Negro," and later becomes "engaged in civic work," helping to weed out corruption in local government (*CL*, 90, 94). And his isn't the only character arc that revolves around a renunciation—in a key narrative strand that Faulkner retains, Zelda has an illegitimate child but "loves it too much to repudiate it completely" (*SL*, 145). She sends the boy, Glynn, away to an orphanage in Atlanta. Zelda marries, and ten years later, after her husband dies, she inherits a Savannah mansion she has always coveted, which turns out to be a high-class brothel. Another seven years go by. Glynn by now has met his birth mother, and he frequently travels with her outside of Savannah. However, once he ventures back to her hometown and discovers her means of income, he is repulsed and refuses to see her again. Carter repudiates his inheritance; Zelda repudiates her son; Glynn repudiates his mother: in the first instance, the Old South gives way to the New, while in the latter two, what Faulkner referred to as "the world's moral set-up" (*SL*, 145) prevents any escape from a Victorian hangover. In rewriting the script for Warner Brothers, Faulkner sold "The Damned Don't Cry" both as a viable, au courant tale of a self-made woman and as a clash of Old and New Souths.

Chapter 4 of "The Bear"—and indeed, the balance of *Go Down, Moses*—concerns itself with repudiation, too: specifically, Isaac McCaslin's "relinquishment" (*N*, 4:188) of land bequeathed to him on his twenty-first birthday. In making this decision, he must draw support from the patchy entries written by his father and uncle in the ledgers, thus validating his disavowal of his birthright to Carothers Edmonds. Although the details are sketchy at best, Isaac is able to cast his grandfather as an incestuous miscegenator who fathers a daughter, Tomasina, with his slave, Eunice, and then another daughter with Tomasina. The horror of all of this drives Eunice to drown herself and persuades Isaac to disown his heritage.

Because the evidence is scanty, however, Isaac must fashion a coherent narrative with adequately fleshed-out characters if he is to convince Carothers (and, by extension, the readers of Faulkner's text) of the propriety of his relinquishment. This ultimately involves the transmuting of words into images, at once asserting the historical evidence of the ledgers and suggesting their ability to give rise to something almost tangible outside of the text. Isaac sees things in the documents that nobody else has borne witness to, enabling him to bring his forebears to life once more as robust characters through their otherwise thinly recorded outlines. Since he has been such an inveterate reader of the ledgers in the years leading up to his twenty-first birthday, Isaac has been able to deduce what he believes was the motivating factor of Eunice's suicide. Indeed, he has dwelled so intently on it that the scene of death becomes a vivid image for him: "And looking down at the yellowed page spread beneath the yellow glow of the lantern smoking and stinking in that rank chill midnight room fifty years later, he seemed to see her actually walking into the icy creek on that Christmas day six months before her daughter's and her lover's ... child was born, solitary, inflexible, griefless, ceremonial, in formal and succinct repudiation of grief and despair who had already had to repudiate belief and hope" (*N*, 4:200). For Isaac, the transformation of Eunice from words on a "yellowed page" to "actually walking into the icy creek" is absolutely crucial. More than anything, he needs her to appear because the entries in the ledger provide, at best, an elliptical account of what actually happened.

And yet after the description of Eunice's drowning, Faulkner punctuates Isaac's thoughts with the peremptory "that was all." Following this decisive phrase, we are told that Isaac "would never need look at the ledgers again nor did he; the yellowed pages in their fading and implacable succession were as much a part of his consciousness and would remain so forever, as the fact of his own nativity" (*N*, 4:200). As Richard Godden and Noel Polk have perceptively observed, the image of Eunice that Isaac conjures relies simultaneously on the information available in the ledgers and on the way that the ledgers subsequently "recede from attention" in order that the image might appear before us. However, they add, this process of image making "must surely depend on an available and traced relation to the documented evidence."[8] Given that the complete and unabridged ledgers are not present to the reader, we must rely instead on Isaac's gloss for our picture of his shameful family history, and it is one we might be justly suspicious of.

It is worth keeping in mind that Faulkner's writing of "The Damned Don't Cry" was equally premised on his ability to make the producers at Warner Brothers see the potential film leap off the page and on to the screen. His concern in his correspondence with the studio—that the "story is already in the script, and I just failed to see it" (*SL*, 145)—also speaks to his desire to ensure that Zelda, and by extension the plot of the treatment, can be imagined visually in the minds of the studio staff. The transition to a fuller screenplay never transpired, however. Two years later, Faulkner revisited the property for producer Jerry Wald, apparently forgetting his earlier treatment. Although he made some useful comparisons between "The Damned Don't Cry" and his 1936 short story "The Brooch," another "story of a southern girl born on wrong side of tracks, trying to raise herself" (*SL*, 183), the idea didn't take.

In marked contrast to his regard for the treatment, Faulkner was highly protective of his latest work on "The Bear," attaching a note for the printer that read "DO NOT CHANGE PUNCTUATION NOR CONSTRUCTION."[9] Indeed, he seemed to think that even a potential Hollywood adaptation would leave the work largely intact. A few months earlier, he had asked Robert Haas to send the manuscript of *Go Down, Moses* to William Herndon in Los Angeles, hoping for a quick sale. "I will have to make a few minor corrections in it before you print it," Faulkner wrote, "but it wont be changed as far as a moom pitcher magnit is concerned" (*SL*, 142). While the studios failed to show interest in (or perhaps never even received) the manuscript, Faulkner would later write a fifty-two-page treatment that was in many ways "the complement of *Go Down, Moses*" and that would allow Faulkner to continue thinking about the past and future of Yoknapatawpha even as he was writing for the screen.[10]

"Country Lawyer"

The structure of the ledgers would have undoubtedly come to Faulkner's mind once again when he sat down to write the treatment for "Country Lawyer" in March 1943, a property that Jack Warner had intended to mark the reunion of "the star, director and producer of 'Mission to Moscow,' Walter Huston, Michael Curtiz and Robert Buckner."[11] In Bellamy Partridge's 1939 novel of the same name, the narrator explains that the story was gleaned from "a little black notebook in which my father had jotted down curious incidents of his practice, of which no other record was ever found. Some of the entries sketched the outline of an incident; others gave pages of dialogue and even bits of description."[12] Like Isaac McCaslin—albeit with greater reverence—Partridge writes the story of his father, pieced together from scraps and embellished where necessary. That piecing together becomes a crucial factor in Faulkner's adaptation.

Faulkner was the sixth writer to work on the script (one Partridge himself had attempted to write and that later Alvah Bessie contributed to), and by that time, the country lawyer was a position that had virtually ceased to exist in many parts of the country.[13] As Partridge recalls, "The first breach in the wall had been made by the telephone. Soon afterwards the motor-car began to bring in the strange people, and the cinema had furnished the new notions. At this point in the century the American country town began to lose its flavor, its individuality, its peculiarities of local custom and local idiom. It was no longer the product of its own environment. Outside influences were now directing its growth and development. The great god Regimentation was in the saddle and ready to go."[14] The influx of new transport and communications media (the cinema singled out here for the second time in the book) rendered the country lawyer superfluous. Although Partridge based his story on his own hometown, Phelps, New York, his hometown was, he pointed out, representative: "The setting could well have been duplicated in any of five thousand small towns scattered over the American landscape; and the country lawyer might as easily have sprung from Kansas or Kentucky origin as from a Vermont-born father and a mother of native New York stock."[15]

Perhaps taking this as his point of departure, Faulkner relocated the narrative to his native Jefferson, treating the finished product as though it were another component of his ongoing Yoknapatawpha chronicle. "I can still invent a little something now and then that is photogenic" (*SL*, 169), he wrote at the time, and indeed, his task here was to bring a property that Warner Brothers had already owned for several years a little closer to the screen. In the space of about three weeks, between March 27 and April 16, 1943, Faulkner would transform Partridge's work into a barely recognizable cross-generational saga structured on a "Romeo and Juliet" framework and would also incorporate the story of a black family (*CL*, 36). In order to effect this transformation, he would modify one of the key events in *Country Lawyer*, finding in the novel of New York State a southern narrative in hiding.

In the book, one of the major cases that Samuel Selden Partridge takes on is that of an arsonist, Jerry Billings, who stands accused of setting fire to a toolshed that then spreads to several nearby premises. While by all accounts

Billings is innocent of the crime, he is nevertheless sent to jail, turned into a scapegoat for the spate of burnings that had recently occurred in the town. Long after Billings has been released and has passed away, Bellamy Partridge finds some suggestive information about the accused in his father's black book. The narrative up to this point has been reconstructed in a seemingly unproblematic way, but now—in a passage that evokes the reading of the McCaslin ledgers—we are told about two pages of newspaper clippings pasted in the book, which give the sense that "there must be a story hidden between the lines."[16] Each of the clippings details an arson attack, and it soon becomes clear that the victims of these attacks, all perpetrated after Billings had served his time, were the very jurors who had found him guilty. The narrator concludes that Billings must therefore be guilty of twelve separate burnings, if not also for the one for which he was initially convicted, but he is never able to ask his father how he had uncovered this mystery, nor why he had kept quiet about it after Billings's death, for his father dies soon after this discovery.

In any case, the fear of a serial arsonist governs both the beginning and the end of *Country Lawyer*, suggesting the possibility of miscarried justice. Arson is also crucial to Faulkner's relocation of the story to the South, where the burning of a barn carries a different kind of weight. Although readers of Faulkner will perhaps most readily associate the poor whites Ab Snopes and Darl Bundren with the crime, acts of arson during Reconstruction were more often than not committed by blacks on white property and are today considered to have been acts both of class and racial warfare.[17] Transported from New York State to Mississippi, the incendiary acts in Partridge's book are recoded as the assumed actions of a poor and shiftless black man, who is out of place in his own town.

The black tramp Tobe in Faulkner's treatment is suspected of burning a banker's stable because he "sleeps around in people's barns, works only when he has to, without ambition, etc" (*CL*, 18). After a lawyer, Galloway, takes up his case, Tobe is found innocent, and he repays the favor by moving his wife, Rachel, and daughter, Caroline, into the lawyer's house, becoming his lifelong servants. Although the lawyer refuses them several times, saying that "he can't afford servants," the family stays, and what develops is "a relationship established upon mutual respect between the white man and the two Negro women which will endure" (*CL*, 19, 20). The blackening of the arsonist in "Country Lawyer" reconfigures the book's narrative completely, as Tobe's racial difference, more than his alleged criminality, attracts the lawyer's attention. Even so, with "Country Lawyer," Faulkner appeared to return to a past he had already done away with. In the Reconstruction South, the idea that Tobe and his family would be willing to work for Galloway for free may be plausible to an extent, and yet Tobe's wife and their descendants remain with the lawyer and grow together harmoniously with his own offspring well into the 1940s. In Yoknapatawpha County, the bonds between black and white had already begun to loosen, so the specific way in which Faulkner revisits them here seems at odds with the direction of his fiction in the same period.

This is most obvious in the different permutations of one particular scene throughout his oeuvre. In *The Unvanquished*, Faulkner develops the relationship between Bayard and Ringo over a number of short narratives. Where there is originally a clear hierarchy between the two boys, with white Bayard sleeping in a bed and black Ringo sleeping on a pallet, the two are soon quite happily sleeping alongside one another on the floor. However, in "The Fire and the Hearth" from *Go Down, Moses*, a similar alliance is overturned. That story depicts the seven-year-old Roth Edmonds peaceably sharing a pallet with Henry Beauchamp, but once he becomes aware of his own whiteness, Roth refuses his companion a place in his bed. In this revision of the Bayard-Ringo scenario, it is Roth's "old haught ancestral pride" (*N*, 4:86) that will forever separate the pair, who "never slept in the same room again and never again ate at the same table" (*N*, 4:87).

Likewise, "Country Lawyer" contains a particular sequence involving the lawyer's son Sam, and Tobe and Rachel's grandson Spoot, which owes an obvious debt to both of these primal pallet scenes:

> The white boy gets into the bed; the Negro takes the pallet. Rachel says goodnight, tells them to be quiet, puts out the lamp and leaves. The lightning glares, thunder rolls. The white boy rises on his elbow, looks down at the Negro.
>
> WHITE BOY
> Come up here with me.
>
> NEGRO BOY
> And have Mammy come in here and whup the tar outen both of us? Naw.
>
> WHITE BOY
> Then I'm coming down there.
>
> NEGRO BOY
> All right. Come on. Then see if you can't shut up and lemme go to sleep.
>
> The white boy gets onto the pallet with the Negro. (*CL*, 32)

Faulkner clearly models this episode from "Country Lawyer" on the exchanges between Bayard and Ringo in *The Unvanquished* and not on the more recent rejection of Henry by Roth in *Go Down, Moses*. To all intents and purposes, then, the return to the earlier romantic novel seems a historically evasive one, calculated to appease a studio system still enamored of the equally fanciful *Gone with the Wind*. This was tantamount to the kind of escape that Faulkner had written of elsewhere, "into a makebelieve region of swords and magnolias and mockingbirds which perhaps never existed anywhere" (*ESPL*, 292).

And yet Faulkner's "Country Lawyer" script does not remain stuck in the past but instead acquits itself well by testing the relationship between black and white right up to the present moment. Perhaps casting his mind back to his early treatments for *Gunga Din*, Faulkner has Spoot and Sam later fight together in the trenches during the Great War, and their camaraderie, which ends with the two dying together under German gunfire, shows "how little the difference in race means to them when they are alone" (*CL*, 47). Far from their homes, the treatment suggests, there is greater scope for the reconciliation of the two races. But the South itself also changes. As the script moves forward to 1942, the lawyer's great-granddaughter Lally delivers a fierce diatribe to the family patriarch about the new global conflict and the way in which it originated in the shortcomings of previous generations: "She tells him calmly how it was the old people like him, with their greed and blundering and cowardice and folly, who brought on this war, brought about this situation in which Carter [Lally's beloved] and Spoot, Junior, will have to risk their lives and perhaps lose them, as her Uncle Sam and Spoot, Junior's, father did in the last war" (*CL*, 56).

Faulkner transports Bellamy Partridge's *Country Lawyer* from New York State to the South. But he also refuses to embrace that work's antimodern reaction to a changed and changing world. Although the return to Jefferson, Mississippi, and the return to the romance of *The Unvanquished*, may seem like conservative maneuvers, Faulkner's rerouting of the narrative through the Reconstruction South paradoxically allows it to move forward. The transposition is crucial, because modernity came belatedly (and was still coming) to the southern states, meaning that Faulkner could extend the scope of his treatment by a further three decades. Where the country lawyer in Phelps, New York, might have been out of a job by the turn of the century, the particular socioeconomic arrangements in towns below the Mason-Dixon line would allow the figure to survive for some time longer (indeed, Faulkner's own country lawyer, Gavin Stevens, would offer him enough material to take him almost to the end of his career). As an adaptation, Faulkner's "Country Lawyer" treatment dislocates an existing narrative, geographically and temporally, in order to make it serve his renewed vision of the South, one that is more progressive than that which Hollywood had to offer.

The Southerner

In the summer of 1944, there was a third opportunity for Faulkner to imagine the South on screen. While in the thick of his Warner Brothers stint, he found time to moonlight on another project closely aligned with his interests: Jean Renoir's *The Southerner* (1945). This was an independent venture, and one on which the contractually tied Faulkner was not supposed to be working. The script was written by Nunnally Johnson, Renoir, and Hugo Butler (who would receive the credit); Faulkner served as advisor. It was adapted from the National Book Award–winning novel *Hold Autumn in Your Hand* (1941) by George Sessions Perry. The title, in the words of Renoir himself, "means you must preserve and store the vegetables that grow in autumn. The truth is it's a book intended mostly to convince American farmers not to eat only canned food in the winter, . . . canned meat, salted food, but to try to eat green beans, and vegetables and fruits, in order to fight against an illness known as pellegra [sic] that was . . . at that time rather widespread in certain southern states."[18]

From novel to screenplay to film, the didactic kernel of the story survived. But the finished version of *The Southerner* seems interested in the idea of preservation in more ways than one. Indeed, it offers a quite nostalgic picture of the region, trumpeting the anachronistic virtues of farming over the more secure option of urban wage labor, occluding black characters from the landscape completely, and holding fast to the image of the rural nuclear family, in this case the Tuckers. Although beset by tragedy and the hardship of the land, the Tucker patriarch, Sam, remains steadfast in his ways, rejecting available factory work and the security of a work camp and resorting to sharecropping so as to grow his own produce. A proud archaism, to be sure, and perfect material for an author who was himself witnessing the slow erosion of the South's agricultural traditions.

As Faulkner contributed to a script that had already been written, one might labor in vain trying to definitively locate his authorial voice. However, Zachary Scott, the star of the film, recalled Faulkner's input in what was the

FIGURE 8. *The Southerner* (Jean Renoir, 1945)

novel's climactic sequence—the scene in which Scott's character, Sam Tucker, finally catches Lead-Pencil, the legendary catfish, only to give it up to his rival neighbor in exchange for the fresh vegetables his family needs.[19]

Faulkner takes the sequence from Perry's novel and injects it with tension, dragging out the big catch in a way the book does not. In *Hold Autumn in Your Hand*, Sam Tucker has resolved to beat his neighbor, Henry Devers, who had earlier denied the family the milk and vegetables they need to cure their son's pellagra. On his way to see Devers, he realizes that Lead-Pencil is caught on his towline in the river, but he is so consumed with feelings of revenge that he only catches the fish "mechanically" and "without joy."[20] In the screenplay, however, the process is far more exciting. By the time this scene occurs, Sam has been begun to see success as a farmer owing to a gift of a cow, and Devers now wants the land that the Tuckers are leasing; the two have just had a fight, and Devers is returning with his shotgun, intending to kill Sam, when he sees the fish. As it turns out, he is far more interested in the fish than in murder; he himself has been pursuing Lead-Pencil for two years and so ends up helping to pull the fish from the water:

> SAM is now seen pulling on the cable. Then we see a BIG FISH, in the middle of the river, leaping around, trying to free himself from the hook, as the scene cuts to a close view of DEVERS and SAM: Fascinated by this spectacle, Devers looks on, all attention. He has forgotten everything, his idea of murder, his fury—Only one thing interests him now—the big fish.

FIGURE 9. *The Southerner* (Jean Renoir, 1945)

        DEVERS.
Holy Smoke!—It's Lead Pencil![21]

 The catch here is crucial, since it forges an uneasy truce between the neighbors and allows Tucker (in the version of the story as it unfolds in the screenplay rather than as it was ultimately shot) to trade the fish for a promise that he can use the vegetables from Devers's garden without any trouble.

 The second identifiable contribution from Faulkner (or, at least, one he reported to Alfred Bezzerides) was the scene in which the Tucker family gathered around on the hearth to light the stove for the first time, a minor episode when compared with the Lead Pencil catch.[22] Although Faulkner's two scenes may not seem to amount to much, Renoir later praised his work, recalling that the "influence of that man of genius had certainly a lot to do with the success of the film."[23] As a whole, *The Southerner* presents a South beleaguered on all sides, the damage effected as much by mechanized agriculture and wage labor as by an illness caused by poor education and a lack of understanding of basic nutritional standards.

The Great Migration to Hollywood 171

But whatever its message, the film was famously banned in Memphis by Lloyd Binford, the notorious chairman of the Memphis Board of Motion Picture Censors, who remarked that "it represents southerners as illiterate mendicants."[24] There was far more to Renoir's film than this criticism suggests, but in some ways Binford was right to be concerned that *The Southerner* did not offer an accurate representation of his region. Set in Texas—although actually filmed mostly in California—Perry's novel, as well as the screenplay and film it gave rise to, are both devoid of African American characters, aside from a few brief instances where they figure as peripheral elements of the mise-en-scène. This perhaps contributed to André Bazin's assessment of the finished film as "more surreal than dramatic" and to James Agee's comment on the unlikely absence of any "racial friction."[25] The opening scene portrays black workers picking cotton and dumping it into a truck, but people of color are largely lacking in the remainder of the screenplay and film.[26] Faulkner's very minor contributions, then, would not make the South any more realistic than the story already suggested, but instead more dramatic. However, even though his next property was not set in the South, Faulkner would include a black southerner in the story, a move that would complicate issues of labor for both white and black alike.

Mildred Pierce and *Intruder in the Dust*

On November 13, 1944, Faulkner was commissioned to work on *Mildred Pierce* and was ushered in as the fifth of seven writers authoring separate scripts. By the time of he came on board, producer Jerry Wald had already elected to rearrange James M. Cain's source material around a crucial narrative flashback, introducing murder into the plot.[27] The emphasis in Cain's novel on the material conditions of the Depression apparently made the story less commercially viable than the unlawful events depicted in *Double Indemnity*, which had been released a couple of months earlier and had proved its worth as a successful Billy Wilder picture for Paramount. So Wald made *Mildred Pierce* into a woman's picture via its flashback sequences and a noir in the form of its present-day murder scenes and Mildred's interrogation. The two genres might appear as strange bedfellows, but the "female gothic" that would come of this union was crucial to the development of noir, with its mostly male-oriented features.[28] Although it is not clear at first glance, there is also an oblique connection to *Intruder in the Dust* (the first novel that Faulkner wrote after his return from Hollywood) that emerges through a curious combination of generic and structural similarities and overlapping ideas about the treatment of African American characters (especially with respect to the changing population of the South).

Cain's 1941 novel *Mildred Pierce* follows the fortunes of a single mother during the Depression after she leaves her husband, Bert, and establishes a successful pie business to support her two daughters, Veda and Ray (who later dies of pneumonia). Ever the entrepreneur, Mildred expands the business and eventually opens a chain of restaurants, finding a new boyfriend, Monty, in the process. Veda, now a budding opera singer, increasingly expects to enjoy the spoils as Mildred's wealth grows, and later has an affair with Monty. Mildred is able to deal with a variety of money troubles and eventually reconciles with Bert, while Veda runs away to New York with Monty. The major variation in the film, as we discover at the end, is that Veda murders her new lover after he refuses to marry her, and although Mildred tries to protect her, Veda is jailed for the crime. As produced, the film casts Cain's narrative as a flashback and frames it with Mildred's revelation of the entire backstory to the police.

The introduction of a crime of passion into the narrative almost completely suppresses the material history of the Depression, which is far too complex and difficult to unravel in the space of ninety minutes. In a bid to eliminate what had become an unwieldy, seemingly extraneous amount of background material in the previous scripts, Faulkner suggested to Wald that "up to the time she [Mildred] meets Monte [her lover], all this finding a job, getting set in the drive-in business, should be almost Montage."[29] In this particular instance, "all this" meant the totality of detailed content in Cain's novel that attempted to show the workaday toils facing a single woman during the Depression. While Faulkner was apparently interested in illuminating some of the film's more intricate financial particulars—especially considering Mildred's seemingly impossible success in a time of economic hardship—the murder story would come to occupy most of his attention in the screenplay, and his version of the story attained no more clarity than that of others on economic matters.[30] In the end, as Karla Oeler has observed, the investment in "social injustice" was displaced by the unraveling of a "solvable and punishable crime."[31]

The way Faulkner executed this generic juggling act was also in keeping with another narrative he had just begun to write. Before he commenced work on the adaptation of *Mildred Pierce*, Faulkner had worked on *The Big Sleep* for Howard Hawks and at the time was planning a novel that would also combine elements from different genres. "Bill," the director asked him, "why don't you do a detective story?" Faulkner replied: "I've been thinking of a nigger in his cell, trying to solve his crime."[32] He had actually thought of the plot for *Intruder in the Dust* (1948) a few years earlier, in 1940, and when it was finally published, the original germ of an idea would remain: "a mystery story, original in that the solver is a negro, himself in jail for the murder and is about to be lynched, solves murder in self defense" (*SL*, 128). The novel revolves around the fate of Lucas Beauchamp, who has been accused of murdering a white farmer, Vinson Gowrie. He sits in the town jail awaiting either his sentence or the lynch mob that gathers outside. Chick Mallison, believing that Lucas is innocent, helps to solve the case, and it is later revealed that Vinson's brother, Crawford, was responsible for his death.

As the manuscript progressed, Faulkner was finding it ever more difficult to synthesize elements of a socially and racially conscious tract with the novel's central murder plot, and he ended up turning to more lasting matters to tie the different strands together. In his own words, the novel "started out to be a simple 150 page whodunit but jumped the traces, strikes me as being a pretty good study of a 16 year old boy who overnight became a man" (*SL*, 266). In its depiction of the changing socioeconomic fortunes of the South, the major shift taking place—the Great Migration—registers in the allusions to the historical movement of African Americans out of the region, which suffuses the murder mystery with an overwhelming sense of melancholy, a mourning for a South that was inevitably slipping away. While there was a considerable amount of movement away from rural areas in the 1930s, the exodus of sharecroppers increased exponentially after the Depression and with the advent of World War II. The South's farm population decreased by 20 percent between 1940 and 1945, with Mississippi alone losing twenty-eight thousand sharecroppers to the war industry.[33] And because the farm population was predominantly black, this in turn meant that a disproportionate number of African Americans were relocating north and west; figures indicate that anywhere up to two million blacks may have vacated the South during the 1940s.[34]

Even as these massive changes were afoot, Faulkner began to concentrate on the black South in his fiction, beginning with a concerted turn to African American narratives in *Go Down, Moses*. In "Country Lawyer," as we have seen, Faulkner revisited the Reconstruction South in order to chart the cross-generational harmony of black and white families, and now, with *Intruder*, he would try to continue this story of interracial coexistence in the present day. What he produced with these works, however, was a narrative that resisted history itself and one in which the characters remained plaintively attached to a fading memory of the Old South. Ward Miner was an early critic who pointed to historical misrepresentation in Faulkner's novels after comparing the real census results of Lafayette County with those listed on the map of Faulkner's fictional county. If the empirical data of the census listed "Negroes" in Mississippi being outnumbered by whites for the first time in 1940, at 49.2 percent, then why did Faulkner list their numbers at 59.6 percent when his Yoknapatawpha map was published for the first time just four years earlier? Miner concludes that for the inhabitants of the fictional county, the psychological awareness of the presence of African Americans makes it seem "as though there were more of them than there actually are."[35]

Whatever one makes of Miner's rather pedantic findings, *Intruder* does seem to bear the thesis out. For in the novel, none of the characters seems aware of the migration taking place, and it is only coded in a number of ephemeral passages, all centering on the young Chick Mallison: "And four years later he had been free almost eighteen months and he thought it was all: old Molly dead and her and Lucas' married daughter moved with her husband to Detroit and he heard now at last by chance remote and belated hearsay that Lucas was living alone in the house, solitary kinless and intractable, apparently not only without friends even in his own race but proud of it" (*N*, 4:301). Here, the move to Detroit is quickly passed over, which makes it easy to overlook the fact that Lucas Beauchamp is not "solitary kinless" because he is "intractable" but rather in spite of it. His pride in separation notwithstanding, there are larger, more ineluctable forces operating to ensure the absence of people of "his own race." As elsewhere in the novel, the Great Migration exists here only as a misjudged domestic issue of one individual's making, but this glossing over of labor's abandonment of the South also codes a latent recognition of what is taking place.

To be sure, Chick is clearly cognizant of the absence of African Americans in the county. As he rides out to the cemetery to meet Aleck Sander and Miss Habersham, for instance, Chick becomes aware that "he had not seen one Negro since leaving town, with whom at this hour on Sunday night in May the road should have been as constant as beads almost" (*N*, 4:355). Of course, blacks are in hiding because Lucas has been arrested, and they fear he will be lynched. The same climate of fear abounds here as did in the earlier short story "Dry September" (1931), in which we are told that after the lynching of Will Mayes there was "not a Negro on the square. Not one" (*CS*, 181). In this instance, however, Chick is also aware that "they were still there, they had not fled, you just didn't see them—a sense a feeling of their constant presence and nearness" (*N*, 4:356). The disappearance of African Americans from the land here has a very particular cause—the threat of lynching—and yet it also gives way to the boy's astute appreciation of the more vital migratory disappearance in the region. For that reason, perhaps, the sudden withdrawal for Chick yields "the deliberate turning as with one back of the whole dark people on which the very economy of the land itself was founded, not in heat or anger nor even regret but in one irremediable invincible inflexible repudiation, upon not a racial outrage but a human shame" (*N*, 4:356).

As John Matthews has helpfully illuminated, the very real danger of violence motivated by Jim Crow began to dissipate in the wake of the changing labor regime in the New South. The movement of southern blacks to the North began to negate the utility of repressive racial policies, because blacks were no longer dependent on landowners for work.[36] The sharecroppers who once lived on the farm now more than ever lived in towns, relying on welfare or the possibility of poorly paid, seasonally commissioned wage work. The days of subsisting and residing perennially on the same farm were all but over. In *Intruder*, as Chick and Stevens drive out to the church to dig up the Gowrie grave for a second time, they observe a solitary black laborer with his mule and plow in the otherwise "empty fields." Stevens comments that "somebody's got to stay home and work" (*N*, 4:395), although over the following decade, and especially with the advent of mechanized labor, this would become less of a necessity.

The African American labor force would instead find work outside the South, in the "*Chicagoes and Detroits and Los Angeleses*" (*N*, 4:446) that come under fire later in the novel and that offer the relative security of waged factory and domestic work. The black population of Los Angeles, for instance, doubled from 63,774 to 133,082 between 1940 and 1946. "By 1950," Eric Avila writes, "that number reached 171,209, giving Los Angeles the West's largest concentration of African Americans." Eventually, over the early years of the next decade, it would creep above 200,000.[37] Nevertheless, the sheer numerical changes weren't reflected in lack of opportunities afforded to people of color in the metropolis. Although the munitions industry and the military seemed to pave the way for a more integrated workforce in the city, there were other areas that would prove more difficult to enter: one of these was Hollywood. As the writer Chester Himes would later attest, the Jim Crow practices in Los Angeles were just as bad as anywhere else: MGM, for example, instituted a segregated eating room on the set of *Cabin in the Sky*, a film with an all–African American cast. Himes also experienced racist treatment on the lot when on the verge of employment at Warner Brothers, he was revealed as a future screenwriter to Jack Warner, who promptly dismissed him: "I don't want no niggers on this lot."[38]

Despite the studio system's mild flirtation with movies about African American life, Hollywood filmmaking hardly reflected the fact that Los Angeles now had a large black constituency. Indeed, popular cultural artifacts claiming to represent the city implied exactly the opposite: the wholesale invisibility of all nonwhite citizens. For Chick in *Intruder*, African American bodies are almost never seen and are felt only through their "constant presence and nearness" precisely because they are vanishing from the South. But curiously, this likewise seems to be the case in one of the metropolitan areas to which those African Americans ventured, where surely the opposite should have been true. While Himes's crime novels proved a rare exception, most films of a noirish bent in postwar Los Angeles practiced the veritable whitening of the city.

This inclination was made all the more apparent in the adaptation process. Raymond Chandler's *Farewell, My Lovely* (1940), for example, begins with the murder of a black man in an African American bar on Central Avenue, but, as James Naremore has written, "it is easy for most readers to forget the first death," but as he suggests, "the neglect of the black man is precisely the point." In the film version of *Farewell, My Lovely*, titled *Murder, My Sweet* (Edward Dmytryk, 1944), however, the bar is full of working-class white men, even in spite of RKO's commitment to social-realist filmmaking.[39] The same is true of many noirs from the period, which, in their occlusion of black characters from the screen, appeared to deliberately ignore the major influx of African American citizens entering the city from the South during the 1940s.[40]

As Eric Lott asserts, the Great Migration was certainly a productive source of noir anxiety, with the films themselves taking the "social energy" associated with this renewed racial threat and "subsuming it into the untoward aspects of white selves." While not dealing explicitly with the racial cause of this anxiety, he writes, film noir tended to sublimate the neurotically projected implications of impending black urbanization into "the criminal undertakings of abjected whites," and in specifically visual terms.[41] In Lott's convincing argument, we are reminded that the postwar cinematic apparatus traded in technical innovations "such as the Norwood exposure meter (which for the first time could take a weighted average of light from all directions rather than a single direction), faster film stock, photoflood bulbs that permitted better location filming, [and] antireflective lens coatings," all of which allowed the camera to locate "a world in the dark."[42] Film noir, then, was technologically predisposed to pit white against black, creating a chiaroscuro scheme that more effectively than ever before displaced the racial difference that was increasingly common in Los Angeles but barely depicted on screen.

With an understanding of noir that is more attuned to its covert stance on racial difference, we can see that at least one aspect of *Mildred Pierce* calls attention to historical reality otherwise ignored in postwar Hollywood cinema. And it was William Faulkner who was responsible for this, for his major contribution to the screenplay was to cast Mildred's maid, Lottie, as a black woman, transformed in the script from the white maid, Letty, of Cain's novel.[43] The property is thus not completely bereft of African American characters, and the sole appearance of Lottie, at Faulkner's behest, sets up an intriguing analogue to the similar impression of African American scarcity in *Intruder in the Dust*. The maid's change in color is more than skin deep and has some subtle effects on the finished product. In novel, screenplay, and film versions of the story, Veda discovers a waitress's uniform in her mother's room. Assuming it is intended for the maid (and not for her mother), she gives it to Letty/Lottie to wear. In Cain's novel, the irony of the situation is a source of shame for Mildred, who is unable to provide her exacting daughter with the wealth and status she desires. But in Faulkner's screenplay and in the film, the anxiety of seeing her maid dressed in her own uniform stems from the fact that the maid is black. With this key shift in the adaptation process, Eric Lott contends that Lottie and Mildred become "versions of each other": Lottie is "less the representative of the hard labor Mildred is perfectly willing to perform for her own interest than of the 'nigger work' this labor echoes."[44] Faulkner's casting of Lottie as a black maid also gestures toward the (relatively) free conditions of wage work in Los Angeles that allowed citizens of the South to exercise their labor mobility for the first time. As she reprimands Veda for her attitude toward her mother, Lottie also reminds the girl of her ability to leave the Pierce house:

LOTTIE
What do you mean, scaring your mamma that way?

VEDA
Did it ever occur to you that you can be discharged?

> LOTTIE
> I sure can, thank the Lord. That's one privilege everybody going to need that works where you live. You come in the house now and go to bed. (she goes on) Come on, now.⁴⁵

Lottie is more than a bit-part player here, as she also proves in her most profound scene, when she attempts to console Mildred after the death of her daughter Ray.

> LOTTIE
> (crying)
> I'm going to sing to you. And that's right; you try to let go and cry good. Then you'll feel better.
> > She sings 'Steal Away.' Her voice is good, untrained, clear and simple and pure. She sings the burden, then a verse. As she begins to repeat the burden, the DISSOLVE BEGINS. She stops singing the words and hums, her voice dying away into the end.⁴⁶

This vignette adds depth to an already heartbreaking point in the narrative. But there is more depth yet in Faulkner's particular choice of song. Lottie is singing a spiritual whose thinly coded lyrics originally allude to the underground railroad of antebellum days, but in the Depression milieu of *Mildred Pierce*, they perhaps find their referent in the city-bound migratory activity, gathering speed at precisely this moment.⁴⁷ Faulkner's note in the margin reads "God damn! How's that for a scene?"

Faulkner's Lottie would need to be played by an actor with tremendous gravitas. Although Hattie McDaniel, who had won the best supporting actress award for her role as Mammy in *Gone with the Wind*, might have been a likely choice, instead, Butterfly McQueen, who had played the flighty servant Prissy in the same film, was cast in the role.⁴⁸ During filming, Jack Warner wrote Wald, expressing his concern at the casting decision, and in the end, McQueen was not credited for her work: "Dear Jerry: Reference my talk on the telephone today about Butterfly McQueen, no one can understand what she is saying or what it is all about. It is advisable that she opens her mouth when she talks so you can understand her. Also be sure that Mike gets wild lines of the important dialogue she says immediately. Jack Warner."⁴⁹ This difficulty probably played a part in the editing out of Faulkner's lines, even if his idea to make the maid a black character was retained. In any case, it is surely no coincidence that the commonly occluded African American presence is given its due in Faulkner's screenplay, the southern author more cognizant than most of the trajectory of black labor at midcentury. Faulkner, too, was a mobile worker, following a now-familiar path from Mississippi to California in search of secure work. His next project would bring home his role as a migratory writer all the more.

The Big Sleep and the Compson Appendix

From August to October 1944 (and again in December that year), Faulkner worked on an adaptation of Raymond Chandler's hard-boiled 1939 novel with Leigh Brackett (who was many years later the screenwriter on another adaptation of a Philip Marlowe story, *The Long Goodbye* [Robert Altman, 1973]). The first screenplay for *The Big Sleep* roughly followed the same complex plot as the novel, with some notable exceptions, including a far more sadistic ending. General Sternwood, facing a blackmail threat involving his daughter, the reckless Carmen, hires Marlowe to defuse the situation. The case as it stands is fairly open and shut, but Marlowe suspects that Sternwood's other daughter, Vivian, knows more than she is letting on. The fact that Shawn Regan, Sternwood's former detective, is missing doesn't help matters, and it is later discovered that Carmen, whose advances he rejected, has killed him. In the end, Marlowe sees off the threat of gangster Eddie Mars, protecting Vivian (who knew that Carmen was a murderer all along) and ruthlessly allowing Carmen to be killed in the crossfire so that she might pay for her crime (Marlowe merely says that he will have her institutionalized in the novel).

Faulkner and Brackett completed the first temporary screenplay for *The Big Sleep* within eight days in September, but it would be almost two months before they had come up with a second complete screenplay, at which point the Mississippian was reassigned to *Mildred Pierce*. Shuttling between the two films, Faulkner certainly would have noticed the ways in which each approached the domestic sphere and charted the changing roles of women in the postwar years. The working title for Faulkner's *Mildred Pierce* screenplay had been "House on the Sand," a reference to the biblical parable. Although it begins from the stability of the American home, the film also ironizes domesticity throughout and gestures toward restless and transient modes of working-class existence in the postwar years. "In noir," as Vivian Sobchack observes, "a house is almost never a home," and indeed—and even though the scenes of the home are not in a noir register—the more time that Mildred spends transforming the homely space of the kitchen into a place of business, the more the family unit disintegrates.⁵⁰

In *The Big Sleep*, the last vestiges of the home as a site of familial harmony are put to rest: two stifled sisters share a mansion with their antiquated father, a lone detective roams the city with no family or home life of which to speak, and the remaining characters restively occupy transitory spaces like bookstores and casinos. Although excised from the final screenplay, one of Faulkner's scenes demonstrated the absolute fragility of the home, depicting Philip Marlowe's only moment of crisis inside his apartment. The private investigator has just thrown the young and unruly Carmen, who has salaciously sucked on one of his chess pieces, out of his place, but she stands outside knocking at his door. The scene ends on a tense note for Marlowe:

> While the knocking still continues, he kneels at the hearth, lays the delicate chess-piece on it and with a heavy fire-dog hammers the chess-piece into dust, still beating even after the piece has vanished, his blows at last drowning out the sound of the knocking on the door.
>
> FADE OUT⁵¹

Howard Hawks apparently redacted the encounter because he didn't like it; Bruce Kawin asserts that Hawks refused to shift the focus from "male honor" to "female dishonor," and not wanting to weaken his hero, he "dropped any indications of strain on Marlowe's part."⁵² However, it seems that there were more powerful forces at work, and that the ultimate decision to pull the scene came from outside the studio. As Faulkner and Brackett completed their pages, the script in progress was intermittently sent to the Hays office for inspection. Joseph Breen, responsible for enforcing the production code, had problems with several elements of "The Big Sleep" screenplay. These included "thumb sucking," "the liquor and drinking" that were almost ever present, and the shocking original plan for the "cold-blooded murder" of Carmen, whom Marlowe would have dressed up in his clothes and sent unwittingly to be gunned down in his place.⁵³ Faulkner's proposed scene, which included liquor as well as the suggestive sucking of the chess piece, was unsurprisingly removed.

Breen also pointed to a series of "nude or lewd photographs" of Carmen, which he noted would have to be replaced with "some other prop" in order "to get away from the present objectionable flavor of depravity."⁵⁴ In Chandler's novel the blackmail photos show "Carmen sitting in Geiger's high-backed teakwood chair on the dais, in her earrings and her birthday suit," but for the screenplay, "the suggestion that these photos are in the nude is unacceptable," although despite Breen's repeated objection, the images would eventually find their way into the finished film in a more sanitized form.[55] It was put to Hawks that "it would be necessary to show the blackmail photograph of Carmen, in an insert, to make it perfectly clear that there was no unacceptable inference connected with this blackmail racket."[56] But all that was filmed in the end was Philip Marlowe's shocked reaction upon seeing the photographs in question.

In Chandler's novel, the nude photographs of Carmen were originally hidden inside classic literary works housed at Arthur Geiger's bookstore: "A heavy book, well bound, handsomely printed in handset type on fine paper. Larded with full-page arty photographs. Photos and letterpress were alike of an indescribable filth. The book was not new. Dates were stamped on the front endpaper, in and out dates. A rent book. A lending library of elaborate smut."[57] Where Faulkner was the author of high literature turned screenwriter, Chandler had always considered himself a modernist writer with a pulp exterior, who had taken a "cheap, shoddy, and utterly lost kind of writing" and "made of it something that intellectuals claw each other about."[58] In this scene, he showed that the inverse was also true: that at the heart of the most venerable, leather-bound tome the easy pleasures of pornography might hide.

The presence of the blackmail photos in the screenplay certainly seemed to stick with Faulkner even after he had finished work on *The Big Sleep*. Two years later, Faulkner published his "Appendix: Compson, 1699–1945," as a new addition to round out *The Portable Faulkner* (1946). This work was written as a follow-up to *The Sound and the Fury*, which, as Faulkner explained, was like "the first moving picture projector—warped lens, poor light, undependable mechanism and even a bad screen—which had to wait until 1946 for the lens to clear, the light to steady, the gears to run smooth" (*ESPL*, 301). And indeed, in its appropriation of Chandler's trope—scandalous photographs housed within novels—the appendix does seem to depend on cinema in a very literal way.

The piece recounts how Melissa Meek, the Jefferson librarian, "spent the rest of her life trying to keep *Forever Amber*, in its orderly overlapping avatars, and *Jurgen* and *Tom Jones* out of the hands of the highschool juniors and seniors who could reach them down" (*SF*, 1133). In the first of those apparently indecent works, she locates a "photograph in color clipped obviously from a slick magazine" (*SN*, 1:1134) of one who resembles Caddy Compson, "ageless and beautiful, cold serene and damned," with "a handsome lean man of middleage in the ribbon and tabs of a German staffgeneral" (*SF*, 1134). Caddy's brother, Jason Compson, first accepts and then deceitfully denies that this is his sister in the photograph—"Don't make me laugh. This bitch ain't thirty yet. The other one's fifty now." (*SN*, 1:1135). The librarian then eagerly seeks out Dilsey's confirmation—"'It's Caddy!' the librarian said. 'It is! Dilsey! Dilsey!'" (*SN*, 1:1136)—but is met with a less than enthusiastic response, Meek reasoning that Dilsey "*didn't want to see it know whether it was Caddy or not because she knows Caddy doesn't want to be saved hasn't anything anymore worth being saved for nothing worth being lost that she can lose*" (*SN*, 1:1137).

The photograph of Caddy Compson offers itself as a proof of life, but it is just as quickly rejected as it is reclaimed, disavowed in part because of the guilty feelings it arouses in its viewers. The image also has ties to *The Big Sleep* in that it is just as scandalous as Carmen Sternwood's photograph, albeit for different reasons. Earlier, in 1920, Caddy was married to "a minor movingpicture magnate" in "Hollywood, California" (*SF*, 1133), but now she is also implicated in nothing less than the rise of Nazism in Germany. Here and in *The Big Sleep*, the images in question fall under the category of what Garrett Stewart has called the "evidentiary photograph" in film noir, part of the impact of which "derives from its sending the private into circulation as the public."[59] For the Compson family, the private image (even if intended for public consumption in a magazine) becomes a problem only retroactively, given the changed relations between the United States and Germany. For the Sternwoods, the shots of Carmen are inherently shocking, taken in private with the threat of publication hovering over them ever after.

The collapsing of public and private is realized in the screenplay in the most obvious way, rendered as the fear of exposure. It is also reflected in the way that Marlowe conducts his work. In Chandler's novel, as Fredric Jameson has remarked, the work of the detective is conducted all across the sprawling city of Los Angeles. In the course of a single day, Philip Marlowe finds himself in all manner of spaces: General Sternwood's hothouse, the oilfields that are visible from his mansion, Geiger's faux bookstore, the lavish Cypress Club, to the highest and lowest parts of the metropolis. All the while he is hard at work. For Chandler, as Jameson points out, the traditional understanding of "the office" encompassed a much wider variety of social activity than it was normally understood to do, making sense of a vast and disparate cityscape by rendering all of its locations as potential workspaces.[60] Even Marlowe's own apartment can become an extension of his office, as working life colonizes the entirety of the detective's world. Private life is surrendered to the call of public duty, and the domestic sphere is invaded by clients, or at least by the problems they bring to the detective's doorstep.

For Marlowe as for Faulkner, the office was everywhere. At this point in time, Faulkner was working mostly on the Warner Brothers lot. But even though he requested a three-month suspension of his contract in December 1944, he continued to work on the script, and his final contributions to *The Big Sleep* were actually penned, as he confirmed in a letter to the studio, when he was "on his way back to Mississippi."[61] Portions of the script were sent from Arizona, New Mexico, and Oxford, with those places typed at the top of the sheets so as to corroborate his story: "With grateful thanks to the studio for the cheerful and crowded day coach which alone saved him from wasting his time in dull and profitless sleep."[62] In the few scenes that Faulkner rewrote on his way back to Oxford, Marlowe returns to the Sternwood house after killing Canino (one of Eddie Mars's henchmen), and demands to speak with the general. He has a tense exchange with Norris, the butler, before being granted entry and then says that although he knows the general does not want him to continue his search for Regan, he is planning to do so anyway. But the general surprises Marlowe by suggesting he should search for Regan. Marlowe then encounters Vivian, who tries to convince him that she killed Regan herself, but it's a ruse he sees straight through.

Unbeknown to Faulkner, Leigh Brackett was rewriting the same scene on the same day, a duplication of labor that probably happened because Faulkner was away from the studio at the time.[63] Although similar in many respects, Faulkner's version of the episode is concerned less with the potential relationship between Marlowe and Vivian and instead privileges the relationship between Marlowe, the general, and Norris, whose conversation centers on the case. As the detective tells his employer:

MARLOWE

In my business, a man's neck is his ordinary stock in trade—that's what he sells.[64]

In the next scene, Vivian picks up on Marlowe's keen work ethic, suggesting that if he were truly obsessed with his job alone, then he would follow her orders as his new employer:

VIVIAN
You keep on telling me how all you're doing is earning a living. All right. I'll pay you to let it alone. I'll pay you a thousand dollars—[65]

Vivian, more than anything, disrupts the triad of former soldiers, first obstructing and then lying to the detective. This was certainly in keeping with Chandler's novel, where the detective knew better than to become involved with the elder Sternwood daughter. But at the studio, there were other matters to consider. Bogart and Bacall had worked well together in *To Have and Have Not*, and it was clear that Warner Brothers needed to capitalize on their dynamic. But in her next film, Bacall had taken a misstep, featuring poorly in *Confidential Agent* (Herman Shumlin, 1945). Now to make matters worse, Martha Vickers (who played Carmen) was threatening to steal the show from Bacall in *The Big Sleep* with her own edgy performance. When it was decided that Bacall's career needed a boost, the release date was put back so that the balance between the two female actors might be righted. Principal photography on the film finished up in January 1945 and, while a version of *The Big Sleep* was screened to U.S. forces in the Pacific theater in April 1945, the final cut was only released in August 1946. This allowed for the shooting of "two new sultry sequences" featuring Bogart and Bacall (not Vickers) and saw more than ten minutes of extraneous footage cut out.[66] While there are notable differences between the two versions of the film, the late push to jumpstart Bacall's career may have also explained why Brackett's and Faulkner's revisions in late 1944 were not incorporated into the script.

Jules Furthman was asked to step in a fortnight later and trim some of the fat so as to accelerate the story. Brackett recalls the change: "Furthman came into it considerably later, because Hawks had a great habit of shooting off the cuff. He had a fairly long script to begin with and he had no final script. He went into production with a 'temporary.' He liked to get a scene going and let it run. He eventually wound up with far too much story left than he had time to do on film. Jules came in and I think he was on it for about three weeks, and he rewrote it, shortening the latter part of the script."[67] Included in these revisions was the scene between Vivian and Marlowe at the Sternwood mansion, to which Furthman added much of the dialogue between them that was included in the finished film. Contrary to Brackett's and Faulkner's approaches to the scene, Furthman removes Sternwood and Norris, manipulating the arrangement of characters to capitalize on the budding Bogart-Bacall dynamic. Furthman also changes the setting from the Sternwood house to the road, as Marlowe drives Vivian to Geiger's house, which makes sense in the final cut. After all, as Kawin points out, Hawks would later forget the intricacies and fault lines of the quest in *The Big Sleep*, and instead focus on simply finishing his film, "directing the picture for speed."[68] Marlowe's car is an abstract space in which he and Vivian can be alone and that, unlike his apartment, allows the narrative to progress at high velocity:

VIVIAN
Why are you driving so fast?

MARLOWE
I've got to get you somewhere pretty quick. Unless you think you can explain everything to Eddie.[69]

In a sense, Furthman's revision suggests the ubiquity of the office all the more, since even the road could turn into a potential workspace. But at the same time, the car in the new scene demonstrates the potential to rapidly accelerate the plot and carves out a private space for romance. Above all else, here we can see the studio's determination to bring Bogart and Bacall together on screen, a task that would require fewer professional discussions between Marlowe and his employer. In place of Faulkner's revisions, written in the "crowded day coach" en route to Mississippi, Furthman's rewrites allowed the narrative to unfold as the two leads drove on together in the intimacy of the automobile.

Stallion Road and "Knight's Gambit"

After sending off the final pages for *The Big Sleep*, Faulkner was back home in Oxford by the end of the year—even if he still felt that he was "morally and spiritually in Hollywood" (*SL*, 187).[70] In March 1945, the studio extended the three-month suspension of his contract he had secured in December for a further three months.[71] Back at Warner Brothers in June, Faulkner commenced solitary work on a screenplay for *Stallion Road*, Stephen Longstreet's novel of life on a California ranch, which the studio had bought even before it was published.[72] Longstreet, whom Faulkner had met years before in New York, had originally put him in touch with his problematic agent, William Herndon, and so it was a rather neat coincidence that the same author would give Faulkner the material for his final Warner Brothers assignment. But there was evidence that Faulkner was trying to make the most of his stay in Los Angeles, as he found time to write after his days at the studio. In a letter to Estelle, Faulkner wrote of his first complete screenplay for *Stallion Road* but also made mention of two other projects. One was a "50 page story" written together with Alfred Bezzerides over a couple of weekends, which they hoped to sell to Hawks. Faulkner had also spent "two weeks working at night and on weekends fixing up a picture for Ginger Rogers" (*SL*, 194)—although there is nothing in the studio records to confirm it, the dates suggest that he may have been working sub rosa over at RKO on *Heartbeat* (Sam Wood, 1946), which was the only film Rogers shot during Faulkner's stay. In addition, he was still finding some spare time for *A Fable*. Bezzerides would later report that Faulkner would wake at four o'clock in the morning to work on his novel for four hours before reporting for duty at the studio in Burbank to work on *Stallion Road* for the remainder of the day.[73]

Although the novel was still almost a decade away from completion, this was certainly a productive period for screenwriting. By the beginning of September, Faulkner had completed a treatment and two full-length screenplays on his own. Longstreet's *Stallion Road* is narrated by Henry Purcell, a writer loosely based on Longstreet himself, who has ventured to California from the East for screenwriting work and is about to begin work on what he believes will be "a very important novel."[74] Purcell stays with rancher and veterinarian Larry Hanrahan and becomes a part of the life of Stallion Road in a number of ways. The two soon find themselves infatuated with the same woman, Fleace Teller, and the romantic struggle plays out against a backdrop of horse breeding and ranch life, culminating in an outbreak of anthrax that threatens horse breeders across the Sierra Madres. Larry finds a cure for the disease, but refuses the advances of a U.S. Army officer who wishes to appropriate it for the exclusive use of the cavalry. In the process, Larry contracts anthrax himself and dies. Purcell honors his memory by staying on the ranch and writing the story of his life.

Faulkner also begins his first version of the story with Purcell's character, although he removed him from the second complete screenplay, an interesting decision, especially since Purcell was a novelist and sometime screenwriter. Various stars had already been announced to play the role before the script was finished, and it was reinstated in the final cut. Initially, Errol Flynn was cast as Purcell alongside Ida Lupino (who would have played Fleace), and there were even rumors of a potential Bogart-Bacall reunion on set.[75] Ultimately, the film starred Zachary Scott (husband of Faulkner's friend Ruth Ford) and Alexis

Smith as two points of the love triangle completed by none other than future president Ronald Reagan. Faulkner's version of the script would have provided even more space for Reagan's Larry, who rather than competing with a male interloper earns the affection of both Fleece Teller (so spelled) and the married Daisy Otis. Longstreet thought the adaptation of his novel was "a magnificent thing, wild, wonderful, mad. Utterly impossible to be made into the trite movie of the period. Bill had kept little but the names and some of the situations of my novel and had gone off on a Faulknerian tour of his own despairs, passions and story telling. Today it could be made as a *New Wave* film."[76]

While these estimations of the screenplay overstate the case (there are certainly remnants of the original storyline, and the script is hardly similar to a New Wave film), perhaps the most interesting aspect of Faulkner's involvement in the project lay in its equestrian focus. Faulkner had always been interested in horses; he had written about them a number of times and had prided himself on his riding ability on several occasions. He later professed to have written *Sanctuary* because he "wanted to buy a horse," and he had purchased his daughter Jill a mare—"Lady Go-lightly"—when she and Estelle came to stay with him in East Hollywood in the summer of 1944.[77] For Faulkner, as for the protagonist of Longstreet's novel, there was a stubborn nostalgia for the horse, even if it had been superseded by the tractor and the automobile. In the novel, Larry Hanrahan is confronted with a major decision: whether to persist with the expensive practice of horse breeding on the ranch or to pursue his career as a veterinarian, potentially for the military. Larry remains uncertain, even as he faces the truth:

> "Nobody wants stud stallions any more. Stallion Road isn't the place it was when Pops or Gramp were alive. Nobody on the range is making money breeding horses."
>
> "Mrs. Major Alcott is."
>
> "That's different. She breeds cheap horses for people who want to keep one horse for the family, on a ten-acre ranch designed by Metro-Goldwyn-Mayer."
>
> "Why don't you sell out the whole stud, the mares and colts, and stick to veterinary?"
>
> "Gramp would turn over in his grave. I'm tradition in these parts, Henry, and like all traditions I'll go down with all flags flying."[78]

Larry Hanrahan stubbornly sticks to tradition, but a tradition that is in some ways future oriented. In the changed and changing postwar world, he offers the continuation of a breed for posterity: unlike the mules that populate the Yoknapatawpha fiction and who are unable to breed, the purpose of the stallion is to prolong the existence of its species, even if only for the spectacle of cinema. In this discussion of the future of horse breeding, the reference to MGM here may not have been merely incidental. As Jerome Christensen points out, with reference to a number of films made by MGM during the war years, there was a near-obsession at the studio with "the bonded themes of breeding and grooming," drawing connections between human reproduction and animal husbandry. In the movie *Thoroughbreds Don't Cry* (Alfred E. Green, 1937), for example, Christensen argues that there is more at stake than merely the future of the horse breed. The film is also concerned about the future of its own "stable" and the new child stars who had begun to populate it, as the presence of the young Mickey Rooney might suggest. Indeed, the eponymous thoroughbred here referred not to the horse but to its owner.[79]

Faulkner himself was interested in the relationship between breeding and grooming and explored that relationship in the budding attraction between Larry and Fleece. When one of Fleece's mares seems close to death, Larry revives her. But in this early scene, he is clearly just as interested in the mare's owner: "She exits. Larry looks after her. As though without knowing he is doing it, he stands stroking the mare's neck. He gives the idea that he might be stroking Fleece's hair. When Fleece is gone, he seems to recover, realize what he is doing, that he was actually stroking Fleece's hair, reacts, turns takes up his bag and begins to open it."[80]

Faulkner also took up the suggestive intersections between grooming and romantic love in "Knight's Gambit," his own story about horses that he had been working on intermittently since 1942 and one he revisited again just after he had finished on the screenplay for *Stallion Road*. It was "about a man who planned to commit a murder by means of an untameable stallion" (*SL*, 203). Both *Stallion Road* and "Knight's Gambit" are concerned with the future of horses in the nation: with their breeding, their uses for leisure and labor, and their health. Both worry about the fate of the species, especially around wartime and make mention of the uses of horses in the military. And just like Longstreet's novel, "Knight's Gambit" briefly considers the difference between sites of honest rural labor and mere simulations of an agrarian past: at the beginning of the story we read of the improved property of the Harriss family, which has matured from "just another plantation" into "something a little smaller than a Before-the-War Hollywood set" (*KG*, 135).

In the most obvious sense, the story revolves around the thwarted murder of Captain Gualdres, an Argentinian interloper who poses a new oedipal threat to Max Harriss after the death of his father by seducing first his sister and then his mother. The murder plot is contingent on Max placing a wild stallion in the Harriss stables, which Gualdres was intended to unwittingly rouse, leading to his brutal demise under its hooves. But that very plot also seems to depend, at least symbolically, on the presence of the horse on the plantation not as a draft animal but as a tool of leisure and murder, which in turn would seem to depend on the survival of the "modest cotton-plantation" (*KG*, 152) that the Harriss patriarch cared little for after it was bequeathed to him; he initially makes an agreement with "Negro tenants" to manage it (*KG*, 152) but later rents "all the farm-land in one lump to a man who didn't even live in the county" (*KG*, 153). Finally, that man himself "brought his own Negro farmhands, and so even the Negroes who had lived and dropped their sweat on the old place longer than she was old, were gone now" (*KG*, 153). At the same time, "horses and mules taken last night from the plow" pass by "gangs of strange men with enough machinery to have built a highway or a reservoir," who have come to "disc and terrace the old fields once dedicated to simple profit-producing corn and cotton, and sow them to pasture grass costing more per pound than sugar" (*KG*, 154).

As mules and horses are slowly sent into retirement by the machines, a new class of leisure animal will come to replace them, mounted by polo players, those "who couldn't ride a horse except in shiny boots and special pants" (*KG*, 157). The black farm hands must also be differently employed, lest they become useless in the county. Accordingly, "two Negro boys" now lay a "trail of torn paper" between each jump in a series, utilizing the practically outmoded equipment of the sharecropper—"two long cotton-pickers' sacks"—for their task (*KG*, 157–58). The mules are now "spanned and tripled," joined in the field by "five- and ten-ton trucks" and "tractors," while the horses, though they still exist as sports equipment, have been shorn of their power on the battlefield by the machinery of modern warfare. Toward the end of the story, Captain Gualdres enlists in an utterly redundant "1942 United States Army cavalry regiment" and exits the story "going to war against Germans not because they had ruined a continent and were rendering a whole race into fertilizer and lubricating oil, but because they had abolished horses from civilised cavalry" (*KG*, 242–43).

The prospective murder weapon itself was "a stallion of first blood and pedigree but absolutely worthless" that had "a hatred for anything walking upright on two legs" (*KG*, 201). For anyone unaccustomed to its behavior—and even to a practiced equestrian like Gualdres—the horse would pose "a considerable worry" (*KG*, 211). Indeed, only the ingenuity of Gavin Stevens and his nephew Chick preserve the Argentinian's life. When mules come to supplement the tractor in the process of sowing and harvesting cotton and horses suddenly disappear from the front lines of battle courtesy of the tank, the use value remaining to horses, the story suggests, is cashed out either in leisure pursuits or in schemes leading to death. The punishment for the intending murderer, Max Harriss, is also tied to this economy of obsolescence, as Stevens ensures that he will enlist, sending him off to fight in the global battle.

Although Faulkner had completed the story as early as 1942, "Knight's Gambit" was initially rejected as a commercial piece of writing. When it was finally published in 1949, the story likewise appears to have renounced the market, with Faulkner's revisions to it constituting what Michael Grimwood has called "a virtual repudiation of the commercial origins of the first five stories" in the collection of the same name.[81] But in so doing, Faulkner in "Knight's Gambit" is able to embrace the onset of modernity in the South, refusing to restrict himself to the more traditional, closed narratives of the five other detective stories that precede it in the collection. Part of this turn, at least, owes itself to Faulkner's *Stallion Road* screenplay. In adapting Longstreet's novel, Faulkner was working through nothing less than the decline of agriculture, the end to the isolation of the rural, and the separation of the old from the new. Horse breeding and grooming had been taken over by MGM, and the plantation now seemed like a Hollywood set. But it was a historical shift now impossible to resist. The South in Faulkner's work, both for the page and for the screen, would never be the same, and although Hollywood might (still) stand accused of perpetuating myths of "magnolias and mockingbirds," at least some of the screenwriting Faulkner completed at Warner Brothers would permit him to think in more contemporary ways about the advance of modernity in his region.

Leaving Hollywood

Although the "Stallion Road" screenplay is registered as Faulkner's last formal contribution at Warner Brothers in the 1940s, it would be another few years until he was able to fully extricate himself from his contract with the studio. There were legal threats from his former agent, William Herndon, as well as concerns over unpaid income tax from 1944, and a letter from Faulkner to Jack Warner trying unsuccessfully to put an end to their relationship. "I feel that I have made a bust at moving picture writing," he wrote, "and therefore have mis-spent and will continue to mis-spend time which at my age I cannot afford" (*SL*, 204). Although his request to be released from the studio was denied, Faulkner was at least given indefinite leave to complete work on *A Fable* before returning to California to see out the rest of his contract (an arrangement that would not pan out as planned).

Although not tethered to the studio in the latter half of the decade, Faulkner did contribute to a number of different properties. In 1946, he wrote a synopsis titled "Continuous Performance," a farcical story about a married couple who are torn apart by the wife's taste for extravagant purchases. In an astute piece of casting, Faulkner had suggested that either Cary Grant or Fred MacMurray play the part of the long-suffering husband, Henry, but ultimately nothing would come of it. "I am sending you today a 40 page synopsis, movie idea. A part of it belongs to another man, who will agree to whatever I do. He says it is rotten, has no chance of sale" (*SL*, 227). Indeed, Tom Reed, the author who had the initial idea for the story, was right, and the "shaggy dog" script failed to sell.[82]

With this screenplay it seemed as though Faulkner was planning to mount a covert assault on Hollywood, whereby he would "go back to the coast, stay away from Warner, and earn some money under the rose" (*SL*, 229). However, it appears that he only ever revisited Los Angeles in 1951, and it is more likely that he undertook some work for Warner Brothers at home in Mississippi. Earlier in March 1943, he had completed a thirty-eight-page treatment with the title "Deep Valley," but he would not take it any further since he was moved over to "Country Lawyer" after that. However—and although there are no records to confirm it—according to *Deep Valley* director Jean Negulesco, Faulkner was hired again on the picture in 1947 to write some additional dialogue, just before it was released.[83]

In the same year, it seems that Faulkner also had a hand in an adaptation of Ben Hecht's story "The Shadow." This is a strange tale about a magician, the "marvelous Sarastro," who seeks revenge on his brother for the mistreatment of his wife. An unproduced screenplay for "The Shadow" dated October 24, 1947, was written by Ivan Goff and Ben Roberts, who had together written the Broadway play *Portrait in Black* and would go on to write the screenplay for *White Heat* (Raoul Walsh, 1949).[84] But there are also thirty-two manuscript pages written by Faulkner that feature characters from the story (although they are untitled). It is unclear whether all three writers collaborated on this property, and the pages that are available only represent perhaps one third of the entire script. In the Faulkner screenplay, Sarastro is married to Anna, who is blind. His fellow magician (and possibly brother) Rico is a malevolent figure, who for an unknown reason is resolved to murder Anna. Although there are some menacing scenes in which Rico lingers around Anna with a noose, it appears that she and Sarastro are safe in the end. Perhaps even more interesting, however, is the fact that a number of pages of the screenplay are printed on the rectos of manuscript pages from *A Fable* (this is a practice that Faulkner would repeat with "The Left Hand of God" and *Requiem for a Nun*).[85] Indeed, it was in 1947 that Faulkner had finally committed to writing *A Fable* as a novel rather than a screenplay, and he was constantly sending pages of his work to Robert Haas at Random House. At the same time, he was still concerned about his contract with Warner Brothers, from which he was "on leave only to write this particular book" (*SL*, 257), and he wondered if Jack Warner would allow him "to come out for one specific job, consultations if possible, a quick treatment" (*SL*, 253).

A two-page synopsis written for Howard Hawks in the following year shared some of *A Fable*'s concerns about unbridled technological advancement, although from comments that Faulkner made about the project, they would have formed the background to a romance plot. In "Morningstar," adapted from a science fiction story by Robert Spencer Carr, a rocket falls to Earth, carrying a Venusian beauty.[86] She meets a scientist named Zweistein (no doubt after the Nobel prizewinning physicist, Einstein), who desires to know more about the state of scientific progress on her home planet: "He is fatherly, wise, extracts information (some of which he has already divined) of her home: a place where war is not known, etc., where science is used for man's happiness, etc. He describes as in a parable this world where science has built 100 storey houses, only for men to hate and starve and suffer in, 300 mph transport only for men to travel 1000 miles in 3 hours to trim each other in slick deals for money, atom bombs to destroy women and children with. Now he wants to explore the secrets of space not to fix just another collection of armed outposts against aggression, but to elevate man, improve the universe as you do horse strains" (n.p., WFFC). Writing in June 1948, Faulkner told Hawks that "we will bring into the story a character something like the one Cary Grant played in *The Bishop's Wife* only ours is a human being." He also mentioned a plot device Hawks had used in *Ball of Fire* (1941).[87] Here, Faulkner showed a familiarity with contemporary cinema, and *The Bishop's Wife* (Henry Koster, 1947), in which Grant plays an angel, might have proved a useful model for his own fish-out-of-water story in "Morningstar," had it ever been produced.

Finally, a few months before *Intruder in the Dust* was published, Warner Brothers and Cagney Productions (an independent company started by James Cagney and his brother in 1942) both showed interest in purchasing the rights to the novel. However, it was sold to MGM in July 1948, and was made into a film directed by Clarence Brown in 1949. Shot in Oxford, Faulkner reported that there was "much excitement" in the town (*SL*, 286), and he later remarked that it was "a good picture, I think" (*SL*, 294). And although it is less than certain, he may have had some very little input on the screenplay by Ben Maddow, as Regina Fadiman has argued.[88] In Faulkner's mind, the release of the film also absolved him of his guilt for the way he had conducted himself at MGM back in 1932. He wrote Sam Marx at the studio, admitting that "I have felt that accounts between me and MGM were not at balance, and my conscience hurt me at times. But since seeing Clarence's 'Intruder in the Dust' here last night, the qualms have abated some. I may still be on MGM's cuff, but at least I am not quite so far up the sleeve" (*SL*, 293). Free from MGM, and effectively free from Warner Brothers, Faulkner's screenwriting career was still not yet over.

CHAPTER 6

Stage Play and Screenplay

Requiem for a Nun and "The Left Hand of God"

Aside from early reviews of plays by Edna St. Vincent Millay and Eugene O'Neill, Faulkner's major foray into theater was *The Marionettes* (1920), one of his first publications.[1] Drawing on the tradition of the commedia dell'arte, the play follows the stock character Pierrot and his seduction of the virgin Marietta, a romantic affair in keeping with the sentiments of the author's early prose. But Faulkner did not persist with the form: indeed, not only would he give up stagecraft in favor of prose, but as Richard Godden points out, the comical figures of his early play would later wind up in *If I Forget Thee, Jerusalem* as mere "show puppets" who are "blasted with syphilis, and being bred by Charlotte for magazine covers."[2] His early experiment in theater was lovingly written in longhand and made available only in a small artisanal print run of six copies for close friends, but when the marionettes reappear in *If I Forget Thee, Jerusalem*, they are completely caught up in the world of shop-window commodities. Abandoning the stage for its even more popular relative, Faulkner thereafter followed the more lucrative trail of the screenplay through most of his career.

But the relationship between cinema and theater in Faulkner's work was always more intertwined than these remarks would suggest. For example, even before it was to become *The Story of Temple Drake*, the rights to Faulkner's *Sanctuary* were acquired by a new theatrical firm, Walker Towne. "Rehearsals start next week, I hear" (*SL*, 53), he wrote Estelle, but, although scheduled for the 1932 season, the play was never produced.[3] And while at Warner Brothers, Faulkner had considered adapting Fitzgerald's short story "The Curious Case of Benjamin Button" (1922) for the stage, but even that motion was raised with the intention of creating a product viable for Hollywood consumption: "I wish I could buy the option myself now," he wrote Harold Ober. "I would make the play first, then sell to the movies" (*SL*, 169). After almost two decades in the studio system, a return to playwriting seemed unlikely for Faulkner. But as I suggest in this chapter, his experience in the studio system actually encouraged Faulkner to engage with theater in a more challenging way, allowing him to think about the shifting destinies of fictional characters between stage, page, and screen. And with *Requiem for a Nun* (1951), a novel that contains three dramatic acts, he also thought keenly about the fate of his characters as they migrated across different media.

In *Requiem* he reintroduces characters that had appeared elsewhere. In particular, Gavin Stevens, who had already made his mark in *Go Down, Moses*, *Intruder in the Dust*, and *Knight's Gambit*, makes an encore. But while Stevens had become something of a Yoknapatawpha fixture by this point—and, indeed, sustained Faulkner's interest for the rest of his career—Temple Drake's arrival back in the fictional county is quite a momentous one. While its prose preambles take in the entire history of Jefferson and its surrounds, the reading plays in *Requiem for a Nun* pick up where *Sanctuary* left off, exploring Temple's eventual marriage to Gowan Stevens, her reliving of the trauma of the earlier novel, and the murder of her baby at the hands of her black maid Nancy Mannigoe. Reflecting on the decision to pursue his infamous early novel in a sequel, Faulkner had wondered, "What would be the future of the girl? and then I thought, what could a marriage come to that was founded on the vanity of a weak man? What would be the outcome of that? And suddenly that seemed to me dramatic and worthwhile" (*FU*, 96). While he remained interested in the characters that first appeared in *Sanctuary*, Faulkner had always seen the novel as being conspicuously implicated in the world of commerce, as a "cheap idea . . . deliberately conceived to make money" (*ESPL*, 176). It would fall to *Requiem* to make something honorable of the earlier work.

The title had come to him as early as October 1933, when he wrote a short story featuring Gavin Stevens having a consultation with a black couple, "the woman's throat bandaged," bringing to mind the events of "That Evening Sun" (1931).[4] But the novel as it stands only really got going in the early months of 1950, when Faulkner began collaborating with a young protégée, Joan Williams, on the play scenes of *Requiem*. "You can begin to work here," he wrote. "This act begins to tell who Nancy is, and what she has done. She is a 'nigger' woman, a known drunkard and dope user, a whore with a jail record in the little town, always in trouble" (*SL*, 298). The work would change considerably over time, but here in embryo (written on stationery from the Hotel Algonquin in New York) was the story of *Requiem*, "not only a few pages of play, but (as I see it now) a kind of synopsis of it" (*SL*, 299). To the short story was added the play, and the whole was reconstituted as a novel, with three prose preambles describing the changing face of Yoknapatawpha and three dramatic acts corresponding to the dramatic events of Temple's life. But in early 1951, enter stage left: Hollywood.

When Faulkner had nearly completed work on *Requiem*, he was called away by Howard Hawks to write a screenplay based on *The Left Hand of God*, a novel by William E. Barrett. The director had acquired the rights under his own production company, Winchester Pictures, as part of a three-film deal with RKO—a studio neither he nor Faulkner had worked for since his failed efforts with *Gunga Din*—making it a quasi-independent feature. The narrative follows an American pilot, Jim Carmody, who, finding himself stranded in China, works as a mercenary for Yang, a local warlord. Carmody, disguising himself as a Catholic priest, escapes and goes into hiding in a remote village, struggling to keep up the ruse even as he falls in love with Ann, a missionary and nurse. Revealed for who he really is, Carmody has a final bloodless showdown with Yang, the pilot successfully gambling his way out of trouble. Although the plot was fairly simple, owing to the fact that its protagonist impersonated a priest, the film quickly came under the fire of the Hays office, so much so that Hawks moved on to other projects. "I understand the Catholic church objected to it," Faulkner later remarked in an interview.[5]

Faulkner may have been unable to find a diplomatic solution to this problem, as he had done for *To Have and Have Not*, but he did make a key modification to the narrative, introducing Hank, Carmody's sidekick who was to take on the responsibility of voice-over narration. The long passages of voice-over dialogue Faulkner wrote for Hank were more notably "Faulknerian" in their syntax than anything he had written before for the screen. Although perhaps a little more constrained than he had been with "Revolt in the Earth," here was Faulkner again writing an independent screenplay, giving free rein now to his tendency toward the lengthy sentence.

Most intriguingly, eleven leaves of the *Requiem for a Nun* typescript share the page with scenes from "The Left Hand of God," often with the designation "F—LH of G" ("Faulkner—Left Hand of God") printed in the upper-left-hand corner, and at other times the screenplay is also superimposed over the draft text of the novel.[6] The material connections between the two are very suggestive, especially so since the contents of both screenplay and novel have certain shared interests—fugitive characters, corporal punishment, and divine justice, to name a few. The two works cross paths in interesting and unpredictable ways, mutually illuminating one another. Before I explore the relationship between these two works, however, it is worth considering some of the major differences between screenplay and stage play and the ways in which each genre is enacted.

Acting for Stage and Screen

In his preface to the third act of *Requiem for a Nun*, Faulkner meditates on Cecilia Farmer, the daughter of the Jefferson town jailer who had already appeared in *The Unvanquished* (as Celia Cook) and as "one of the daughters of the jailer" (N, 4:321) in *Intruder in the Dust*. In her most extended appearance in *Requiem*, Cecilia scratches her name on the windowpane of the town's jail, bidding for her remembrance alongside the more famous historical notables alluded to in the passage. Cecilia's scratched name on the window invites speculation about exactly who the young girl was, and the narrator, refusing to pin down her identity, leaves open the possibility that she might have been just as historically important as "Jenny Lind" or "Mark Twain" or "Maximilian of Mexico" (N, 4:648).

Eleonora Duse and Sarah Bernhardt, the two great ladies of European theater at the turn of the twentieth century, are also comparable to Cecilia in this regard, pitched "among the roster and chronicle, the deathless murmur of deathless faces, the faces omnivorous and insatiable and forever incontent" (N, 4:648). Aside from their exploits in theater, the pair later became known for their appearances on film; intriguingly, Duse and Bernhardt both passed from the stage to the cinema screen near the end of their careers, a move that allowed them to forestall their retirement from the world of acting. And both were excited by the promise of such a move. After her performance in *Camille* (Louis Mercanton, 1911), Bernhardt was full of praise for the new medium: "I never thought . . . that I would ever be a film," she proclaimed, "but now that I am two whole reels of pictures I rely for my immortality upon these records."[7] Duse, meanwhile, both starred in and cowrote the screenplay for *Cenere* (Febo Mari, 1916), embracing the new medium as a chance to reorient her acting style.[8] Composing several other scenarios for potential films, she made sure "to exclude any subject from the usual dramatic repertory" and was pleased to remark on the vital innovation of *Cenere* relative to theater: "Throughout the whole film *I never speak*."[9] However varied their experiences of acting for the camera, the fact remains that, as André Bazin has observed, it is ironically "the cinema that has preserved their bones, fossilized in the *films d'art*."[10]

Just as Cecilia Farmer's signature in *Requiem* indicates "not *might* have been, nor even *could* have been, but *was*" (*N*, 4:648), the "deathless faces" of Duse and Bernhardt, recorded or "fossilized" on film, refuse to fade into the ether but are immortalized for generations to come. And to cement the likeness between the young girl and the older actors, Cecilia's written name conjures not just a voice but the very origins of photographic media: "speaking, murmuring, back from, out of, across from, a time as old as lavender, older than album or stereopticon, as old as daguerreotype itself" (*N*, 4:644). As for the actors, so too for the unknown girl: voice, presence, and the written record of that presence, are in the final analysis augmented by the possibilities of the photographic image, a more definitive method of preservation. As I detail, Faulkner's invocation of the two actors who resisted retirement—plus another who went from stage to screen ("Mistinguette, too, invincibly possessed of a half-century more of years than the mere three score or so she bragged and boasted" [*N*, 4:648])—was not incidental.

Cinema could not preserve the careers, or lives, of every actor who came knocking on Hollywood's door. Tallulah Bankhead, for whom Faulkner had written "Night Bird" and then "The College Widow" while at MGM, was not long for the cinema and returned to the stage shortly after her film debut. If twenty years before he had tried to help a fellow southerner move from stage to screen, now Faulkner was called on to assist another Mississippian—Ruth Ford—to make a move in the opposite direction, with *Requiem* as the conduit. Ford was the sister of poet Charles Henri Ford and was married to Zachary Scott, whom Faulkner had worked with on *The Southerner* several years before. As an actor, she had been a member of Orson Welles's Mercury Theater, starring in his play *Too Much Johnson* (1938), a screwball comedy adapted from an 1894 farce by William Gillette. In a structure that offers some suggestive parallels with *Requiem*, each act of the play was supposed to be preceded by a short, silent film that would introduce the characters and provide a counterpart to the action on stage. The footage—not finished on time, in true Wellesian fashion—would have seen actors like Ford present both on stage and screen during the production.

And indeed, Ford did move between the two throughout her career. Not having much luck in Hollywood, she asked Faulkner to write her a play—in which she would be the lead—a request freighted with more than a little anxiety about her future in show business. Later, as he revised *Requiem* into the play that Ford would indeed star in, Faulkner noted that his friend was "shooting the works on this," even "missing radio and t.v. jobs because her known commitment to the play had removed her from availability in people's minds" (*SL*, 325). Ignoring the financial certainties of the newer cultural outlets, Ford had opted for the tradition of the theater, and it was here that her career would flourish or flounder: the theater, Faulkner mused, was Ford's "last-best-chance to make tops as an actress" (*SL*, 326). The stage had the potential to give Ford what the screen had offered for Duse and Bernhardt: a new lease of life. But what was the difference between these two avenues for the twentieth-century actor? And more importantly, what separated the writing of a screenplay from the writing of a stage play (and in Faulkner's case, the writing of a stage play within a novel)?

The most obvious differences between film and theater acting can be discovered both in terms of production and presentation. In film production, the actor does not perform for an audience, but for the camera. Bankhead, as we have seen, had a voice that was perhaps better suited for the film industry than stage, even if her image was not. But the opposite could also be true, especially in the silent era. Sarah Bernhardt, who was perhaps unaccustomed to performing without an audience, apparently overacted her part when she appeared in *Les amours de la Reine Elisabeth* (Louis Mercanton and Henri Desfontaines, 1912). After seeing the film, John Howard Lawson bluntly remarked that Bernhardt's "ludicrous" performance derived from its inappropriateness for cinema, where "the camera exposed and mocked the gestures that had emotional validity on the stage."[11]

For Walter Benjamin, the film actor is always exiled from her audience, separated by the "mechanical contrivance" of the camera, which becomes a spectatorial surrogate. Because many of the actor's histrionic achievements on film are altered after the fact, with the aid of editing, she is also denied the immediacy of human encounter granted by the stage. Unlike the single event of the stage play, motion pictures are instead "assembled from many individual performances," as the actor's work ruptures "into a series of episodes capable of being assembled."[12] As opposed to an enacted stage play, where the actors follow the script chronologically, film production allows for scenes to be shot in any order the director desires.

The mechanical aspect of filmmaking also brings itself to bear on the screenplay, both in terms of the image and sound of the film it imagines. Mark O'Thomas, while remarking on its similarities with the stage play, writes that "from the very beginning the format of the screenplay was dependent on and determined by technology."[13] The camera dictates the dramatic action of the screenplay even before it makes its bulky presence felt on set, the page clearing sufficient space for the technical object that will make its progression from page to screen possible. As we have seen, Faulkner understood the special exigencies of the screenplay, and he put that understanding into practice in his earliest treatments for MGM, which are conspicuously unlike stage plays in their use of camera angles and effects.

Although the inclusion of camera directions in the scene text might at times prove disruptive in the reading of a screenplay, the camera is also key to its unbounded sense of narrative freedom. Budgets of course constrain the number of shooting locations a screenwriter might suggest, but even the most innocuous changes in scene can have a profound effect on a story. In *Requiem*, both the constraints of the stage and the gaze of the camera determine how the plot unfolds. Faulkner was certainly aware of the impact that each genre would have on his work, and while he presented the dramatic action in the form of a "reading play" (itself another genre altogether), he was conscious of how it would have appeared were it written for the screen.[14] Indeed, the importance of the camera for the screenplay is evident in an early discarded scene from the novel.

In the first act of the published novel, Temple is on holiday in California, where she has fled with her family after Nancy's sentencing. Stevens sends her a telegram from Mississippi, wondering what she would do after Nancy had been hanged: "But where will you go then?" he goads her. Wracked with guilt over her part in Nancy's murder of her child and over withholding this information from Stevens, who suspects she knows more than she has said, Temple returns to Mississippi to save Nancy. But rather than admitting that it was Stevens's remonstrance that compelled her to return, Temple "invent[s] the coincidence" (*N*, 4:532) that her son, Bucky, had uttered the exact same words to her that Stevens uses in his telegram on the day Stevens had written them. This is the lie she uses to go back to Jefferson, where she offers her assistance to Stevens and hopes to appeal to the governor for a stay of execution. It only sounds a minor note in the finished novel, but is important in revealing Temple's potential to bend the truth, and it matters that the lie she tells details action that could only have occurred offstage.

In August 1950, before Faulkner had finalized the scene as it stands, he wondered about how it might appear on film, describing it in a letter to Joan Williams:

> What do you think of this? This is what sends Temple back to Jefferson. If this were film, we could show the scene: a California beach say. But in a play, Temple had probably better tell Gavin (the lawyer) this: she and the little boy on a beach, Temple reading perhaps, the boy with a toy shovel and pail.
>
> CHILD
> Mama, we're a long way from Jefferson now, aren't we?
>
> TEMPLE
(reading)
> Yes, a long way.
>
> CHILD
> How long are we going to stay here?
>
> TEMPLE
> As long as we want to.
>
> CHILD
> Will we stay here until they hang Nancy?
>
> TEMPLE
(reacts now, listening, probably knows what's coming but it's too late to stop now.)
>
> CHILD
> Where will we go then? (*SL*, 306–7)

Here Faulkner hits on the most rudimentary of differences between film and enacted theater: the older craft is subject to spatial restrictions that its successor is not. Importantly, the potential intrinsic to the camera's freedom of movement also permits the taking of certain narrative liberties in the text itself, whereby a false memory could be filmed as a flashback. But if the scene were to be written in this way, it would appear as a factual occurrence, suggesting to the reader that Temple is not the liar she turns out to be.

In the scene as published, Temple tells Stevens about the conversation between her and Bucky on the California beach. As such, the invented "coincidence" is at first convincing because of Temple's dramatic reenactment—we are not privy to any other recounting of the event, and so, along with Stevens, we believe her—but soon enough, Bucky's words are revealed as Temple's own fabrications. In response to his question whether his telegram was the coincidence that moved her to return (*N*, 4:525), she responds:

> TEMPLE
> No. This is.
>   (she drops, tosses the folded paper onto the table, turns)
>   It was that afternoon—the sixth. We were on the beach, Bucky and I. I was reading, and he was—oh, talking mostly, you know—"Is California far from Jefferson, mamma?" and I say "Yes, darling"—you know: still reading or trying to, and he says, "How long will we stay in California, mamma?" and I say, "Until we get tired of it" and he says, "Will we stay here until they hang Nancy, mamma?" and it's already too late then; I should have seen it coming but it's too late now; I say, "Yes, darling" and then he drops it right in my lap, right out of the mouths of—how is it?—babes and sucklings? "Where will we go then, mama?" And then we come back to the hotel, and there you are too. Well? (*N*, 4:525)

In this published version of the same passage, the difference is clear: without the screenplay's camera to film Temple's fantasy in California, the burden is on her to play both her and her son's parts in this flashback, and it is her unconvincing performance that gives the game away to Stevens. Temple is also forced to enunciate the scene text here, leading to an uncertain explanation of Bucky's actions ("he was—oh, talking mostly, you know"). Such faltering speech patterns are common in Temple's dialogue throughout *Requiem*. However, if Faulkner were to have "shown the scene" as though in a screenplay, this particular fabrication would have appeared less strained, as Temple would have had the support of the camera to confirm her invented coincidence, as well as the props and setting necessary to round out the episode.

Later on, Temple does narrate act 2, scene 2, in its entirety in a reenactment, recounting the death of her child at Nancy's hands. But this is a different flashback entirely, wherein Temple narrates the events to the governor and Stevens, while the reader follows them on the page as different characters play out their roles in the reading play. Dramatic dialogue takes place between Temple, Pete, and Nancy, and although the death of the baby occurs offstage, there is no obvious sense in which Temple has lied about any of the events as they happened. Again, it is crucial for the narrative that this scene takes place in this way, as Temple is forced to relive the most horrifying experience of her life for the questionable benefit of Stevens. In these scenes and elsewhere throughout *Requiem for a Nun*, Faulkner demonstrates awareness of the limitations of the stage but also makes deliberate and productive use of those limitations in a way that drives the narrative. But he would soon find himself writing for the camera once more.

"The Left Hand of God"

At the beginning of February 1951, Faulkner returned to Hollywood. He had agreed to work on the script for *The Left Hand of God*, which at that stage was still very much a Howard Hawks project but was eventually directed by Hollywood Ten member Edward Dmytryk in 1955. Meta Carpenter Wilde, whom Faulkner encountered once more during his stay, has suggested that he "did not share Hawks' belief in the property as the basis for a successful motion picture, but he said nothing."[15] However, in a letter to Joan Williams he wrote ecstatically about the "fantastic place, fantastic work, almost worth the 2000 a week they pay me" (*SL*, 312). By all accounts he worked hard, producing a 170-page script in less than a month. His mood was still buoyant just before he left for Oxford on March 4, as he had received a bonus for completing the script within four weeks. Yet he still couldn't resist firing a parting shot at the city from which he could soon distance himself: "This is a nice town full of very rich middle class people who have not yet discovered the cerebrum, or at best the soul" (*SL*, 313). Although seemingly finished with the property, Faulkner would continue to work on "Left Hand of God" back home, finishing up on March 21.[16]

This overtime might be explained by the fact that the script still had to overcome one major obstacle: the objection from the Hays Office to its protagonist masquerading as a Catholic priest. A *New York Times* article confirms that this had already been a sticking point for another studio: Paramount "originally wanted to buy the story but was advised that the Roman Catholic Church would view as sacrilegious any film in which the Sacraments were administered by an imposter."[17] What was being suggested was an imitation of an imitation, with the actor playing Jim Carmody (eventually Humphrey Bogart) conducting a ritual that amounted to nothing less than the making present of the body and blood of Christ. Of course, such an act could only be carried out by an ordained Catholic priest, and so dressing an actor up in the vestments and having him imitate the sacred procedure would be tantamount to blasphemy. Even with the additional revisions he completed in Oxford, Faulkner was unable to find a solution to Hawks's pretend priest, and the director later sold the rights to Zanuck at Twentieth Century–Fox.

Faulkner's screenplay survived, however, and it remains fascinating both in spite and because of its rejection. For while at times it offers a fairly straightforward adaptation of Barrett's novel, it also draws surprising inspiration from *Requiem for a Nun*. Faulkner had written most of his novel when he started writing scenes for the film on the verso pages of his typescript, returning to his habit of reusing manuscript pages as he finished work on his script for Hawks. While most of the recycled pages from *Requiem* derive from the novel's second act, the scenes from "Left Hand" are from both the beginning and end of the script, suggesting that Faulkner was reworking much of his "completed" screenplay.

An early sequence from "Left Hand" in which Hank and Carmody make good on their escape both overlays the text of a scene from *Requiem*'s act 2 in which Nancy and Temple argue before her child is killed and also figures on the back of a page of the typescript from the same act, where Stevens articulates his theory about Temple to the governor. The escape scene does not appear in Barrett's novel: there, the seven-day journey Carmody makes after fleeing Mieh Yang's lamasery is outlined in a number of short pages, and there is little sense of urgency or danger attached to it, incognito as Carmody is now without his beard.[18] Faulkner's rendering of this episode involves Hank's voice-over narration and dramatizes the getaway by adding a landslide that injures Hank's leg.

Faulkner emended at least part of Hank's narration as he wrote, and the changes to the script are worth commenting on. The final passage expresses Hank's concerns that Yang will track the pair down: "Because as soon as Yang found out the next morning that Jim and I were missing, and that the priest's robe was gone too, he would know what had happened, he just didn't know where" (*WFATCF*, 793). Following on from this are the original lines, typed over the top of the *Requiem* manuscript. They further convey Hank's misgivings about Carmody's sudden departure from the compound, and were originally more expansive, suggesting the sidekick's anxiety in his compulsive, repetitive syntax: "I mean, about Yang's new idea for fun and games with the whip, which after all would have been my business, since it was my face Yang aimed to use, and like I told Jim, I'd a heap rather take a whip across it than jump out of that 54 again onto a hundred miles of jagged mountain with nothing on top of it but one thin cloud——." Here, Hank refers to the plane, the Douglas C-54 Skymaster, out of which he and Carmody had to jump. As Carmody later reveals, Hank saved his life by helping to drag him to safety down a mountain, an incident already hinted at in Hank's earlier narration in scene 7. But Faulkner, writing in his own hand, replaced this long sentence with the line that remained in the script: "And still Jim never had told me why he decided to leave when we did, what it was that happened so sudden that we had to pull out practically carrying our shoes in our hands" (*WFM*, 19.2:65). This revision leaves Hank far less vocal in his concerns about Carmody's decision, and the suggestion that corporal punishment would be less disquieting a prospect compared with their previous travails has been eliminated. Additionally, Faulkner's truncation of the line reveals something about his estimations of the voice-over more broadly, which is here reined in from taking one of its more candid turns.

One reason for such an edit might be suggested by the ghostly presence of *Requiem for a Nun*. Revealed beneath the edited lines from "Left Hand"—which are dated "3/14"—is Temple's flashback to the death of her baby, the text upside-down and reversed but still legible. In this passage, which appears to match that in the published novel, Nancy challenges Temple's decision to take her six-month-old daughter with her as she elopes with her lover, Pete, suggesting that instead Temple should "just leave it in there in that cradle; it'll cry for a while, but it's too little to cry very loud and so maybe wont nobody hear it and come meddling, especially with the house shut up and locked until Mr Gowan gets back next week, and probably by that time it will have hushed—" (*N*, 4:598). Temple then threatens to hit Nancy, though Nancy continues to taunt her but is eventually cut off as "Temple makes a convulsive movement, then catches herself" (*N*, 4:599).

Comparing this scene from *Requiem* with the lines from "Left Hand," there is a curious correlation between the two. Both detail plot points in which the major character will make or has already made an escape from their current situation; both characters become or will become fugitives for doing so; and both scenes recount a particular violent threat that is never realized. In "Left Hand," the hint of violence is not realized because it was excised from Faulkner's final draft screenplay. In *Requiem*, although Temple does slap Nancy "across the face" (*N*, 4:596), she doesn't hit her again, and it is in fact Nancy who threatens Temple's children and husband (*N*, 4:599). There is a clear connection between the two texts, insofar as Yang from the script "would know what had happened, he just didn't know where," while Gowan Stevens from the novel, on vacation at the Aransas Pass in Texas (*N*, 4:589), would find out what happened a week later; the first would pursue his escapees, but at Nancy's suggestion, the second may not have done so (*N*, 4:598).

Another page of the typescript setting copy of *Requiem* on which a discussion about theological matters unfolds curiously mirrors a similar conversation on the verso of that page—a concluding scene from "Left Hand." In the episode from the novel (*N*, 4:583), Stevens tells Temple that "God either would not or could not—anyway did not—save innocence just because it was innocent." In the scene from the screenplay, Sigman, the chief doctor and religious skeptic at the village where Carmody and Hank seek refuge, tells the discouraged Ann, whose faith has thus far prevented her from marrying Carmody, that "your church can't meddle in your dreams" (*WFM*, 19.3:259–60). On the manuscript page, Sigman convinces Ann that she is free to abandon her faith in order to go with Carmody, while on the overleaf, Stevens convinces the governor of precisely the opposite: that Temple's "armistice with God" had made her "ready and willing—nay, eager—to suffer at any time" (*N*, 4:583).

In contrast to the way he is characterized in his final appearances in Barrett's novel, here Sigman is an emboldened figure, and religion certainly seems to be on its way out at the story's close. In Barrett's *Left Hand of God*, Sigman does not assert himself so strongly, and there is a sense of melancholy at the end surrounding the romance between Anne (so spelled) and Carmody. She must stay behind at the mission, while Carmody goes on ahead, fairly certain of their future together but despondent and impatient to see her again: "He would not hear Anne's answer before he went away. She was less than fifty yards away from him, yet she was months away. She would follow him as Beryl had followed Dave Sigman and, like Beryl, she would share what he had. He knew that with certainty. Yet tonight there was urgency in him, the urgency that a quiet priest had called emotional risk."[19]

Although the rather thinly veiled "urgency" or "emotional risk" is not mentioned in Faulkner's script, lust is implied in another form. Father Cornelius, the priest who visits the mission to pass judgment on Carmody and Ann, speaks to the nurse of her need to "suffer" for the sins committed by the American pilot, by which he means she should avoid giving into the "urgency" that comes from falling in love:

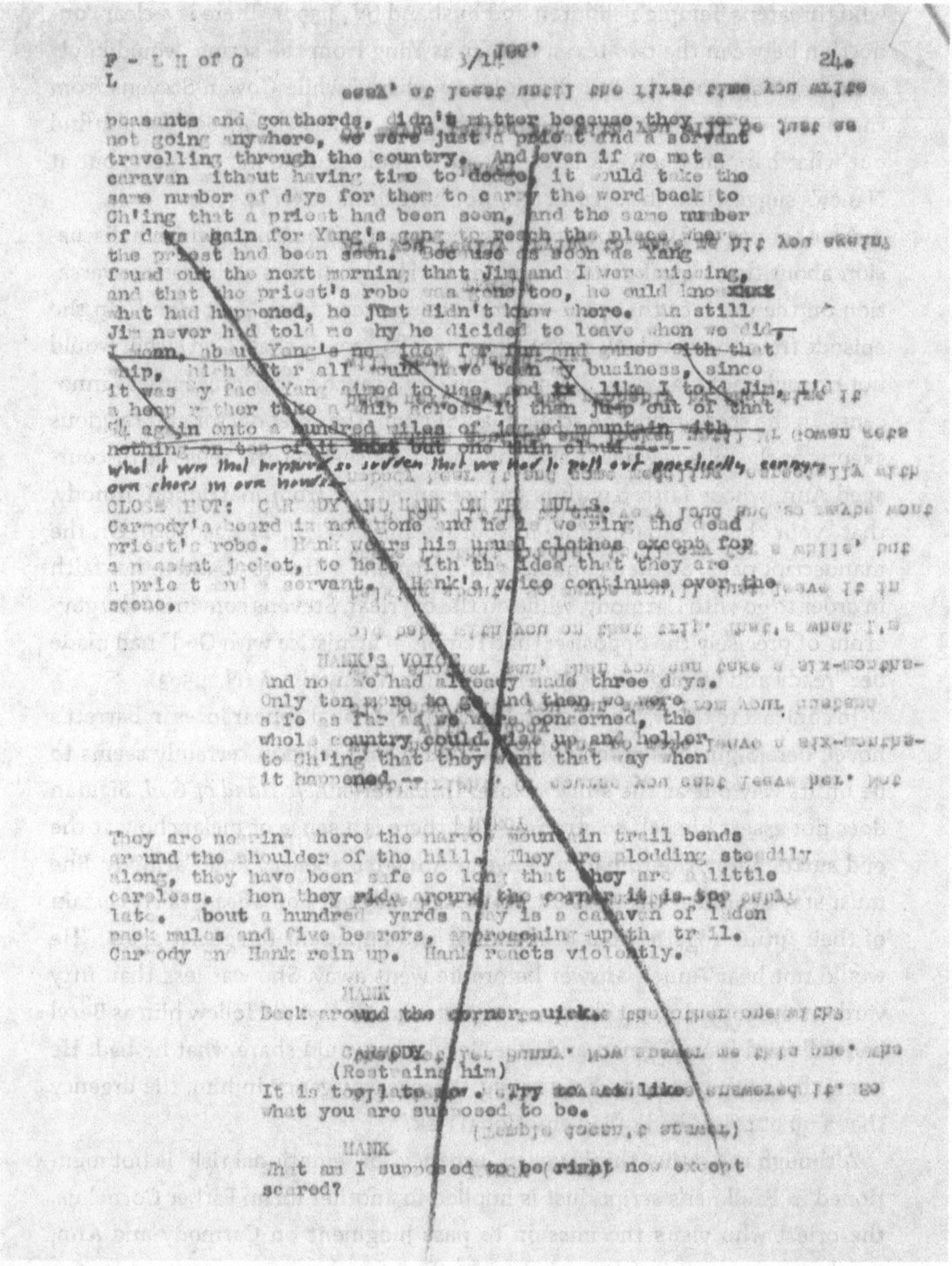
F - L H of G 3/14 24.
L

peasants and goatherds, didn't matter because they were not going anywhere, we were just a priest and a servant travelling through the country. And even if we met a caravan without having time to dodge, it would take the same number of days for them to carry the word back to Ch'ing that a priest had been seen, and the same number of days again for Yang's gang to reach the place where the priest had been seen. Because as soon as Yang found out the next morning that Jim and I were missing, and that the priest's robe was gone too, he could know what had happened, he just didn't know where. Jim still Jim never had told me why he dicided to leave when we did, I mean, about Yang's new idea for him and games with that whip, which after all would have been my business, since it was my face Yang aimed to use, and like I told Jim, I'd a heap rather take a whip across it than jump out of that 'Ch again onto a hundred miles of jagged mountain with nothing on top of it but one thin cloud ----
what it was that happened so sudden that we had to pull out practically carrying our shoes in our hands.
CLOSE SHOT: CARMODY AND HANK ON THE MULES.
Carmody's beard is now gone and he is wearing the dead priest's robe. Hank wears his usual clothes except for a peasant jacket, to help with the idea that they are a priest and a servant. Hank's voice continues over the scene.

HANK'S VOICE
And now we had already made three days. Only ten more to go and then we were safe as far as we were concerned, the whole country could rise up and holler to Ch'ing that they went that way when it happened --

They are nearing where the narrow mountain trail bends around the shoulder of the hill. They are plodding steadily along, they have been safe so long that they are a little careless. When they ride around the corner it is too late. About a hundred yards away is a caravan of laden pack mules and five bearers, approaching up the trail. Carmody and Hank rein up. Hank reacts violently.

HANK
Back around the corner, quick.

CARMODY
(Restraining him)
It is too late now. Try to act like what you are supposed to be.

HANK
What am I supposed to be right now except scared?

FIGURE 10. *Requiem for a Nun*, carbon typescript page, from William Faulkner Manuscripts by William Faulkner. Used by permission of W. W. Norton & Company, Inc.

CORNELIUS

You thought your sin was that you had fallen in love with a priest. You could not confess it because you believed the only priest available was the man you had fallen in love with. But this man was not a priest, so there is no sin in your love. But there is a sin in his masquerade, his sacrilege, and because of your love for him, you must suffer a part of his penance. (WFATCF, 926)

For readers familiar with the ethical quandary at the heart of *Requiem for a Nun*, the end of this passage should ring a bell. For Faulkner's novel dwells on the nature and meaning of suffering: the suffering of Temple's murdered baby, of Nancy on death row, and of Temple herself, who has suffered for eight years with the trauma of the events that transpired in *Sanctuary*. In act 2— the scene that shares the page with this material from "Left Hand"—Gavin Stevens misinterprets one of Christ's parables from the gospel of Luke, as he discusses suffering with the governor: all of Temple's experiences had "shown her that God either would not or could not—anyway, did not—save innocence just because it was innocent; that when He said 'Suffer little children to come unto Me' He meant exactly that: He meant suffer; that the adults, the fathers, the old in and capable of sin, must be ready and willing—nay, eager—to suffer at any time, that the little children shall come unto Him unanguished, unterrified, undefiled" (*N*, 4:583).

As Noel Polk has argued, not only is Stevens's reading completely off the mark, but he himself ignores the suffering that he is now inflicting on Temple and the suffering that his interrogation might bring to Temple's family: the very family that Nancy's suffering was supposed to preserve.[20] Father Cornelius in "Left Hand" also uses "suffer" in the sense of "endure," but unlike Stevens, he does not conflate the two senses of the word, and the suffering to which Ann is condemned seems far lighter than Temple's. These thematic connections offer proof of the intimate relationship between Faulkner's novel and screenplay that the shared space of the drafts literalizes. This empirical, material connection of *Requiem* and "Left Hand" also appears to have worked on the content of each text in this clearest overlap between Faulkner's screenwriting and novel-writing practices. But there is another, less direct way in which the two share common ground, and in this case it is a unique aspect of *Requiem* that develops from one of the screenplay's innovations.

Faulkner's major intervention in William Barrett's narrative was not only the addition of Carmody's sidekick, Hank, but also and more importantly the voice-over that he bestowed on the new character. It is this voice-over that takes the screenplay away from the novel form (intended as it is to be spoken) and directs it toward the screen, where real, living actors could imitate the characters ordained for them. Although atypical in the course of his career, Howard Hawks had used a voice-over just a few years earlier for Walter Brennan's narration in *Red River* (1948). Indeed, two versions of that film were released, another with textual narration that ran almost eight minutes longer.[21] And in what stands as a quasi sequel to that film, the RKO picture *The Big Sky* (Hawks, 1952), the director used voice-over narration once more. This may have been the decision of the studio rather than Hawks's own, but nevertheless, it is a trend in the director's career at this point.[22] This is perhaps why Faulkner opted to begin his screenplay the way he did, with Hank's initial voice-over setting the scene for the action to come. The mode of Hank's voice-over, which we hear in thirteen separate scenes in the film, is what Claudia Sternberg, following Gérard Genette, would call embedded or "homodiegetic," since his words are spoken from a place external to the world of the film, even as he is also a character within that world.[23] Paradoxically, Hank is both integral and peripheral to the plot: an accident that befalls him and prevents the two fugitives from moving on ultimately confines the narrative action to one village, but at the same time, and particularly in the voice-over, Hank is only a "micro-narrator"—although he has a part to play here, he is essentially telling Carmody's story, and though his expository remarks and reflections on their travails might reveal something about himself, they are mostly concerned with his partner.[24]

And indeed, Faulkner initially presents him as a minor character: his introduction to Hank goes nowhere near to suggesting the character who so idiosyncratically delivers his first lines: "The second white man is Hank. He is about the same age is obviously a subordinate though he is loyal to Carmody rather than to Carmody's superior. He is faithful probably has plenty of guts, is a good man to have on your side though you do have to do some of his thinking for him" (*WFATCF*, 761–62). This is not the most flattering entrance. But then, as if from nowhere and in a way that suggests a far more complex character, Hank's voice-over begins, the narration running across several pages:

HANK'S VOICE
China, 1951 right under the edge of Tibet a thousand miles from nowhere and for my nickel you could have had the country and the job both two years ago, and by now even Jim too was going around to that idea. Not that Mieh Yang wasn't a right guy for a Chinese and the dough was right

dough—when you got it that is whenever the dice fell right. Which they did sometimes because at least Yang wasn't a crook since why should he be since he owned the whole country in the thirteen days hard ride. Because even Jim's welcome was wearing out now. Yang took us—Jim—on because he needed and liked tough men and had faith in his judgment of men enough to pick one, so to prove his judgment was right he would have to find tougher and tougher things for Jim to do, and so the tougher the job Jim brought off, the bigger Jim got, until after awhile there would not be any space between Jim and Yang, not enough for just one district thirteen days wide anyway. So me and Jim both probably knew it wouldn't be long now. Though we never thought that morning that this would start it. Because he had done it before: one of the usual Soviet gangs moving in across what Yang called his boundary, deadline. Not that Yang cared anything about Soviets or of anybody except himself, he just did not allow any other gang to chisel into his territory. (WFATCF, 762)

Compared to most dialogue Faulkner wrote for cinema, this is certainly a radical and unexpected contribution. What is immediately striking about Hank's first address—aside from the fact that it belies his initial characterization—is its undeniably "Faulknerian" quality: the use of conjunctions to begin sentences; the way that each sentence worriedly modifies the one before it; the near tautology ("boundary, deadline"). It is the kind of writing that Faulkner was accused of concocting for "Banjo on My Knee," what David Hempstead, the film's second unit director, referred to as "practically blank verse."[25]

More than ever before, "The Left Hand of God" allowed Faulkner to build a character replete with the same anxious habit of qualification that marks the author's narrative voice, broadly speaking. This is partly evident, too, in Hank's desire to cautiously downplay his involvement in the story, narrating for Carmody even as he undergoes many of the same experiences ("Yang took us—Jim—on because he needed and liked tough men"). Hank's extended commentary on the history of the Chinese warlord Mieh Yang's relations with Carmody and himself also constitutes the most unique utterances in the screenplay, which are spoken as though to the audience itself, in the second person. Hank's voice usually stands in for the lack of intensive conflict in a scene—most of his voice-overs accompany long shots or close shots without dialogue and are especially prevalent in transitional scenes involving long journeys. As Hank and Carmody—dressed as a priest—escape Yang's fortress, they are met by a caravan of the warlord's men but continue on, unfazed:

27. CLOSE SHOT. Carmody in front of Hank, riding slowly and gravely and steadily on, not looking back.

CARMODY
(to Hank behind Him)

Don't look back.
Hank's voice over scene.

HANK'S VOICE

Not me. I'd already seen too much. Because that tore it. But at least we had six days—three of them until the caravan reached the lamasery, and the three more it would take Yang to reach the corner. So we might have got away with it even then, only four days after that— (*WFATCF*, 794)

At this point, Hank injures his leg and is bedridden for almost all of the remaining pages. And, perhaps not coincidentally, he has by this stage already spoken his lengthiest narrative asides. Seemingly introduced as an expedient for exposition or maybe even to satisfy the desires of Hawks or RKO for a voice-over narrator, Hank now gives way to Carmody, whose story this truly is. Faulkner has had his fun with the sidekick's protracted sentences and now finds a reason to have him retreat from the story.

Hank's voice-overs in "The Left Hand of God," as imagined by Faulkner, were themselves never incorporated into the filmed version of the story, precisely because they resisted the explanatory simplicity required of them. Although Todd McCarthy suggests that "the results, while craftsman-like, were disappointing—rather dull and sincere, with an abundance of narration," this is also clearly what is most fascinating about Faulkner's script.[26] The bold introduction of Hank might have even piqued Hawks's interest, but once the rights were handed over to Fox, the sidekick and his voice-over seemed completely out of place. When William Bacher (one of the original contributors to the plot of *A Fable*) prepared a treatment for Fox on March 16, 1954, Zanuck commented that "the added character of Hank and his function is entirely unnecessary. He gives value to certain scenes but he also destroys a great many important elements. I think it is entirely wrong to have anyone share or know about the great 'deception'" (*WFATCF*, 757). Where screen dialogue had previously merely weathered Faulkner's peculiar touch, the expository voice-over was more capable of harboring his style. Perhaps partly for this reason, Faulkner's voice-over never survived after the first draft of the screenplay. If there was a potential for blasphemy inherent in an actor administering the sacraments, then more worrying for the studio was the narrator's own authoritative pretense in "Left Hand of God." Hank's voice-over was eventually sacrificed, while Humphrey Bogart's role as a Catholic priest was retained.

Requiem Redux

The role of another medium—radio—is crucial in assessing Faulkner's voice-over for "The Left Hand of God" and the way it seems to have influenced his later revision of *Requiem*. In her important work on film dialogue, Sarah Kozloff demonstrates that along with the novel, "radio was cinema's major role-model for first-person narration."[27] Before it would appear in feature films, the idea of voice-over narration was borrowed from the radio for use in newsreels and documentaries. The radio voice would also suggest itself to other cultural objects, perhaps even altering the way in which first-person narration of prose fiction was transcribed. Indeed, Fredric Jameson, in his work on Raymond Chandler, has asserted the presence of a "radio aesthetic" at the heart of the voice-over common to detective film and fiction. For Jameson, the voice-over in Chandler's prose signals "in advance the closure of the events to be narrated," and it also depends on "the omnipresence of a radio culture" in the 1930s that veered away from the relatively traditional "yarn-spinning" of an author like Conrad and toward a fresh coupling with cinematic images.[28] Moving away from the more exclusive voice of the storyteller to a voice that was premised on mass circulation and presence, radio drove not only the talkies but also the hard-boiled detective novel, which would supplement its retelling of past events with a certain present-tense feeling of "doom and foreboding."[29] From radio to cinema to the novel, this "reproducible oral aesthetic" would continue to spread in the first decade of the talkies, and the voice-over would come to attach itself to a particular star and a particular studio, Orson Welles at RKO.[30] In the late 1930s, Welles had been an instrumental figure in the history of radio narration, making waves with his "The War of the Worlds" broadcast in 1938, and he subsequently made the move to Hollywood. Here he began recording voice-over narration for feature films and went on to direct *Citizen Kane* (1941) and *The Magnificent Ambersons* (1942)—two of Faulkner's favorite films—which both make prominent use of voice-over narration.[31] Each of these films was produced by RKO, a company that had formed out of the merger of a theater consortium and a film studio, brought together under the auspices of the Radio Corporation of America (RCA) in 1928. From the beginning, RKO had had designs on bringing together the best of radio and the movies, and by the time that Welles signed for the company in 1939, this vision—which underlined the continued importance of radio—was still very much alive.[32] But by the 1940s, as Kozloff points out, the voice-over had taken a slightly different turn: it was now ubiquitous on television, which often made use of on-screen narrators, and so cinema no longer had a monopoly on the technique.[33] With RKO in disarray under the leadership of Howard Hughes between 1948–52 and cinema forced to reorient itself to a new postwar media landscape, the voice-over did not seem to enjoy the same positive association with radio that the studio had earlier fostered.[34] In any case, although it was certainly an interesting addition to the film, once "Left Hand" had made its way to Fox, the voice-over was discarded altogether.

When Faulkner returned to *Requiem* in late March, the manuscript was mostly finished. One section he revised, however, was "The Jail," the typescript for which wasn't sent to the printer until the beginning of June, a month after the other two acts.[35] Before he had left for Hollywood, Faulkner wrote his collaborator, Joan Williams, requesting "our act three section," the "two or so pages" of the "scene in the jail" that they had evidently worked on together. At the time of writing, Faulkner considered that he was "getting the mss. in good shape," but he was worried that "this job will interrupt it for a while" (*SL*, 312). Not only was he working on the play scenes for that section but also the prologue. Indeed, as he would soon remind Saxe Commins, "the prose is not at all a prologue, but is an integrated part of the act itself" (*SL*, 316).

Faulkner's work on "The Left Hand of God" did indeed put a brief stop to the progress of the novel, but at the same time, it appeared to push the prologue for "The Jail" section in an interesting new direction that closely resembled the voice-over. Although it has many virtues, perhaps the key oddity of Faulkner's preamble to act 3 of *Requiem* is, as Polk has indicated, that it is the only prose in his entire oeuvre written in the second person.[36] What is equally as interesting is that Faulkner only wrote "The Jail" in the second person *after* he had completed work on Hank's voice-over for "The Left Hand of God."

This is a chain of events that is certainly worth contemplating further. Compare, as Polk does, an earlier version of this section of narrative with the final published version of the same passage:

> The visitor would descry . . . a name and a date; not at first of course, but after a moment, a second, because at first he would be a little puzzled, a little impatient because of his illness-at-ease from having been dragged here into the kitchen of

a strange woman busy cooking a meal; he would think merely *What? So what?* until suddenly, even while he was still thinking it, something would happen: the faint frail illegible meaningless even inferential-less scratchings in the ancient poor-quality glass would seem to move, to coalesce, actually to enter into other senses than vision—— (*WFM*, 19.3:394)

. . .

you will descry to be a name and a date;

Not at first, of course, but after a moment, a second, because at first you would be a little puzzled, a little impatient because of your illness-at-ease from having been dragged without warning or preparation into the private kitchen of a strange woman cooking a meal; you would think merely *What? So what?* annoyed and even a little outraged, until suddenly, even while you were thinking it, something has already happened: the faint frail meaningless even inference-less scratching on the ancient poor-quality glass you stare at, has moved, under your eyes, even while you stared at it, coalesced, seeming actually to have entered into another sense than vision. (*N*, 4:643)

The principal change from the first to the final version of the passage is clear: the impersonal "he," the "visitor," enunciated in the third person, becomes the reader, the "you" addressed in the second person. This intimate mode of address, unlike the narrative voice in the rest of the prologues, interpellates us directly, reaching to the present reader, at over a century's remove, through the power of the direct voice. And, although not exactly the same as Hank's second-person voice-over, it seems more than coincidental that Faulkner made this change to the manuscript just after he had finished "The Left Hand of God." This shift in perspective is extended over several pages of the section, positioning the reader as a visitor to Jefferson: "You, a stranger, an outlander say from the East or the North or the Far West, passing through the little town by simple accident" (*N*, 4:642). The voice that was formerly limited to addressing a "visitor" within the book now goes outside of its jurisdiction, calling beyond the time of the novel's setting—and even its future projection of 1965 (*N*, 4:642)—and on into the present.

This shift to the second person also intensifies the end of the prologue, announcing its kinship less with the pastness of the novel genre and more with the presentness of the stage and also with the vast reach of radio. Here, Cecilia Farmer's spoken proof of life—"*Listen, stranger; this was myself: this was I*" (*N*, 4:649)—which she adds to her inscribed name on the glass, arrives to us at long last, "the clear undistanced voice as though out of the delicate antenna-skeins of radio" (*N*, 4:648). It is a simile, as Spencer Morrison has noted, that maintains "a crucial gap between the actual patter and screams of mass culture and the acoustical clarity aspired to by radio but, in *Requiem*, achieved by the storyteller's voice."[37] In Morrison's view, the narrator here makes a claim for the importance of the voice, not as recorded and transmitted on radio waves from the past into the present but as passed down over time in the form of oral history. While radio might seem to be the more reliable means of transmission, the endurance of Cecilia's story instead bears witness to the power of "knowledge or memory of leisure" (*N*, 4:642). Counterintuitively, those who remember enough to tell it, "instead of dying off as they should as time passed . . . were actually increasing in number" (*N*, 4:642).

But the simile seems to register instability between old and new forms of storytelling rather than the victory of one over the other—not exactly the complete triumph of the radio aesthetic that Jameson sees in the detective fiction of the 1930s, then, but a shift in the recalcitrant South nevertheless. In the prologue to "The Jail," Faulkner is juggling the seemingly irreconcilable balls of technological modernity and classical literary humanism, expertly tying the contradictions of a rapidly expanding American media ecology to the very stuff that resists it: the more traditional representation of Yoknapatawpha as registered in the novel form. In his brief analysis of the section, Julian Murphet points out that this last mention of the radio, which follows hard on the heels of a catalogue of modern mediations across the county, is part of a "wholly unexpected figural chiasmus" that begins several pages earlier. Faulkner begins by invoking "an oak leaf" (*N*, 4:633), its networked veins forming "a natural semaphore," as "the only way to figure forth mediation," but now, Murphet suggests, that image is inverted: "The most effective way of figuring the unmediated, 'undistanced' voice of the living past, to make its 'vast instantaneous intervention' aesthetically comprehensible, is to compare it to the radio voice itself."[38] While here as elsewhere Faulkner rails against the seemingly inevitable drive of the modern world to subsume all that is particular about the South, it is clear that he at the same time relies on such modern devices as the radio for making the past present once more.

The changes wrought in the South usher in not only "a new century and a new way of thinking, but of acting and behaving too" (*N*, 4:634). The radio is only one among many material innovations creeping over the Mississippi horizon between the Civil War and 1951, preceded by the railroad, electricity, and paved roads, and followed by domestic appurtenances like "automatic stoves and washing machines and television antennae" that transform "little lost lonely farmhouses" into "glittering and gleaming" (*N*, 4:638) beacons of the modern. It is not the radio alone that carries Cecilia's voice from 1861 through to the mid-twentieth century, but its sphere of influence is such that it registers more acutely what is happening all over the South, namely, the eradication of local institutions (such as the jailhouse) and their replacement by immense national flows of power and capital and noise: "the county's hollow inverted air one resonant boom and ululance of radio: and thus no more Yoknapatawpha's air nor even Mason and Dixon's air, but America's: the patter of comedians, the baritone screams of female vocalists, the babbling pressure to buy and buy and still buy arriving more instantaneous than light, two thousand miles from New York and Los Angeles; one air, one nation" (*N*, 4:637). Taking charge of the voice, radio takes control of the air, thereby enveloping all and pressuring those that hear its call to consume. And just as radio in Faulkner's account seems inspired by the oak leaf's veins and the twinned grids of road and rail, so too does it stimulate other media to follow its example, colonizing public and private spaces alike.

One such medium was cinema, where the radio voice had also managed to locate itself, appealing to a generation of moviegoers by providing voice-over narration for the images projected before them. Hank's voice-over in "The Left Hand of God" was intended to introduce the viewer to the unfamiliar world of postwar China. But although it went unappreciated in the production process, Faulkner's creation made its way to the South, a radio voice reaching all the way on "delicate antenna-skeins" from Los Angeles. In *Requiem for a Nun*, the second-person voice is similarly designed so as to guide "you, a stranger" through Jefferson's long history. It is a southern voice, to be sure, purpose built to make sense of the Mississippi landscape for the interloping reader and, more particularly, to demonstrate the importance of Cecilia Farmer's scratchings on the glass. But it is a voice that is also a product of California. Here, revitalized by the power of the voice-over with which Faulkner had been recently wrangling in "Left Hand," those statements in the second person preserve a small part of the South, creating out of the name on the windowpane a past that is "never dead. It's not even past" (*N*, 4:535). While Faulkner's version of "Left Hand" was not produced, here something of the screenwriting process is preserved, as words become sounds, become life: "And again one sense assumes the office of two or three: not only hearing, listening, and seeing too, but you are even standing on the same spot, the same boards she did that day she wrote her name into the window" (*N*, 4:645).

CHAPTER 7

Writing for the Small Screen

Faulkner and Television

From November 1952 until August 1953, the German philosopher Theodor Adorno occupied the position of scientific director of the Hacker Foundation in Beverly Hills. He spent his time there analyzing a randomly generated collection of television scripts in a bid to understand the new medium—both in terms of genre distribution and the way in which it addressed its audience—as the latest manifestation of the inexorable culture industry. He would later remark on the difficulty of his research—"the industry does not in the least like to part with its scripts"—but, although it would not prove very fruitful, it still stands as an interesting chronicle of one medium exploring its new horizon of possibilities, ushering in what is now known as television's "Golden Age."[1] Indeed, almost a decade earlier, Adorno had gestured toward the fact that television's star was rising as classical Hollywood's was falling, remarking that the newer medium was even then showing its potential to "force the Warner Brothers into what would certainly be the unwelcome position of serious musicians and cultural conservatives."[2]

Ultimately, Adorno only completed a few short pieces of television criticism, his chief observation being that the stereotypes of the new form were "defended with technological imperatives, such as the need to produce in a minimal period of time a terrific quantity of material."[3] While predictably taking this most modern medium to task, the Frankfurt School critic also notes the similarities between the episodic programs on screen and the form of the short story. Television's commercial structure, whereby airtime was sold in blocks to various sponsors, generated "the dramaturgical necessity of concentrating lengthy and elaborate psychodynamic processes into a half-hour episode."[4] This was clearly a problem for the medium. There was something crippling about shorter narratives in and of themselves, even before they made their way to the screen. "These television dramas," Adorno remarks, "relate to films in a manner similar to the way detective novellas compare to detective novels: in both cases the formal shallowness serves an intellectual one."[5]

We need not take such criticisms too seriously, however, since the ease with which they sweep away everything valuable about both "television dramas" and "detective novellas" itself smacks of a kind of shallowness. Short stories (even those featuring a detective) have always had their defenders: no less a figure than Edgar Allan Poe, reviewing Hawthorne's *Twice Told Tales* (1842), argued that "the demands of high genius" were best fulfilled by "the short prose narrative," primarily since it should contain "no word written, of which the tendency, direct or indirect, is not to the one pre-established design."[6] Over a century later, William Faulkner himself followed suit, insisting that this was indeed the privileged mode of narrative construction. In a letter to his protégée Joan Williams, he wrote that a "short story is a crystallised instant, arbitrarily selected, in which character conflicts with character or environment or itself. We both agreed long since that, next to poetry, it is the hardest art form" (*SL*, 345). It is evident that Faulkner held the short story in high regard, but what was his assessment of television, the newer medium that also traded in compressed narratives?

At the same time as Theodor Adorno assumed his post in Los Angeles, on the other side of the country, Faulkner began his brief foray into television—not as its incisive critic but as a paid employee. In New York, in the spring of 1953, he produced two television screenplays (teleplays) based on his own short stories—"The Brooch" (1936) and "Shall Not Perish" (1943)—for *Lux Video Theatre*, a weekly anthology drama that originated with half-hour installments broadcast live from studios in New York. It was relocated to Hollywood in 1954, and in 1955, the half-hour segments were extended to an hour. A third teleplay, a treatment based on the "Old Man" sections of *If I Forget Thee, Jerusalem*, was written at the same time but never produced. These three pieces joined Faulkner's catalogue of earlier self-adaptations—"Today We Live," "War Birds," and "Revolt in the Earth"—and all depart rather radically from the original publications. A fourth teleplay, titled "The Graduation Dress," was coauthored with Joan Williams earlier in 1952, in response to

Faulkner's suggestion that she "establish [herself] as a television writer or rewriter," completing "hack work, for pay, while you do your own writing" (*SL*, 336). The duo received $500 for their efforts, and it was broadcast, somewhat belatedly, in October 1960 on the CBS program *General Electric Theater* (*SL*, 337).[7]

These works represent Faulkner's first taste of composing for the small screen after twenty years of working in the film industry, and the two modes of writing differed in several important ways. However, his letter to Williams and another he sent from New York as he was writing for *Lux Video Theatre* in March 1953 suggested that working for television on the East Coast was not so far removed from working for film out west. Indeed, Faulkner would cast the teleplay in the same light as the studio screenplay, namely, as a simple interruption to his preferred craft: "Am writing television scripts now, to have money to go somewhere and get at my own novel again" (*SL*, 347). A few months earlier, after completing the "Old Man" treatment, Faulkner was equally dismissive of television's capacity to enter into conversation with his literary work: "I may be obtuse, but I doubt if what a tv screen shows is going to hurt what Random House prints in books, any more that [sic] what movie screens have shown that I did" (*F*, 2:104). His indifference was not just limited to his contributions to the medium but also extended to his own understanding of the television's place in society. Speaking to Gore Vidal—who had adapted both "Smoke" and "Barn Burning" for the CBS *Suspense* anthology—he claimed that "I don't have the television."[8] And with Robert Oppenheimer, who had seen Faulkner's televised version of "The Brooch," he would share the unfortunate opinion that "television is for niggers."[9]

Nevertheless, Faulkner clearly had some interest in television, both as a writer and as a viewer. In late 1952, he reluctantly played a part in a seventeen-minute program in the *Omnibus* series, focused on his life at home in Oxford, Mississippi. Sponsored by the Ford Foundation, *Omnibus* aimed to bring awareness of various social, cultural, and political issues to a mass audience and offered intimate portraits of figures such as Orson Welles, Leonard Bernstein, Frank Lloyd Wright, and now Faulkner.[10] For his shoot, which he told Joan Williams offered a different perspective on the "history of my apocryphal county" (*SL*, 340), Faulkner had to reenact his being notified of receiving the Nobel Prize and his delivering the commencement address at his daughter's high school.

A few years later, a well-received NBC telecast of the Dilsey section of *The Sound and the Fury* fetched the author $3,500.[11] Just before it aired, Faulkner

FIGURE 11. *William Faulkner* (*Omnibus*, December 28, 1952)

sent a comment on the program to Harold Ober, evidently in order to clear up his views on the adaptation: "CORRECTED QUOTE STORY CHANGED FROM ONE TO ANOTHER MEDIUM BOUND TO LOSE SOME MEANING THOUGH MAY GAIN COMPLETELY NEW SIGNIFICANCE. WHICH YOU LIKE DEPENDS WHERE YOU STAND. THIS MAKES TV VERSION MORE INTERESTING TO ME QUOTE. FAULKNER" (*SL*, 389). And although he refused to buy a television set, Faulkner would regularly report to his friends' house in the last year of his life to watch his favorite series, *Car 54, Where Are You?*[12] If Adorno had once balked at the idea of the detective novella, then this program, about two bumbling police officers working in the Bronx, would have been utterly unthinkable to him.

Whatever Faulkner might have said of television and however others may have adapted his works for the medium, the proof is in the pudding: his teleplays certainly differ from the screenplays he had written throughout his career and demonstrate his acute awareness of the technical restrictions of early television drama. In this chapter, I analyze in some detail the three Faulkner teleplays that are currently available—"The Brooch," "Shall Not Perish," and "Old Man"—but I also consider how Faulkner altered these particular narratives to prepare them especially for the television screen. While Faulkner's adaptations of his own works are interesting for many different reasons, each of these stories also contains intriguing details that speak to the relative value of various modes of cultural representations: the narrator of "The Brooch" contemplates his fiancée in relation to popular culture; "Shall Not Perish" invokes a variety of media by which a dead brother might be remembered; and "Old

Man" has been pulled out of its original context as one half of a novel, its narrative now tested as a freestanding piece of work without "The Wild Palms" to keep it company.

Faulkner's work for television, I argue, is most fascinating when one considers that he was writing for a relatively young medium. A good deal of experimentation came with the territory, and there were a variety of technical constraints introduced here that were less problematic in the world of filmmaking. This is evident in a 1944 adaptation of Faulkner's "Two Soldiers," written by Gilbert Seldes and shown on CBS, "the first [story] they had bought for television" ("FH," 121). The obstacles of television in these years were such that it was "hard to give a sense of depth in a scene, when the action required medium close-ups of two or three people."[13] When Faulkner himself wrote teleplays almost a decade later, there were still many impediments he had not encountered in Hollywood. One of these lay in the recording of the programs. Prior to the introduction of videotape in 1956, live television broadcasts were recorded by way of kinescope, with a film camera mounted in front of the video monitor, filming the images before it. And yet although both "The Brooch" and "Shall Not Perish" were broadcast and likely recorded, it is not known if archived footage of these programs still exists. The written words of the teleplays are all that remain, and these only by virtue of their being archived in the files of the J. Walter Thompson advertising agency ("FH," 122).

Golden Age television also had a strange relationship with the South, both in terms of its transmission and its content. In late 1952, when the *Omnibus* program on Faulkner was going to air on CBS, his own hometown was unable to see it. The Federal Communications Commission had put a freeze on station allocations in 1948 as a way of preventing interference with the reception of stations that already existed.[14] Oxford, Mississippi, was one of the towns to miss out, and although transmission became easier with time, residents of Oxford were unable to see the broadcast of the Faulkner special and instead had to organize a makeshift screening in their civic auditorium.[15] *Omnibus* would later court controversy in the South with its airing of a bold adaptation of *Uncle Tom's Cabin*, which it then tried to balance out by offering another program named *The Four Flags of the Confederacy*, which openly celebrated the efforts of the South in the Civil War.[16] The sensitivity of southern viewers (and program sponsors) tempered the racial politics of television in the civil rights era, with NBC vice president Edward D. Madden ensuring that his network approached the race issue by way of the infamous notion of integration without identification.[17] In this climate, it is of no little interest that Faulkner's first two teleplays, both with southern settings, feature peripheral—but important—African American characters.[18]

"The Brooch"

Faulkner had first started writing "The Brooch" in 1931, but it was rejected twice by different magazines and wasn't published for another five years. It tells of the courtship of Howard and Amy Boyd, which is stifled by Howard's mother's bedridden state, making it difficult for her son to ever venture out on his own. Amy becomes frustrated with her husband's fidelity to Mrs. Boyd; Howard sympathizes, and they concoct a scheme whereby they pretend to leave the house to go dancing, but in reality, only Amy leaves, while Howard sneaks back upstairs past his mother's bedroom and then back down later when Amy comes home, so they can pretend to be entering the house together. One night a friend calls to say that she found the brooch the mother gave Amy when she and Howard got married; being awoken by the phone, the mother then guesses the secret, and Howard realizes that Amy, who is not in fact home yet, must be having extramarital affairs. When Amy does finally show up, the mother, still awake, demands that Amy leave the house immediately, and when Howard won't leave with her, she leaves alone. Utterly defeated by his mother, Howard ends the story with a gun in his mouth. Faulkner did not make many changes when he revised the story for publication in 1936, although in the lead-up to Howard's suicide he added a two-hundred-word passage detailing the man's reading of *Green Mansions* (1904), an exotic South American romance by W. H. Hudson.[19] This revision would also play a small part in the adaptation.

At the CBS studios in New York, Faulkner composed the teleplay for the story in forty-eight hours in late March 1953, with the help of writer Dick McDonagh and story editor Ed Rice. It was written for a minimal cast of five and made use of only two rooms: a hallway and a bedroom in the house. Even in this confined space, a reviewer remarked that "the script flowed along so effortlessly that its overall mood of frustration and despair seemed a natural outgrowth of the conflict between the three participants, rather than a deliberate contrivance by writer, director, and performer."[20] There are more than three participants, however. Faulkner added a black maid, Clara, to the plot, a move that William Furry has argued "clarifies Mrs. Boyd's character as a Southern matriarch, and gives her someone else to bully besides her son and

FIGURE 12. William Faulkner and Dan Duryea on the *Lux Video Theatre* set of "The Brooch," April 1953. Photo courtesy of the Center for Faulkner Studies, Southeast Missouri University, Cape Girardeau.

daughter-in-law" ("FH," 126). Indeed, although Clara (played by Tillie Born) has only three scenes, her introduction helps underscore the vindictive nature of Mrs. Boyd, provides a source of knowledge of the couple's comings and goings, and finally emphasizes the tight spatial dynamics of the house:

CLARA, A COLORED MAID, ENTERS.

MRS. BOYD
Hasn't Mr. Howard come in, yet?

CLARA
No, ma'am.

MRS. B
How long did he tell you to stay tonight?

> CLARA
> SHE DOES NOT LIKE THIS LINE OF QUESTIONING. SHE WANTS TO ESCAPE.
>   He said he wouldn't be late.
>
> MRS. B
>   Is he out with that Foster girl?
>
> CLARA
> MOVING TOWARD THE DOOR
>   I don't know.
>
> MRS. B
>   Don't lie to me!
>
> CLARA
> AT DOOR
>   I don't know where he went.
> IN THE DISTANCE THE FRONT DOOR OPENS ("FH," 151)

It is clear that Clara does not wish to be there, a suspicion confirmed later when Howard explains to Amy that he can't leave his mother alone with the maid:

> HOWARD
>   Clara can't stay. Clara has her own family. Whenever I have to be out after six o'clock I have to pay Clara extra to stay. And every time I come back I expect to find that Clara's quit, too. ("FH," 158)

Here, the claustrophobia of the narrative emerges not just from the tense dialogue and Clara's desire to escape but also from the opening and closing of doors that signals the beginning and ending of the first scene, drawing attention to the close quarters of the Boyd house and of the television studio itself.

There are several other major divergences between the teleplay and the short story: Amy and Howard get married in secret; Amy's excursions after dark are completely innocent, involving no more than quiet reading in a lodging house; and the couple (or rather, Amy, on behalf of her milquetoast husband) conquer the cruel mother in the end and leave together. The cutting of the suicide was criticized by one reviewer in the *New York Times*, who lamented that "even under the television industry's purity code there was no reason for

Mr. Faulkner to capitulate so completely to the video mores."[21] In truth, given the more positive tone of the adaptation overall, it would have been quite difficult to justify ending the program on the same note as the story. Morality notwithstanding, however, there were other, more technical restrictions that dictated what Faulkner could and couldn't do with his adaptation.

In 1953, much of the programming on television was still performed live, as suggested by the iterations of "theater" and "playhouse" in many of the titles of anthology dramas in this period. Live telecast was also theatrical in that it required extensive rehearsals before going to air and permitted only a minimal amount of camera movement, since the actors were confined to small soundstages. In the productions of the *Lux Video Theatre*, several fixed cameras dictated a set of largely static character positions. Furthermore, in imitation of the stage, so-called proscenium-style shooting regulated movement mostly along the x-axis (side to side), reinforcing the sense of television as a flat medium, as Caren Deming has observed.[22] The small screen and small sets, as well as the lack of location shooting, meant that there was not a great deal of room to move, a problem the cinema had seldom experienced. The restrictions of live television were, however, also serendipitously suited to the narrative content and mood of Faulkner's story, with its suffocating setting. In "The Brooch," much of the action centers around the axial figure of Mrs. Boyd, who is completely stationary in her bed and dictates the blocking of the other characters. Howard and Amy are forced to enter her room to speak with her, and if Mrs. Boyd wishes to summon Clara, she has a bell on her bedside table for that purpose. Mrs. Boyd's detective work is all done from the comfort of her room, as she makes telephone inquiries regarding Amy's whereabouts and hears Howard sneaking around the house when he should be with his wife at the country club. Although it can offer the semblance of movement—at one point the teleplay suggests a "DOLLY IN SLOWLY FOR A SCREENFUL OF THE OLD LADY'S EYES"—the camera itself mostly matches Mrs. Boyd's immobility, with the action taking place off-screen either narrated in voice-over or reported by one of the characters ("FH," 158).

And yet there was also a push to break through such restrictions. Even at the stage of the teleplay, Faulkner added another dimension to proceedings, resisting the lack of shooting options and the lack of narrative options for the Boyd couple. This is evident in a deleted passage from the teleplay's second act, which features several quick cuts and which, more importantly, introduces a new room to the set. As Amy returns home from one of her weekly escapes to the hotel, Mrs. Boyd hears her footsteps. In the scene, Faulkner suggests that the camera briefly cross-cut between the two antagonists as a means of heightening tension before making a final cut to the couple's bedroom, seen here for the first time, as Amy surreptitiously enters it and then sits down and begins to cry:

> FADE UP ON MRS. BOYD'S CLOCK. IT NOW READS 12.45. ONCE MORE WE HEAR THE FRONT DOOR OPEN AND MRS. BOYD'S EYES TELL US SHE'S ALSO HEARD. CUT TO FRONT DOOR, WHERE AMY IS COMING IN, CLOSING THE DOOR QUIETLY. SHE TAKES OFF HER SHOES AND CARRIES THEM AS SHE TIPTOES GENTLY PAST HER MOTHER-IN-LAW'S ROOM, LITERALLY HOLDING HER BREATH. CUT TO MRS. BOYD. WITH HER EYES SHE IS FOLLOWING AMY'S PROGRESS, AS IF NO WALL WERE BETWEEN THEM. CUT TO AMY. SHE IS NOW ENTERING HOWARD'S BEDROOM. CUT TO INTERIOR OF BEDROOM. HOWARD IS IN BED, HIS EYES CLOSED, AS HIS WIFE ENTERS. SHE QUICKLY TAKES OFF HER WRAP AND THEN GOES TO LOOK AT HER HUSBAND. SHE HALTS AT THE FOOT OF THE BED. HIS EYES REMAIN CLOSED. THEN AMY SITS AT HER DRESSING TABLE AND GAZES AT HERSELF IN THE MIRROR. SHE'S THINKING OF WHAT HAS HAPPENED TO HER LIFE. SHE TURNS AND LOOKS AT HOWARD IN THE BED AND THEN BREAKS INTO QUIET TEARS, BURYING HER FACE IN HER ARMS ON THE DRESSER-TOP. ("FH," 170–71)

This scene, which imagines the space of the house without the inconvenience of the joining wall, is clearly problematic under the conditions of live television and was excised from the teleplay. Such a sequence was certainly possible, but it would have necessitated the construction of another room on set and another camera to film it. Instead of expanding the space of the house, Faulkner's more experienced cowriters or perhaps the director, Fielder Cook, evidently went for a more economical option. As Cook says of the period, directors "had 100 percent control, something that doesn't exist much any more," and so Faulkner's suggestion was here not included.[23]

Although television in this instance curtailed the potential of the adaptation, one scene from Faulkner's short story makes a very interesting transposition indeed. As published in 1936, "The Brooch" closes with Howard's preparations for suicide. Immediately before he begins these preparations, he contemplates passages he once read from his "coat-pocket size, Modern Library *Green Mansions*." Since his adolescence, Howard has interpreted the world through this book, "with peaceful despair justifying, vindicating, what he was through (so he believed) no fault of his own, with what he read in books, as the young do" (*CS*, 663). He sees himself as the novel's protagonist, Abel, a wealthy Venezuelan man who stumbles across a lost tribe and falls in love with Rima, a young indigenous woman and for him a representation of Amy. Like Abel, Howard is separated from the one he loves in the end, and although he shares Rima's and Amy's "desire and need to flee and escape" (*CS*, 663), his solution is suicide.

Earlier in "The Brooch," Howard looks on Amy and reflects on how she is the negation of the various commercial artifacts of the world. She is "not of the face whose impeccable replica looks out from the covers of a thousand magazines each month, nor of the figure, the shape of deliberately epicene provocation into which the miles of celluloid film have constricted the female body of an entire race" (*CS*, 658–59). Instead—and undoubtedly as filtered through the pages of *Green Mansions*—she possesses "a quality completely female in the old eternal fashion, primitive assured and ruthless" (*CS*, 659). Although Howard's vision of Amy is still filtered through a fictional narrative, it is a vision that is more singular than those offered by magazines and movies, and it is one he takes to his death.

In the teleplay, Amy's own connection to written and visual media (notwithstanding her adaptation here to the television screen itself) is reimagined in a quite unexpected way. As she grows frustrated with life in the Boyd house, Amy escapes each Saturday night, claiming to attend the country club dances but instead retreating to a private lodging house. Mrs. Boyd discovers her whereabouts after Amy misplaces the story's eponymous brooch and suspects the worst. And yet the truth is hardly scandalous, as the lodge manager, Mrs. Murchison, confirms:

> MRS B
>
> PLEASANTLY STILL
> Yes. What does she do there?
>
> MRS M
> Why, nothing. Just reading books and magazines. I thought it was funny too—a pretty young girl like that, sitting alone in a furnished room every Saturday night, reading, then about midnight telling me goodnight and leaving. ("FH," 172)

Although Mrs. Murchison assures her that her guest entertains no visitors, Mrs. Boyd chooses to ignore what she is told and accuses Amy of deceiving

Howard. After Howard finally stands up to his mother, Mrs. Boyd throws the pair out of her house, Amy taking the prized brooch along with her, and the drama comes to a close. All of this seems securely contained within the diegetic confines of the narrative, until *the Lux Video Theatre* logo appears, and the announcer introduces "Miss Sally Forrest," who has played Amy in the program. The actor, who goes on to advertise Lux Toilet Soap, first speaks about the author of the story:

> MISS FORREST
> Practically all my life I have been one of the millions of people who admire William Faulkner and consider him to be one of the truly great writers of our time. . . . Speaking for myself, as well as the rest of our cast, I feel it a particular honor to have appeared in Mr. Faulkner's first television play, which he wrote especially for the Lux Video Theatre. ("FH," 178).

The appearance of an actor in a commercial capacity like this was customary in anthology drama. And yet the celebration of Faulkner's work here, especially by the actor whose character regularly escaped her situation by reading books, is an intriguing one. Literature is voraciously consumed by a character within the confines of the drama, but the literature of the teleplay writer, William Faulkner, was not so readily devoured in the real world, having only recently achieved critical acclaim. The irony of Forrest's hyperbolic statement—a complete fabrication—is certainly telling of the lopsided relationship between popular and modernist cultural production: had "millions of people" not just admired but bought Faulkner's works, then he may not have needed to adapt one of them for television at all! In valorizing an oeuvre that had been commercially unsuccessful up to that point and then drawing attention to the teleplay written by the same author, *Lux Video Theatre* was connecting high and low culture, bridging the gap between Faulkner's difficult prose fiction and his first foray on the small screen. Although Howard Boyd had attempted to prevent the "thousand magazines" and "miles of celluloid film" from compromising the "old eternal fashion" of Amy and of literature, here his wife and the actor who played her were bringing them together once more, as though there were nothing to separate them.

Although the ending of Faulkner's freshman teleplay is completely different from the ending of the short story from which it derives, the teleplay also underscored two crucial aspects of the story: on the one hand, the spatial restrictions of the television set enhanced the claustrophobic mood of the story, almost too much for Faulkner's liking, and, on the other, the flattening of the distinction between high and low culture in the *Lux* production called into question Howard's disdain for popular media in the story and served as a reminder that the short story form itself occupied a fraught position somewhere between literature and the culture of "a thousand magazines." As a teleplay, "The Brooch" demonstrates the kind of modifications that were required to take a short story to the television screen, a journey that in this case also throws new light on the source text.

"Shall Not Perish"

Faulkner wrote "Shall Not Perish" in 1943 as the sequel to his successful story "Two Soldiers" from the year before. Both depict the Grier family, and in particular the two boys, Pete and his unnamed brother, as they witness the nation being plunged into the Second World War. As I mention in chapter 4, "Two Soldiers" begins with the Grier brothers listening to the powerful messages on their neighbor's radio, as it brings news of the attack on Pearl Harbor. Pete quickly enlists, and the much younger Grier, who also wants to fight for his country, follows him to Memphis to join the rest of the new recruits. Sure enough, the boy is sent home, but he returns in "Shall Not Perish" as a more mature figure, albeit this time without his southern dialect.

In this follow-up story, the family receives a telegram notifying it of Pete's death in the Pacific and struggles to come to terms with the news. The narrator's disbelief in the news conveyed by the vague telegram—"*A ship was. Now it is not. Your son was one of them*" (*CS*, 101)—motivates him to look elsewhere for confirmation of his death. While the Memphis newspaper provides an obituary with "Pete's name and picture" (*CS*, 102), the whereabouts of his body at sea remain a mystery, leading to the narrator's hopeful conclusion: "It's like, since nobody can tell us exactly where he was when he stopped being *is*, instead of just becoming *was* at some single spot on the earth where the people who loved him could weight him down with a stone, Pete still *is* everywhere about the earth, one among the fighters forever, *was* or *is* either" (*CS*, 104). Evaluating the absence of a physical record of Pete in this way, the narrator comes to doubt the modern media's capacity to capture the words and image of the deceased. Where in "Two Soldiers" the radio provided a crucial link between the South and the rest of the world, now it is merely "a little wooden box" designed to "catch the voices of them that saw the courage and the sacrifice" (*CS*, 104).

Such wariness of new media is elsewhere offset by a respect for older, seemingly more honest forms of representation. When another boy from the county, the son of the wealthy Major de Spain, also dies in battle, Mrs. Grier and her remaining child visit him in Jefferson to offer condolences. After a tense encounter in which the bereaved argue over the value of sacrifice for the war effort, the Grier mother and son have some time to kill before the bus back home to Frenchman's Bend is scheduled to leave, and so they visit a museum in which there were "pictures of men and women and children who were the same people that we were even if their houses and barns were different and their fields worked different, with different things growing in them" (CS, 111).

However, where painting appears to the narrator as a more respectful medium in its ability to render the human, the story ends with his reminiscence about the way in which the photorealism of film functions as a painful illusion: on an earlier family trip to the cinema, his grandfather mistakes the charging cowboys in a serial western for the Union army returning for vengeance in the South after their victory in the Civil War. His panicked outburst and hasty exit from the theater embarrass all except for Mrs. Grier, who recognizes the contemporary relevance of Grandpap's reaction: "He wasn't running from anybody! He was running in front of them, hollering at all clods to look out because better men than they were coming, even seventy-five years afterwards, still powerful, still dangerous, still coming!" (CS, 114).

The evocation of the Civil War here, as well as in the story's title (derived from the Gettysburg Address), recalls Faulkner's use of Abraham Lincoln in the World War II setting of "Battle Cry." And in the "Shall Not Perish" teleplay, which he wrote in February 1954, Faulkner would update the story once more, now using the recent struggle in Korea to frame the narrative. While this aspect of the adaptation had little impact on the overall plot, the original story's guarded fascination with various media—the telegram, the newspaper, radio, the visual arts, and film—was certainly affected in the transposition of "Shall Not Perish" to television. The narrator in the two Grier family stories clearly rejects the telegram bearing news of his brother's death, as well as the radio that can reproduce the voices of soldiers lost in battle. But at the same time he is attracted to the paintings in the Jefferson museum, and one of his lasting memories of Pete derives from an experience in the cinema. In representing the South and the nation more broadly, some media were evidently more trustworthy than others, a position that Faulkner himself seems to have adopted earlier when writing "Two Soldiers." "I like it," he said, "because it portrays a type which I admire—not only a little boy, and I think little boys are all right, but a true American: an independent creature with courage and bottom and heart—a creature which is not vanishing, even though every articulate medium we have—radio, moving pictures, magazines—is busy day and night telling us that it has vanished, has become a sentimental and bragging liar" (*SL*, 184). Faulkner and his young narrator may part ways in their specific ideas about the value of "every articulate medium," but it is nevertheless clear that modern media are of paramount importance to both "Two Soldiers" and its sequel, as I have argued elsewhere.[24] What is intriguing about the teleplay of "Shall Not Perish," then, is the way in which it skirts around these questions, minimizing references to and contemplation of nonliterary modes of representation.

Where Pete's death in the story is relayed by the telegram, the adaptation supplements its inadequacy with human presence—a minister and a captain of the American Legion accompany the postmaster, Willie, to deliver the wired messages to the Grier family and to a banker, Major Blakestone, whose son was killed by the same shell blast. But even this personal touch is not enough; the captain insists that "it doesn't seem right to deliver these just the way they are. I'm going to call Washington. We need all the details we can get" ("FH," 183). Although the following lines were omitted from the final script, they gesture toward the inability of media to adequately record the vanishing of American boys at sea:

CAPTAIN
I'm going to call the War Department. We elected them, too—or anyway the men who appointed them.

WILLIE
Wait, Captain. I'm supposed to deliver wires as quick as I can. It's a company rule. A government order, too.

CAPTAIN
REFERRING TO MESSAGES IN HIS HAND
I'll take the responsibility for this. These boys never did belong to the Western Union. And they don't belong to the government anymore now. They belong to us. ("FH," 185)

With these lines, which speak of the singularity of a human life and the inability of a hastily wired message to approximate it, the teleplay alters the original narrative in one very important respect. For, after the tragic announcements to the Grier family, and Major Blakestone, there follows no consideration of other media: there is no disavowal of radio's "wooden box," no approval of the local gallery's folk art, and most conspicuously, no misperception of reality in the cinema. While the scenes were conceivably sacrificed due to time constraints, the lines that remained in the teleplay—depicting the captain's personal conveyance of the telegram's message—appear to have rendered the story's later negotiations of a range of diverse media moot.

This seems especially noteworthy given that this story about the capacity of media to represent life was being prepared for what was undoubtedly the most threatening "articulate medium" in 1953: television. A veritable unknown quantity that would forever change the way that life in the postwar United States was depicted and experienced, television had already made its presence felt in a number of different ways. One of television's most obvious hallmarks was that its programming was from the very beginning organized around advertising, a structural feature that associated it with radio even more than cinema. Anthology drama, one of the earliest forms of TV programming, was broken up by an advertisement for the sponsor's product in between its two acts and featured another advertisement at the close of the show. Lever Brothers, the company that owned Lux Soap, were at the forefront of production, and a representative from the J. Walter Thompson advertising agency—in this instance Ed Rice—was always on hand to ensure its interests were protected "from the first word of a story to the last sprocket hole of a film."[25]

These featured advertisements often included cast members from the program being screened. The actors would step off the set in between scenes to deliver a word from the sponsor. So, in "The Brooch," Sally Forrest plays her part as Amy Boyd before acknowledging Faulkner's authorship of the teleplay and then recommending the use of Lux Soap for a "beautiful complexion" ("FH," 179). The involvement of actors in this way blurred the lines between the fictional narratives of the anthology drama and the straightforward commercial messages of the program sponsor, which resulted in interesting and unintended overlaps. "Shall Not Perish," for example, begins perhaps not coincidentally with a scene in which Mr. Grier and his son, Jody, clean themselves up before the noonday dinner, the father making his own judgments about the value of complexion and the necessity of soap:

GRIER WASHES, SPLASHING AND BLOWING. FUMBLES FOR TOWEL UNTIL JODY HANDS IT TO HIM. WHILE HIS FATHER IS DRYING HIS FACE, JODY TOSSES BASIN OF DIRTY WATER OUT THE DOOR, RE-

FILLS THE BASIN AND GINGERLY DIPS HIS HANDS
INTO IT. THEN HE REACHES FOR THE TOWEL WHICH HIS FATHER IS
STILL USING.

GRIER

You call that washing? Don't you know your Maw ain't going
to let you eat without she can see your eyebrows? Go on—wash! ("FH," 187)

Unconscious product placement, perhaps? Or something more deliberate? Either way, the appearance of the sponsor's product here accords with what Raymond Williams once designated as the "flow" of television programming. Writing in Britain in the mid-seventies, Williams suggested that it was no longer appropriate to look at television programming as a sequence "of discrete units with particular insertions" of commercials and trailers for other programs.[26] Instead, he wrote, programming was becoming a more seamless flow, where advertisements did not so much interrupt the program as form a crucial part of it. And importantly, this flow was planned, such that programs often featured "violent or bizarre" moments that would capture the audience through the breaks. In such cases, Williams asserted, "a quality of the external sequence becomes a mode of definition of an internal method."[27]

The Lux advertisements that were included in Faulkner's teleplays were not written by him. Nevertheless, advertisements ultimately determined the two-act structure of the anthology drama and were an integral part of the program, especially given that they relied on the actors of the drama, who were called on to shift in and out of their roles as part of the flow. In his review of Faulkner's "Shall Not Perish" teleplay, writer Dick McDonagh emphasizes the importance of this structure, suggesting that he reorganize his narrative around moments of heightened tension that are accompanied by commercial breaks. Faulkner follows up on this suggestion in connection with Major Blakestone's contemplation of suicide. In "The Brooch," Faulkner had omitted the scene from the short story in which Howard Boyd shoots himself, but this second attempt saw Faulkner introducing the element of suicide more openly into a narrative that had only hinted at its possibility. "The word 'suicide' is never used," Faulkner wrote in a scene outline for the teleplay (archived in the WFFC), but this was precisely the kind of enticement that would string the spectator along, especially through the commercial interludes.[28]

In accord with this logic, McDonagh's response suggested rewriting the first scene by only letting on that the Griers and Major Blakestone have each lost a son, before providing more background about the families. What should be revealed at this point, however, McDonagh noted, is that the Griers have been tenant farmers fifteen years, a fate that befell them after the bank owned by Blakestone foreclosed a mortgage on them. In the second scene, McDonagh likewise recommended that the deaths themselves not be elaborated. In Faulkner's version, as in the story, Mrs. Grier makes a decision early on to go and visit the major, though McDonagh suggests in notes on the script that the declaration of this decision be held off until she actually acts on it, because then "the drama of her decision would be heightened."[29] The decision to visit Major Blakestone is hinted at just before the sponsor's announcement, and so the viewer is carried through the advertisement by the prospect of an imminent dramatic confrontation.

Because there is an imperative here to remain glued to the screen, the break in the narrative perhaps functions less as a break than a tangent, and although not a part of the story itself, it certainly augments the viewing experience and alters the way that the content is viewed. The introduction of tension in the teleplay, strategically mediated by the bridging advertisement, transports the narrative into a different realm once it appears on television, emphasizing the capacity of the medium to take an element of the original and enhance its effect by extending it over a commercial interlude. While this maneuver directly implicates the narrative tension in the seductive power of advertising, it also expands the reach of the story and deftly translates its tone into another medium for another audience.

Television could hardly be called a progressive medium in the 1950s, considering its direct marketing of consumer goods, on the one hand, and its inhospitable approach to the race question, on the other. Fresh in terms of its technological innovations, television was rather regressive where opportunities for African American representation were concerned. There were very few roles created for black actors in the 1950s, since race did not seem a subject that was particularly helpful for the purposes of entertainment. So scarce were the opportunities, in fact, that Sidney Poitier was the only black lead in an anthology drama in the decade, playing a railroad worker in a 1955 episode of *Philco Television Playhouse*.[30] But however unkind Golden Age television might have been to black actors, Faulkner's work ever so slightly rectified the cruel imbalance, showing that the teleplay could even improve on the original in this regard.

In "Shall Not Perish," Major Blakestone's black servant Albert, referred to as the "houseman" in the teleplay, is key to preventing his suicide. In the short story, the name of Major de Spain's servant is never spoken: he is referred to derogatively by Mr. Grier as a "monkey nigger in a white coat" (*CS*, 104), and that same label is also taken up by the impressionable narrator. Even when Mrs. Grier asks Major de Spain for the man's name, and it is spoken, the narrator deigns not to report it: "He called the name then. And the nigger wasn't so far away after all" (*CS*, 109). The servant does not speak in the short story, and indeed he manages to show the Griers into the house "without making any more noise on the floor than a cat" (*CS*, 109).

In the teleplay, Albert has a greater role to play, standing up to his employer when asked to destroy the only remaining photograph of Blakestone's dead son and later helping to prevent the major from killing himself. Albert is also paid more respect here, too, and even manages to arouse the sympathy of Major Blakestone at his most furious. When the major refuses to attend the memorial service for his son and the Griers' boy, Albert pleads with him, but his words fall on deaf ears:

> MAJOR
> Today, Albert, I'll have my own services. Get out!
> THE HOUSEMAN HESITATES. THE MAJOR SHOUTS
> GET OUT!!!
> THE HOUSEMAN NOW HURRIES TO DOOR. WITH THE DOOR OPEN, HE LOOKS AT THE MAJOR IMPLORINGLY. THE MAJOR SPEAKS IN LOWER, CONTRITE, ALMOST GENTLE VOICE.
>
> MAJOR
> I'm sorry, Albert. You loved my boy too. Leave now. I wish to be alone.
> HOUSEMAN
> Y-yes, sir. ("FH," 206)

In a different way from the introduced character Clara in "The Brooch" teleplay, Albert in "Shall Not Perish" manages to avoid the most racist of characterizations that marked him in the earlier short story. On the one hand, the adaptation process here seems to have offered a reprieve from racism to the black character from the South, who is afforded better treatment for the national broadcast a decade after the publication of the original story. On the other, the presence of the character here—especially given the dearth of black characters in television more broadly—may have been contingent on the regional nature of the program; the very inclusion of Albert in the teleplay may not have been possible in a story set outside of the South. Here Albert may only play a servile role, but by suggesting to Faulkner that he should moderate the depiction of a character he had created, television was subtly pointing the way forward for cultural representation, both in the South and in the nation as a whole.

"Old Man"

Both "The Brooch" and "Shall Not Perish" had been custom made for television: each was written to fit a two-act program that ran for around thirty minutes (including advertisements), and each was designed for a small set featuring a minimal number of actors. Encouraged by his success with these two teleplays, Faulkner then tried to take the initiative by adapting the "Old Man" section of *If I Forget Thee, Jerusalem* for television, writing a treatment in April 1953 under his own steam. It wasn't the first time that he had repurposed this half of the novel, and by the time he sat down to adapt it as a teleplay, "Old Man" had already had varied success elsewhere. In 1945, prior to his recognition of its potential for television, Faulkner had agreed to include "Old Man" as a freestanding piece in the *Portable Faulkner*, seemingly content to decouple the narrative from its original partner, "The Wild Palms." And yet while Faulkner consented to this use of the work, he also resisted the New American Library's decision, in the same year, to print the two parts of his novel consecutively rather than alternately: "Dismembering THE WILD PALMS will in my opinion destroy the over-all impact which I intended" (*SL*, 352).[31] On the one hand, separating "Old Man" from "The Wild Palms"—for print and for television—was acceptable, while rearranging the way they were presented was not.

"Old Man" follows a convict who escapes from jail and lives a free but fleeting existence outside during the 1927 Mississippi flood. Taking up with a pregnant woman, the convict helps to deliver her baby and then finds work with a Cajun man in the bayous of Louisiana, before he honorably reports back to Parchman Prison, an additional ten years added to his sentence. In its first appearance within the pages of *If I Forget Thee, Jerusalem*, "Old Man" was punctuated with sections from "The Wild Palms," the tale of lovers Charlotte Rittenmeyer and Harry Wilbourne. The two halves of the novel offered separate yet connected worldviews: "Old Man," with its scenes of utopian freedom outside of civilization is an idyllic romance and adventure story, while "The Wild Palms," which underscores the restrictions of modern society, ruminates on the relationship between commercial culture and high art.

Although the alternation of these two stories positions a bucolic (though turbulent) life in Mississippi and Louisiana against the real struggles of the market and of itinerant labor in Chicago and Utah, it also allows for their mutual cross-pollination. Reading *If I Forget Thee, Jerusalem* requires a cognitive shuttling back and forth between rural and urban, South and the North, even as similarities emerge along the way. Although Harry Wilbourne and the convict have led very different lives, in the end, their imprisonments illustrate the fact that both are prisoners of "the same 'objective' reality, where," as Richard Gooden writes, "reification touches every sphere of life."[32] Wherever the characters roam, they are in the same United States and subject to the same social, political, and economic regime, with only some minor variations. Read in isolation, each story contains its own discrete plot, characters, and worldview. Read in tandem, the differences between them are less pronounced, and the "over-all impact" that Faulkner referred to becomes clear.

The "Old Man" teleplay is initially faithful to its source text, as Faulkner points out a number of times in the script. From the very moment the convict is freed, unfettered from the demands of the state that views him as "a valuable commodity," he is dragged back into a bond of bourgeois domesticity the likes of which he has never experienced before (4).[33] Faulkner provides the following instructions: "We now follow the story line in the book, except that it is a love story now, a love story between two people who are so busy saving their own lives that they have no time even to hold hands and speak of love" (5). By the time the woman has given birth, both characters have slipped easily into their new roles: "Her attitude toward him is already that of a secure and comfortable wife of about a year, say, the marriage just old enough for the first child to have come; without being conscious of it, they have settled into a sort of domesticity" (17–18).

If there is fidelity here to the original, then the resolution—which owes itself, at least in part, to the absence of the more pessimistic "Wild Palms" and the dialectical effect that text had on the convict's story—alters the entire narrative. The convict and the girl eventually "kiss" and, without his prison stripes, he now has a new reason to try and escape; indeed, this realization "changes his nature completely" (21). After that point, the original narrative is less in evidence, and allusions to it become more cursory in nature: "We follow the book, page 251 et seq. When they find refuge with the Cajun trapper and the convict goes into the alligator business" (22). Although freedom is within the convict's reach in the television treatment, he foregoes it for the prospect of raising a family, returning to the prison even as he has the chance to leave it: "Then she tells him: if they go now, they will be fugitives in hiding for the rest of their lives; they can live nowhere long enough to have a peaceful home; the child itself will grow up a fugitive, knowing nothing of security and peace" (22).

Absent the doomed romantic relationship of "Wild Palms," the teleplay introduces its own "sort of domesticity" into the proceedings, and the relationship between the convict and the woman is allowed to succeed against all odds. While in the final sequence, the other prisoners revel in the "orgiastic" conjugal visits of the Midnight Special train, he and the woman refuse to give into temptation and patiently await their future matrimony (4). At the end of the teleplay, as the convict prepares to face another three years in prison, he shows signs of a complete rehabilitation:

> The girl has come, with the baby. She and the convict stand holding hands, watching the frantic couples rushing away into the bushes, until they are alone. The same thought seems to occur to both of them, but the girl says,
>
> GIRL
> No. Not yet. We're going to do it right. We've waited this long; we can last out the rest of it. (26)

This final scene seems to sanitize the original story, as indeed does the "overtone of tenderness" (17) that pervades the teleplay in general, the narrative no longer bearing the "grief or nothing" of "Wild Palms" nor even its own sense of fated resignation to the dictates of the law. It is perhaps unexpected, then, that Faulkner includes a scene in which the woman gives birth, the convict cutting the baby's umbilical cord with a "can's jagged edge" (15). Even more surprising, his final censored line from the original story—"Women, shit"—is here returned to the convict's mouth, a seemingly unnecessary profanity for a writer undoubtedly now aware of the sensitivities of sponsored anthology dramas (4).

In the treatment as Faulkner wrote it, there is the paradoxical combination of a saccharine finale—which may have appealed to the networks—and two decidedly odd and dangerous moments that could have prevented its being aired at all. But in actual fact, "Old Man" probably deterred potential buyers not because of the graphic birth scene or the cursing but because of its requirement for location shooting, the special effects necessitated by its flood scenes, and its longer overall running time. A few months after he had written the teleplay, Faulkner still held out hope: "Have heard nothing about OLD MAN thing" (*SL*, 351). And in August or September of that year, in a letter to his editor, he mentioned that he was still hopeful that "the OLD MAN script may materialise" (*SL*, 352).

But while "Old Man" never made it to the small screen under Faulkner's watch, it was developed for the CBS anthology series, *Playhouse 90*, and was screened in 1958. Horton Foote, who would go on to write the screenplay for *To Kill a Mockingbird* (Robert Mulligan, 1962), adapted "Old Man" as a ninety-minute program, apparently overcoming some of the obstacles that likely prevented its earlier filming.[34] While the director, John Frankenheimer, had wanted to film the drama live, this was evidently very difficult, given the content of the story. To depict the flood, for instance, he "had two enormous water tanks built, which he planned to use for the river scenes, but as rehearsals moved from an empty soundstage to the sets, trouble began immediately." Accepting the need to "use videotape and shoot the scenes out of sequence," "Old Man" actually "became the first TV drama to be so taped and, because of its instant success, did much to end the era of live television."[35] Just as Faulkner's "Two Soldiers" would have the honor of being one of the earliest dramas on CBS, so too would his "Old Man" find its own place in television history.

Although it was a medium for which the author had little outward affection, it is clear that television had an affection for his work. Faulkner's time working for television was brief, and he did not contribute nearly as much as he did to cinema. Despite the success of his two teleplays for *Lux Video Theatre*, after 1953 it seemed that outside interest in Faulkner working directly for television had decisively cooled. Even so, his few teleplays remain fascinating documents for understanding the craft of writing for television in its early years and for understanding how Faulkner thought about his own works as they were adapted for the newer, smaller screen.

CURTAIN CALL

Land of the Pharaohs

In Jean-Luc Godard's satirical *Grandeur et décadence d'un petit commerce de cinéma* (*The Grandeur and Decadence of a Small-Time Filmmaker* [1986]), two directors set about the task of producing a made-for-TV movie based on a pulp detective novel by James Hadley Chase. At one point in this mocking take on the commercial moviemaking process, a parade of somnambulant actors auditioning for the film file past a video camera for four minutes, mechanically voicing words that form a long sentence. The fragmentary lines are not drawn from Chase's novel but instead from Faulkner's short story "Sepulture South: Gaslight" (1954).[1] Godard had already borrowed from Faulkner—quoting from *If I Forget Thee, Jerusalem* in both *À bout de souffle* (*Breathless*, 1960) and *2 ou 3 choses que je sais d'elle* (*Two or Three Things I Know about Her*, 1966)—and would do so again, most notably alluding to *Light in August* and *Absalom, Absalom!* in his essayistic love letter to the filmic medium, *Histoire(s) du Cinéma* (1988–98).[2]

But here, Faulkner's words—decontextualized and delivered in French in an expressionless way—hail from a minor, late story that was published in *Harper's Bazaar*. "Sepulture South" is narrated by a young boy whose grandfather has recently died, a loss prompting the boy to "something like hysterics" and a fierce denial of his own mortality: "I won't die! I won't! Never" (*US*, 452). Later, however, his fear of death is reversed, the narrator realizing something different about the marble effigies in the cemetery representing his deceased relatives: "And three or four times a year I would come back, I would not know why, alone to look at them, not just at Grandfather and Grandmother but at

FIGURES 13 to 16. *Grandeur et décadence d'un petit commerce de cinéma* (Jean-Luc Godard, 1986)

all of them looming among the lush green of summer and the regal blaze of fall and the rain and ruin of winter before spring would bloom again, stained now, a little darkened by time and weather and endurance but still serene, impervious, remote, gazing at nothing, not like sentinels, not defending the living from the dead by means of their vast ton-measured weight and mass, but rather the dead from the living; shielding instead the vacant and dissolving bones, the harmless and defenseless dust, from the anguish and grief and inhumanity of mankind" (*US*, 455). And it is these final words of the story that would later hold unexpected appeal for Jean-Luc Godard.

Just as Godard's movie drew inspiration from the story, so too Faulkner drew inspiration from a photographic image for his writing: "Sepulture South" was composed after he was shown a photograph by Walker Evans of the Wooldridge Family Monument in Kentucky, and the image appeared alongside his words when the piece was published.

The image and the words that accompany it also appear to closely correspond with the concerns of Faulkner's writing more generally in the mid-1950s. In the same year that he published "Sepulture South," Faulkner had worked on

FIGURE 17. Walker Evans, *Wooldridge Family Monument, Maplewood Cemetery, Mayfield, Kentucky*, 1945–47. Gelatin silver print, 19.9 × 19.2 cm (7 ⅚ × 7 ⁹⁄₁₆ in.). J. Paul Getty Museum, Los Angeles © Walker Evans Archive, Metropolitan Museum of Art.

another story about immense tombs that divided the living from the dead: the screenplay for Howard Hawks's *Land of the Pharaohs* (1955). Faulkner first worked on the script with Hawks and Harry Kurnitz, a young screenwriter, in December 1953, but the workplace was nothing like the studio backlot he was used to. At first, the team was located in a northern Italian villa for two weeks. From there they shifted to St. Moritz, Rome, and Cairo, for casting and location scouting, during which time Kurnitz apparently did most of the writing. A second draft screenplay was completed by February 17, 1954, and although the final script is dated October 2 of that year and bears only Faulkner's name, it is unlikely that he had much to do with it, since he had left for Paris in late March. Indeed, a short note from Faulkner to Finlay McDermid, head of the story department at Warner Brothers, suggests his input was minimal: "In my opinion Kurnitz did most of job. Will support any credit suggestion he makes provided Hawks concurs. Faulkner."[3]

One other credited writer on the film, Harold Jack Bloom, would go further, suggesting that Hawks had employed Faulkner simply for the prestige of having his name on the screen: "as window dressing, so to speak."[4] Faulkner would later reluctantly use his newfound celebrity to help advertise the film, making a public appearance at a preview of the film in Memphis as a favor to Hawks.[5] But in spite of the fact that Faulkner seems to have contributed very little to the screenplay, Hawks himself maintained that his writer of choice was instrumental in the project (in much the same way that Jean Renoir had emphasized Faulkner's very small contributions to *The Southerner* in the previous decade). In an interview, Hawks confirmed that Faulkner "contributed enormously" to the project, and he was "the man for the assignment" for many reasons: "because his imagination was challenged by these men, their conversations, the reasons for their belief in a second life, how they happened to achieve these tasks for beliefs we would find it difficult to understand today, such as the slight importance attached to the present life in comparison with the future life, the rest that was to be assured to the Pharaoh in a place where his body would be secure."[6]

On the face of it, *Land of the Pharaohs* is a simple story about the construction of the pyramids, and one that Faulkner knew all too well. "*Land of the Pharaohs* is nothing new," he pointed out. "It's the same movie Howard . . . has been making for 35 years. It's *Red River* all over again. The Pharaoh is the cattle baron, his jewels are the cattle, and the Nile is the Red River. But the thing about Howard is, he knows it's the same movie, and he knows how to make it."[7] An overstated comparison, perhaps, but one that at least draws attention to the fact that the film is less interested in local detail than it is in more transversal themes and character types. Perhaps owing to the property's lack of attachment to the specificities of Egyptian history, Faulkner was able in one discarded scene to insinuate something of his own Mississippi. In this scene, which features the Egyptian ruler and his deputy Hamar, Faulkner reportedly wrote a physical conflict into the script, the pharaoh demanding that Hamar "leave go of my arm," a throwback perhaps to a similar gesture in *Absalom, Absalom!*, in which Clytie twice grabs Rosa's arm in an effort to prevent her from discovering some difficult family secrets. Harry Kurnitz noted that

Faulkner was unsure of the likely speech patterns of a pharaoh, and understandably this southern scene in hiding did not survive the final cut.[8]

In the finished film, the pharaoh Khufu (Jack Hawkins) hires a foreign architect (James Robertson Justice) for the job of building a burial edifice that would be secure against grave robbers. All is going according to plan, until the pharaoh's treacherous second wife, Nellifer (Joan Collins), who has designs on stealing his hoards of treasure and ultimately ruling Egypt, plots his murder. In the end, however, she is buried alive with her late husband, with traditional custom taking its revenge on the would-be usurper. Hamar delivers her chilling death sentence before shutting her inside:

HAMAR

Yes, the treasure is yours now. This is your kingdom—for the same twenty years it will take to tear it down stone by stone, that it took the husband you betrayed and murdered, to build it—It is yours now—all yours now—[9]

Although the story as a whole has its many points of interest, and this closing scene is certainly very effective, there is a real sense that the narrative was never of paramount importance in *Land of the Pharaohs*. More than words, here it is the images—shot on location and screened in beautiful WarnerColor—that are absolutely central to the film.

In the early 1950s, a new film format had emerged, dictating the importance not of complex dialogue and storylines but primarily of a monumental spectacle and the spectacle of monuments: CinemaScope. Indeed, in a later interview, Hawks confessed that he "made this film for one simple reason: Cinemascope," a format that he had almost used for a similar story about the construction of an American Army airfield in China.[10] The CinemaScope camera, which had been invented in 1953, was purpose-built to take in a more panoramic vision, its cylindrical lenses capable of an angle of view twice that of normal lenses.[11] Effectively, the anamorphic images it created on screen, with an aspect ratio of up to 2.66:1, stretched each scene out horizontally, allowing more action to fit in each frame. With the potential to show multiple characters at the same time, the format promised longer takes and a shift away from the familiar shot/reverse-shot patterns that were ubiquitous in classical Hollywood cinema. And indeed, there are a few clear early examples of directors experimenting with the form: in *The Robe* (Henry Koster, 1953), a shot from a Roman archer at one extreme of the screen hits a Christian on the other, all without a cut.[12] In general, CinemaScope films made between 1953

FIGURE 18. *Land of the Pharaohs* (Howard Hawks, 1955)

and 1955 suggest overall changes in editing patterns: in those years, as one study points out, "the typical range is between 180 and 350 shots per hour for 'Scope films, as opposed to 300–520 shots per hour for non-Scope ones."[13]

Although he didn't much appreciate the new format, Howard Hawks nevertheless grasped the value of CinemaScope for *Land of the Pharaohs*; "it can show things impossible otherwise," he observed, because "you don't have to bother about what you should show—everything's on the screen."[14] And what better material for this more capacious aspect ratio than the construction of one of the seven wonders of the world? Not coincidentally, many films in widescreen formats (such as Paramount's VistaVision and MGM's Panavision) would be set in the ancient world, with swords and sandals stories such as Fox's *The Egyptian* (Michael Curtiz, 1954), Paramount's *The Ten Commandments* (Cecil B. DeMille, 1956), and MGM's *Ben Hur* (William Wyler, 1959) all calling for ambitious, epic sequences shot in color. And Hawks had apparently planned two biblical epics to be made in Egypt—one about Solomon, the other about Ruth—both of which he wanted Faulkner to have a hand in: "It looks like I will be rich at last," Faulkner wrote his wife about the anticipated contracts.[15]

Riches wouldn't follow for Faulkner from these unrealized projects, but CinemaScope itself was associated with the prospect of great financial return in the face of the decline of the studio system. Its fondness for the exotic past was also soon cemented. In a scene from Godard's *Le mépris* (*Contempt*, 1962)—itself shot in the wide-angle Franscope—the German director Fritz Lang (playing himself) expressed his understanding of the new format: "It wasn't meant for human beings," he makes clear at one point in the film. "It's only good for filming snakes and funerals."

Land of the Pharaohs, a film that shows more interest in picturesque landscapes than intricate storylines, contains both. Whether the new format would affect the craft of screenwriting or not, CinemaScope films would nevertheless still require writers. At Fox, Nunnally Johnson quipped that he would "have to put the paper in the typewriter sideways," in order to accommodate the lengthened screen. Although "the emphasis at Fox under Zanuck has always been less on visual spectacle and more on story elements," Johnson noted that the format "wouldn't have altered anything in the writing."[16] Indeed, it is difficult to discern the influence of CinemaScope in Faulkner's and Kurnitz's scripts for *Land of the Pharaohs*: the heightened attention to the visual is certainly there, but there are no special directions indicated in either of the screenplays for longer takes or alterations to the shot/reverse-shot patterns of dialogue. The second draft screenplay for *Land of the Pharaohs* contains 225 scenes, while the final screenplay contains 249, suggesting more rather than fewer shots in the final production as it edged closer to the screen. The scripts do not exactly bear the hallmarks of CinemaScope, then. But in its content and its form, this film does forge a subtle allegorical connection between the future of cinema and the future of the human. For what *Land of the Pharaohs* demonstrates and what the format seemed to promise in general—the precarious survival of cinema amid the sudden rise of television, greater durability of film stock—went hand in hand with Faulkner's work in the period more broadly, stressing as it did the indomitability of the human spirit in the face of atomic fallout and the difficulties of representing what Mark Greif points to in Faulkner's writing as "a strictly abstract, universalized man."[17]

With his almost-completed novel, *A Fable*, Faulkner had moved further than ever from the South, seeking to make good on his declaration in his 1950 Nobel Prize speech: "I decline to accept the end of man" (*ESPL*, 120). But this is equally his aim in *Land of the Pharaohs*, which is to all intents and purposes an Egyptian story but at the same time signifies far beyond the nation. The written narrative is mostly buried within the exotic monuments on display, but in the tradition of the pharaohs, this grants it even greater power; although the words of the screenplay are seldom read, they live on in the images committed to celluloid in the film. While Nunnally Johnson would downplay the influence of the new film format on the screenwriter, the tension between words and images in *Land of the Pharaohs* as a CinemaScope film in the making is already

FIGURE 19. *Land of the Pharaohs* (Howard Hawks, 1955)

presupposed in the very first scene of the screenplay. Continuing Hawks's turn to the voice-over in his RKO films from earlier in the decade, at the start of the script Hamar begins to speak over a montage of images. And interestingly, this voice-over itself emerges from Hamar's historical notations, as the high priest engages in a specifically pictorial mode of writing: hieroglyphics. The American poet Vachel Lindsay, in his *Art of the Moving Picture* (1915), had seen in the Egyptian hieroglyphs nothing less than a "moving-picture alphabet," a universal language of pictures that could be read by anyone.[18] And here, at the beginning of the film, Hamar's written record of history promises to create a lasting document of Egyptian civilization:

15.   CLOSE SHOT . . . PAST HAMAR.
        The manuscript form of Egyptian writing.

                    HAMAR'S VOICE
                     (as he writes)
    . . . this was the beginning . . . in the twelfth year of the reign of our
    Pharaoh, Cheops, the Second of that name, he returns in triumph to his
    palace in our great city of Luxor . . .[19]

In the film as produced, before anything else we see Hamar writing the chronicle of his pharaoh, speaking in voice-over at the same time as he inscribes hieroglyphs on the papyrus in front of him. The image suggests the enduring power of writing, especially picture writing, for posterity. But it also mimes the composition of the screenplay, in which Faulkner, Kurnitz, and Bloom, in consultation with Hawks, were crafting an original narrative, the words of which were always already subservient to the images they would create. Struggling over the appropriate language for the pharaoh to speak, the words that Faulkner would end up writing here were ultimately less memorable than the CinemaScope images Hawks created, building his shots—as Pedro Costa has written so poetically—"brick over brick like a mausoleum, like a huge graveyard."[20]

Here a written narrative surrenders to the more powerful grammar of cinematic images. But like Hamar's hieroglyphs, the words of the script did in fact manage to circulate beyond Hawks's cinematic tomb, not only surviving in screenplay form in the Warner Brothers archive but also migrating into Faulkner's prose after they had been written. As I have suggested, it is unlikely that Faulkner contributed much to the final screenplay. However, Nellifer's last lines in that version of the script (as spoken by Joan Collins in the film) are suggestively Faulknerian in tone, especially when compared with two other bits of dialogue the author had written around the same time. As the queen's fate is all but sealed, she pleads with Hamar to spare her:

242da *(cont.)*
    INT. MAIN BURIAL CHAMBER:
    Nellifer is now distraught and frantic, and terribly frightened. The noise is getting louder and louder as the stones fall—she clutches her head to try and shut out the noise.

                    NELLIFER
No...No....
    She throws herself on her knees, grasping Hamar's arm—begging him, imploring him—but he is firm...

                    NELLIFER
I don't want to die...please, don't let me. please...I don't want to die....[21]

This last desperate appeal bears an uncanny resemblance to the hysterical words of the narrator of "Sepulture South" ("I won't die! I won't! Never"), but it also reminds us of the final lines of *A Fable*, which Faulkner completed just after he had worked on *Land of the Pharaohs*.[22] These are uttered by the runner, a key character in the narrative who has ventured to the grave of the Unknown Soldier in Paris for the state funeral of the old general at the heart of the novel. The runner was horribly maimed by friendly fire during a mutiny that he instigated, which the military command averted by bombarding their own troops. In an effort to embarrass the criminally liable top brass, he throws his service medals on the general's coffin and is promptly turned on and nearly beaten to death by the angered civilian crowd. Lying half conscious in the arms of an old veteran, he is last seen "laughing up at the ring of faces enclosing him," and manages to speak his final lines through "blood and shattered teeth": "That's right," he said: "Tremble. I'm not going to die. Never" (*N*, 4:1072). The runner, as Richard Godden points out, is the "everlasting deformity that cannot die," produced by the brutality of war.[23] And he is here counterposed against the other eternal product of the war, the tomb of the Unknown Soldier, who, as an abstraction, is likewise immortal.

Just as his final contributions as a screenwriter seemed thoroughly entombed in filmmaking history, William Faulkner's words escaped once more: back to the South in a short story and to France in a novel, from screenwriting and into the fiction that has always seemed so far away from the studio back lot. Perhaps, with the narrator of "Sepulture South," we as readers might now cease "defending the living" novels "from the dead" screenplays and instead understand that the two locked rooms of Hollywood and Mississippi were always more permeable than we thought.

Timeline

William Faulkner between Cinema and Literature

YEAR	EMPLOYMENT HISTORY	CINEMA	LITERATURE
1932	Arrives at MGM; on payroll at $500 a week for six weeks (May 7)		"Turnabout" published (*Saturday Evening Post*, March 5)
		"Manservant" (treatment, 21 pages, May 25)	
		"The College Widow" (treatment, 13 pages, May 26)	
		"Absolution" (treatment, 9 pages, June 1)	
		"Flying the Mail" (treatment, 16 pages, June 3)	
		"Turn to the Right" (story conferences, June 23–26)	
	Contract terminated (June 26)		
		"Turn About" (screenplay, July)	
		On payroll at $250 a week (July 26)	
		"Turn About" (second draft screenplay, 122 pages, August 24)	
	Returns to MGM (3 October)		*Light in August* published (October 6)
		"Turn About" (third draft screenplay, 131 pages, October 25)	Rights to *Sanctuary* sold to Paramount (October 17)

YEAR	EMPLOYMENT HISTORY	CINEMA	LITERATURE
1933	On MGM payroll at $600 a week (November 28)	"War Birds" (screenplay, 143 pages, November 28, 1932–January 12, 1933) "Honor" (possible revisions, January 28–February 27)	
	Salary reduced to $300 a week (March 18)	"Mythical Latin American Kingdom Story" (screenplay, March–April) "Louisiana Lou/Lazy River/Bride of the Bayou" (screenplay, 62 pages, April–May)	*A Green Bough* published (April 20)
	Fired from MGM (May 13)	"Mythical Latin American Kingdom Story" (screenplay, 110 pages, August 26)	Revisions on "Elly" (July 1933)
1934			Revisions on "Christmas Tree/Two Dollar Wife" (winter 1933–34) *Dr. Martino and Other Stories* published (April 16)
	Reports to Universal Studios (July 1)	"Sutter's Gold" (treatment, 108 pages, July)	
1935			*Pylon* published (March 25)
	Reports to Twentieth Century–Fox (December 10) On payroll of Twentieth Century–Fox at $1,000 a week for four weeks (December 16)		

YEAR	EMPLOYMENT HISTORY	CINEMA	LITERATURE
1936		"Zero Hour/Wooden Crosses/The Road to Glory" (screenplay with Joel Sayre, 170 pages, December 16–31; "taken off due to temporary illness," January 7, 1936)	Writes final two scenes for *Absalom, Absalom!* (January 1–7)
	Reports to Twentieth Century–Fox; on payroll at $1,000 a week (February 26)		
		"Banjo on My Knee" (two sequences in treatment, 32 pages, February 26– March 3; story conference, March 5; revised treatment, 44 pages, March 10) "Zero Hour/Wooden Crosses/The Road to Glory" (possible revisions on set, March)	
	On payroll at RKO at $1,000 a week for five weeks (April 9)	"Gunga Din" (Notes, April 10–13; sequence and story outlines, May 14–16)	
	Reports to Twentieth Century–Fox; on payroll at $750 a week for twenty weeks (August 1)		
		"The Last Slaver" (temporary screenplay with Nunnally Johnson, 149 pages, August 7–September 1, dated September 24) "Four Men and a Prayer" (reader, September 2–3) "Splinter Fleet" (screenplay with Kathryn Scola, 129 pages, September 4– November 30)	First chapter of *Absalom, Absalom!* published (*American Mercury*, August) *Absalom, Absalom!* published (October 26)

YEAR	EMPLOYMENT HISTORY	CINEMA	LITERATURE
1937	On Twentieth Century–Fox payroll at $1,000 a week (February 26)		
		"The Giant Swing/Dance Hall" (minor contributions, March 9–11)	
		"Drums along the Mohawk" (treatment, 26 pages, March 15)	
		"One Way to Catch a Horse" (treatment, 36 pages, undated, probably June)	
		"Drums along the Mohawk" (dialogue treatment, 238 pages, July 3)	
		"Revolt in the Earth" (screenplay with Dudley Murphy, 62 pages, undated, probably July)	"An Odor of Verbena" completed (July 24)
	Contract ends with Twentieth Century–Fox (August 15)		
1938			*The Unvanquished* published and rights sold to MGM (February 15)
1939			*If I Forget Thee, Jerusalem* published (January 19 as *The Wild Palms*)
1940			*The Hamlet* published (April 1)
1941		"The Damned Don't Cry" (treatment, 19 pages, late November–early December)	Revisions on "The Bear" (mid-November–mid-December)
1942			*Go Down, Moses* published (May 11)
	Reports to Warner Brothers; on payroll at $300 a week for fifty-two weeks (July 26)		
		"The De Gaulle Story" (treatment and screenplays, July 28–September)	
		"Air Force" (screenplay scenes, 17 pages, September 14–October 5)	

YEAR	EMPLOYMENT HISTORY	CINEMA	LITERATURE
		"The De Gaulle Story" (revisions, late September–October 30)	
		"The Life and Death of a Bomber" (report on visit to Consolidated Aircraft Factory, November 14)	
		"Background to Danger" (revised final screenplay with Dan Fuchs, November 23–December 7)	
1943	Reports to Warner Brothers (January 16)		
		"The Life and Death of a Bomber/Liberator Story" (outline for original screenplay, 21 pages, January 21)	
		"Northern Pursuit" (screenplay with Frank Gruber, Thomas Job, Robert Rossen, Alvah Bessie, A. I. Bezzerides, early February–February 26)	
		"Deep Valley" (screenplay, 38 pages, March 5–9)	
		"Country Lawyer" (treatment, 53 pages, March 27–April 16)	
		"Battle Cry" (treatments, April 21; expanded treatments and sequences, June; screenplays, July)	
	On Warner Brothers payroll at $400 a week for fifty-two weeks (August 1)		
		"Who?" (treatment, 51 pages, September–November)	
1944	Reports to Warner Brothers (February 14)		
		"God Is My Co-Pilot" (notes on Steve Fisher script, 15 pages, February 17–March 4)	

Timeline 255

YEAR	EMPLOYMENT HISTORY	CINEMA	LITERATURE
		"To Have and Have Not" (screenplay with Jules Furthman, 140 pages, February 21–April 1; revised screenplay with Furthman, 118 pages, April 2–May 6)	
		"The Damned Don't Cry" (treatment, 79 pages, May 15–June 10)	
		"The Adventures of Don Juan" (revised screenplay, 158 pages, June–July 13)	
		"Fog Over London" (outline, 23 pages, July 3–July 15)	
		"Escape in the Desert/ Strangers in Our Midst" (extensive revisions with A. I. Bezzerides, July 12–August 19)	
		"God Is My Co-Pilot" (revisions, August 7–19)	
		"The Southerner" (revisions on two scenes, summer)	
		"The Big Sleep" (first draft screenplay with Leigh Brackett, August 29– September 14)	
		"Fog over London/ The Amazing Dr. Clitterhouse" (revisions, 3 pages, September 14)	
		"The Big Sleep" (revised temporary screenplay with Leigh Brackett, 172 pages, September 30; final screenplay with Leigh Brackett, October 26)	
		"Mildred Pierce/House on the Sand" (screenplay, 124 pages, November 13–December 12)	
		"The Big Sleep" (story changes, 13 pages, December 12–15)	

YEAR	EMPLOYMENT HISTORY	CINEMA	LITERATURE
		"Dreadful Hollow" (screenplay, 160 pages, undated, possibly December)	
1945	Reports to Warner Brothers; on payroll at $500 a week for fifty-two weeks (June 7)		
		"Stallion Road" (story line, 18 pages, June 12–16; screenplay, 138 pages, June 25–July 28; screenplay, 153 pages, August 17–September 1)	
1946		"Continuous Performance" (treatment, 37 pages, February 1946)	
			The Portable Faulkner published (April 29)
1947		"The Shadow" (screenplay possibly with Ivan Goff and Ben Roberts, 32 pages, October) "Deep Valley" (possible contributions to additional dialogue, undated)	
1948		"Morningstar" (outline, 2 pages, June)	
			Rights to *Intruder in the Dust* sold to MGM (July 11) *Intruder in the Dust* published (September 27)
1949		"Intruder in the Dust" (possible revisions to screenplay by Ben Maddow, February)	
			Knight's Gambit published (November 27)
1950			*Collected Stories* published (August 21)
1951		"The Left Hand of God" (first draft screenplay, 170 pages, February 1–March 4)	
			Requiem for a Nun published (September 27)

YEAR	EMPLOYMENT HISTORY	CINEMA	LITERATURE
1953		"The Brooch" (teleplay, 51 pages, March 31; aired April 2) "Shall Not Perish" (teleplay, 58 pages, March; aired February 11, 1954) "Old Man" (teleplay, 42 pages, April)	
1954		"Land of the Pharaohs" (screenplay with Harry Kurnitz and Harold Jack Bloom, 111 pages, December 1953–February 17, 1954)	*A Fable* published (August 2) "Sepulture South: Gaslight" published (*Harper's Bazaar* 88, December)

Notes

Title Sequence. William Faulkner, Screenwriter

1. Faulkner often omitted the apostrophe from contractions like "won't" and "don't," both in his letters and in his fiction (although not in his screenplays).
2. Dardis, *Some Time in the Sun*, 80.
3. Kawin, "*Faulkner and Film*," 89.
4. Blotner, *Faulkner*, 1:787.
5. Fine, *West of Eden*, 98–99.
6. Jameson even calls Faulkner "the greatest novelist in the world" (*The Modernist Papers*, 361).
7. Langford, "Beyond McKee," 252.
8. King, "Faulkner's Brazen Yoke," 303. In this vein, see also Fiedler, "Pop Goes the Faulkner."
9. Schwartz, *Creating Faulkner's Reputation*, 46.
10. Matthews, "Faulkner and the Culture Industry," 51. One recent example of this is Philip Weinstein's biography, *Becoming Faulkner*; Weinstein seems to take Faulkner's dissatisfaction with Los Angeles almost as grounds for the dismissal of cinema in his work altogether: "Hollywood could never, for Faulkner, be other than a perversely willed invention, a huge stage set, a scene of bloated egos and untrustworthy performances: all of this resting on a meretricious art form. It was a place of exploitative machinations disguised by tinselly mirages—alluring surfaces with nothing reliable underneath. It battened on sentimental illusion. The unceasing hum of high profit—greed—bespoke its subterranean motor if one listened hard enough" (*Becoming Faulkner*, 88). While it is certainly true that Faulkner seems to have detested both the Hollywood industry and the city that housed it, we need not simply accept as true his own comments on the matter, and we should certainly not allow them to exclude the screenwriting work from our research altogether.

11. In this regard, see Baldwin, "Putting Images into Words," Folks, "William Faulkner and the Silent Film," Murphet, "Faulkner in the Histories of Film," Murray, "Faulkner, the Silent Comedies, and the Animated Cartoon," Nyerges, "Immemorial Cinema," Rhodes and Godden, "*The Wild Palms*," and Watson, "The Unsynchable William Faulkner."

12. Lurie does not engage the screenplays directly, since he views them as being too implicated in the culture industry to perform the same kind of dialectical critique as the novels. While I would agree with Lurie to an extent, I believe that an attentive reading of the screenwriting work reveals that it has a critical edge as well as shows how various screenplays were themselves foundational for Faulkner's "enormously ambitious novels of social and historical questioning" (*Vision's Immanence*, 177).

13. See Bloom, "The Hollywood Challenge," Brinkmeyer, *The Fourth Ghost*, 188–195, Gleeson-White, "Auditory Exposures," Gleeson-White, "Faulkner Goes to Hollywood," Gleeson-White, *William Faulkner at Twentieth Century–Fox*, Gleeson-White, "William Faulkner, Screenwriter," Hamblin, "The Curious Case of Faulkner's 'The De Gaulle Story,'" Hayhoe, "Faulkner in Hollywood," Hulsey, "'I Don't Seem to Remember a Girl in the Story,'" Kawin, "*Faulkner and Film*," Liénard-Yeterian, *Faulkner et le cinéma*, Liénard-Yeterian, "William Faulkner and Howard Hawks," Ramsey, "'Touch Me While You Look at Her,'" Robbins, "Inscrutable Images and Cultural Migrations," Robbins, "The Pragmatic Modernist," Solomon, "Faulkner and the Masses," and Urgo, "*Absalom, Absalom!*."

14. Strychacz, *Modernism, Mass Culture, and Professionalism*, 7–8. This passing statement on Faulkner's writing process anticipates Lurie's far more in-depth argument about the complex divestment of Hollywood in the novels of the 1930s.

15. Blotner, *Faulkner*, 2:927.

16. Throughout this book, I distinguish between a screenplay and a finished film by placing the screenplay in quotation marks—"The Big Sleep"—and italicizing the film title—*The Big Sleep*. Although this system at times ignores the italicized titles of published screenplays (in the volume of Faulkner's MGM screenplays edited by Bruce Kawin, for instance), it makes for a much simpler distinction between the two, and often saves an unnecessary explanation of the distinction.

17. Jameson, afterword, 232.

18. Pasolini, "The Screenplay as a 'Structure That Wants to Be Another Structure,'" 193, italics in original.

19. Boozer, introduction, 1–2.

20. See Boon, *Script Culture and the American Screenplay*, Maras, *Screenwriting*, Nannicelli, *A Philosophy of the Screenplay*, Price, *A History of the Screenplay*, Price, *The Screenplay*, Sternberg, *Written for the Screen*, and Tieber, "'Story Conferences and the Classical Studio System.'"

21. Price, *A History of the Screenplay*, 4.

22. See Stempel, *Framework*, 78.

23. LaValley, introduction, 18–19.

24. Bazin, "De la politique des auteurs," 154.

25. Schatz, *The Genius of the System*, 6.

26. Christensen, *America's Corporate Art*, 2.

27. Ibid., 7.

28. See Kawin, "Faulkner and Film," 96–100, McCarthy, "Phantom Hawks," Phillips, *Fiction, Film, and Faulkner*, 40–42. In her helpful comparative analysis of this screenplay and *Absalom, Absalom!*, Michelle E. Moore points out that Karlova wrote Hawks on 1 October 1945 asking why the film was not yet in production ("'The Unsleeping Cabal,'" 55). Also missing are extended considerations of the farcical "One Way to Catch a Horse," the romantic comedy "Continuous Performance," the Nazi thriller "Escape in the Desert/Strangers in Our Midst," the convict drama "Deep Valley," and the Jekyll and Hyde story "Fog over London." For a brief analysis of "One Way to Catch a Horse" and "Fog over London," see Grimwood, *Heart in Conflict*, 16, 306.

1. First Run: MGM

1. "Metro-Goldwyn-Mayer," *Fortune* 6 (December 1932), 54.

2. Blotner, *Faulkner*, 1:772.

3. Ibid., 1:773.

4. Ibid., 1:774n19.

5. "Greta Garbo Expected to Return," *New York Times*, January 29, 1933, X5.

6. Hammill, *Women, Celebrity, and Literary Culture between the Wars*, 63.

7. Faulkner was well aware of Loos's Hollywood fame, having written to his mother about her in 1925: "She is rather nice, quite small—I doubt it if she is five feet tall. Looks like a flapper. But she and [husband John] Emerson get $50,000.00 for photoplays" (*Thinking of Home*, 189–90).

8. Vieira, *Irving Thalberg*, 164–66, 177.

9. Adela Rogers St. Johns, "Can Mary Pickford Come Back?," *New Movie Magazine*, August 1932, 24.

10. Haskell, *From Reverence to Rape*, 79.

11. Ibid., 125.

12. Rogin, *Blackface, White Noise*, 161.

13. See ibid., 161.

14. Another antebellum film from the year before *Gone with the Wind* places its female lead on a similar trajectory. In *Jezebel* (William Wyler, 1938), as Ida Jeter has observed, Julie (Bette Davis) "originally violates the Southern codes of proper behavior," which is acceptable to viewers as it may seem "anachronistic and quaint." However, once she attempts "to transgress the more universal moral and religious codes of society which

sanctify marriage and the family," she is labeled a sinner—a Jezebel ("*Jezebel* and the Emergence of the Hollywood Tradition of a Decadent South," 42, 43). Once again, female rebellion is permissible in the South only if it is rebellion against a code that is no longer binding.

15. For a good overview of the tensions between the New Woman and southern womanhood, see Fujie, "Modern Sexuality." See also Jones, "Faulkner, Sexual Cultures, and the Romance of Resistance," and Roberts, *Faulkner and Southern Womanhood*.

16. Fiedler, *Love and Death in the American Novel*, 311–12.

17. "Writers War on Filth," *Hollywood Reporter*, February 27, 1933, 1–2.

18. Blotner, *Faulkner*, 1:729.

19. Ibid., 1:729.

20. "Chatter," *Variety*, December 8, 1931, 56.

21. Kawin, *Faulkner's MGM Screenplays*, 34.

22. Ibid., 36.

23. Ibid., 34.

24. Bankhead, *Tallulah*, 1.

25. Burns Mantle, "Tallulah Bankhead Splendid in Quieter Parts of 'Rain,'" *Chicago Sunday Tribune*, February 24, 1935, 33.

26. See Lawrence, *Echo and Narcissus*, 88.

27. Silverman, *The Acoustic Mirror*, 61.

28. Price, *A History of the Screenplay*, 148–49.

29. Blotner, *Faulkner*, 1:773.

30. Ibid., 1:781. For more on the disruption of Faulkner's short story in the adaptation process, see Hulsey, "'I Don't Seem to Remember a Girl in the Story.'"

31. The screenplay that Kawin includes in his edited MGM volume is attributed to both Hawks and Faulkner and is dated August 24, 1932.

32. Matthews, "Faulkner and the Culture Industry," 66.

33. See Kawin, *Faulkner and Film*, 78.

34. "Dorothy Gray," *Hollywood Filmograph*, December 3, 1932, 6.

35. Kawin, "Howard Hawks," 90.

36. Kozloff, *Overhearing Film Dialogue*, 92.

37. For a reading attentive to the influence of the star system and that connects Ann to some of Faulkner's other female characters, see Ramsey, "'Touch Me While You Look at Her.'"

38. Aronowitz, *Dead Artists, Live Theories*, 54.

39. See Kawin, *Faulkner's MGM Screenplays*, 106.

40. Ibid., 106.

41. Ibid., 108.

42. Blotner, *Faulkner*, 1:798.

43. See Sklar, *Movie-Made America*, 175ff. Although a useful division for thinking

about Faulkner's career, such a schematic ordering of Hollywood film history does not ring true with many films of the era. For a more robust discussion of pre- and post-code cinema in the United States, see Lugowski, "Queering the (New) Deal."

44. Pravadelli, *Classic Hollywood*, 46.
45. Faulkner cowrote the original story with Estelle Oldham Faulkner, but it was rejected by *Scribner's* for being "too febrile" (*SL*, 42).
46. See Petry, "Double Murder," 231–32.
47. See Volpe, *A Reader's Guide to William Faulkner*, 88.
48. Petry, "Double Murder," 229.
49. Blotner, *Faulkner*, 1:899; Ferguson, *Faulkner's Short Fiction*, 39.
50. See Blotner, *Faulkner*, 2:491.
51. Faulkner, "The Christmas Tree," 29.
52. See Volpe, *A Reader's Guide to Faulkner*, 62. Indeed, Patricia C. Willis suggests that the story may have been written first as "Christmas Tree" around 1921, which would also explain its affinities with flapper culture. See Faulkner, "The Christmas Tree," 26.
53. Volpe, *A Reader's Guide to William Faulkner*, 62.
54. See Cavell, *Pursuits of Happiness*, 18–19.
55. Ibid., 86.
56. Christensen, *America's Corporate Art*, 5.
57. Kawin, *Faulkner's MGM Screenplays*, 545.
58. Vieira, *Irving Thalberg*, 226–27.
59. Blotner, *Faulkner*, 1:699–700.
60. Frow, *Character and Person*, 1.
61. Ibid., 1.
62. Ibid., 35.
63. See Dyer, *Stars*, 126.
64. Ibid., 20.
65. Sternberg, *Written for the Screen*, 109.
66. See Kawin, *Faulkner's MGM Screenplays*, 73.
67. See Sternberg, *Written for the Screen*, 116.
68. Mulvey, *Death 24x a Second*, 36.
69. See Kawin, *Faulkner's MGM Screenplays*, 257.
70. "Faulkner on 'Birds,'" *Variety*, February 7, 1933, 29.
71. Blotner, *Faulkner*, 1:648. In September 1934, he would write a piece for the Memphis *Commercial Appeal* about his chance encounter with Grider's son, also a pilot. See Faulkner, "Mac Grider's Son" (*ESPL*, 264–69).
72. Towner, *The Cambridge Introduction to William Faulkner*, 15.
73. Faulkner, however, refers to the film as *Secrets* (Kawin, "Howard Hawks," 90).
74. "Thru the Lens of the Critic," *American Cinematographer*, November 1932, 12.
75. Turim, *Flashbacks in Film*, 108.

76. Grider and Springs, *War Birds*, 128.

77. Kawin, *Faulkner's MGM Screenplays*, 430.

78. "Mayer Tells MG Execs to Work Only," *Variety*, January 10, 1933, 4.

79. Vieira, *Irving Thalberg*, 224ff.

80. Kawin, *Faulkner's MGM Screenplays*, xxxii.

81. Ibid., 431.

82. Ibid., xxxv.

83. Ibid., xxxvii.

84. Apparently he wasn't the only southerner working on the screenplay; Erskine Caldwell had been assigned to the film around the same time. See "New Writer for MGM," *Hollywood Reporter*, May 9, 1933, 4.

2. Second Run: Universal, Twentieth Century–Fox, RKO

1. "Faulkner's Briefs," *Variety*, May 1, 1934, 49.

2. As Faulkner only made very small, indefinable contributions to "Four Men and a Prayer" and "Dance Hall," I do not address those screenplays here.

3. See Montagu, *With Eisenstein in Hollywood*, 109, and Eisenstein, *Beyond the Stars*, 284–85.

4. Eisenstein, *Beyond the Stars*, 292.

5. "O'Neil Scripts 'Gold,'" *Variety*, November 28, 1933, 31.

6. Schatz, *The Genius of the System*, 233–34.

7. "Nine New Production Companies Organize," *Motion Picture Herald*, May 26, 1934, 26.

8. Gleeson-White, "William Faulkner, Screenwriter," 433.

9. Eisenstein, Alexandrov, and Montagu, "Sutter's Gold," 159; see Gleeson-White, "Auditory Exposures," 88.

10. Gleeson-White, "Auditory Exposures," 88.

11. Eisenstein, Pudovkin, Alexandrov, "Statement on Sound," 234–35.

12. See Price, *A History of the Screenplay*, 140–62. Price also points out (148–49) that the master-scene format was more routinely used at Warner Brothers than at MGM, who preferred its own in-house format throughout the 1930s—Faulkner, who worked at both studios, would have experienced the transition firsthand.

13. Ibid., 118.

14. Ibid., 116.

15. Montagu, *With Eisenstein in Hollywood*, 107.

16. Ibid., 150.

17. Eisenstein, Alexandrov and Montagu, "Sutter's Gold," 151.

18. Ibid., 178–79.

19. Gleeson-White, "Auditory Exposures," 91.

20. Price, *A History of the Screenplay*, 151.

21. See Riley, *Frankenstein*, Riley, *The Bride of Frankenstein*, and Riley, *Dracula*.

22. This screenplay is archived in the HHP and is cited by page number in the text.

23. Dolar, *A Voice and Nothing More*, 14; Barthes, "The Grain of the Voice," 179–89.

24. Zeitlin, "Pylon, Joyce, and Faulkner's Imagination," 182.

25. Ross, *Fiction's Inexhaustible Voice*, 60–61.

26. Zeitlin, "Pylon, Joyce, and Faulkner's Imagination," 201.

27. Matthews, *Seeing through the South*, 61.

28. For a reading of *Pylon* that is acutely aware of its incorporation of different media, see Hagood, "Media, Ideology, and the Role of Literature in *Pylon*," 112–14. Hagood's interpretation of the presence of the loudspeaker amplifies my own reading.

29. Murphet, introduction, 5.

30. Chion, *The Voice in Cinema*, 3.

31. Jackson, *Seeking the Region in American Literature and Culture*, 59. For another careful interpretation of the story, see Ramsey, "'All That Glitters.'"

32. Gomery, *The Hollywood Studio System*, 119.

33. Red Kann, "Insiders' Outlook," *Motion Picture Daily*, May 29, 1935, 2.

34. Lev, *Twentieth Century–Fox*, 26.

35. Kawin, "Howard Hawks," 106.

36. "Fox Takes Natan's War Film For U.S.," *Variety*, August 9, 1932, 15.

37. Stempel, *Screenwriter*, 59.

38. See *Sheets vs. Twentieth Century–Fox Film Corporation*, 33 F. Supp. 389 (DDC 1940), 4.

39. Frank S. Nugent, "An Objective War Film Is 'The Road to Glory,' at the Rivoli," *New York Times*, August 6, 1936, 22.

40. See Phillips, *Fiction, Film, and Faulkner*, 26–27.

41. This version of the screenplay has been published, however it does not incorporate the revisions that Faulkner (at least until January 7) and Sayre continued to make. See Sayre and Faulkner, *The Road to Glory*.

42. Tieber, "Story Conferences and the Classical Studio System," 234.

43. There were two further screenplays—dated January 24 and 27, 1936—that bore Faulkner's name, even though by this time he had returned to Oxford.

44. James Fisher to Estelle Faulkner, July 14, 1965, Twentieth Century–Fox Archives, University of Southern California, Los Angeles.

45. Weinstein, *Becoming Faulkner*, 179.

46. Carpenter Wilde and Borsten, *A Loving Gentleman*, 96.

47. Bob Stern, "Paris," *Variety*, March 11, 1936, 62.

48. "$1,000,000 Plagiarism Suit Over 'Road to Glory,'" *Variety*, July 14, 1937, 33.

49. "20th-Fox Wins Suit Brought by Soldier," *Motion Picture Daily*, June 5, 1940, 2.

50. "Swing along with 20th Century-Fox," *Motion Picture Herald*, June 13, 1936, 50.

51. Max Wilk, "A 'Little' from Hollywood 'Lots,'" *Film Daily*, March 20, 1936, 10.

52. "Chatter," *Variety*, February 26, 1936, 66.

53. "20th Cent-Fox Wins First Clash with Play Producer," *Film Daily*, December 22, 1936, 2.

54. Nunnally Johnson gave this information to George Sidney in an interview. See Sidney, "Faulkner and Hollywood," 159n1.

55. Price, *A History of the Screenplay*, 153–54.

56. Faulkner, "Banjo on My Knee," March 3, 1936, 19, Twentieth Century–Fox Collection, University of Southern California, Los Angeles.

57. Ibid., 20.

58. Blotner, *Faulkner*, 2:960.

59. Ibid., 2:930.

60. Ibid., 2:941.

61. Although, as Sean Cubitt has pointed out, "its lack of house style and apparent disinterest in searching for one is typical of classicism" (*The Cinema Effect*, 160).

62. Balio, *Grand Design*, 195.

63. "RKO Film Budget Biggest Ever," *Motion Picture Daily*, June 16, 1936, 1; Jewell, *RKO Radio Pictures*, 116.

64. Jewell, *RKO Radio Pictures*, 170, 168.

65. Behlmer, *America's Favorite Movies*, 88; Blotner, *Faulkner*, 2:901.

66. Faulkner, "Pukka Sahib," April 10, 1936, Rudy Behlmer Papers, Margaret Herrick Library, Los Angeles.

67. Faulkner, untitled story, April 15, 1936, Rudy Behlmer Papers, Margaret Herrick Library, Los Angeles.

68. Faulkner, sequence outline, May 14, 1936, Rudy Behlmer Papers, Margaret Herrick Library, Los Angeles.

69. Brecht, "Two Essay Fragments," 209–10.

70. Faulkner, notes for an original story, April 15, 1936, Rudy Behlmer Papers, Margaret Herrick Library, Los Angeles.

71. Faulkner, sequence outline, May 14, 1936, Rudy Behlmer Papers, Margaret Herrick Library, Los Angeles.

72. Carpenter Wilde and Borsten, *A Loving Gentleman*, 136.

73. Blotner, *Faulkner*, 2:936.

74. Ibid., 2:933–34.

75. Rascoe, "An Interview with William Faulkner," 70.

76. Blotner, *Faulkner*, 2:135.

77. B. R. Crisler, "Footnotes on Pictures and People," *New York Times*, June 21, 1936, X3; King, *The Last Slaver*, 54.

78. Ibid., 55–56.

79. Karem, "Fear of a Black Atlantic?," 166.

80. Quoted in Cripps, *Slow Fade to Black*, 289.
81. See Scott, *Cinema Civil Rights*, 223n18.
82. Blotner, *Faulkner*, 2:945.
83. Karem, "Fear of a Black Atlantic?," 171.
84. Scott, *Cinema Civil Rights*, 112.
85. Karem, "Fear of a Black Atlantic?," 167.
86. See Matthews, "Recalling the West Indies," 240.
87. Waid, *The Signifying Eye*, 164.
88. Urgo, "*Absalom, Absalom!*," 60.
89. Blotner, *Faulkner*, 2:946–47.
90. Williamson, *William Faulkner and Southern History*, 256.
91. Matthews, "Faulkner and the Culture Industry," 264.
92. Blotner, *Faulkner*, 2:946.
93. Ibid., 2:945. Among other films, Markey and Scola together worked on two Barbara Stanwyck pictures at Warner Brothers—*Baby Face* (Alfred E. Green, 1933) and *A Lost Lady* (Green, 1934)—and one picture—*Luxury Liner* (Lothar Mendes, 1933)—that was set at sea, giving them at least some credentials for their current project.
94. Millholland, *The Splinter Fleet of the Otranto Barrage*, 48.
95. Burrows, *A Familiar Strangeness*, 131–32.
96. Gomery, *The Hollywood Studio System*, 6–7.
97. Blotner, *Faulkner*, 2:950–51.
98. Ibid., 2:953.
99. "Book Notes," *New York Times*, November 12, 1936, 25; "Purely Personal," *Motion Picture Daily*, October 8, 1936, 2; "20th-Fox Buys Two," *Motion Picture Daily*, November 30, 1936, 8.
100. An annotated copy of this treatment is included in Sidney, "Faulkner in Hollywood," 113–51.
101. Ibid., 111.
102. See Gleeson-White, "William Faulkner, Screenwriter," 437–38; see also Sidney, "Faulkner in Hollywood," 130.
103. In between the treatment and the continuity for *Drums along the Mohawk*, Faulkner may have developed one of his own stories for the screen. "One Way to Catch a Horse" is a thirty-six-page screenplay centered around Ernest V. Trueblood, a farcical character and proxy for himself, that was initially thought to have been written in 1946. However, given a number of contextual factors in the screenplay (especially the inclusion of a Hollywood address at the top of the typescript) Michael Grimwood has suggested that it may have been written around the same time that Faulkner shared another Trueblood story with his French translator Maurice Coindreau (*Heart in Conflict*, 308n14).
104. Edmonds, *Drums along the Mohawk*, 345.

105. Gleeson-White, "William Faulkner, Screenwriter," 437.
106. Blotner, *Faulkner*, 2:968.
107. Of the proceeds, 20 percent went to his publisher, Random House, and 5 percent of what remained went to his agent, Morty Goldman, leaving Faulkner with $19,000 (Ibid., 2:984).

3. Independence: *Absalom, Absalom!* and "Revolt in the Earth"

1. Kawin, *Faulkner and Film*, 130; Baldwin, "Putting Images into Words," 55; Schoenberg, *Old Tales and Talking*, 68.
2. B. R. Crisler, "Footnotes on Pictures and People," *New York Times*, July 18, 1937, X3.
3. Ibid.
4. "Associated Artists Plan Four Pictures First Season," *Film Daily*, June 14, 1937, 2.
5. The last day Faulkner was charged to this project was June 16, although the treatment is dated July 3 (Blotner, *Faulkner*, 2:960).
6. Schoenberg, *Old Tales and Talking*, 64.
7. Although, as Schoenberg points out, Wash's curse ignores the fact that he himself has Sutpen blood (*Old Tales and Talking*, 66).
8. Kawin, *Faulkner and Film*, 135.
9. This screenplay is archived in the WFFC and is cited by page number in the text.
10. Friedman, *Hollywood's African-American Films*, 23.
11. Ibid., 25.
12. See Delson, *Dudley Murphy*, 89.
13. Donald, "Jazz Modernism and Film Art," 46.
14. Cripps, *Slow Fade to Black*, 258.
15. For a thorough account of this phenomenon, see Maurice, "'Cinema at Its Source,'" 31–71.
16. Cripps, *Slow Fade to Black*, 204.
17. Donald, "Jazz Modernism and Film Art," 41.
18. Ibid., 46.
19. "Sam Coslow Will Head 'Soundies' Production," *Film Daily*, October 14, 1941, 2. See also Delson, *Dudley Murphy*, 168–75.
20. Moritz, "Americans in Paris," 131.
21. Kawin, *Faulkner and Film*, 134.
22. Delson, *Dudley Murphy*, 110.
23. Murphet, *Faulkner's Media Romance*, n.p. For more on the significance of the photographic negative in Faulkner's work, see Morrell, "Kodak Harlot Tricks of Light."
24. Delson, *Dudley Murphy*, 160.
25. Louella O. Parsons, "Howard to Head New Company of Film Producers," *Milwaukee Sentinel*, April 3, 1937, 3.

26. Urgo, "*Absalom, Absalom*," 58.
27. Ibid., 69.
28. Schoenberg, *Old Tales and Talking*, 67.
29. Blotner, *Faulkner*, 2:927.
30. Owada, "Faulkner, Haiti, and Questions of Imperialism," 221.
31. Blotner, *Faulkner*, 2:947.
32. Ibid., 2:1129.
33. Ibid., 2:1138.

4. Winning the War with Warners

1. See Polan, *Power and Paranoia*, 194.
2. Faulkner, notes on Steve Fisher's "God Is My Co-Pilot," 2, February 22, 1944, box 1653, folder 4.12, series 9, subseries 1, Louis Daniel Brodsky Collection, Kent Library, Southeast Missouri University, Cape Girardeau.
3. Blotner, *Faulkner*, 2:1155.
4. Hawks appears to have borrowed this idea for a self-referential joke in one of his later films: when asked if he knows how to use a pistol, Lieutenant Ken MacPherson in *The Thing from Another World* (1951) responds by stating that he "saw Gary Cooper in *Sergeant York*."
5. Schatz, *The Genius of the System*, 300.
6. Blotner, *Faulkner*, 2:1112.
7. As Ben Robbins has noted in a recent article on Faulkner's work for Warner Brothers, Mrs. Brix emerges as an obviously noirish femme fatale in the story, such that "Snow" evokes more than the grand affairs of national conflict ("Inscrutable Images and Cultural Migrations," 60–61).
8. Additionally, as Jessica Follansbee has argued, Faulkner creates another kind of fascist character in Thomas Sutpen, and so in a sophisticated fashion *Absalom, Absalom!* "depicts fascism emerging from American culture," offering "access to a moment *before* 'democracy' became fascism's 'other'" ("'Sweet Fascism in the Piney Woods,'" 70).
9. Mann, "What's Wrong with Anti-Nazi Films," 28.
10. Birdwell, *Celluloid Soldiers*, 78.
11. Warner, "Harry Warner's Testimony to a Senate Subcommittee on War Propaganda in Film, 1941," 244.
12. Hamblin and Brodsky, *F*, 3:x.
13. Schatz, *Boom and Bust*, 280.
14. For more on these adaptations, see Arnold, "Faulkner Writ Large/Faulkner Ritt Small," and Wald, "Faulkner and Hollywood."
15. Stempel, *Framework*, 127. In 1956, Faulkner worked with Wald again, completing a "9-page story line" for an unsatisfactory script called "A Stretch on

the River," based on the novel by Richard Bissell. However, he resisted any further involvement in the project, suggesting that he "act as advisor to the script writer," rewriting scenes and dialogue as required rather than working full time on the screenplay (SL, 396–97).

16. See Schatz, *Boom and Bust*, 50.

17. "W. B. to Film War Leaders," *Motion Picture Daily*, August 28, 1942, 2.

18. Hamblin and Brodsky, *F*, 3:xiii.

19. Later, when he was working on the screenplay for *Mildred Pierce* (Michael Curtiz, 1945), Faulkner would write out a similar formula, which Jerry Wald found in his desk: "Boy meets girl . . . Boy gets girl . . . Boy loses girl . . . Boy sues girl. . . ." It continued for pages (Blotner, "Faulkner in Hollywood," 293).

20. Nichols would earn an Academy Award nomination for Best Original Screenplay in 1944 for *Air Force*, but Faulkner's name was not mentioned. See Hamilton, *Writers in Hollywood, 1915–1951*, 204–5.

21. See Nichols, *Air Force*, 115–17.

22. Faulkner, "Air Force," screenplay scene, 71, October 5, 1942, box 1650, folder 016, Louis Daniel Brodsky Collection, Kent Library, Southeast Missouri University, Cape Girardeau.

23. Nichols, *Air Force*, 169.

24. Kawin, *Faulkner and Film*, 95, 108.

25. Faulkner, "Air Force," screenplay scene, September 14, 1942, box 1650, folder 016, Louis Daniel Brodsky Collection, Kent Library, Southeast Missouri University, Cape Girardeau.

26. For Robert Jackson, this scene exemplifies Faulkner's capacity for collaborative authorship and for knowing what was required in a particular moment in a film: "There's something in the smallness of this scene, both its modest contribution to the film's larger narrative and its diminutive size as evidence of Faulkner's collaborative persona, that invites us to think about other overlooked details in Faulkner's life and work" ("Images of Collaboration," 41).

27. Hamblin and Brodsky, *F*, 3:xxx.

28. Hedda Hopper, "Looking at Hollywood," *Chicago Daily Tribune*, May 29, 1944, 10. In November 1990, Faulkner's work for "The De Gaulle Story" was adapted for French television as *Moi, General De Gaulle*. For more on this see Hamblin, "The Curious Case of Faulkner's 'The De Gaulle Story.'"

29. Blotner, *Faulkner*, 2:1129.

30. McCall and Plimpton, "The Art of Fiction LXX," 11.

31. Blotner, *Faulkner*, 2:1097.

32. Fussell, *Wartime*, 191.

33. Agee, *Agee on Film*, 28.

34. Ibid., 153.

35. Faulkner, report on visit to Consolidated Aircraft factory for "Liberator," box 1651, folder 003, Louis Daniel Brodsky Collection, Kent Library, Southeast Missouri University, Cape Girardeau.

36. Faulkner, "Liberator" notes, box 1651, folder 003, Louis Daniel Brodsky Collection, Kent Library, Southeast Missouri University, Cape Girardeau. Thanks to Ben Robbins for pointing this out.

37. Geller to Buckner, November 13, 1942, Warner Archive, University of Southern California, Los Angeles.

38. Farmer, *Celluloid Wings*, 189.

39. Kerouac, *Road Novels, 1957–1960*, 220.

40. Fuchs, *The Golden West*, 5.

41. Faulkner and Fuchs, retakes for "Background to Danger," 60, May 12, 1942, in "Background to Danger," revised final, November 6, 1942, Warner Archive, University of Southern California, Los Angeles.

42. Wald, "Faulkner and Hollywood," 130.

43. Fuchs, *The Golden West*, 6.

44. "In the Short Shops," *Showmen's Trade Review*, December 23, 1939, 32.

45. Carruthers, suggestions on "To the Last Man" script, February 26, 1943, 4, Warner Archive, University of Southern California, Los Angeles.

46. Ibid., 14.

47. Bessie, *Inquisition in Eden*, 63–64.

48. As Charles Hannon has pointed out, Faulkner had likely been aware of crediting standards in Hollywood from day one, for it was in 1932, the year he arrived at MGM, that the Academy of Motion Pictures' writer's agreement was struck. The guidelines it laid out determined that all writers on a script would review the cutting continuity and finished film and decide which one or two among them was most deserving of the credit. However, as we see in this instance, there was also a provision that allowed a writer to voluntarily relinquish his credit in favor of another (*Faulkner and the Discourses of Culture*, 85; see also Bordwell, Staiger, and Thompson, *The Classical Hollywood Cinema*, 313).

49. Blotner, *Faulkner*, 2:1140.

50. Hamblin and Brodsky, *F*, 4:xix.

51. William Weaver, "Hollywood," *Motion Picture Daily*, May 12, 1943, 4; "Warner Film to Hail Allies," *Motion Picture Herald*, June 12, 1943, 36.

52. Red Kann, "Insider's Outlook," *Motion Picture Daily*, March 31, 1943, 2. In July, Gary Cooper, Claudette Colbert, Charles Boyer, and Irene Dunne joined the cast ("Add to 'Battle' Cast," *Motion Picture Daily*, July 12, 1943, 4).

53. William Weaver, "Hollywood," *Motion Picture Daily*, March 31, 1943, 7.

54. Hamblin and Brodsky, *F*, 4:xxv.

55. "24 Writers Contributing to 18-Reel 'Battle Cry,'" *Film Daily*, May 14, 1943, 2.

56. Roberts, "John Wayne Goes to War," 147.

57. Carpenter Wilde and Borsten, "Faulkner," *F*, 4:xiii.

58. Hamblin and Brodsky, *F*, 4:xxix, xxx.

59. Ibid., 4:xxxv.

60. Blotner and Polk, "Note on the Texts," 1109.

61. Hamblin, "Faulkner and Hollywood"; Solomon, "Faulkner and the Masses."

62. Phillips, *Fiction, Film, and Faulkner*, 56.

63. Godden, *William Faulkner*, 156.

64. Blotner, *Faulkner*, 2:1155–56.

65. Faulkner, notes on Steve Fisher's "God Is My Co-Pilot," 3, February 22, 1944, box 1653, folder 4.12, series 9, subseries 1, Louis Daniel Brodsky Collection, Kent Library, Southeast Missouri University, Cape Girardeau.

66. Kawin, "Howard Hawks," 95–96.

67. Hemingway, *To Have and Have Not*, 225.

68. Kawin, *To Have and Have Not*, 32.

69. Ibid., 27.

70. Robbins, "The Pragmatic Modernist," 248.

71. Breen to Warner, March 2, 1944, Motion Picture Association of America, Production Code Administration Records, Margaret Herrick Library, Los Angeles.

72. Furthman, "To Have and Have Not," temporary, 142, October 14, 1943, Warner Archive, University of Southern California, Los Angeles.

73. Ibid., 168.

74. Furthman and Faulkner, *To Have and Have Not*, 123.

75. Ibid., 174–75.

76. McBride, *Hawks on Hawks*, 56–57. For more on this rivalry, see Fruscione, *Faulkner and Hemingway*.

5. The Great Migration to Hollywood

1. This chapter is heavily indebted to Richard Godden's analysis of the changing South in Faulkner's work during the interwar period and owes a great deal to his careful and ambitious historicizing of the novels in both *Fictions of Labor* and *William Faulkner: An Economy of Complex Words*.

2. On the other hand, while code-era Hollywood might have repressed female sexuality, Patricia White has argued that it also unwittingly "revived forms of homosocial culture that were now suspiciously sexual" (*Uninvited*, 20).

3. Although perhaps, as Mary Anne Doane argues, most films of the time were less concerned with social class: "In the '40s, the issues of social class so important to the maternal melodrama of the '30s are repressed or marginalized." She suggests that *Mildred Pierce* is a possible exception, as "Mildred's problems are a direct result of her desire to move up the social scale)" (*The Desire to Desire*, 80).

4. Cripps, *Slow Fade to Black*, 374–83.

5. Suid, *Air Force*, 24.

6. Ellison, *Shadow and Act*, 277.

7. As Faulkner's letters to Robert Haas and Commins confirm, this incomplete sentence was from "page 295" of the manuscript, which he sent in late December (*SL*, 146, 147).

8. Godden and Polk, "Reading the Ledgers," 337.

9. Blotner, *Faulkner*, 2:1090.

10. Kawin, *Faulkner and Film*, 108.

11. "Production Notes from the Studios," *Showmen's Trade Review*, February 20, 1943, 26.

12. Partridge, *Country Lawyer*, 11.

13. "Name News," *Motion Picture Herald*, 17 February 1940, 35; Bessie, *Inquisition in Eden*, 49.

14. Partridge, *Country Lawyer*, 312.

15. Ibid., 12.

16. Ibid., 308.

17. See Godden, *William Faulkner*, 15. For more on this particular act, see Smith, "'Southern Violence' Reconsidered."

18. Renoir, "Jean Renoir Presents Twenty of His Films," 239.

19. Blotner, *Faulkner*, 2:1184. Bruce Kawin makes an association between this scene and Faulkner's detective story "Hand upon the Waters" because both feature a body snagged on a line. However, Kawin cautions that the film itself is such a collaborative effort that one would be hard pressed to uphold connections of this kind: "The parts of *The Southerner* that most directly echo Renoir's other pictures—in this case the Tuckers' battle with despair, the contrast between city and country, and the complex ways nature is presented—can also be described as Faulknerian" (*Faulkner and Film*, 122).

20. Perry, *Hold Autumn in Your Hand*, 241.

21. Butler, "The Southerner," 367.

22. Blotner, *Faulkner*, vol. 2, 1184.

23. Renoir, *My Life and My Films*, 234–35.

24. "Memphis Censor Hits Advertising," *Motion Picture Herald*, August 4, 1945, 45.

25. Bazin, *Jean Renoir*, 93; Agee, *Agee on Film*, 167.

26. For an interpretation of the lack of black characters in the film, see Poague, "Jean Renoir, American Artist."

27. LaValley, introduction, 29–30.

28. Schatz, *Bust and Boom*, 233. Albert LaValley suggests that the overly gothic tones of some scenes in Faulkner's screenplay might have ultimately ruled it out of contention as the final shooting script (introduction, 34–35).

29. Faulkner to Wald, interoffice communication, November 16, 1944, Warner Archive, University of Southern California, Los Angeles.

30. See LaValley, introduction, 34–35.

31. Oeler, *A Grammar of Murder*, 167.

32. Blotner, *Faulkner*, 2:1245–46.

33. Wiener, "Class Structure and Economic Development in the American South, 1865–1955," 990.

34. See Woodward, *The Strange Career of Jim Crow*, 128, and Mandle, *The Roots of Black Poverty*, 84.

35. Miner, *The World of William Faulkner*, 88. Cheryl Lester is correct to point out that Miner is "seemingly indifferent to the perspectives of the Afro-Mississippians" and ignorant of population increases in Oxford itself ("Changing the Subject of Place in Faulkner," 210). However, irrespective of his analytical weaknesses, Miner's county-wide migratory statistics are usefully suggestive, and his preliminary question helped motivate some of the concerns of this chapter.

36. Matthews, *Seeing through the South*, 231.

37. Avila, *Popular Culture in the Age of White Flight*, 30; Kurashige, *The Shifting Grounds of Race*, 207–8.

38. Williams, "My Man Himes," 56.

39. Naremore, *More Than Night*, 234–35.

40. As Ben Robbins helpfully reminded me, noir was even more notably shaped by the influx of Jewish émigrés to Hollywood throughout the 1930s, a contingent that included Fritz Lang, Billy Wilder, and Otto Preminger. For more on how this particular exiled population helped to develop the genre, see Brook, *Driven to Darkness*.

41. Lott, "The Whiteness of Film Noir," 551. For a cognate argument, see Murphet, "Film Noir and the Racial Unconscious."

42. Lott, "The Whiteness of Film Noir," 548.

43. LaValley, introduction, 35–36.

44. Lott, "The Whiteness of Film Noir," 560.

45. Faulkner, "Mildred Pierce," scene 107, November 14, 1944, Warner Archive, University of Southern California, Los Angeles.

46. Ibid., scene 115.

47. Meta Carpenter Wilde writes of Faulkner singing "Steal Away to Jesus" on Mulholland Drive en route to a cocktail party during his time at Fox in the late 1930s (Carpenter Wilde and Borsten, *A Loving Gentleman*, 141).

48. LaValley, introduction, 35–36. Malcolm X remarked that "when Butterfly McQueen went into her act, . . . I felt like crawling under the rug." (*Autobiography*, 32). Thanks to Ben Robbins for alerting me to this.

49. Warner to Wald, memo, December 28, 1944, Warner Archive, University of Southern California, Los Angeles.

50. Sobchack, "Lounge Time," 144.

51. Faulkner and Brackett, "The Big Sleep," 267.

52. Kawin, *Faulkner and Film*, 119.

53. Breen to Warner, September 27, 1944, *The Big Sleep*, 1944–48, Motion Picture Association of America, Production Code Administration records, Margaret Herrick Library, Los Angeles.

54. Breen, "Memo reporting on conversation with Howard Hawks," and Breen to Warner, September 27, 1944, *The Big Sleep*, 1944–48, Motion Picture Association of America, Production Code Administration records, Margaret Herrick Library, Los Angeles.

55. Chandler, *The Big Sleep*, 36; Breen to Warner, September 27, 1944, *The Big Sleep*, 1944–48, Motion Picture Association of America, Production Code Administration records, Margaret Herrick Library, Los Angeles.

56. Breen, memo reporting on conversation with Howard Hawks, October 5, 1944, *The Big Sleep*, 1944–48, Motion Picture Association of America, Production Code Administration Records, Margaret Herrick Library, Los Angeles.

57. Chandler, *The Big Sleep*, 19.

58. Chandler, *Selected Letters of Raymond Chandler*, 48.

59. Stewart, *Between Film and Screen*, 59.

60. Jameson, "Synoptic Chandler," 39.

61. Blotner, *Faulkner*, 2:1175.

62. Faulkner to Geller, interoffice communication, December 12, 1944, Warner Archive, University of Southern California, Los Angeles.

63. Brackett describes the nature of his and Faulkner's collaboration on *The Big Sleep*: "I went to the studio the first day absolutely appalled. I had been writing pulp stories for about three years, and here is William Faulkner, who was one of the great literary lights of the day, and how am I going to work with him? What have I got to offer, as it were? This was quickly resolved, because when I walked into the office, Faulkner came out of his office with the book *The Big Sleep* and he put it down and said: 'I have worked out what we're going to do. We will do alternate sections. I will do these chapters and you will do those chapters.' And that was the way it was done. He went back into his office and I didn't see him again, so the collaboration was quite simple. I never saw what he did and he never saw what I did. We just turned our stuff in to Hawks" (Swires, "Leigh Brackett," 17).

64. Faulkner, "The Big Sleep," additional scenes, December 12, 1944–December 15, 1944, 154, Warner Archive, University of Southern California, Los Angeles, California.

65. Ibid., 155.

66. See Thomson, *The Big Sleep*, 58–59.

67. Ibid., 55.

68. Kawin, *Faulkner and Film*, 117.

69. Furthman, "The Big Sleep," story changes, December 30, 1944, 1, Warner Archive, University of Southern California, Los Angeles.

70. Indeed, it is highly likely that Faulkner completed work on "Dreadful Hollow" around this time, given that Hawks had recently acquired the rights to the property. Although Kawin's suggestion that the screenplay was written between October 1942 and May 1944 is inaccurate (given that Hawks only purchased the rights to Irina Karlova's novel in November 1944), it is likely that "once he had the rights he would have started the adaptation process promptly" ("*Faulkner and Film*," 97).

71. Blotner, *Faulkner*, 2:1175, 1180.

72. "WB Buys Hoss Yarn," *Variety*, April 18, 1945, 7.

73. See Blotner, *Faulkner*, 2:1184.

74. Longstreet, *Stallion Road*, 14.

75. "Studio Size-Ups," *Film Bulletin*, September 17, 1945, 25; "Studio Size-Ups," *Film Bulletin*, November 26, 1945, 25.

76. Blotner, *Faulkner*, 2:1190. This sentiment echoes Robert Buckner's earlier interpretation of "The De Gaulle Story" as "nouvelle vague."

77. Jelliffe, *Faulkner at Nagano*, 9; Blotner, *Faulkner*, 2:1166–67.

78. Longstreet, *Stallion Road*, 11.

79. Christensen, *America's Corporate Art*, 107.

80. Faulkner, *Stallion Road*, 16.

81. Grimwood, *Heart in Conflict*, 188.

82. Blotner, *Faulkner*, 2:161.

83. See Negulesco, *Things I Did and Things I Think I Did*, 95.

84. See Goff and Roberts, "The Shadow," October 24, 1947, 12I: Scripts, 1935–54, box 1090, folder 2, Selznick Collection, Harry Ransom Center, University of Texas at Austin.

85. See the untitled script concerning "Sarastro," "Anna," "Rico" in the WFFC.

86. See McCarthy, "Phantom Hawks," 73.

87. Blotner, *Faulkner*, 2:166.

88. See Fadiman, *Faulkner's "Intruder in the Dust,"* 60–61.

6. Stage Play and Screenplay: *Requiem for a Nun* and "The Left Hand of God"

1. See Faulkner, *ESPL*, 312–16.

2. Godden, "The Authorship of William Faulkner," 342.

3. "New Theatrical Firm: Walker Towne Inc., Acquires Four Plays for Next Season," *New York Times*, May 29, 1931, 28.

4. Blotner, *Faulkner*, 2:826–28.

5. Howard, "Faulkner Steps Out of His 'Land of Pharaohs' into Memphis," 118.

6. Polk writes that the material "on versos of 160–161, 163–172" of the third volume of the manuscripts in Garland Publishing's series "appears to be from a movie script" (*F*, 3:xii).

7. "Bernhardt Conquers New World," *Motion Picture Weekly*, March 9, 1912, 874.
8. Remshardt, "The Actor as Intermedialist."
9. Weaver, *Duse*, 303, 312.
10. Bazin, *What Is Cinema?*, 122.
11. Lawson, *Theory and Technique of Playwriting and Screenwriting*, 318.
12. Benjamin, "The Work of Art in the Age of Its Material Reproducibility," 112, 113.
13. O'Thomas, "Analysing the Screenplay," 238.
14. In his discussion of the idiosyncracies of the form, Fredric Jameson suggests that the reading play gives us "the seeming immediacy of a theatrical representation which is in reality the unmediated experience of the printed book" (*The Modernist Papers*, 148).
15. Carpenter Wilde and Borsten, *A Loving Gentleman*, 320.
16. All of this suggests that Faulkner was still working on the screenplay back home in Oxford. Meta Carpenter Wilde writes that there "was more work to be done for Howard Hawks on *The Left Hand of God*" (*A Loving Gentleman*, 321) even after he had returned from a trip to Europe in April 1951, but there is no record of his ever having visited Hollywood again.
17. Thomas F. Brady, "Hollywood in China," *New York Times*, April 1, 1951, 101.
18. See Barrett, *The Left Hand of God*, 40–43.
19. Ibid., 261.
20. Polk, *Faulkner's "Requiem for a Nun,"* 92.
21. Mast, *Howard Hawks, Storyteller*, 338.
22. Ibid., 342.
23. Sternberg, *Written for the Screen*, 136.
24. Kozloff, *Invisible Storytellers*, 49.
25. Blotner, *Faulkner*, 2:930.
26. McCarthy, *Howard Hawks*, 486.
27. Kozloff, *Invisible Storytellers*, 28.
28. Jameson, "Synoptic Chandler," 36.
29. Ibid., 37.
30. Ibid., 36.
31. Thompson, "Through Faulkner's View-Finder," 162.
32. See Jewell, *RKO Radio Pictures*, 21, 179.
33. Kozloff, *Invisible Storytellers*, 35. Indeed, Faulkner would later make brief use of off-screen voiceover narration in his teleplay for "The Brooch."
34. For more on this history, see Jewell, *Slow Fade to Black*.
35. See Polk, *Faulkner's "Requiem for a Nun,"* 243.
36. Ibid., 162.
37. Morrison, "*Requiem*'s Ruins," 324.
38. Murphet, introduction, 4.

7. Writing for the Small Screen: Faulkner and Television

1. Adorno, *Critical Models*, 239.
2. Adorno and Horkheimer, "The Culture Industry," 130–31.
3. Adorno, *Critical Models*, 55.
4. Ibid., 65.
5. Ibid., 60.
6. Poe, "*Twice-Told Tales*," 572.
7. The final teleplay for this program is dated August 23, 1960 and was an adaptation Faulkner's and Williams's initial work by William Cox. See William Cox, teleplay of William Faulkner's "The Graduation Dress," accession #6251-bz, Special Collections, University of Virginia Library, Charlottesville.
8. Vidal, *Palimpsest*, 277.
9. Blotner, *Faulkner*, 2:1705. For a more detailed account of this comment, see Kodat, "What Is Television For?," 34–48.
10. See Polk, *Children of the Dark House*, 242ff. Footage from the *Omnibus* episode was later used in a documentary written by A. I. Bezzerides, and the script is included in Bezzerides, *William Faulkner*. For more on the *Omnibus* episode and its afterlife, see Phillips, *Fiction, Film, and Faulkner*, 182–83.
11. Blotner, *Faulkner*, 2:1587.
12. Ibid., 2:1812.
13. Gilbert Seldes, "Regarding Video Experiments," *New York Times*, December 24, 1944, 35.
14. Kraszewski, *New Entrepreneurs*, 50.
15. Blotner, *Faulkner*, 2:1452.
16. For more on the tension between these two *Omnibus* programs, see McCarthy, *The Citizen Machine*, 141–54.
17. Kraszewski, *New Entrepreneurs*, 50.
18. For a more thoroughgoing analysis of television in the South, from midcentury to the present day, see the forthcoming collection edited by Lisa Hinrichsen, Gina Marie Caison, and Stephanie Rountree, *Small-Screen Souths*.
19. Blotner, *Faulkner*, 2:884.
20. June Bundy, "Faulkner Adaptation Proves TV Can Be Great, tho Simple," *Billboard*, April 11, 1953 2, 11.
21. Jack Gould, "'The Brooch' on TV," *New York Times*, April 12, 1953, 11.
22. Deming, "Locating the Televisual in Golden Age Television," 138.
23. Billips and Pierce, *Lux Presents Hollywood*, 516.
24. See Solomon, "A Little Boy and an Idea."
25. Gross, "Turning an Idea into a Print," 97.
26. Williams, *Television*, 91.

27. Ibid., 93.

28. Interestingly, the lines that most openly allude to suicide—Major Blakestone's instructions to his servant to "Leave now. You'll know when to come back"—were culled from the final teleplay, as they clearly implied an act that was verboten for the program to engage with ("FH," 206).

29. McDonagh et al., "Points on Shall Not Perish," WFFC.

30. MacDonald, *Blacks and White TV*, 54.

31. For the history of this dismemberment, see Kodat, "C'est Vraiment Dégueulasse," 69.

32. Godden, *Fictions of Labor*, 221.

33. This screenplay is archived in the WFFC and is cited by page number in the text.

34. Foote also wrote a screenplay for another Faulkner adaptation, *Tomorrow* (Joseph Anthony, 1972), and a teleplay for *Barn Burning* (Peter Werner, 1980).

35. Hampton, *Horton Foote*, 127.

Curtain Call: Land of the Pharaohs

1. See Warner, "*Contempt* Revisited," 209n9.

2. For a more comprehensive account of the uses of Faulkner in Godard's cinema, see Du Graf, "What Is a Digital Author?"

3. Faulkner to McDermid, November 27, 1954, Margaret Herrick Library, Los Angeles.

4. Wilk, "Faulkner and the Pyramids," 285.

5. Blotner, *Faulkner*, 2:1538.

6. Becker, Rivette, and Truffaut, "Howard Hawks Interview," 4.

7. Howard, "Faulkner Steps Out," 117–18.

8. Blotner, *Faulkner*, 2:1490.

9. Faulkner, "Land of the Pharaohs," basis of second draft, 109, February 17, 1954, Warner Archive, University of Southern California, Los Angeles.

10. Becker, Rivette, and Truffaut, "Howard Hawks Interview," 229.

11. Belton, "Glorious Technicolor, Breathtaking CinemaScope, and Stereophonic Sound," 195–96.

12. Ibid., 197.

13. Bordwell, Staiger, and Thompson, *Classical Hollywood Cinema*, 361.

14. Becker, Rivette, and Truffaut, "Howard Hawks Interview," 229.

15. Blotner, *Faulkner*, 2:1483.

16. Stempel, *Screenwriter*, 145, 170.

17. Greif, *The Age of the Crisis of Man*, 125.

18. Lindsay, *The Art of the Moving Picture*, 117.

19. Faulkner, "Land of the Pharaohs," basis for second draft," 4, February 17, 1954, Warner Archive, University of Southern California, Los Angeles.

20. Costa, "The Mystery of the Great Pyramid," n.p.

21. Faulkner, "Land of the Pharaohs," 120, October 2, 1954, Warner Archive, University of Southern California, Los Angeles.

22. The lines from the film may also recall the famous closing negations of Quentin Compson in *Absalom, Absalom!*: "I dont. I dont! I dont hate it! I dont hate it!" (N, 3:311).

23. Godden, *William Faulkner*, 201.

Works Cited

Adorno, Theodor W. *Critical Models: Interventions and Catchwords.* Trans. Henry W. Pickford. New York: Columbia University Press, 1998.

Adorno, Theodor W., and Max Horkheimer. "The Culture Industry: Enlightenment as Mass Deception." In *Dialectic of Enlightenment: Philosophical Fragments*, ed. Gunzelin Schmid Noerr, trans. Edmund Jephcott, 120–67. Stanford, CA: Stanford University Press, 2002.

Agee, James. *Agee on Film.* Vol. 1. London: Peter Owen, 1963.

Arnold, Edwin T. "Faulkner Writ Large/Faulkner Ritt Small." *Faulkner Journal* 16.1–2 (2000–2001): 3–6.

Aronowitz, Stanley. *Dead Artists, Live Theories, and Other Cultural Problems.* New York: Routledge 1994.

Avila, Eric. *Popular Culture in the Age of White Flight: Fear and Fantasy in Suburban Los Angeles.* Berkeley: University of California Press, 2004.

Baldwin, Doug. "Putting Images into Words: Elements of the 'Cinematic' in William Faulkner's Prose." *Faulkner Journal* 16.1–2 (2000–2001): 35–64.

Balio, Tino. *Grand Design: Hollywood as a Modern Business Enterprise, 1930–1939.* Berkeley: University of California Press, 1995.

Bankhead, Tallulah. *Tallulah: My Autobiography.* Jackson: University Press of Mississippi, 2004.

Barrett, William E. *The Left Hand of God.* New York: Pocket Books, 1955.

Barthes, Roland. "The Grain of the Voice." In *Image, Music, Text*, ed. and trans. Stephen Heath, 179–89. London: Fontana Press, 1977.

Bazin, André. "La politique des auteurs." In *The New Wave*, ed. and trans. Peter Graham, 137–55. New York: Doubleday, 1968.

———. *Jean Renoir.* Ed. Francois Truffaut. London: W. H. Allen, 1974.

---. *What Is Cinema?* Vol. 1. Ed. and trans. Hugh Gray. Berkeley: University of California Press, 2005.

Becker, Jacques, Jacques Rivette, and François Truffaut. "Howard Hawks Interview." In *Howard Hawks: Interviews*, ed. Scott Breivold, 3–15. Jackson: University of Mississippi Press, 2006.

Behlmer, Rudy. *America's Favorite Movies: Behind the Scenes.* New York: Frederick Ungar, 1982.

Belton, John. "Glorious Technicolor, Breathtaking CinemaScope, and Stereophonic Sound." In *Hollywood in the Age of Television*, ed. Tino Balio, 185–212. Boston: Unwin Hyman, 1990.

Benjamin, Walter. "The Work of Art in the Age of Its Material Reproducibility." Trans. Edmund Jephcott and Harry Zohn. In vol. 3, *Selected Writings, 1935–1938*, ed. Howard Eiland and Michael W. Jennings, 101–33. Cambridge, MA: Belknap Press of Harvard University Press, 2002.

Bessie, Alvah. *Inquisition in Eden.* New York: Macmillan, 1965.

Bezzerides, A. I. *William Faulkner: A Life on Paper.* Ed. Ann J. Abadie. Jackson: University Press of Mississippi, 1980.

Billips, Connie, and Arthur Pierce. *Lux Presents Hollywood: A Show-by-Show History of the "Lux Radio Theatre" and the "Lux Video Theatre," 1934–1957.* Vol. 2. Jefferson, NC: McFarland, 1995.

Birdwell, Michael E., *Celluloid Soldiers: The Warner Bros. Campaign against Nazism.* New York: New York University Press, 1999.

Bloom, James D. "The Hollywood Challenge." In *William Faulkner in Context*, ed. John T. Matthews, 79–90. New York: Cambridge University Press, 2015.

Blotner, Joseph. *Faulkner: A Biography.* 2 vols. New York: Random House, 1974.

---. "Faulkner and Hollywood." In *Man and the Movies*, ed. W. R. Robinson, with assistance from George Garrett, 261–303. Baton Rouge: Louisiana State University Press, 1967.

---, ed. *Selected Letters of William Faulkner.* New York: Random House, 1975.

Blotner, Joseph, and Noel Polk. "Note on the Texts." In William Faulkner, *Novels: Go Down, Moses, Intruder in the Dust, Requiem for a Nun, A Fable*, 1104–10. New York: Library of America, 1994.

Boon, Kevin. *Script Culture and the American Screenplay.* Detroit, MI: Wayne State University Press, 2008.

Boozer, Jack. Introduction to *Authorship in Film Adaptation*, ed. Jack Boozer, 1–30. Austin: University of Texas Press, 2008.

Bordwell, David, Janet Staiger and Kristin Thompson. *The Classical Hollywood Cinema: Film Style and Mode of Production to 1960.* London: Routledge, 1988.

Brecht, Bertolt. "Two Essay Fragments on Non-professional Acting." In *Brecht on Theatre*, rev. ed., ed. Marc Silberman, Steve Giles, and Tom Kuhn, 206–11. New York: Bloomsbury, 2015.

Brinkmeyer, Robert. *The Fourth Ghost: White Southern Writers and European Fascism, 1930–1950*. Baton Rouge: Louisiana State University Press, 2009.

Brook, Vincent. *Driven to Darkness: Jewish Émigré Directors and the Rise of Film Noir*. New Brunswick, NJ: Rutgers University Press, 2009.

Burrows, Stuart. *A Familiar Strangeness: American Fiction and the Language of Photography, 1939–1945*. Athens: University of Georgia Press, 2008.

Butler, Hugo. "The Southerner." In *Best Film Plays—1945*, ed. John Gassner and Dudley Nichols, 331–80. New York: Crown, 1946.

Carpenter Wilde, Meta, and Orin Borsten. "Faulkner: Hollywood, 1943." In *Faulkner: A Comprehensive Guide to the Brodsky Collection*, vol. 4: *Battle Cry, a Screenplay by William Faulkner*, ed. Louis Daniel Brodsky and Robert W. Hamblin, ix–xiv. Jackson: University Press of Mississippi, 1985.

———. *A Loving Gentleman: The Love Story of William Faulkner and Meta Carpenter*. New York: Simon and Schuster, 1976.

Cavell, Stanley. *Pursuits of Happiness: The Hollywood Comedy of Remarriage*. Cambridge, MA: Harvard University Press, 1981.

Chandler, Raymond. *The Big Sleep*. In *The Raymond Chandler Omnibus: Four Famous Classics*, 1–140. New York: Knopf, 1964.

———. *Selected Letters of Raymond Chandler*. Ed. Frank MacShane. New York: Columbia University Press, 1981.

Chion, Michel. *The Voice in Cinema*. Ed. and trans. Claudia Gorbman. New York: Columbia University Press, 1999.

Christensen, Jerome. *America's Corporate Art: The Studio Authorship of Hollywood Motion Pictures*. Stanford, CA: Stanford University Press, 2012.

Costa, Pedro. "The Mystery of the Great Pyramid." Trans. Ricardo Matos Cabo and Andy Rector. *Film Comment*, July 16, 2015. www.filmcomment.com/blog/the-mystery-of-the-great-pyramid.

Coughlan, Robert. *The Private World of William Faulkner*. New York: Harper, 1954.

Cripps, Thomas. *Slow Fade to Black: The Negro in American Film, 1900–1942*. New York: Oxford University Press, 1977.

Cubitt, Sean. *The Cinema Effect*. Cambridge, MA: MIT Press, 2004.

Dardis, Tom. *Some Time in the Sun*. New York: Charles Scribner's Sons, 1976.

Delson, Susan. *Dudley Murphy: Hollywood Wild Card*. Minneapolis: University of Minnesota Press, 2006.

Deming, Caren. "Locating the Televisual in Golden Age Television." In *A Companion to Television*, ed. Janet Wasko, 126–41. Oxford, UK: Wiley-Blackwell, 2010.

Doane, Mary Ann. *The Desire to Desire: The Woman's Film of the 1940s*. Bloomington: Indiana University Press, 1987.

Dolar, Mladen. *A Voice and Nothing More*. Cambridge, MA: MIT Press, 2006.

Donald, James. "Jazz Modernism and Film Art: Dudley Murphy and *Ballet mécanique*." *Modernism/Modernity* 16.1 (2009): 25–49.

Dreiser, Theodore. "The Real Sins of Hollywood." *Liberty* 9.24 (1932): 6–11.

Du Graf, Lauren. "What Is a Digital Author? The Faulknerian Author Function in Jean-Luc Godard's *Film Socialisme*." *Comparative Literature Studies* 51.4 (2014): 533–56.

Dyer, Richard. *Stars: New Edition*. London: BFI, 1998.

Edmonds, Walter D. *Drums along the Mohawk*. New York: Vintage, 2015.

Eisenstein, Sergei M. *Selected Works*, vol. 4, *Beyond the Stars: The Memoirs of Sergei Eisenstein*. Ed. Richard Taylor, trans. William Powell. London: BFI, 1996.

Eisenstein, Sergei M., Grigori V. Alexandrov, and Ivor Montagu. "Sutter's Gold: Scenario." In *With Eisenstein in Hollywood: A Chapter of Autobiography*, 148–205. New York: International Press, 1969.

Eisenstein, Sergei M., Vsevolod Pudovkin, and Grigori V. Alexandrov. "Statement on Sound." In *The Film Factory: Russian and Soviet Cinema in Documents, 1896–1939*, ed. Richard Taylor and Ian Christie, 234–35. Cambridge, MA: Harvard University Press, 1988.

Ellison, Ralph. *Shadow and Act*. New York: Random House, 1964.

Everson, William K. "Rediscovery: Raymond Bernard and *Les Croix de Bois*." *Films in Review* 36.3 (1985): 171–75.

Fadiman, Regina K. *Faulkner's "Intruder in the Dust": Novel into Film*. Knoxville: University of Tennessee Press, 1978.

Farmer, James H. *Celluloid Wings: The Impact of Movies on Aviation*. Blue Ridge Summit, PA: TAB Books, 1984.

Faulkner, William. "Absalom, Absalom." *American Mercury* 38.132 (1936): 466–74.

———. "The Christmas Tree." *Yale Review* 83.1 (1995): 26–30.

———. *Collected Stories of William Faulkner*. New York: Vintage, 1977.

———. *Country Lawyer and Other Stories for the Screen*. Ed. Louis Daniel Brodsky and Robert W. Hamblin. Jackson: University Press of Mississippi, 1987.

———. *Essays, Speeches, and Public Letters*. New York: Random House, 2011.

———. *Faulkner: A Comprehensive Guide to the Brodsky Collection*. 5 vols. Ed. Louis Daniel Brodsky and Robert W. Hamblin. Jackson: University Press of Mississippi, 1982–1988.

———. *Faulkner in the University: Conferences at the University of Virginia, 1957–1958*. Ed. Frederick L. Gwynn and Joseph L. Blotner. New York: Knopf, 1965.

———. *Faulkner's MGM Screenplays*. Ed. Bruce Kawin. Knoxville: University of Tennessee Press, 1982.

———. *Knight's Gambit*. New York: Vintage, 1978.

———. *Novels*. 5 vols. New York: Library of America, 1990–2006.

———. *Stallion Road: A Screenplay*. Jackson: University of Mississippi Press, 1989.

———. *Thinking of Home: William Faulkner's Letters to His Mother and Father, 1918–1925*. Ed. James G. Watson. New York: Norton, 1992.

———. *Uncollected Stories of William Faulkner*. Ed. Joseph Blotner. New York: Random House, 1979.

———. *William Faulkner at Twentieth Century–Fox: The Annotated Screenplays.* Ed. Sarah Gleeson-White. New York: Oxford University Press, 2017.

———. *William Faulkner Manuscripts.* 25 vols. New York: Garland Publishing, 1986–87.

Faulkner, William, Leigh Brackett, and Jules Furthman. "The Big Sleep." In *Film Scripts*, vol. 1, ed. George P. Garrett, O. B. Hardison Jr., and Jane R. Gelfman, 137–329. New York: Appleton, Century, Crofts, 1971.

Ferguson, James. *Faulkner's Short Fiction.* Knoxville: University of Tennessee Press, 1991.

Fiedler, Leslie A. *Love and Death in the American Novel.* New York: Criterion, 1960.

———. "Pop Goes the Faulkner: In Quest of *Sanctuary.*" In *Faulkner and Popular Culture*, ed. Doreen Fowler and Ann J. Abadie, 75–92. Faulkner and Yoknapatawpha 1988. Jackson: University Press of Mississippi, 1990.

Fine, Richard. *West of Eden: Writers in Hollywood, 1928–1940.* Washington, DC: Smithsonian Institution Press, 1993.

Folks, Jeffrey J. "Faulkner and the Silent Film." In *The South and Film*, ed. Warren French, 171–82. Jackson: University Press of Mississippi, 1981.

Follansbee, Jessica. "'Sweet Fascism in the Piney Woods': *Absalom, Absalom!* as Fascist Fable." *Modernism/Modernity* 18.1 (2011): 67–94.

Friedman, Ryan Jay. *Hollywood's African American Films: The Transition to Sound.* New Brunswick, NJ: Rutgers University Press, 2011.

Frow, John. *Character and Person.* Oxford: Oxford University Press, 2014.

Fruscione, John. *Faulkner and Hemingway: Biography of a Literary Rivalry.* Columbus: Ohio State University Press, 2012.

Fuchs, Dan. *The Golden West: Hollywood Stories.* Boston: Black Sparrow Press, 2006.

Fujie, Kristin. "Modern Sexuality." In *William Faulkner in Context*, ed. John T. Matthews, 111–18. New York: Cambridge University Press, 2015.

Furry, William. "Faulkner in a Haystack: The Search for Faulkner's Television Adaptations of 'The Brooch' and 'Shall Not Perish.'" *Faulkner Journal* 16.1–2 (Fall 2000–2001): 119–25.

Furthman, Jules, and William Faulkner. *To Have and Have Not.* Ed. Bruce F. Kawin. Madison: University of Wisconsin Press, 1980.

Fussell, Paul. *Wartime: Understanding and Behavior in the Second World War.* Oxford: Oxford University Press, 1990.

Gleeson-White, Sarah. "Auditory Exposures: Faulkner, Eisenstein, and Film Sound." *PMLA* 128.1 (2013): 87–100.

———. "Faulkner Goes to Hollywood." In *William Faulkner in Context*, ed. John T. Matthews, 194–206. New York: Cambridge University Press, 2015.

———, ed. *William Faulkner at Twentieth Century–Fox: The Annotated Screenplays.* New York: Oxford University Press, 2017.

———. "William Faulkner, Screenwriter: 'Sutter's Gold' and 'Drums along the Mohawk.'" *Mississippi Quarterly* 62.3–4 (2009): 427–42.

Godden, Richard. "The Authorship of William Faulkner: An Under-Authorized Version." *Mississippi Quarterly* 42.3 (1989): 339–46.

———. *Fictions of Labor: William Faulkner and the South's Long Revolution*. New York: Cambridge University Press, 1997.

———. *William Faulkner: An Economy of Complex Words*. Princeton, NJ: Princeton University Press, 2007.

Godden, Richard, and Noel Polk. "Reading the Ledgers." *Mississippi Quarterly* 55.3 (2002): 301–59.

Gomery, Douglas. *The Hollywood Studio System: A History*. New ed. London: BFI, 2005.

Greif, Mark. *The Age of the Crisis of Man: Thought and Fiction in America, 1933–1973*. Princeton, NJ: Princeton University Press, 2015.

Grider, John McGavock, and Elliott White Springs. *War Birds: The Diary of an Unknown Aviator*. Philadelphia: Temple University Press, 1966.

Grimwood, Michael. *Heart in Conflict: Faulkner's Struggles with Vocation*. Athens: University of Georgia Press, 1987.

Gross, Jack J. "Turning an Idea into a Print: A Step-By-Step Analysis of How a TV Film is Made." *Broadcasting Telecasting*, October 12, 1953, 90–97.

Hagood, Taylor. "Media, Ideology, and the Role of Literature in *Pylon*." *Faulkner Journal* 21.1–2 (Fall 2005–6): 107–19.

Hamblin, Robert W. "The Curious Case of Faulkner's 'The De Gaulle Story.'" *Faulkner Journal* 16.1–2 (2000–2001): 79–86.

———. "Faulkner and Hollywood: A Call for Reassessment." In *Faulkner and Film*, ed. Peter Lurie and Ann J. Abadie, 3–25. Faulkner and Yoknapatawpha 2010. Jackson: University Press of Mississippi, 2014.

Hamblin, Robert W., and Louis Daniel Brodsky, eds. *Faulkner: A Comprehensive Guide to the Brodsky Collection*, 5 vols. Jackson: University Press of Mississippi, 1982–88.

Hamilton, Ian. *Writers in Hollywood, 1915–1951*. London: Heinemann, 1990.

Hammill, Faye. *Women, Celebrity, and Literary Culture between the Wars*. Austin: University of Texas Press, 2007.

Hampton, Wilborn. *Horton Foote: America's Storyteller*. New York: Free Press, 2009.

Hannon, Charles. *Faulkner and the Discourses of Culture*. Baton Rouge: Louisiana State University Press, 2005.

Haskell, Molly. *From Reverence to Rape: The Treatment of Women in the Movies*. New York: Holt, Rinehart, and Winston, 1975.

Hayhoe, George F. "Faulkner in Hollywood: A Checklist of His Film Scripts at the University of Virginia." *Mississippi Quarterly* 31.3 (1978): 407–19.

———. "Faulkner in Hollywood: A Checklist of His Film Scripts at the University of Virginia: A Correction and Some Additions." *Mississippi Quarterly* 32.3 (1979): 467–72.

Hemingway, Ernest. *To Have and Have Not*. New York: Scribner's, 1937.

Hinrichsen, Lisa, Gina Marie Caison, and Stephanie Rountree, eds. *Small-Screen Souths: Interrogating the Televisual Archive*. Baton Rouge: Louisiana State University Press, 2017.

Howard, Edwin. "Faulkner Steps Out of His 'Land of Pharaohs' into Memphis." In *Conversations with William Faulkner*, ed. M. Thomas Inge, 117–19. Jackson: University Press of Mississippi, 1999.

Hulsey, Dallas. "'I Don't Seem to Remember a Girl in the Story': Hollywood's Disruption of Faulkner's All-Male Narrative in *Today We Live*." *Faulkner Journal* 16.1–2 (Fall 2000–2001): 65–77.

Jackson, Robert. "Images of Collaboration: William Faulkner's Motion Picture Communities." In *Faulkner and Film*, ed. Peter Lurie and Ann J. Abadie, 26–46. Faulkner and Yoknapatawpha 2010. Jackson: University Press of Mississippi, 2014.

———. *Seeking the Region in American Literature and Culture: Modernity, Dissonance, Innovation*. Baton Rouge: Louisiana State University Press, 2005.

Jameson, Fredric. Afterword to *True to the Spirit: Film Adaptation and the Question of Fidelity*, ed. Colin McCabe, Kathleen Murray, and Rick Warner, 215–34. New York: Oxford University Press, 2011.

———. *The Modernist Papers*. London: Verso, 2007.

———. "Synoptic Chandler." In *Shades of Noir: A Reader*, ed. Joan Copjec, 33–56. London: Verso, 1993.

Jelliffe, Robert A., ed. *Faulkner at Nagano*. Tokyo: Kenkyusha, 1956.

Jeter, Ida. "*Jezebel* and the Emergence of the Hollywood Tradition of a Decadent South." In *The South and Film*, ed. Warren G. French, 31–46. Jackson: University Press of Mississippi, 1981.

Jewell, Richard B. *RKO Radio Pictures: A Titan Is Born*. Berkeley: University of California Press, 2012.

———. *Slow Fade to Black: The Decline of RKO Radio Pictures*. Berkeley: University of California Press, 2016.

Jones, Ann Goodwyn. "'Like a Virgin': Faulkner, Sexual Cultures, and the Romance of Resistance." In *Faulkner in Cultural Context*, ed. Donald M. Kartiganer and Ann J. Abadie, 39–74. Faulkner and Yoknapatawpha 1995. Jackson: University Press of Mississippi, 1996.

Karem, Jeff. "Fear of a Black Atlantic? African Passages in *Absalom, Absalom!* and *The Last Slaver*." In *Global Faulkner*, ed. Annette Trefzer and Ann J. Abadie, 162–73. Faulkner and Yoknapatawpha 2006. Jackson: University Press of Mississippi, 2009.

Kawin, Bruce. *Faulkner and Film*. New York: Frederick Ungar, 1977.

———. "*Faulkner and Film*: An Update." In *Faulkner at Fifty: Tutors and Tyros*, ed. Marie Liénard-Yeterian and Gérald Préher, 89–102. Newcastle, UK: Cambridge Scholars Publishing, 2014.

———. "A Faulkner Filmography." *Film Quarterly* 30.4 (1977): 12–21.

———. ed. *Faulkner's MGM Screenplays*. Knoxville: University of Tennessee Press, 1982.

———. "Howard Hawks." In *Selected Film Essays and Interviews*, 89–128. London: Anthem Press, 2013.

———, ed. *To Have and Have Not*. Madison: University of Wisconsin Press, 1980.

Kerouac, Jack. *Road Novels, 1957–1960*. Ed. Douglas Brinkley. New York: Library of America, 2007.

King, George S. *The Last Slaver*. New York: G. P. Putnam's Sons, 1933.

King, Vincent Allan. "Faulkner's Brazen Yoke: Pop Art, Modernism, and the Myth of the Great Divide." In *A Companion to William Faulkner*, ed. Richard C. Moreland, 301–17. Oxford, UK: Wiley-Blackwell, 2007.

Kodat, Catherine Gunther. "'C'est Vraiment Dégueulasse': Meaning and Ending in *A bout de souffle* and *If I Forget Thee, Jerusalem*." In *A Companion to William Faulkner*, ed. Richard C. Moreland, 65–84. Oxford, UK: Wiley-Blackwell, 2007.

———. "What Is Television For? (or, from 'The Brooch' to *The Wire*)." In *William Faulkner in the Media Ecology*, ed. Julian Murphet and Stefan Solomon, 34–48. Baton Rouge: Louisiana State University Press, 2015.

Kozloff, Sarah. *Invisible Storytellers: Voice-Over Narration in American Fiction Film*. Berkeley: University of California Press, 1988.

———. *Overhearing Film Dialogue*. Berkeley: University of California Press, 2000.

Kraszewski, Jon. *New Entrepreneurs: An Institutional History of Television Anthology Writers*. Middletown, CT: Wesleyan University Press, 2010.

Kurashige, Scott. *The Shifting Grounds of Race: Black and Japanese Americans in the Making of Multiethnic Los Angeles*. Princeton, NJ: Princeton University Press, 2008.

Langford, Barry. "Beyond McKee: Screenwriting in and out of the Academy." In *Analysing the Screenplay*, ed. Jill Nelmes, 251–62. London: Routledge, 2011.

LaValley, Albert J. Introduction to *Mildred Pierce*, ed. Albert J. LaValley, 9–53. Madison: University of Wisconsin Press, 1980.

Lawrence, Amy. *Echo and Narcissus: Women's Voices in Classical Hollywood Cinema*. Berkeley: University of California Press, 1991.

Lawson, John Howard. *Theory and Technique of Playwriting and Screenwriting*. New York: G. P. Putnam's Sons, 1949.

Lester, Cheryl. "Changing the Subject of Place in Faulkner." In *A Companion to William Faulkner*, ed. Richard C. Moreland, 202–19. Oxford, UK: Wiley-Blackwell, 2007.

Lev, Peter. *Twentieth Century–Fox: The Zanuck-Skouras Years, 1935–1965*. Austin: University of Texas Press, 2013.

Liénard-Yeterian, Marie. *Faulkner et le cinéma*. Paris: Michel Houdiard, 2010.

———. "William Faulkner and Howard Hawks: How to 'Speak the Same Language.'" In *Faulkner at Fifty: Tutors and Tyros*, ed. Marie Liénard-Yeterian and Gérald Préher, 69–88. Newcastle, UK: Cambridge Scholars Publishing, 2014.

Lindsay, Vachel. *The Art of the Moving Picture*. New York: Modern Library, 2000.
Longstreet, Stephen. *Stallion Road*. New York: Julian Messner, 1945.
Lott, Eric. "The Whiteness of Film Noir." *American Literary History* 9.3 (1997): 542–66.
Lugowski, David M. "Queering the (New) Deal." In *American Film History: Selected Readings, Origins to 1960*, Ed. Cynthia Lucia, Roy Grundmann, and Art Simon, 264–81. Oxford, UK: Blackwell, 2016.
Lurie, Peter. *Vision's Immanence: Faulkner, Film, and the Popular Imagination*. Baltimore, MD: Johns Hopkins University Press, 2004.
Malcolm X, with Alex Haley. *The Autobiography of Malcolm X*. New York: Grove Press, 1965.
Mandle, Jay R. *The Roots of Black Poverty: The Southern Plantation Economy after the Civil War*. Durham, NC: Duke University Press, 1978.
Mann, Klaus. "What's Wrong with Anti-Nazi Films." *Decision* 2.2 (1941): 27–35.
Maras, Steven. *Screenwriting: History, Theory and Practice*. London: Wallflower Press, 2009.
Mast, Gerald. *Howard Hawks: Storyteller*. Oxford: Oxford University Press, 1982.
Matthews, John T. "Faulkner and the Culture Industry." In *The Cambridge Companion to William Faulkner*, ed. Philip Weinstein, 51–74. Cambridge: Cambridge University Press, 1995.
———. "Recalling the West Indies: From Yoknapatawpha to Haiti and Back." *American Literary History* 16.2 (2004): 238–62.
———. *William Faulkner: Seeing through the South*. Malden, MA: Blackwell, 2009.
Maurice, Alice. "'Cinema at Its Source': Synchronizing Race and Sound in the Early Talkies," *Camera Obscura* 17.1 (2002): 31–71.
McBride, Joseph. *Hawks on Hawks*. Berkeley: University of California Press, 1982.
McCall, John, and George Plimpton. "The Art of Fiction LXX: Malcolm Cowley." In *Conversations with Malcolm Cowley*, ed. Thomas Daniel Young, 3–18. Jackson: University Press of Mississippi, 1986.
McCarthy, Anna. *The Citizen Machine: Governing by Television in 1950s America*. New York: New York University Press, 2013.
McCarthy, Todd. *Howard Hawks: The Grey Fox of Hollywood*. New York: Grove Press, 1997.
———. "Phantom Hawks." *Film Comment* 18.5 (1982): 63–66, 68, 70–76.
MacDonald, J. Fred. *Blacks and White TV: African Americans in Television since 1948*. 2nd ed. Chicago: Nelson Hall, 1992.
Millholland, Ray. *The Splinter Fleet of the Otranto Barrage*. London: Cresset Press, 1936.
Miner, Ward L. *The World of William Faulkner*. New York: Grove Press, 1952.
Montagu, Ivor. *With Eisenstein in Hollywood: A Chapter of Autobiography*. New York: International Press, 1969.
Moore, Michelle E. "'The Unsleeping Cabal': Faulkner's Fevered Vampires and the Other South." *Faulkner Journal* 24.3 (2009): 55–76.

Moritz, William. "Americans in Paris: Man Ray and Dudley Murphy." In *Lovers of Cinema: The First American Avant-Garde, 1919–1945*, ed. Jan-Christopher Horak, 118–36. Madison: University of Wisconsin Press, 1995.

Morrell, Sascha. "Kodak Harlot Tricks of Light: Faulkner and Melville in the Darkroom of Race." In *William Faulkner in the Media Ecology*, ed. Julian Murphet and Stefan Solomon, 172–93. Baton Rouge: Louisiana State University Press, 2015.

Morrison, Spencer. "*Requiem*'s Ruins: Unmaking and Making in Cold War Faulkner." *American Literature* 85.2 (2013): 303–31.

Mulvey, Laura. *Death 24x a Second: Stillness and the Moving Image*. London: Reaktion Books, 2006.

Murphet, Julian. "Faulkner in the Histories of Film: 'Where Memory Is the Slave.'" In *Faulkner and Film*, ed. Peter Lurie and Ann J. Abadie, 197–219. Faulkner and Yoknapatawpha 2010. Jackson: University Press of Mississippi, 2014.

———. "Film Noir and the Racial Unconscious." *Screen* 39.1 (1998): 22–35.

———. Introduction to *William Faulkner in the Media Ecology*, ed. Julian Murphet and Stefan Solomon, 1–14. Baton Rouge: Louisiana State University Press, 2015.

———. *Faulkner's Media Romance*. Oxford: Oxford University Press, 2016.

Murray, D. M. "Faulkner, the Silent Comedies, and the Animated Cartoon." *Southern Humanities Review* 9.3 (1975): 241–57.

Nannicelli, Ted. *A Philosophy of the Screenplay*. New York: Routledge, 2013.

Naremore, James. *More Than Night: Film Noir in Its Contexts*. Rev. ed. Berkeley: University of California Press, 2008.

Negulesco, Jean. *Things I Did and Things I Think I Did*. New York: Linden Press/Simon and Schuster, 1984.

Nichols, Dudley. *Air Force*. Ed. Laurence Howard Suid. Madison: University of Wisconsin Press, 1983.

Nicolaisen, Peter. "Collective Experience and Questions of Genre in *A Fable*." In *The Artist and His Masks: William Faulkner's Metafiction*, ed. Agostino Lombardo, 397–414. Rome: Bulzone, 1991.

Nyerges, Aaron. "Immemorial Cinema: Film, Travel, and Faulkner's Poetics of Space." *Faulkner and Film*, ed. Peter Lurie and Ann J. Abadie, 47–70. Faulkner and Yoknapatawpha 2010. Jackson: University Press of Mississippi, 2014.

Oeler, Karla. *A Grammar of Murder: Violent Scenes and Film Form*. Chicago: University of Chicago Press, 2009.

O'Thomas, Mark. "Analysing the Screenplay: A Comparative Approach." In *Analysing the Screenplay*, ed. Jill Nelmes, 237–250. London: Routledge, 2011.

Owada, Eiko. "Faulkner, Haiti, and Questions of Imperialism." PhD diss., State University of New York at Albany, 1999.

Partridge, Bellamy. *Country Lawyer*. London: G. G. Harrap, 1940.

Pasolini, Pier Paolo. "The Screenplay as a 'Structure That Wants to Be Another Structure.'" In *Heretical Empiricism*, ed. and trans. Ben Lawton and Louise K. Barnett, 187–196. Bloomington: Indiana University Press, 1988.

Perry, George Sessions. *Hold Autumn in Your Hand*. Albuquerque: University of New Mexico Press, 1999.

Petry, Alice Hall. "Double Murder: The Women of Faulkner's 'Elly.'" In *Faulkner and Women*, ed. Doreen Fowler and Ann J. Abadie, 220–234. Faulkner and Yoknapatawpha 1985. Jackson: University Press of Mississippi, 1986.

Phillips, Gene D. *Fiction, Film, and Faulkner: The Art of Adaptation*. Knoxville: University of Tennessee Press, 1988.

Poague, Leland. "Jean Renoir, American Artist." *South Central Review* 28.3 (2011): 63–83.

Poe, Edgar Allan. "Twice-Told Tales." In *Essays and Reviews*, ed. G. R. Thompson, 569–77. New York: Library of America, 1984.

Polan, Dana. *Power and Paranoia: History, Narrative, and the American Cinema, 1940–1950*. New York: Columbia University Press, 1986.

Polk, Noel. *Children of the Dark House: Text and Context in Faulkner*. Jackson: University Press of Mississippi, 1996.

———. *Faulkner's "Requiem for a Nun."* Bloomington: Indiana University Press, 1981.

———. Introduction to *Requiem for a Nun: Preliminary Holograph and Typescript Materials. William Faulkner Manuscripts 19, Vol. 1*. New York: Garland Publishing, 1987.

Pravadelli, Veronica. *Classic Hollywood: Lifestyles and Film Styles of American Cinema, 1930–1960*. Trans. Michael Theodore Meadows. Champaign: University of Illinois Press, 2015.

Price, Steven. *A History of the Screenplay*. Basingstoke, UK: Palgrave Macmillan, 2013.

———. *The Screenplay: Authorship, Theory, and Criticism*. Basingstoke, UK: Palgrave Macmillan, 2010.

Ramsey, D. Matthew. "'All That Glitters': Reappraising 'Golden Land.'" *Faulkner Journal* 12.1–2 (2005–6): 51–64.

———. "'Touch Me While You Look at Her': Stars, Fashion, and Authorship in *Today We Live*." In *Faulkner and Material Culture*, ed. Joseph R. Urgo and Ann J. Abadie, 82–103. Faulkner and Yoknapatawpha 2004. Jackson: University Press of Mississippi, 2007.

———. "Turnabout Is Fair(y) Play: Faulkner's Queer War Story." *Faulkner Journal* 15.1–2 (1999–2000): 61–81.

Rascoe, Lavon. "An Interview with William Faulkner." In *Conversations with William Faulkner*, ed. M. Thomas Inge, 66–72. Jackson: University Press of Mississippi, 1999.

Remshardt, Ralf. "The Actor as Intermedialist: Remediation, Appropriation, Adaptation." In *Intermediality in Theatre and Performance*, ed. Freda Chapple and Chiel Kattenbelt, 41–53. Amsterdam: Rodopi, 2006.

Renoir, Jean. "Jean Renoir Presents Twenty of His Films." In *Renoir on Renoir: Interviews, Essays, and Remarks*, trans. Carol Volk, 213–47. Cambridge: Cambridge University Press, 1989.

———. *My Life and My Films*. London: William Collins Sons, 1974.

Rhodes, Pamela, and Richard Godden. "*The Wild Palms*: Faulkner's Hollywood Novel." *Amerikastudien* 28.4 (1983): 449–66.

Riley, Philip J., ed. *The Bride of Frankenstein*. Vol. 2, *Universal Filmscripts Series, Classic Horror Films*. Absecon, NJ: Magic Image Filmbooks, 1989.

———. *Dracula*. Vol. 13, *Universal Filmscripts Series, Classic Horror Films*. Absecon, NJ: Magic Image Filmbooks, 1989.

———. *Frankenstein*. Vol. 1, *Universal Filmscripts Series, Classic Horror Films*. Absecon, NJ: Magic Image Filmbooks, 1989.

Robbins, Ben. "Inscrutable Images and Cultural Migrations: Wartime Noir and the Compson Appendix," *Faulkner Journal* 28.1 (2014): 55–77.

———. "The Pragmatic Modernist: William Faulkner's Craft and Hollywood's Networks of Production." *Journal of Screenwriting* 5.2 (2014): 239–58.

Roberts, Randy. "John Wayne Goes to War." In *Hollywood's America: Twentieth-Century America through Film*, 4th ed., ed. Steven Mintz and Randy W. Roberts, 144–62. Malden, MA: Wiley-Blackwell, 2010.

Roberts, Diane. *Faulkner and Southern Womanhood*. Athens: University of Georgia Press, 1994.

Rogin, Michael. *Blackface, White Noise: Jewish Immigrants in the Hollywood Melting Pot*. Berkeley: University of California Press, 1996.

Ross, Stephen M. *Fiction's Inexhaustible Voice: Speech and Writing in Faulkner*. Athens: University of Georgia Press, 1989.

Sayre, Joel, and William Faulkner. *The Road to Glory: A Screenplay*. Ed. Stephen W. Smith. Carbondale: Southern Illinois University Press, 1981.

Schatz, Thomas. *Boom and Bust: American Cinema in the 1940s*. Berkeley: University of California Press, 1999.

———. *The Genius of the System: Hollywood Filmmaking in the Studio Era*. New York: Pantheon, 1988.

Schoenberg, Estelle. *Old Tales and Talking: Quentin Compson in William Faulkner's Absalom, Absalom! and Related Works*. Jackson: University Press of Mississippi, 1977.

Schwartz, Lawrence H. *Creating Faulkner's Reputation: The Politics of Modern Literary Criticism*. Knoxville: University of Tennessee Press, 1988.

Scott, Ellen C. *Cinema Civil Rights: Regulation, Repression, and Race in the Classical Hollywood Era*. New Brunswick, NJ: Rutgers University Press, 2015.

Sidney, George R. "Faulkner in Hollywood: A Study of His Career as a Scenarist." PhD diss. University of New Mexico, 1959.

Silverman, Kaja. *The Acoustic Mirror: The Female Voice in Psychoanalysis and Cinema*. Bloomington: Indiana University Press, 1988.

Sklar, Robert. *Movie-Made America: A Cultural History of American Movies*. Rev. ed. New York: Vintage, 1994.

Smith, Albert C. "'Southern Violence' Reconsidered: Arson as Protest in Black-Belt Georgia, 1865–1910." *Journal of Southern History* 51.4 (1985): 527–64.

Sobchack, Vivian. "Lounge Time: Postwar Crises and the Chronotope of Film Noir." In *Refiguring American Film Genres: Theory and History*, ed. Nick Browne, 129–70. Berkeley: University of California Press, 1998.

Solomon, Stefan. "Faulkner and the Masses: A Hollywood Fable." In *Faulkner and Film*, ed. Peter Lurie and Ann J. Abadie, 98–119. Faulkner and Yoknapatawpha 2010. Jackson: University Press of Mississippi, 2014.

———. "A Little Boy and an Idea: 'Two Soldiers' and 'Shall Not Perish.'" In *William Faulkner in the Media Ecology*, ed. Julian Murphet and Stefan Solomon, 49–66. Baton Rouge: Louisiana State University Press, 2015.

Stempel, Tom. *Framework: A History of Screenwriting in the American Film*. 3rd ed. Syracuse, NY: Syracuse University Press, 2000.

———. *Screenwriter: The Life and Times of Nunnally Johnson*. San Diego, CA: A. S. Barnes, 1980.

Sternberg, Claudia. *Written for the Screen: The American Motion-Picture Screenplay as Text*. Tübingen: Stauffenburg, 1997.

Stewart, Garrett. *Between Film and Screen: Modernism's Photo Synthesis*. Chicago: University of Chicago Press, 1999.

Strychacz, Thomas. *Modernism, Mass Culture, and Professionalism*. New York: Cambridge University Press, 1993.

Suid, Lawrence H., ed. *Air Force*. Madison: University of Wisconsin Press, 1983.

Swires, Steve. "Leigh Brackett: Journeyman Plumber." In *Backstory: Interviews with Screenwriters of the 1940s and 1950s*, vol. 2, ed. Patrick McGilligan, 15–26. Berkeley: University of California Press, 1997.

Thompson, Howard. "Through Faulkner's View-Finder." In *Conversations with William Faulkner*, ed. M. Thomas Inge, 161–162. Jackson: University Press of Mississippi, 1999.

Tieber, Claus. "'A Story Is Not a Story but a Conference': Story Conferences and the Classical Studio System." *Journal of Screenwriting* 5.2 (2014): 225–37.

Towner, Theresa M. *The Cambridge Introduction to William Faulkner*. Cambridge: Cambridge University Press, 2008.

Turim, Maureen. *Flashbacks in Film: Memory and History*. New York: Routledge, 1989.

Urgo, Joseph. "*Absalom, Absalom!*: The Movie." *American Literature* 62.1 (1990): 56–73.

Vidal, Gore. *Palimpsest: A Memoir*. New York: Random House, 1995.

Vieira, Mark A. *Irving Thalberg: Boy Wonder to Producer Prince*. Berkeley: University of California Press, 2010.

Volpe, Edmund L. *A Reader's Guide to William Faulkner: The Short Stories*. Syracuse, NY: Syracuse University Press, 2004.

Waid, Candace. *The Signifying Eye: Seeing Faulkner's Art*. Athens: University of Georgia Press, 2013.

Wald, Jerry. "Faulkner and Hollywood." *Films in Review* 10.3 (1959): 129–33.

Warner, Harry. "Harry Warner's Testimony to a Senate Subcommittee on War Propaganda in Film, 1941." In *America between the Wars, 1919–1941: A Documentary Reader*, ed. David Welky, 243–45. Oxford: Blackwell, 2012.

Warner, Rick. "*Contempt* Revisited: Godard at the Margins of Adaptation." In *True to the Spirit: Film Adaptation and the Question of Fidelity*, ed. Colin MacCabe, Kathleen Murray, and Rick Warner, 195–214. New York: Oxford University Press, 2011.

Watson, Jay. "The Unsynchable William Faulkner: Faulknerian Voice and Early Sound Film." In *William Faulkner in the Media Ecology*, ed. Julian Murphet and Stefan Solomon, 93–114. Baton Rouge: Louisiana State University Press, 2015.

Weaver, William. *Duse: A Biography*. London: Thames and Hudson, 1984.

Weinstein, Philip. *Becoming Faulkner: The Art and Life of William Faulkner*. New York: Oxford University Press, 2009.

White, Patricia. *Uninvited: Classical Hollywood Cinema and Lesbian Representability*. Bloomington: Indiana University Press, 1999.

Wiener, Jonathan. "Class Structure and Economic Development in the American South, 1865–1955." *American Historical Review* 84.4 (1979): 970–92.

Wilk, Max. "Faulkner and the Pyramids: Harold Jack Bloom, 1972." In *Schmucks with Underwoods: Conversations with Hollywood's Classic Screenwriters*, 279–94. New York: Applause Theatre and Cinema Books, 2004.

Williams, John A. "My Man Himes: An Interview with Chester Himes." In *Conversations with Chester Himes*, ed. Michael Fabre and Robert E. Skinner, 29–82. Jackson: University Press of Mississippi, 1995.

Williams, Raymond. *Television: Technology and Cultural Form*. Ed. Ederyn Williams. London: Routledge, 2003.

Williamson, Joel. *William Faulkner and Southern History*. Oxford: Oxford University Press, 1993.

Woodward, C. Vann. *The Strange Career of Jim Crow*. New York: Oxford University Press, 1966.

Zeitlin, Michael. "*Pylon*, Joyce, and Faulkner's Imagination." In *Faulkner and the Artist*, ed. Donald M. Kartiganer and Ann J. Abadie, 181–207. Faulkner and Yoknapatawpha 1993. Jackson: University Press of Mississippi, 1996.

Index

Absalom, Absalom! (Faulkner), 101, 104–5, 110, 244, 280n22; fascism in, 269n8; and "Gunga Din," similarities with, 79; and Hollywood, attempts to sell to, 87, 97, 113; and "The Last Slaver," similarities with, 55, 85–87; map of Yoknaptawpha County in, 41–42; photography in, 107; publication of first chapter of, 85–87; and *Pylon*, relationship to, 62–63; slavery in, 57, 86, 113; and "Sutter's Gold," similarities with, 57; writing process of, 7, 12, 68, 72, 85

adaptation, 10–11, 13, 27, 28, 37, 45–46, 58, 70–71, 88–90, 92–93, 98; as competition between media, 8; as dependent on the screenplay, 8–9; as devaluation of literary writing, 54; of Faulkner by other writers, 15, 23, 124, 159

"Ad Astra" (Faulkner), 46

Adorno, Theodor W., 218–19, 221

Agee, James, 134, 172

Air Force (1943), 126–30, 133–34, 135, 136; collective efforts in, 130, 152

"Air Force" (screenplay), 128, 129–30, 151

Alabamy Bound (1941), 104

"All the Dead Pilots" (Faulkner), 46

American Revolutionary War, 92, 95

"Appendix, Compson: 1699–1945" (Faulkner), 149, 182–83

Arnold, Edward, 56

As I Lay Dying (Faulkner), 63

Associated Artists, 12, 97–98, 108–9, 113, 147

Bacall, Lauren, 116, 152, 158, 185, 187

Bacher, William, 148, 212

Background to Danger (1943), 136–40

Ballet mécanique (1924), 103, 109

Banjo on My Knee (1936), 76; lawsuit against, 74

"Banjo on My Knee" (screenplay), 73–77, 119, 211

Bankhead, Tallulah, 23–24, 26, 199

"Battle Cry" (screenplay), 62, 119, 142–47, 151, 231

Bazin, André, 10, 172, 199

"Bear, The" (Faulkner), 7, 160–61, 162–64, 165

Beery, Wallace, 17, 25, 43–44

Benjamin, Walter, 200

Bernhardt, Sarah, 198–99, 200

Bessie, Alvah, 141, 165

Bezzerides, Alfred, 141, 171, 187

Big Sky, The (1952), 210

Big Sleep, The (1946), 10, 11, 116, 158, 173–74; different versions of, 185

Big Sleep, The (Chandler), 180, 181–82

"Big Sleep, The" (screenplay), 180–82, 184–86, 275n63

Binford, Lloyd T., 172
Bishop's Wife, The (1947), 193–94
Black and Tan (1929), 98, 102, 103
Bloom, Harold Jack, 244
Bogart, Humphrey, 116, 152, 158, 185, 187, 204
Bow, Clara, 21
Brackett, Leigh, 180, 184–85, 275n63
Brecht, Bertolt, 78–79
Breen, Joseph, 23, 181–82
"Brooch, The" (Faulkner short story), 164, 221, 223, 227–28
"Brooch, The" (Faulkner teleplay), 220, 223–30
Browning, Tod, 52
Buckner, Robert, 98, 113–14, 132, 136, 145

Cabin in the Sky (1943), 159, 176–77
Car 54, Where Are You? (television series), 221
Carpenter Wilde, Meta, 73, 204, 274n47
Cather, Willa, 4
Chandler, Raymond, 213
character (fiction), 42–43
Civil Rights Movement, 159, 222–23
Civil War: in "Battle Cry," 143–44; in *Flags in the Dust*, 46; in *Gone with the Wind*, 21; in "My Grandmother Millard and General Bedford Forrest and the Battle of Harrykin Creek," 118; in "Revolt in the Earth," 98–99; in "Shall Not Perish," 231; on television, 222; in *The Unvanquished*, 95
Clarkson, Thomas, 82
"College Widow, The" (Faulkner) 24–25, 78
comedy of remarriage, 34, 39
Commins, Saxe, 161, 214
"Compson Appendix" (Faulkner), 149, 182–83
Confessions of a Nazi Spy (1939), 123
conscription, 117, 155
"Continuous Performance" (Faulkner), 192
Cooper, Gary, 119, 125, 269n4
Cooper, James Fenimore, 92
"Country Lawyer" (Faulkner), 159–60, 164–69, 174, 192; arson in, 165–66
Country Lawyer (Partridge), 165, 168
Cowley, Malcolm, 2, 132
Crawford, Joan, 26, 27, 28, 31, 33, 158

"Curious Case of Benjamin Button, The" (Fitzgerald), 150, 195

"Damned Don't Cry, The" (Faulkner), 7, 13, 158, 160–62, 164
"Dance Hall" (screenplay), 92
De Gaulle, Charles, 125–26, 130–32, 151
"De Gaulle Story, The" (Faulkner), 113–14, 125–26, 130–32, 147, 151, 152, 155
death, film's relationship to, 45, 199
"Deep Valley" (Faulkner), 192
depression (economic), 39, 41, 51, 54, 56, 70, 74, 174; in *Mildred Pierce*, 172, 173, 179
Dmytryk, Edward, 204
Dos Passos, John, 4
double exposure (special effect), 48–49
Double Indemnity (1944), 172
"Dreadful Hollow" (Faulkner), 15, 261n28, 276n70
Dressler, Marie, 20, 41, 43–44
Drums along the Mohawk (Edmonds), 92–93
"Drums along the Mohawk" (Faulkner), 92–95, 98, 143
"Dry September" (Faulkner), 21–22, 35, 175
Duse, Eleonora, 198–99, 200

Eisenstein, Sergei, 54, 55, 57–60
"Elly" (Faulkner), 34–37, 40
Emperor Jones, The (1933), 97, 102, 103, 105
"Evangeline" (Faulkner), 91, 98, 107–8, 110–11
Evans, Walker, 242

Fable, A (Faulkner), 13, 148–51, 187, 193, 212, 249–50; as Warner Brothers allegory, 149
Farewell, My Lovely (Chandler), 177
Faulkner, Estelle Oldham, 263n45
Faulkner, William: *Absalom, Absalom!*, 7, 12, 55, 57, 62–63, 72, 79, 85–87, 97, 101, 104–5, 107, 110, 113, 244, 269n8, 280n22; "Ad Astra," 46; alcoholism of, 72; "All the Dead Pilots," 46; "Appendix, Compson: 1699–1945," 149, 182–83; *As I Lay Dying*, 63; and Balzac, influence of, 41; "The Bear," 7, 160–61, 162–64, 165; "The Brooch" (short story), 164,

221, 223, 227–28; "The Brooch" (teleplay), 220, 223–30; and Carpenter Wilde, Meta, affair with, 73, 204; "The College Widow," 24–25, 78; "Continuous Performance," 192; "Country Lawyer," 159–60, 164–69, 174, 192; "The Damned Don't Cry," 7, 13, 158, 160–62, 164; "Deep Valley" (Faulkner), 192; "The De Gaulle Story," 113–14, 125–26, 130–32, 147, 151, 152, 155; "Dreadful Hollow," 15, 261n28, 276n70; "Drums along the Mohawk," 92–95, 98, 143; "Dry September," 21–22, 35, 175; "Elly," 34–37, 40; "Evangeline," 91, 98, 107–8, 110–11; *A Fable*, 13, 148–51, 187, 193, 212, 249–50; *Flags in the Dust*, 45, 46; "Flying the Mail," 43–44; *Go Down, Moses*, 13, 91, 122, 160, 167–68, 174; "Golden Land," 54, 65–68; "Gunga Din," 77–79, 168, 197; "Hand upon the Waters," 273n19; "Honor," 51; "Idyll in the Desert," 24; *If I Forget Thee, Jerusalem*, 14, 52, 195, 221, 237–38; *Intruder in the Dust*, 115, 149, 160, 172–73, 174–76, 177, 178, 194, 198; *Knight's Gambit*, 160; "Knight's Gambit," 133, 189–91; "The Left Hand of God," 13–14, 193, 197–98, 204–13, 214, 215, 217, 277n16; "The Life and Death of a Bomber," 134–36, 150; *Light in August*, 122–23; "Manservant," 18, 78; *The Marionettes*, 195; and manuscript pages, use of by, 161, 164, 192–93, 205–9, 214, 215, 273n7, 276n6; "Mildred Pierce/House on the Sand," 180; "Morningstar," 193–94; "My Grandmother Millard and General Bedford Forrest and the Battle of Harrykin Creek," 118; "Mythical Latin-American Kingdom Story," 51; and Nobel Prize, 5, 6, 13, 220, 250; "Old Man," 220, 237–40; "One Way to Catch a Horse," 267n103; opinions of Hollywood, 1–3, 259n10; *Pylon*, 20, 51, 62–65, 75, 135, 265n28; *Requiem for a Nun*, 4, 13–14, 149, 193, 197–209, 214–17, 277n14; "Revolt in the Earth," 12, 97–114, 197; *Sanctuary*, 18, 22–23, 25, 40, 63, 188, 195, 196; *Sartoris*, 45, 46; "Sepulture South: Gaslight," 241–43, 249, 250; "Shall Not Perish" (short story), 117–18, 221, 230–32; "Shall Not Perish" (teleplay), 232–37; short story schedule of, 53; "Snow," 120–23, 269n7; *The Sound and the Fury*, 27–28, 182; "Stallion Road," 187–88; "A Stretch on the River," 269n15; studio contracts of, 72, 73, 79, 92, 95–96, 191–92, 204; "Sutter's Gold," 54, 55–64, 146; "The Tall Men," 117; "That Evening Sun," 196; "Turn About" (screenplay), 27, 89–90; "Turnabout" (short story), 26–27, 53; "Two Dollar Wife," 34–35, 37–40; "Two Soldiers," 117, 127, 128–29, 230, 232; *The Unvanquished*, 95–96, 118, 167–68; "War Birds," 45–51; and war effort, contributions to, 120, 132; "Wash," 98; "Who?," 148–51; "With Caution and Dispatch," 47

film noir, 158, 172, 177–78, 180–81, 274n40
Fitzgerald, F. Scott, 20
Flags in the Dust (Faulkner), 45, 46
flashback, 36, 121, 172
"Flying the Mail" (Faulkner), 43–44
Flynn, Errol, 140, 187
Ford, Ruth, 187, 199–200
Fuchs, Dan, 138
Furthman, Jules, 151, 152, 153, 154, 155

Gable, Clark, 3–4, 96
Gilbert, John, 18
Gish, Lillian, 21
Go Down, Moses (Faulkner), 13, 91, 122, 160, 167–68, 174; attempt to sell to Hollywood, 164
God Is My Co-Pilot (1945), 119, 134
"God Is My Co-Pilot" (screenplay), 151
"Golden Land" (Faulkner), 54, 65–68; print media in, 67–68
Goldman, Morton, 54, 68, 87
Gone with the Wind (1939), 21, 87, 96, 142, 157, 160, 167–68, 179
"Graduation Dress" (Faulkner and Williams), 219–20
Grand Hotel (1932), 26
Grandeur et décadence d'un petit commerce de cinéma (1986), 241–42

Great Migration, 115–16, 157, 159, 174–75, 176, 179
Green Mansions (Hudson), 223, 227–28
"Gunga Din" (Faulkner), 77–79, 168, 197

Haas, Robert, 164, 193
"Hand upon the Waters" (Faulkner), 273n19
Handy, W. C., 76
Harlow, Jean, 20, 41
Hathaway, Henry, 148
Hawks, Howard, 3, 56, 77, 119, 124, 187; on *Air Force*, 126–27, 133; on "Battle Cry," 142, 147; on *The Big Sleep*, 181, 185, 186; on "Dreadful Hollow," 15, 261n28; on *To Have and Have Not*, 151–53, 155; on *Intruder in the Dust*, 174; on *Land of the Pharaohs*, 243–44, 245, 246; on "The Left Hand of God," 197, 204; on "Morningstar," 193–94; and *Pylon*, adaptation of, 56; on *The Road to Glory*, 69, 70, 73; on *The Thing from Another World*, 269n4; on *Today We Live*, 27, 29; and voiceover, use of, 210, 212, 248; on "War Birds," 45, 47
Hays Code (Motion Picture Production Code), 23, 108
Hemingway, Ernest, 4, 151–52
Hempstead, David, on Faulkner's screenwriting, 76, 211
Herndon, William, 120, 160, 164, 191
hieroglyphs, 248–49
Himes, Chester, 176–77
Hold Autumn in Your Hand (Perry). See *Southerner, The* (1945 film)
Hollywood Party (1934), 17–18
"Honor" (Faulkner), 51
Howard, Leslie, 109

"Idyll in the Desert" (Faulkner), 24
If I Forget Thee, Jerusalem (Faulkner), 14, 52, 195, 221, 237–38
Informer, The (1935), 77
Inter-American Affairs Office, 152
Intruder in the Dust (1949), 194

Intruder in the Dust (Faulkner), 115, 149, 160, 172–73, 174–76, 177, 178, 194, 198
I Walked with a Zombie (1943), 105

Jezebel (1938), 261n14
Johnson, Nunnally, 71, 80, 82, 85, 87, 169

Knight's Gambit (Faulkner), 160
"Knight's Gambit" (Faulkner), 133, 189–91
Kurnitz, Harry, 243–44

labor, 57, 86, 98, 115, 124, 159, 175–78; in *The Big Sleep*, 183–84; in "Knight's Gambit," 189–90; in "The Life and Death of a Bomber," 134–36; in *The Southerner*, 169, 172
Laemml, Carl, Jr., 55–56
Land of the Pharaohs (1955), 11, 14, 243–49; use of CinemaScope in, 14, 245–49
"Land of the Pharaohs" (screenplay), 243–49
Lasky, Jesse L., 55, 125
The Last Slaver (King), 79–80
"Last Slaver, The" (screenplay), 79–87, 104; Sam Hellman and Gladys Lehmann, screenplays by, 80
Lazy River (1934), 41, 52
"Left Hand of God, The" (Faulkner), 13–14, 193, 204–13, 277n16; Catholic Church objects to, 205, 212–13; and *Requiem for a Nun*, similarities with, 197–98, 205–9, 214, 215; voiceover in, 209–13, 215, 217
Left Hand of God, The (Barrett), 197, 207, 209
Les croix de bois (Dorgelès), 73
Les croix de bois (*Wooden Crosses*, 1932), 70, 72
"Life and Death of a Bomber, The" (Faulkner), 134–36, 150
Light in August (Faulkner), 122–23
Lincoln, Abraham, 143–44, 146, 151, 231
Lindsay, Vachel, 248
Loos, Anita, 19–20, 261n7
Los Angeles, 65–66, 134, 157, 159, 176–77
"Louisiana Lou" (Faulkner). See *Lazy River* (1934)
"Love" (Faulkner), 18

Lupino, Ida, 187
Lux Video Theatre (television series), 14, 219, 226; sponsorship strategies of, 229, 233–34
lynching, 174, 175–76

Magnificent Obsession (1935), 56
Maltese Falcon, The (1941), 116
Mann, Thomas, 4
"Manservant" (Faulkner), 18, 78
Marion, Frances, 20
Marionettes, The (Faulkner), 195
Markey, Gene, 88, 267n93
Marx, Sam, 17, 33, 51–52, 194
Mary of Scotland (1936), 77
Mayer, Louis B., 51
McDaniel, Hattie, 179
McQueen, Butterfly, 179, 274n48
Metro-Goldwyn-Mayer (MGM), 1, 9, 11–12, 70, 194; hiring of screenwriters at, 16; star system at, 17, 19, 40–45, 50
Mickey Mouse, 17
Mildred Pierce (1945), 10, 13, 158, 160, 172–73, 178–81, 272n3
Mildred Pierce (Cain), 172, 173, 178
"Mildred Pierce/House on the Sand" (Faulkner), 10, 173, 178–79, 180
Min and Bill (1930), 25, 43–44
miscegenation: in *Absalom, Absalom!*, 87; in "The Bear," 162–63; in "Gunga Din," 78, 79; in "Revolt in the Earth," 98, 107–8, 110
"Morningstar" (Faulkner), 193–94
Motion Picture Production Code (Hays Code), 23, 108
Murder, My Sweet (1944), 177
Murphy, Dudley, 12
music, 76, 103–4, 143, 146–47
Mutiny on the Bounty (1935), 82
"My Grandmother Millard and General Bedford Forrest and the Battle of Harrykin Creek" (Faulkner), 118
"Mythical Latin-American Kingdom Story" (Faulkner), 51

Native Americans, 93
Nazism, 121–24, 140
New Woman, 19–23, 37, 39, 262n15
Nichols, Dudley, 126–27, 129, 270n20
"Night Bird" (Faulkner). *See* "College Widow, The" (Faulkner)
Northern Pursuit (1943), 140–41; dispute over screen credits for, 141

Office of War Information (OWI), 124, 152
"Old Man" (Faulkner), 220, 237–40; CBS adaptation of, 240. See also *If I Forget Thee, Jerusalem* (Faulkner)
Omnibus (television series), 220, 222, 278n10
"One Way to Catch a Horse" (Faulkner), 267n103
On the Road (Kerouac), 136
Oppenheimer, Robert, 220

Paramount Pictures, 23, 26, 55, 204
Pasolini, Pier Paolo, 8
photography, 106–8, 181–83
Poe, Edgar Allan, 219
Portable Faulkner, The, 41–42, 182, 237
primitivism, 102, 103–5, 228
propaganda, 123–24, 131, 134
Pylon (Faulkner), 20, 51, 63–65, 75, 135, 265n28; and *Absalom, Absalom!*, relationship to, 62–63; attempt to sell to Hollywood, 65

race: in "Battle Cry," 144–45; in "Country Lawyer," 167; and discrimination in Los Angeles, 176–77; in "Elly," 36; in Golden Age television, 235; in "Gunga Din," 79; in Hollywood cinema, 159; in "Revolt in the Earth," 102–4, 108, 112–13; in "Shall Not Perish," 235–37; in *The Southerner*, 172
Radio Keith Orpheum (RKO), 77, 197; importance of radio to, 213–14; roadshow releases from, 77
Raft, George, 137, 138–40
Rain (Somerset Maugham), 26
Reagan, Ronald, 188

realism, 57, 82, 84, 85, 140, 231
Red River (1948), 210
Renoir, Jean, 11, 169, 244
Requiem for a Nun (Faulkner), 4, 13–14, 149, 193, 214–17; and distinctions between theatre and film, 201–4; historical figures in, 198; "The Left Hand of God," similarities with, 197–98, 205–9, 214, 215; radio in, 215–17; reading plays in, 201, 277n14
"Revolt in the Earth" (Faulkner), 12, 97–114, 197; as collaborative work, 109–10; photography in, 106–8; racism in, 112–13; voodoo in, 105–6
Road to Glory, The (1936), lawsuit against, 73
"Road to Glory, The" (screenplay), 68–73, 142, 265n41
Robeson, Paul, 97, 102, 144
Rogers, Ginger, 187
Rooney, Mickey, 189

St. Louis Blues (1929), 102–3
Sanctuary (Faulkner), 18, 22–23, 25, 40, 63, 188, 195, 196; adaptation of, as a play, 195. See also *Story of Temple Drake, The* (1933)
Sartoris (Faulkner), 45, 46
Sayre, Joel, 70, 71–72
Schenck, Nicholas, 41
Scola, Kathryn, 88, 267n93
Scott, Zachary, 169–70, 187, 199
screenplays: as blueprints for films, 8, 58; as crucial to adaptation process, 8–9; master-scene format of, 58, 264n12; segmented sequences in, 74; split-page format of, 60, 61, 62, 63, 146–47
Screen Writers' Guild, 23
screenwriting: character profiles in, 43, 210–11; as collaborative labor, 10–11, 72, 88, 97–98, 109–10, 141, 192–93, 270n26, 273n19, 275n63; credits for, 3, 141, 271n48; dialogue in, 18–19, 24–25, 28–31, 33–34, 59–61, 83, 88, 203; effect on literary writing of, 5–6, 7, 54; practice of, 5, 10; studies of, 9; studio house styles of, 9

"Sepulture South: Gaslight" (Faulkner), 241–43, 249, 250
Sergeant York (1941), 118–20, 123–24, 125, 269n4
sexual desire, 20, 158, 207
"Shadow, The" (screenplay), 192–93
"Shall Not Perish" (Faulkner short story), 117–18, 221, 230–32
"Shall Not Perish" (Faulkner teleplay), 232–37
Skin of Our Teeth, The (Wilder), 150
Slave Ship (1937), 55; Carl van Vechten's opinion of, 84. See also "Last Slaver, The" (screenplay)
slavery: in *Absalom, Absalom!*, 57, 86, 113; in *Gone with the Wind*, 21; in "Revolt in the Earth," 104; in *Slave Ship*, 79–87
Smilin' Through (1932), 47–48
Smith, Alexis, 187–88
"Snow" (Faulkner), 120–23, 269n7; optical technology in, 121–22
Sound and the Fury, The (Faulkner), 27–28, 182; NBC telecast of Dilsey section from, 221
sound cinema: comedy of remarriage and, 39; distinctions between voice and sound in, 60–61; Eisenstein's theory of, 57–58; at MGM, 16–17; "Revolt in the Earth" and, 99–104, 106; synchronization with images in, 65; transition to, 59
soundies, 104
southern states: modernity in, 157, 159, 162, 169–72, 174, 176, 190–91, 216–17; nutritional standards in, 169; representations of, 157, 160
Southerner, The (1945), 11, 13, 160, 169, 199, 244, 273n19
"Southerner, The" (screenplay), 170–71
"Splinter Fleet" (screenplay), 87–92; problems with dialogue in, 88; stereopticon in, 91–92
Splinter Fleet of the Otranto Barrage, The (Millholland), 87–88
Sports Parade, The (1932), 106
Stallion Road (1945), 160
Stallion Road (Longstreet), 186–87

"Stallion Road" (Faulkner), 187–88
Stella Dallas (1937), 158
Story of Temple Drake, The (1933), 23, 195
"Stretch on the River, A" (Faulkner), 269n15
studio system, 9–11, 40–41, 97–98, 109–10, 246
Submarine Patrol (1938), 87, 92. See also "Splinter Fleet" (screenplay)
Sutter's Gold (Cendrars), 55, 56–57
"Sutter's Gold" (Eisenstein), 58–59
"Sutter's Gold" (Faulkner), 54, 55–64, 146
Swanson, Gloria, 79

"Tall Men, The" (Faulkner), 117
television, 14, 218, 222; live telecast on, 226, 228; problems in the South with, 222–23
Thalberg, Irving, 19, 27, 33, 41, 44
"That Evening Sun" (Faulkner), 196
theater, 26, 74, 195–96, 198–200
Thomas, Lowell, 75
Tobacco Road (Kirkland), 74
Today We Live (1933), 9, 11, 19, 26–34, 88. See also "Turn About" (Faulkner screenplay); "Turnabout" (Faulkner short story)
To Have and Have Not (1944), 13, 116, 158, 185, 197
To Have and Have Not (Hemingway), 152
"To Have and Have Not" (screenplay), 152–55
Too Much Johnson (Welles), 199
"Turn About" (Faulkner screenplay), 27, 89–90
"Turnabout" (Faulkner short story), 26–27, 53
Twentieth Century-Fox, 2, 9–10, 12; story conferences at, 69, 72, 74, 75–76, 85, 88, 212
"Two Dollar Wife" (Faulkner), 34–35, 37–40. See also "College Widow, The"
"Two Soldiers" (Faulkner), 117, 127, 128–29, 230, 232
"Two Soldiers" (Seldes), 222, 240

Uncle Tom's Cabin (Stowe), 84–85
Universal Pictures, 54, 55–56, 60
Unvanquished, The (Faulkner), 95–96, 118, 167–68

Vickers, Martha, 185
Vidal, Gore, 220
voice, 28–31, 33, 39, 61, 65, 75
voiceover narration, 14, 209–13, 215, 217
voodoo, 105–6

Wald, Jerry, 124, 140, 172, 173, 179, 269n15
Wallis, Hal, 124, 151
Walsh, Raoul, 136–41
"War Birds" (Faulkner), 45–51
War Birds (Springs), 45–46, 49
Warner Brothers, 2, 10, 12–13, 113–14, 125; war films produced by, 133
Warner, Harry, 123–24
Warner, Jack, 2, 120, 124, 142, 164, 179, 191–92, 193
"Wash" (Faulkner), 98
Welles, Orson, 213–14
"Who?" (Faulkner), 148–51. See also *Fable, A* (Faulkner)
Wild Palms, The (Faulkner). See *If I Forget Thee, Jerusalem* (Faulkner)
Williams, Joan, 196–97, 214, 219–20
"With Caution and Dispatch" (Faulkner), 47
Works Progress Administration (WPA), 117
World War I, 46, 47, 87–88, 91–92, 117, 127, 150, 168
World War II, 115–16, 158, 159, 190

Yankee Doodle Dandy (1942), 138
Yoknapatawpha County, 4, 11–12, 17, 19, 45, 47, 65, 118, 149, 157, 165, 167; character system of, 41–42, 196; maps of, 41–42, 175

Zanuck, Darryl F., 12, 54, 69, 72, 74, 75–76, 80, 85, 88, 119, 212

The South on Screen

Truman Capote: A Literary Life at the Movies,
BY TISON PUGH

William Faulkner in Hollywood: Screenwriting for the Studios,
BY STEFAN SOLOMON

Unwhite: Appalachia, Race, and Film,
BY MEREDITH MCCARROLL

Queering the South on Screen,
EDITED BY TISON PUGH

www.ingramcontent.com/pod-product-compliance
Lightning Source LLC
Chambersburg PA
CBHW011622250426
43672CB00038B/2959